Advanced Machine Learning Algorithms for Complex Financial Applications

Mohammad Irfan
CMR Institute of Technology, India

Mohamed Elhoseny
American University in the Emirates, UAE

Salina Kassim
International Islamic University of Malaysia, Malaysia

Noura Metawa
University of Sharjah, UAE

A volume in the Advances in Finance, Accounting, and Economics (AFAE) Book Series

Published in the United States of America by
    IGI Global
    Engineering Science Reference (an imprint of IGI Global)
    701 E. Chocolate Avenue
    Hershey PA, USA 17033
    Tel: 717-533-8845
    Fax: 717-533-8661
    E-mail: cust@igi-global.com
    Web site: http://www.igi-global.com

Copyright © 2023 by IGI Global. All rights reserved. No part of this publication may be reproduced, stored or distributed in any form or by any means, electronic or mechanical, including photocopying, without written permission from the publisher.
Product or company names used in this set are for identification purposes only. Inclusion of the names of the products or companies does not indicate a claim of ownership by IGI Global of the trademark or registered trademark.

Library of Congress Cataloging-in-Publication Data

Names: Irfan, Mohammad, 1986- editor. | Elhoseny, Mohamed, editor. |
   Kassim, Salina H., editor. | Metawa, Noura, editor.
Title: Advanced machine learning algorithms for complex financial
   applications / Mohammad Irfan, Mohamed Elhoseny, Salina Kassim, and
   Noura Saad Metawa, editors.
Description: Hershey, PA : Business Science Reference, [2022] | Includes
   bibliographical references and index. | Summary: "This book clarifies
   the vital role of artificial intelligence and machine learning on the
   performance of complex financial applications processing a complex
   banking and financial environment"-- Provided by publisher.
Identifiers: LCCN 2022001826 (print) | LCCN 2022001827 (ebook) | ISBN
   9781668444832 (hardcover) | ISBN 9781668444849 (paperback) | ISBN
   9781668444856 (ebook)
Subjects: LCSH: Finance--Data processing. | Machine learning. | Artificial
   intelligence.
Classification: LCC HG173 .A345 2022 (print) | LCC HG173 (ebook) | DDC
   332.0285--dc23/eng/20220329
LC record available at https://lccn.loc.gov/2022001826
LC ebook record available at https://lccn.loc.gov/2022001827

This book is published in the IGI Global book series Advances in Finance, Accounting, and Economics (AFAE) (ISSN: 2327-5677; eISSN: 2327-5685)

British Cataloguing in Publication Data
A Cataloguing in Publication record for this book is available from the British Library.

All work contributed to this book is new, previously-unpublished material.
The views expressed in this book are those of the authors, but not necessarily of the publisher.

For electronic access to this publication, please contact: eresources@igi-global.com.

Advances in Finance, Accounting, and Economics (AFAE) Book Series

Ahmed Driouchi
Al Akhawayn University, Morocco

ISSN:2327-5677
EISSN:2327-5685

MISSION

In our changing economic and business environment, it is important to consider the financial changes occurring internationally as well as within individual organizations and business environments. Understanding these changes as well as the factors that influence them is crucial in preparing for our financial future and ensuring economic sustainability and growth.

The **Advances in Finance, Accounting, and Economics (AFAE)** book series aims to publish comprehensive and informative titles in all areas of economics and economic theory, finance, and accounting to assist in advancing the available knowledge and providing for further research development in these dynamic fields.

COVERAGE

- Economics of Intellectual Property Rights
- Banking
- Behavioral Economics
- Applied Accounting
- Internet Banking
- International Trade
- Comparative Accounting Systems
- Investments and Derivatives
- Environmental and Social Accounting
- Evidence-Based Studies

IGI Global is currently accepting manuscripts for publication within this series. To submit a proposal for a volume in this series, please contact our Acquisition Editors at Acquisitions@igi-global.com or visit: http://www.igi-global.com/publish/.

The Advances in Finance, Accounting, and Economics (AFAE) Book Series (ISSN 2327-5677) is published by IGI Global, 701 E. Chocolate Avenue, Hershey, PA 17033-1240, USA, www.igi-global.com. This series is composed of titles available for purchase individually; each title is edited to be contextually exclusive from any other title within the series. For pricing and ordering information please visit http://www.igi-global.com/book-series/advances-finance-accounting-economics/73685. Postmaster: Send all address changes to above address. Copyright © 2023 IGI Global. All rights, including translation in other languages reserved by the publisher. No part of this series may be reproduced or used in any form or by any means – graphics, electronic, or mechanical, including photocopying, recording, taping, or information and retrieval systems – without written permission from the publisher, except for non commercial, educational use, including classroom teaching purposes. The views expressed in this series are those of the authors, but not necessarily of IGI Global.

Titles in this Series

For a list of additional titles in this series, please visit: http://www.igi-global.com/book-series/

Blockchain Applications in Cryptocurrency for Technological Evolution
Atour Taghipour (Normandy University, France)
Business Science Reference • © 2023 • 308pp • H/C (ISBN: 9781668462478) • US $250.00

The Past, Present, and Future of Accountancy Education and Professions
Nina T. Dorata (St. John's University, USA) Richard C. Jones (Hofstra University, USA) Jennifer Mensche (St. Joseph's College, USA) and Mark M. Ulrich (CUNY Queensborough Community College, USA)
Business Science Reference • © 2023 • 300pp • H/C (ISBN: 9781668454831) • US $215.00

Handbook of Research on Changing World Economic Order in the Post-Pandemic Period
Sushanta Kumar Mahapatra (IBS Hyderabad, The ICFAI Foundation for Higher Education, India) and Vishal Sarin (Lovely Professional University, India)
Business Science Reference • © 2023 • 470pp • H/C (ISBN: 9781799868965) • US $325.00

Transforming Economies Through Microfinance in Developing Nations
Yahaya Alhassan (University of Sunderland in London, UK) and Uzoechi Nwagbara (University of Sunderland in London, UK)
Business Science Reference • © 2023 • 300pp • H/C (ISBN: 9781668456477) • US $250.00

Handbook of Research on Artificial Intelligence and Knowledge Management in Asia's Digital Economy
Patricia Ordóñez de Pablos (The University of Oviedo, Spain) Xi Zhang (Tianjin University, China) and Mohammad Nabil Almunawar (Universiti Brunei Darussalam, Brunei)
Business Science Reference • © 2023 • 531pp • H/C (ISBN: 9781668458495) • US $295.00

Future Outlooks on Corporate Finance and Opportunities for Robust Economic Planning
Siraj Kariyilaparambu Kunjumuhammed (Modern College of Business and Science, Oman) and Nithya Ramachandran (University of Technology and Applied Science, Oman)
Business Science Reference • © 2023 • 335pp • H/C (ISBN: 9781668453421) • US $240.00

701 East Chocolate Avenue, Hershey, PA 17033, USA
Tel: 717-533-8845 x100 • Fax: 717-533-8661
E-Mail: cust@igi-global.com • www.igi-global.com

Table of Contents

Preface.. xvi

Chapter 1
Opportunities and Challenges for Artificial Intelligence and Machine
Learning Applications in the Finance Sector.. 1
    Ruchi Sawwalakhe, RICS SBE, Amity University, Noida, India
    Sooraj Arora, RICS SBE, Amity University, Noida, India
    T. P. Singh, RICS SBE, Amity University, Noida, India

Chapter 2
Blockchain and Smart Contracts for Secure and Sustainable Development........ 18
    Sunil Kumar, AURO University, India
    Rohit Singh, The Assam Royal Global University, India

Chapter 3
Cryptocurrency and the Indian Monetary System 31
    Ranjana R. Kamath, SHSS, Jain University (Deemed), India
    Mahammad Habeeb, SHSS, Jain University (Deemed), India

Chapter 4
A Theoretical Perspective of Artificial Intelligence in Hostility of Cyber
Threats in the Banking Sector.. 43
    Diksha Verma, Chandigarh Group of Colleges, India
    Pooja Kansra, Lovely Professional University, India
    Sarabjit Kaur, Chandigarh Business School of Administration, India

Chapter 5
Role of Technology in Improving the Quality of Financial Advisory for
Personal Financial Management 55
    Niranjan Kulkarni, Vishwakarma University, India
    Omvir Gautam, Vishwakarma University, India
    Swapnil Pradeep Shah, FinoGlobin Financial Services Pvt. Ltd., India

Chapter 6
Blockchain in the Healthcare Industry: Process and Applications 81
    Vedica Awasthi, Lovely Professional University, India
    Pooja Kansra, Lovely Professional University, India

Chapter 7
Does the Cryptocurrency Index Provide Diversification Opportunities With
MSCI World Index and MSCI Emerging Markets Index? Cryptocurrency and
Portfolio Diversificaiton 94
    Miklesh Prasad Yadav, Amity University, India
    Sudhi Sharma, FIIB Delhi, India
    Babita Parmar, CHRIST University (Deemed), India

Chapter 8
Role of AI in the Inventory Management of Agri-Fresh Produce at
HOPCOMS 115
    Raghavendra A. N., CHRIST University (Deemed), India
    Amalanathan S., CHRIST University (Deemed), India

Chapter 9
Emergence of Crypto Currency and the Digital Financial Landscape: A
Critique 132
    Nidhi U. Argade, Faculty of Commerce, The Maharaja Sayajirao
        University of Baroda, Vadodara, India
    Parag Shukla, Faculty of Commerce, The Maharaja Sayajirao
        University of Baroda, Vadodara, India
    Madhvendra Pratap Singh, Management Institute, Kamla Nehru
        Institute of Physical and Social Sciences, India

Chapter 10
The Exploratory Study of Machine Learning on Applications, Challenges,
and Uses in the Financial Sector..156
    Tripti Pal, RATM, India

Chapter 11
Transforming Retail Markets Through IoT and AI-Enabled Architecture to
Identify COVID-19 Shoppers 166
    Mohan N., CMR Institute of Technology, India
    Sanjeev Kumar Thalari, CMR Institute of Technology, India

Chapter 12
Data Modeling in Finance Challenges 183
Prasanth Kumar Ra, University of Hyderabad, India
Santosh Kumar, PNC Financial Services, USA
Vikas Singh, Ministry of Consumer Affairs, Government of India, India

Chapter 13
Review of Machine Learning Techniques in the Supply Chain Management
of Indian Industry: A Future Research Agenda 199
Rashmi Ranjan Panigrahi, Siksha 'O'Anusandhan, India
Meenakshee Dash, Rajdhani College of Engineering and Management,
India
Zakir Hossen Shaikh, Bahrain Training Institute, Bahrain
Mohammad Irfan, CMR Institute of Technology, India

Chapter 14
The Effect of Good Corporate Governance on Financial Distress in
Companies Listed in Sharia Stock Index Indonesia: Machine Learning
Approach 220
Sylva Alif Rusmita, Airlangga University, Indonesia
Moh.Saifin Ami An-Nafis, Airlangga University, Indonesia
Indria Ramadhani, Airlangga University, Indonesia
Mohammad Irfan, CMR Institute of Technology, India

Compilation of References 252

About the Contributors 286

Index 291

Detailed Table of Contents

Preface.. xvi

Chapter 1
Opportunities and Challenges for Artificial Intelligence and Machine
Learning Applications in the Finance Sector.. 1
    Ruchi Sawwalakhe, RICS SBE, Amity University, Noida, India
    Sooraj Arora, RICS SBE, Amity University, Noida, India
    T. P. Singh, RICS SBE, Amity University, Noida, India

This book chapter primarily discusses various applications and historical developments
of artificial intelligence (AI) and machine learning (ML) applications in financial
sectors, specially from the perspective of Indian capital markets. AI and ML are
unique technologies that may be used in a variety of sectors. Especially for financial
sectors, these bring a lot of advantages, such as Lesser human bias; quicker resolution
of issues; cheaper than human labor; greater reach and impact; increasing client
involvement; and reducing fraudulent activity. It also talks about various challenges,
and charts the future outlook of AI and ML applications. AI and ML will persist to
have a growing influence on the finance industry in the upcoming times.

Chapter 2
Blockchain and Smart Contracts for Secure and Sustainable Development........ 18
    Sunil Kumar, AURO University, India
    Rohit Singh, The Assam Royal Global University, India

Smart contracts play an important role of simplifying business and trade between
the identified and anonymous parties without need of any intermediary to handle the
transaction, as well as the intermediary's associated fees and time delays. A business
can easily bring the transparency and build the trust of the customers by storing
the encrypted records of transaction across participants. It also prevents hackers
from breaking the integrity of the transaction because each record is connected on
a distributed ledger, and if hackers want to alter any particular record, he/she would
have to modify the entire chain for a single record. Therefore, a smart contract

has huge potential to streamline and automate the business work across industries around the world. In this chapter, the authors will explore the potential of blockchain and smart contracts in the different aspects of business world, like supply chain, insurance, mortgage loans, financial settlements, and many more applications in the financial industry.

Chapter 3

Cryptocurrency and the Indian Monetary System 31

    Ranjana R. Kamath, SHSS, Jain University (Deemed), India
    Mahammad Habeeb, SHSS, Jain University (Deemed), India

"Change is the only constant," wrote the ancient Greek philosopher Heraclitus of Ephesus. And in today's world, one of the greatest changes is the changing nature of money. As the world embraces the ease in accessibility to high-speed internet services across all spectrums, the medium of exchange is transforming from fiat currency to virtual and cryptocurrencies. The exchange of cryptocurrency heavily revolves around speculation by professionals, and institutional investors dealing with large sums of money. The global adoption of cryptocurrency has increased over the last few years and has seen an 880% increase in year-to-year transactions in the last year, reflecting the increased acceptance in cryptocurrency usage in emerging markets. India ranks second in the overall crypto-adoption index ranking, backing the increased interest of Indian investors in the cryptocurrency markets. The major focus of this paper is regarding the next phase of transition into digital and cryptocurrency and its implications on monetary policies with a specific focus on the Indian monetary system.

Chapter 4

A Theoretical Perspective of Artificial Intelligence in Hostility of Cyber
Threats in the Banking Sector 43

    Diksha Verma, Chandigarh Group of Colleges, India
    Pooja Kansra, Lovely Professional University, India
    Sarabjit Kaur, Chandigarh Business School of Administration, India

With the progress of new know-how and technology, various cyber centers are utilized by illegal persons to augment cyber related crime. To alleviate this digital crime and cyber threats, artificial intelligence is being implemented by banks and financial institutions. A variety of avenues are offered by artificial intelligence techniques, which facilitate the banks to amplify affluence plus wealth. As per various literatures it has been observed that the expenses of cybercrime were around $ 450 million globally. Therefore, it becomes imperative to introduce certain security programs for guarding cyber threats in banking area. To battle and overcome hackers many banks are moving hands to employ artificial intelligence. Various kinds of cybercrimes are prohibited and recognized by AI-based fraud detection systems. However, execution and preservation of artificial intelligence consist of the high cost. After it, joblessness rate is also augmented by AI techniques. In this study various artificial intelligence techniques will be discussed along with their utilization and limitations.

Chapter 5
Role of Technology in Improving the Quality of Financial Advisory for Personal Financial Management 55
  Niranjan Kulkarni, Vishwakarma University, India
  Omvir Gautam, Vishwakarma University, India
  Swapnil Pradeep Shah, FinoGlobin Financial Services Pvt. Ltd., India

Increased per capita income, improved life span, families changing from joint to nuclear ones, and absence of robust social security system; justify the need for a shift in management of personal finance for many. As a result of it, financial advisory is needed. This chapter tries to explore the relation between significance of technology in financial advisory with special reference to personal financial management. The study focuses on describing current use of technology, areas of improvements, and impact on quality of financial advice in personal financial management. The financial advisory field is also witnessing technology disruption with help of machine learning and artificial intelligence getting democratized in the hands of individuals. A lot of information is available at the fingertips, but the role of an advisor will always play a crucial role in achieving the objectives of financial inclusion, financial independence, financial maturity, and financial stability.

Chapter 6
Blockchain in the Healthcare Industry: Process and Applications 81
  Vedica Awasthi, Lovely Professional University, India
  Pooja Kansra, Lovely Professional University, India

Blockchain was first conceptualized in 2008, but became all the rage with Bitcoin. Blockchain is a digital ledger that records the transactions, excluding any third party. It has many features like transparency, security, privacy, accuracy, reliability, and decentralization. In the present study, the process and applications of blockchain in healthcare, and how and where blockchain is helpful for the healthcare industry, are discussed. The study shows that blockchain helps in generating a private key for its use, which can be accessed by that key only, ensuring privacy and security. Blockchain can record and manage the data of patients, which improves doctor-patient interaction with accuracy. It can also keep track of any upcoming outbreak of disease by helping epidemiologists and can help in claiming health insurance, which is helpful for both parties, i.e., insurer and insured. Lastly, it can help trace and secure the medical supplies without any fraud or manipulation, which can increase the product lifecycle by protecting the rights.

Chapter 7
Does the Cryptocurrency Index Provide Diversification Opportunities With
MSCI World Index and MSCI Emerging Markets Index? Cryptocurrency and
Portfolio Diversificaiton 94
Miklesh Prasad Yadav, Amity University, India
Sudhi Sharma, FIIB Delhi, India
Babita Parmar, CHRIST University (Deemed), India

The study is extending the ongoing discussion on Bitcoin as a diversification asset
with the stock market. Some studies analysed cryptocurrencies as a diversification
asset, and few challenged the same. During times of turbulence, it is crucial to gauge
further diversification opportunities. Henceforth, the study revisits the opportunities
of hedging and diversification with the crypto market from a broader perspective.
The study captures the spillover from MSCI World Index and MSCI Emerging
Markets Index to Bitwise 10 Crypto Index Fund (BITW). The study has contributed
methodologically to the existing literature by applying DY with symmetric and
asymmetric dynamic conditional volatility models. The results provide in-depth
shreds of evidence that BITW is insulated, neither taking volatilities from other
countries nor contributing to the volatilities of other countries. The study provides
insight to policymakers and investors.

Chapter 8
Role of AI in the Inventory Management of Agri-Fresh Produce at
HOPCOMS 115
Raghavendra A. N., CHRIST University (Deemed), India
Amalanathan S., CHRIST University (Deemed), India

Inventory management is vital for maintaining the efficiency of supply chain
management. Fruits and vegetables being perishable in nature should involve
inventory management to avoid wastage and loss in terms of over stocking and stock
out situations. The present study focuses on the role of artificial intelligence (AI)-
powered inventory management of fruits and vegetables at HOPCOMS, a cooperative
society founded in Bangalore. In the road to satisfy the customers, it is necessary for
the society to come up with different strategies to manage the inventories in which a
retailer confronts overstock and stock out situation, affecting the profit of the society.
Therefore, a study was conducted with the help of structured questionnaire among
122 retailers of HOPCOMS outlets in Bangalore. The results obtained from the study
suggest that inventory valuation method positively influences AI-powered demand
forecasting and customer order fulfillment, and AI-powered demand forecasting is
positively related to customer order fulfillment.

Chapter 9
Emergence of Crypto Currency and the Digital Financial Landscape: A
Critique 132
Nidhi U. Argade, Faculty of Commerce, The Maharaja Sayajirao
University of Baroda, Vadodara, India
Parag Shukla, Faculty of Commerce, The Maharaja Sayajirao
University of Baroda, Vadodara, India
Madhvendra Pratap Singh, Management Institute, Kamla Nehru
Institute of Physical and Social Sciences, India

The reality of the new normal induced by the pandemic has resulted in a radical
transformation of the financial sector, where it is undergoing a dramatic digital
change. With this backdrop, the purpose of this study is conceptualizing the role of
crypto currencies and the effects on the digital financial (DiFi) landscape in India
and worldwide. It has led to disruptive technological innovation and accelerated
change in the financial system. In this light, the present study attempts to highlight the
different digital initiatives undertaken by various developed and developing countries
and the pros and cons associated with the same. This research study shall serve as
a primer to demonstrate the effects of use of digitalization and technology-enabled
initiatives for crypto currencies and is also aimed to encapsulate the restraining and
facilitating forces that drive adoption of digital financial models and the hybrid role
of government as we usher in the new financial landscape.

Chapter 10
The Exploratory Study of Machine Learning on Applications, Challenges,
and Uses in the Financial Sector..156
Tripti Pal, RATM, India

Artificial intelligence (AI) and machine learning (ML) have become essentials part
of our lives by having their applications in various fields. Artificial intelligence is
a technology that allows a machine to behave like a human. Machine learning is a
subdivision of artificial intelligence that helps a machine to automatically learn from
past data with more accurate predicting outcomes. In today's life, especially during
the COVID-19 pandemic, our lives run online and almost all work is done online
like office work, education, shopping, medical facilities, etc., as are so many cases
where machine learning is used in the finance sector like financial monitoring, making
investment predictions, process automation, secure transactions, risk management,
financial advisory, customer data management, decision making, business analysis,
and customer service-level improvement.

Chapter 11
Transforming Retail Markets Through IoT and AI-Enabled Architecture to
Identify COVID-19 Shoppers 166
    Mohan N., CMR Institute of Technology, India
    Sanjeev Kumar Thalari, CMR Institute of Technology, India

The novel corona virus disease (COVID-19) is a pandemic, and quarantines are helping to stop it. However, defections of confined individuals around the world are causing considerable concern. This study examines the impact of artificial intelligence methods in the retail business utilizing a qualitative concept research approach. It's encouraging to see the retail sector steadily getting back on track following the impact of COVID-19. This hand band device will easily find the COVID-19 affected. Persons are identified by a 5-metre radius, and they are warned by vibrating. Finally, this chapter provides a conceptual framework for speeding up the struggle to prevent the spread of COVID-19 in India by combining IoT and AI technologies used to combat COVID-19 outbreaks around the world. Business decision-makers and managers should prepare their organizations and workers for the upcoming market shifts based on the findings of this research.

Chapter 12
Data Modeling in Finance Challenges 183
    Prasanth Kumar Ra, University of Hyderabad, India
    Santosh Kumar, PNC Financial Services, USA
    Vikas Singh, Ministry of Consumer Affairs, Government of India, India

This chapter aims to draw readers' attention on the challenges of modeling in finance. The new quantitative methods offer extraordinary capabilities with the latest algorithms using AI, ML, etc., aided by high technological computational power. However, the adoption of the latest tools and techniques comes with many challenges that are limited by human resources and nuances of financial industries. Unlike the recommendation-based models in the technology industry, real money is at stake in the financial industry. Hence, it is not very prudent to accept the result of quantitative methods without understanding the inherited risks. Despite the hype created by data scientists, the financial industry cautiously adopted the highly complicated learning tools after due diligence because investor and shareholder money is at stake and experts want to strategize financial decisions based on the data model outputs. Further, the chapter brings the key highlights of financial models.

Chapter 13
Review of Machine Learning Techniques in the Supply Chain Management
of Indian Industry: A Future Research Agenda 199
    Rashmi Ranjan Panigrahi, Siksha 'O'Anusandhan, India
    Meenakshee Dash, Rajdhani College of Engineering and Management, India
    Zakir Hossen Shaikh, Bahrain Training Institute, Bahrain
    Mohammad Irfan, CMR Institute of Technology, India

The technologies have increased the role of IT in evolving the path for the future. A sense of belonging and significance to the market is felt by current industries. Procurement, assembly, and supply were affected by the digital revolt that has swept the world. Now machine learning is a hot area among scholars and industry professionals. Two decades ago, there were few publications of machine learning and supply chain management. SCM-related ML application research hasn't been thoroughly examined in the literature till date with respect to the Indian steel industry. As a result, this study examined articles from Jan. 2010 to Dec. 2020 in five major databases to present the latest research trends. A quantitative analysis of 112 shortlisted articles revealed that there were not enough publications to form a strong group force in this field. This study's comprehensive look at ML techniques used in SCM will help future research. A true reflection of today's industries, the chapter accurately reflects prospects to express feelings, thoughts, and contribute to future industries.

Chapter 14
The Effect of Good Corporate Governance on Financial Distress in
Companies Listed in Sharia Stock Index Indonesia: Machine Learning
Approach..220
    Sylva Alif Rusmita, Airlangga University, Indonesia
    Moh.Saifin Ami An-Nafis, Airlangga University, Indonesia
    Indria Ramadhani, Airlangga University, Indonesia
    Mohammad Irfan, CMR Institute of Technology, India

This study aims to examine the effect of good corporate governance (GCG) on financial distress in companies listed on the Indonesian Sharia Stock Index. The purposive sampling method was used, obtaining 23 samples that met the criteria. Panel regression and machine learning were used to test the hypothesis. Based on the results, the variables of GCG, which consist of institutional ownership (IO), managerial ownership (MO), board of commissioners size (BoC), and proportion of independent commissioners (PI), affect financial distress simultaneously, whereas BoC and PI are partially the most significant variables. The machine learning method shows that extra trees is the best model to analyze financial distress. The model indicates the most significant variable is IO, followed by BoC and PI. From the result, Islamic issuers should manage their GCG by reducing the number of BoC, IO, and adding a proportion of PI to minimize the case of financial distress.

Compilation of References 252

About the Contributors 286

Index 291

Preface

Finance is vital to the applications of machine learning. Several complex problems, such as investment decision making, macroeconomic analysis, asset credit evaluation, etc., widely exist in the field of finance. Machine learning (ML) is used in many financial companies which is making significant impact in the financial services. With the increasing complexity of financial transaction processes, ML can reduce operational costs through process automation which can automate repetitive tasks and increase productivity. Among others, ML can analysis large volumes of historical data and make better trading decisions to increase revenue.

AI/ML (subsuming computational intelligence, deep learning, reinforcement learning) has become a new phenomenon and caught every researcher in almost all domains by surprise with its spectacular success accompanied by unprecedented accuracies. The resurgence of AI/ML is so pervasive that it could virtually solve any problem from any field-be it theoretical or empirical with astounding results. It came very close to human intelligence and cognition, and in some cases even surpassed human experts. Banking, finance and insurance (BFSI) sector is no exception to this modern tsunami. Here, these technologies include traditional ML based predictive analytics, computational intelligence, deep learning, and reinforcement learning and deep reinforcement learning as well.

The advancement in fin-tech especially artificial intelligence (AI) and machine learning (ML), has significantly affected the way financial services are offered and adopted today. Important financial decisions such as investment decision making, macroeconomic analysis, and credit evaluation are getting more complex in the field of finance. ML is used in many financial companies which is making significant impact in the financial services. With the increasing complexity of financial transaction processes, ML can reduce operational costs through process automation which can automate repetitive tasks and increase productivity. Among others, ML can analysis large volumes of historical data and make better trading decisions to increase revenue.

Preface

The main objective of this book is to provide an exhaustive overview on the roles of AI and ML algorithms in financial sectors with special reference to complex financial applications such as financial risk management in big data environment. In addition, it aims to provide a collection of high-quality research works that address broad challenges in both theoretical and application aspects of AI in the field of finance. We invite colleagues to contribute original book chapters that will stimulate the continuing effort on the ML algorithms that leads to solve the problem of big data processing in a complex banking and financial environment. Ideas and contributions are also invited from practitioners who are developing algorithms, systems, and applications, to share their results, ideas, and experiences.

Target Audience: Researchers, Academicians, Industrialists, Investors, Regulatory Bodies, Enthusiastic Expert, Inspired Innovator, and Considerate Conventionalist.

IMPORTANCE OF THE CHAPTER SUBMISSIONS

1. Opportunities and Challenges for Artificial Intelligence and Machine Learning Applications in the Finance Sector

The growth of technology is an unavoidable phenomenon and must be integrated in the future to maximize the output and efficiency of valuable systems such as Capital Markets in India. Artificial intelligence in finance has a lot of benefits. Perhaps the most significant advantage of AI is that it opens a plethora of automation opportunities. As a result, automation may help financial firms enhance the productivity and efficiency of a variety of activities. Furthermore, since AI may replace humans in some instances, it aids in the elimination of human biases and different failures caused by sensitive or psychological elements. AI is also better at analysing data than humans. On the other hand, machine learning enables computers to discover data trends, give critical insights to decision-makers and assist companies in producing highly accurate information. ML as a subset of AI, collects and store data from their experience and come up with different and better solutions every time to cope with the problem better next time. Artificial intelligence has been widely embraced in every sector during the last few decades. Companies used AI to gain a competitive advantage by: Making better, data-driven decisions; Increasing profits effectively through efficient targeting or pinpoint suggestions; Increasing actual sales by recognising "hesitating" customers early; Automating repetitive tasks that AI does faster than an average person among other benefits.

AI and ML integration is necessary in developing markets like India to capture all global news, understand patterns and behaviour of the market based on past trends, study annual financial statements and to finally give an opinion after progressive analysis using ML. These can be integrated with automation so that consumers can simply enter their expected returns or risk capacity and using the algorithm, a portfolio could be curated for everyone. Also, these technologies must be made available to small, medium investors to ensure market stabilisation otherwise the risk of income disparity is likely to grow.

Conclusively, the plan for the future should be to leverage technological advancements and execute its application creatively to make the capital market flourish & act as a stimulus of recovery post COVID and also act as a springboard towards our dream of a 5 Trillion-dollar economy.

2. Blockchain and Smart Contracts for Secure and Sustainable Development

The use of machine learning in finance is essential. In the realm of finance, there are many complicated issues that need to be addressed, including asset credit evaluation, macroeconomic analysis, and investment decision-making. Many financial firms use machine learning (ML), which is having a big impact on the financial services industry. Because financial transaction processes are becoming more complicated, machine learning (ML) can lower operational costs by automating repetitive procedures and boosting productivity. Among other things, ML can analyse vast amounts of previous data and improve trading decisions to boost profits.

3. Cryptocurrency and the Indian Monetary System

Cryptocurrency and blockchain is a topic of significant importance in the current global scenario as they are a means of decentralised transactions worldwide. The transition to an economic system consisting of increasing digitisation in financial services will require strong monetary frameworks supporting it. Understanding the underlying algorithms governing the functioning of such financial systems is key to framing monetary policies. At present, the Reserve Bank of India does not recognise cryptocurrency as a safe means of digital transaction. The Indian government is also evaluating the various models and its effects. Along with the existing global cryptocurrencies, the Reserve Bank of India (RBI) is in the process of implementing the Central Bank Digital Currency (CBDC) in a phased manner for wholesale and retail segments and the CBDC will be a sovereign backed digital currency. This chapter provides an overview of the digital algorithms, th uses and application of cryptocurrencies and the possible implications on the Indian Monetary system. The readers will have an increased understanding on the functioning of the Indian banking system and the financial services provided by them.

Preface

4. A Theoretical Perspective of Artificial Intelligence in Hostility of Cyber Threats in the Banking Sector

Nowadays, the numbers of users who are using devices and programs have increased considerably in the modern enterprise that generates a large amount of data, many of which are sensitive or confidential. Thus, here comes the importance of cyber security as in this age, the data theft on these systems continues to grow. The increase in volume and more sophistication in methods which are used by the cyber attackers through many attack techniques create many problems even further. Maintaining cyber security is a challenge for all organizations in this threat landscape which is constantly evolving. In Traditional reactive approaches, the resources were put towards protecting systems against the biggest known threats, while lesser-known threats were undefended, which is no longer a sufficient tactic. A more proactive and adaptive approach is necessary in order to keep up with changing security risks. There are several key cybersecurity advisory organizations that recommend good guidance. Like if we adopt continuous monitoring and perform assessments in real-time, it can help us to defend if any known and unknown threats occur, as part of a risk assessment framework and is also endorsed by the National Institute of Standards and Technology (NIST). Therefore, the present chapter tries to highlight the issues of cyber threats in the field of Artificial Intelligence.

5. Role of Technology in Improving the Quality of Financial Advisory for Personal Financial Management

Financial Advisory is a need of an hour. This chapter tries to explore the relation between significance of technology in financial advisory with special reference to personal financial management. The study focuses on describing current use of technology, areas of improvements and impact on quality of financial advice in personal financial management. There is a strong case for adoption of technology by the financial advisors in personal financial management which need to be extended to rural areas as well. Author aims to see the outcome of this research to add value to financial service providers, regulators, Fintech players and individual investor. Suggestions for further research include studies in the area of technology adoption by investors and the financial advisors. More research is desirable to study the reasons for lower rates of technology adoption despite proven benefits.

Preface

6. Blockchain in the Healthcare Industry: Process and Applications

This chapter helps in enhancing the learning of blockchain in the healthcare sector. Various research articles have been reviewed which helped in improving the content and quality of the chapter. The chapter shows how blockchain works and helps in improving the healthcare sector. Applications of blockchain in healthcare are also mentioned in this book chapter. Knowledge about what is blockchain, the characteristics of blockchain, and how it maintains the privacy of the user's data has made a prior concern, all these topics have been covered in this chapter.

7. Does the Cryptocurrency Index Provide Diversification Opportunities With MSCI World Index and MSCI Emerging Markets Index? Cryptocurrency and Portfolio Diversification

This study unravels an attempt to investigate the spillover from MSCI World Index and MSCI Emerging Markets Index with Bitwise 10 Crypto Index Fund (BITW) so that cryptocurrency can be identified whether it will provide diversification opportunity. Further, the results of the dynamic conditional models captured no significant short-term volatility transmissions from MSCI Emerging Markets Index to BITW. However, significant short-term evidence has been found from the MSCI World Index to BITW. Henceforth, there is an opportunity for diversification with BITW while investing in MSCI Emerging Markets Index. This study is important for all the stakeholders of the market who believe in the investing cryptocurrency and stock market. It will provide an insight to policymakers and investors encompassing that the technology-based asset could be considered as a diversification asset while investing in these emerging market indexes.

8. Role of AI in Inventory Management of Agri-Fresh Produce at HOPCOMS

Globalization has increased the relevance of supply chain management in recent years. In the current business environment, supply chain management, which is a strategic, tactical, and operational strategy, is necessary to bring about transformation in an inter-organizational process that includes customers, suppliers, and partners. Inventory management is vital for maintaining the efficiency of the supply chain management. The present study focuses on the role of artificial intelligence (AI) powered inventory management of fruits and vegetables at HOPCOMS, a cooperative society founded in Bangalore. Lack of awareness regarding inventory valuation method will result in improper ordering decisions affecting the purchase planning,

Preface

sales planning and product planning. Practicing AI powered Demand Forecasting as part of inventory management at the retail outlet of HOPCOMS is a significant driver for increasing customer satisfaction. Hence, the present book chapter helps the farmers, wholesalers and retailers to plan their inventory through technological interventions thereby achieving the individual, organizational and societal objectives.

9. Emergence of Crypto Currency and Digital Financial Landscape: A Critique

The reality of the new normal induced by the pandemic has resulted in a radical transformation of the financial sector, where it is undergoing a dramatic digital change. With this backdrop, the purpose of this study is conceptualizing the role of crypto currencies and the effects on the Digital financial (DiFi) landscape in India and Worldwide. It has led to disruptive technological innovation, and accelerated change in the financial system. In this light, the present study attempts to highlight the different digital initiatives undertaken by various developed and developing countries and the pros and cons associated with the same. This research study shall serve as a primer to demonstrate the effects of use of digitalization and technology enabled initiatives for crypto currencies and is also aimed to encapsulate the restraining and facilitating forces that drive adoption of digital financial models and the hybrid role of government as we usher in the new financial landscape.

10. The Exploratory study of Machine Learning on Applications, Challenges, and Uses in the Financial Sector

AII changed globally the finance services industry. Machine learning is an automated, streamlined, and optimized process to increase work efficiency and reduced cost and time. When AI comes to the finance sector it predicts loan risk, trading, stock marketing, sales forecasting, Investment predictions, and credit score. It reduces money laundering. Machine learning algorithms are superb to find out transactional fraud by examine millions of data points. The fraud detection tools analyse client behaviours, track the allocation therefore they can quickly detect and prevent any unusual activities.AI provides finance companies to complete replacement of manual work to RPA for enhance business productivity. The aim of process optimization to reduce operation cost and drive profitably in both front and backend activities.

AI provides many tools that gives solution regarding how to happy your customer. These are some points that tells the important of AI in finance industry. After these we can only say that now AI is an essential part of finance industry without, we cannot imagine the financial services. This technology gives us a better, compact and accurate methods regarding our services.

11. Transforming Retail Markets Through IoT and AI-Enabled Architecture to Identify COVID-19 Shoppers

The novel corona virus disease (COVID-19) is spreading like a pandemic, and quarantines are helping to stop it. However, defections of confined individuals around the world are causing considerable concern. This study examines the impact of Artificial Intelligence Methods in the retail business utilizing a qualitative Concept research approach. It's encouraging to see the retail sector steadily getting back on track following the impact of Covid-19. Many of the tedious and repetitive duties of a marketer's life can already be replaced by IoT and AI technology, as evidenced by the study. This Hand band device designed by us will easily deduct Covid effects. Persons are identified by a 5-meter radius, and they are warned by vibrating.

12. Data Modeling in Finance Challenges

The chapter on modeling in finance and its challenges is based on the existing published works. The chapter suggests that the new quantitative methods offer extraordinary capabilities with the latest algorithms using AI, ML etc. aided by very high technological computational power. However, the adoption of the contemporary tools may bring certain challenges including skillful human resources. Both the quantitative and qualitative methods inherit their own challenges. Despite the hype created by data science with the use of AI, ML, and increased computational power, the financial industry is cautiously taking the steps to adopt the highly complicated Machine learning tools after a thorough understanding of the limitations or challenges.

13. Review of Machine Learning Techniques in Supply Chain Management of the Indian Industry: A Future Research Agenda

The increasing importance of cutting-edge technology means that IT-enabled systems will play an ever-growing role in shaping the future of the economy. Companies in the modern economic climate have a deep commitment to their local communities and a desire to improve the globe. The proliferation of digital technologies has affected every facet of real-world operations, from sourcing and production to distribution and customer service. There is a lot of talk about machine learning right now in a wide range of settings, from the commercial world to the academic world. Up to the last two decades, there was a dearth of scholarly work connecting ML with SCM (SCM). Until now, there hasn't been a systematic analysis of the research done on ML's use in India's steel industry with regard to supply chain management. This article provides a thorough evaluation of ML methods for SCM, which might serve as a useful resource for future research. This paper provides a realistic picture of

Preface

today's industries by focusing on how the free flow of information and the exchange of ideas might shape tomorrow's market.

14. The Effect of Good Corporate Governance on Financial Distress in Companies Listed in the Sharia Stock Index Indonesia: Machine Learning Approach

Good Corporate Governance (GCG) is one of the things that significantly affect the company's sustainability. Thus, it is necessary to pay attention to factors that can affect the performance of GCG in terms of minimizing the risk of bankruptcy. By using two research methods, (regression of panel data as traditional statistical tools and machine learning which is a modern tool), the results of this study become relevant to answer problems that have always been the scourge of companies related to managerial GCG. By using several external variables (independent commissioners and institutional ownership) and internal variables (managerial ownership and board of commissioners), this research can provide an overview of companies related to managerial GCG. From the investor side, this result can be an assessment of investment preferences by considering the implementation of GCG in the company. Different results between panel data methods and machine learning show that these two methods are complementary. In the research panel data, the study's results can indicate the direction of the significance of variables. At the same time, machine learning can minimize errors in the research model to determine an ideal model. However, the result shows that both support agency theory, where companies need to pay attention to the implementation of GCG in terms of external and internal aspects to minimize the risk of bankruptcy. Future research can add independent variables or focus on case studies of certain sector companies.

CONCLUSION

The book has the potential to provide new source of reference in the areas of fintech, artificial intelligence, blockchain, machine learning, big data, data science, and data mining. In the era of disruptive innovation in finance and technology, knowledge advancements in various aspects of engineering, management, data science, and cloud computing are highly sought to ensure that companies remained competitive edge and able to achieve sustainability in new era. The book can be the main source of reference for institutions of higher learning and training institutions offering and deliberating on these issues.

Mohammad Irfan
CMR Institute of Technology, India

Mohamed Elhoseny
American University in the Emirates, UAE

Salina Kassim
International Islamic University of Malaysia, Malaysia

Noura Metawa
University of Sharjah, UAE

Chapter 1

Opportunities and Challenges for Artificial Intelligence and Machine Learning Applications in the Finance Sector

Ruchi Sawwalakhe
RICS SBE, Amity University, Noida, India

Sooraj Arora
RICS SBE, Amity University, Noida, India

T. P. Singh
RICS SBE, Amity University, Noida, India

ABSTRACT

This book chapter primarily discusses various applications and historical developments of artificial intelligence (AI) and machine learning (ML) applications in financial sectors, specially from the perspective of Indian capital markets. AI and ML are unique technologies that may be used in a variety of sectors. Especially for financial sectors, these bring a lot of advantages, such as Lesser human bias; quicker resolution of issues; cheaper than human labor; greater reach and impact; increasing client involvement; and reducing fraudulent activity. It also talks about various challenges, and charts the future outlook of AI and ML applications. AI and ML will persist to have a growing influence on the finance industry in the upcoming times.

DOI: 10.4018/978-1-6684-4483-2.ch001

Copyright © 2023, IGI Global. Copying or distributing in print or electronic forms without written permission of IGI Global is prohibited.

AI AND ML IN THE FINANCE INDUSTRY

Starting from the early 1990s, the finance sector has evolved tremendously. Due to emergence of technologies like online and mobile banking, the industry has been significantly affected by digitalization. In today's world, speed and efficiency are the most important competitive advantages in every business.

Millennials and Generation Z are emerging as a major part of the working population and they prefer getting their information, buying goods and getting services online by simply operating their phones and devices. As a result, the sector has become increasingly dynamic and competitive. Firms must stay up to date with new innovative advancements in order to survive competitive pressure.

Artificial intelligence (AI) and its subset machine learning (ML) are technologies that help organisations better serve their customers by automating tasks. By 2030, experts believe that AI and ML could save financial institutions around 1 trillion USD.

As per research, over 35% of institutions are now utilising AI to improve responsiveness, personalization, and to recognise speech and predictive data modelling. Companies are learning to apply AI technology towards their unique goals and promising application fields are expected to emerge.

The application of AI technology to enhance customer satisfaction is amongst the high potential developments in technology. Certain customer-centric solutions, such as chat-bots, are becoming commonplace. Simultaneously, computational analysis, activity mechanisation, and automation systems are becoming increasingly common in banking as companies highlight the value they provide.

Despite the fact that automating processes with robots follows sets of rules, rather than intelligent methods, it is frequently utilised in conjunction using AI-powered technologies. When contrasted to AI, machine learning is a more popular form since it has a critical contribution in the development of banking and finance industry in general.

In a wide range of uses, machine learning has so far demonstrated its enormous promise, and indeed the banking industry is no exception. The key benefits of ML in the banking business include the ability to acquire, analyse, and organise massive volumes of data. Human intervention is minimal to non-existent in ML-based approaches.

Computers may look at the historical information, spot correlations, and apply such inferences to retrieve information having potential. Such algorithms can also be used with several variables and information to build a predictive model.

Whenever it comes to AI Technology, the terms machine learning and automating get frequently used. Such Artificially Intelligent applications are really valuable, and they may yield excellent outcomes rapidly, allowing visitors to immediately assess the benefits of the recent innovation as well as the return on investment. However, there may be less obvious aspects of Artificial Intelligence that are equally amazing.

The banking industry businesses have recently evolved considerably as a result of technological advancements. This evolution had been ongoing for several years, but the rate of growth has suddenly accelerated dramatically. Such solutions have been used by the financial technology industry to challenge the larger business by improving consumer satisfaction and disrupting the long-standing client gaining strategies.

Both back-end and intermediary office applications that help run the finance industry would be the area of prime interest of the next generation of finance technology. Only a Handful of prominent players recognise that use of such emerging financial technology has been shiny in front-end client experiences but are typically still supported via old infrastructure.

Financial technology's potential to flourish is being hampered by a lack of invention at the back end of financial services during the last years. That is, nevertheless, improving.

In the near future, the banking and finance technology sectors would be revolutionized by machine learning while the impact of AI would be greater appreciated eventually in the following decades.

Many businesses, particularly banking institutions, have massive volumes of consumer, company, transactional, and income statements. Such innovations may benefit banks in 2 manners: better client handling and engagement, and seamlessly streamlined back-office procedures.

Deeper Understanding of Artificial intelligence and Machine learning

Artificial intelligence and machine learning help increase effective execution of laborious tasks and serving as a tool to make management decisions. Artificial intelligence and machine learning are two aspects of computer science that are interlinked. They are gaining popularity since they help to develop relevant and useful solutions.

Despite the fact that they are interrelated techniques that are frequently referenced interchangeably, their area of usage and utilities are quite distinct. For simplification, we may distinguish artificial intelligence and machine learning as follows:

"Artificial intelligence is an all-encompassing idea which aims to produce smart computers and machines which could replicate human-like thought processes, capabilities, and behaviour to innovate and solve complex problems."

On the other hand, ML is a sub-type, part or branch of Artificial Intelligence which enables computers to understand given data and learning from the patterns automatically, not having to be coded or re-programmed repeatedly. Following are a few key distinctions within Artificial Intelligence and Machine Learning technologies, as well as an explanation of AI and ML.

Artificial Intelligence

AI is an area of digital technology which aims to create computers or devices which could 'think' and perform tasks like a person. AI is constructed by using the 2 terms: "artificial" which signifies man-made and "intelligence," which refers to a brain-like thought process. Together they signify a "man-made thinking ability."

One may describe AI as a method which allows development of advanced machines which could imitate humans' intellect to solve complex problems. AI systems don't need frequent re-programming or manual upgrades; rather, they use 'Machine Learning' to employ processes which function in combination to record, analyse, re-program and 'learn' all by themselves.

AI devices actively use 'Reinforced learning' systems and'deep- learning' structures which are examples and types of ML systems. ' Cortana', Alphabet's 'Alpha-Go', computer learning to play competitive chess-moves and other applications of Intelligence are all applications.

Artificial Intelligence may be divided into 3 categories as per its abilities: Weak, General and Strong Artificial Intelligence. As of, now Financial Sector is dealing with both weaker and general Artificial Intelligence. Stronger AI seems to become a possibility in the future, which is predicted to be more credible, accurate and smarter than a human brain.

Machine Learning

We use ML specifically to generate useful information by analysing and cleaning large datasets. This could be described in the following manner:

"ML is a branch of AI technology that allows computers to keep learning without the need to be specially taught using prior information or events."

They don't need to be specifically re-coded to upgrade themselves or 'learn', instead ML allows a computerized device to generate estimates or draw conclusions based on past data. ML makes use of a large quantity of unstructured and partially structured data, cleans and organises it in order for a ML model to analyse it, figure out patterns and correlations, learn from it and perform better considering its learnings.

4

Artificial Intelligence uses ML to create smart machines or devices. AI has a broader scope since it considers how a machine interacts with its environment, the different forms by which they consume or record data, such as by using speech recognition, visual inputs and finally AI converts this data into simplified data sets which are organised and analysed by Machine Learning to upgrade the software and make the machine and its artificial brain-like intelligence smarter and capable of dealing with its environment more efficiently as time progresses.

ML is based on a system that learns by itself with the use of previous data. A limitation of ML is that the system will function only if a particular type of dataset is provided into it as an input; for example, the designers must develop a complex code for ML system to recognise photographs of birds, once coded, the software will be able to interpret only bird pictures but will not be able to analyse or comprehend other kinds of images as well such as car pictures.

Hence either the code must be sophisticated enough to analyse different types of data or by using AI or manual methods, datasets must be converted into a form which the ML software could easily interpret.

ML is utilised in a variety of applications, including digital recommendation systems, Google or other web searching engines, block mails which are spammy by using filters, and social media automatically detecting our friends' faces to give tag suggestions, among others.

It is broken into 3 categories: supervised, reinforced, or unsupervised machine learning.

Advantages of Artificial Intelligence and Machine Learning

Banks and finance-providing firms may use machine learning and artificial intelligence to better comprehend company customers and corporate verticals. ML is being used by numerous companies for powering financing product personalization and client engaging cues to relationships maintenance team, for instance. It integrates confidential information, such as how anyone manages debt, their credit score, or outstanding liabilities and afterwards recommends goods which would meet each user's requirements.

Regarding cards and payment processing, lenders are starting to employ Machine Learning and Artificial Intelligence to generate predictive modelling about client patterns, purchase preferences, or anomalous scam identification. Banking and finance organisations that offer personal loans and digital payment choices can employ Artificial Intelligence systems to determine usage which is unusual to determine and block cards after theft, thanks to better fraud prevention.

Table 1. Key differences between Artificial Intelligence and Machine learning (ML)

Artificial Intelligence	Machine learning
AI is a technique that uses technologies to make computer mimic human thinking and problem solving.	ML is a part of AI that enables a computer to understand and self-evolve from prior data, not needing manual reprogramming.
A major objective of AI would be to create intelligent machines/devices that can resolve complicated challenges.	Machine learning aim is limited to enabling computers to analyse and keep learning from data to become more efficient.
AI helps create sophisticated computers that can interact with the environment to retrieve data, the same way a human can.	In machine learning, we use data to train computers how to do an activity better to produce reliable results.
The 2 primary subgroups of artificial intelligence are machine learning and 'deep learning'.	The only major subgroup of ML is 'Deep learning'.
It is attempting to develop an advanced machine capable of performing a variety of challenging activities.	It constructs devices with comprehensive coding but solely accomplish the functions for which they were programmed.
Cortana, client service with chatbots, Intelligent systems, virtual videogames, smart lifelike robots andother AI devices are among the most common.	ML is used for online recommendation tools like Netflix, refining Google search-engines for personalised results and social media automatically detecting friends faces to give tag suggestions, among others.
It may be classified into 3 categories based on its functionality: weak, general and strong Artificial Intelligence.	Supervised, Unsupervised and Reinforced learning are the 3 primary categories of ML.
Interacting with environment, collecting data, to learn and evolve are all part of it.	Whenever presented with fresh facts, it incorporates analysis and self-improvement.
Organized, partially organized and unorganized data are all dealt with.	It can only handle Data that is organised or partially-organised.

This could integrate system info, IP address, geographical region and activity pattern, then evaluate these to a "normal" solitary customer's benchmark. Machine Learning /Artificial Intelligence firms are allowing innovative banks and financial technology to contend against latest tech. Previously, just big credit agencies provided such innovations.

Using automation processes, Artificial Intelligence provides large-scale client support, with the computer evolving throughout times. Companies could minimise overall purchase prices and other client focused KPIs by eliminating disruptions to the client's experience with artificial intelligence services.

Artificial Intelligence driven technologies like customer support queries may automatically redirect questions depending on context. Organizations can avoid using ticketing custodians and route queries towards appropriate verticals or utilise algorithms to respond quickly.

Financial organizations which employ Artificial Intelligence and Machine learning to enhance prediction models instead of depending only on human workforce can analyse massive volumes of datasets, enhance operational procedures and prevent fraudulent acts. To sum up, these are some instances of how ML strategies are applied in the finance domain to ensure client satisfaction and move the business ahead:

- **Advantage 1: Lesser Human bias**

Bias comes without realisation in our actions. Individuals may utilise facts selectively and form judgments on the basis of intuitions about other individuals with regard to their attitude, personality, behaviour, or multiple other factors. Machines would, within majority situations, act with lesser lapse of judgement compared to us. This would not rule out the possibility of AI having lapses in acting entirely with objectivity. Whenever a machine learning code is taught on a consistently flawed data, it would generate biased and skewed results. (Vargas, 2021)

Organisations would have to keep updated on all company matters in order to recognise when artificial intelligence could promote impartiality and when machine learning and humans' cognition could work together to decrease biases. It might be especially beneficial in sectors like mortgage handling and assessing any acceptable credit score with minimal human input.

- **Advantage 2: Quicker resolution of issues**

Since algorithms are modified across all connected devices in the split of a second, if not in real time, Artificial Intelligence/Machine learning is quicker than human operators. Any computer with this updated algorithm could forecast the behaviour of thousands of clients as per requirement, accurately, within moments once it is incorporated inside an automatic mechanism for analysis and to make decisions (Vargas, 2021).

In contrast, if such forecasting mechanisms remain in a manual form controlled by humans, then to make similar decisions of updating entire algorithms frequently and notifying all stakeholders, will become extremely expensive to create a comparable capacity to process. Such perks come in handy when it comes to taking difficult business actions.

- **Advantage 3: Cheaper than Human Labour**

Since forecasting analytics could generate quicker, accurate and hence less expensive, conclusions even compared to traditional finance specialist professionals, technologies work with professionals to help us save time, money and effort but may soon entirely replace traditional talents. Since the improvements are handled via Machine learning programs rather than people, Artificial Intelligence/Machine learning are considerably less expensive to implement than people-centric work processes. Both, capital expenses and recurring expenses are cheaper when compared to the price of employing highly skilled human professionals.

- **Advantage 4: Greater reach and Impact**

Artificial Intelligence/Machine learning can handle a huge amount of datasets. Sub- division of clients into small segments powered by AI technology breaks apart big consumer groups formed by conventional segmenting processes, allowing businesses to connect with clients in an increasingly personalised and tailor - made manner. Such sub-segmenting implies qualified leads and more precise advertising. (Vargas, 2021)

- **Advantage 5: Increasing client involvement**

Client involvement may be increased via utilising artificial intelligence for further understanding the client by reaping the benefits of real-time updating of algorithms to conduct advanced and deep analytics. Service suggestion algorithms, for instance, have been shown to be beneficial in providing a customized content for clients while also increasing income. Service recommending systems are a type of artificial intelligence that makes recommendations for every client depending on a variety of characteristics such as previous behaviour, activity during the interactions, products pricing and the interests and habits of clients with similar demographics. (Vargas, 2021)

- **Advantage 6: Reduces fraudulent activity**

Worldwide, cybercrime is growing at a faster rate than banking institutions are able to neutralise it. While artificial intelligence and machine learning don't instantly resolve all concerns, they can help develop algorithms for reducing malicious attempts by recognising such attempts early by machine learning different activities and behaviours to immediately freeze, report and raise alert against such attempts. Identifying such activities so early and setting off alerts across the vulnerable devices are not possible by Traditional human methods. (Vargas, 2021)

Furthermore, artificial intelligence/machine learning could significantly minimise the number of deceitful instances that need to be assessed by individuals. Prior to actually compiling a database of "highly suspicious" instances requiring appropriate assessment, the systems could first accurately categorise and reject a higher number of situations which were not actually criminal attempts. Doing so provides its users with a greater sense of trust on the banking system's protection. (Vargas, 2021)

- **Advantage 7: Quicker resolution of issues**

The Artificial Intelligence prediction system could provide a real-time evaluation of the client's credit rating, enabling client service agents to provide a tailored proposition. Such an approach improves the effectiveness of proposals by speeding up the total borrowing risk-assessment procedure.

The above listed examples are merely a few of the multitude of possibilities of using AI/ machine learning in the workplace. They may be used to improve conventional evaluation with human knowledge whenever employed correctly. AI and machine learning would persist to have a growing influence on the finance industry in the upcoming times.

Ultimately such innovations are currently more inclined towards providing finance professionals with tools to enable users to perform the tasks efficiently or more successfully rather than creating self-functioning innovations, since creating that with credibility may take a few more years. (Vargas, 2021)

Potential Applications of AI and ML by 2025

The Covid outbreak and continuous curfews brought new opportunities for upcoming virtual solutions by AI and ML in 2020. Within the finance sector, there has been a pressing need for many years, and presently an increasing need, for innovative solutions. Clients demand rapid and efficient ML and AI adoption to create reliable, accurate, and tailored solutions, from banking institutions to Small and medium sized lenders in the foreseeable future.

In recent times, AI and ML have been the trendiest topics in the banking industry. Businesses gain a significant edge over its competitors by implementing clever measures to deal with the evolving industrial scenario. Artificial Intelligence allows businesses to have a better grasp of their customers' demands while also empowering corporate operations. For the dynamic environment, businesses may optimise and enhance existing marketing plan swiftly.

Artificial intelligence tech has an international market worth of more than USD 30 billion. Artificial intelligence's application in financial technology alone was valued around 7 billion USD in 2019 and was predicted to increase to around 23 billion USD by 2025. The financial technology industry is expected to develop at a CAGR around 24 percent till 2025, with a multitude of elements accelerating expansion. So now is the greatest chance to search into financial technology developments in order to ensure a great era. Listed below are a few areas which could have growing potential applications:

Process Control and Optimization (PCO)

Process control and optimization are commonly used methodologies in the financial technology industry, and they'll be a crucial business asset for the company in the upcoming years. PCO assists the company in decreasing or eliminating physical labour task. It improves the efficiency and speed of company operations, as well as productiveness. Service companies and marketing divisions utilise PCO, which improves staff training sessions by shifting it digitally and allows faster financial transactions.

The technologies will be extensively popular in the upcoming times, driving additional processes closer to automation. AI financing application is capable of responding to consumers relatively quickly, deliver accurate insights, and analyse large amounts of data (Dmitry, 2021).

Customer Service

A company would be more profitable if you provide better client experiences. Naturally, following a series of failures on one's part, clients may move to rivals. To avoid such mistakes, companies are turning to AI and machine learning, which address two major issues: quick responsiveness and customized client service.

Clients will not be waiting for longer duration, just a few moments, for a solution. A business has a higher probability of making a transaction when clients are given solutions which they desire, quickly. Chatbots incorporating AI and machine learning will response in milliseconds. With the increasing competitiveness in the industry, timely user satisfaction will be more important than anything else (Dmitry, 2021).

Insights about client wants and dislikes may also be gained through technologies. Because of the substantial quantity of evaluated data, a more tailored client experience may be created. AI can indeed respond to customers in a chat box, but it can also capture information from online platforms, evaluate online web pages, create personalised mails to targeted audiences for input, and much more (Dmitry, 2021).

Credit Scoring and Churn Prediction

Most of credit rating systems that are available have become obsolete. Their judgments are dependent on population trends, ages, relationship status, and probable interests of a predicted client base. As a result, the system does not gather genuine data; instead, it identifies potential clients. On the other hand. Newer credit rating and churning prediction tools, deal with the problem of analysing real customers (Dmitry, 2021).

Each consumer that makes a mortgage loan request will be considered by Artificial Intelligence / Machine learning churning predictions. In the coming days of banking sector, you will get a fantastic advertising strategy dependent on genuine consumer requirements, then you will recognize how to reach customers if situation of churning occurs. Churn prediction using artificial Intelligence may eliminate a lot of lapsed clients by 45 percent and boost the advertising and selling effort as a whole (Dmitry, 2021).

Credit rating based on artificial intelligence and machine learning is indeed the solution of managing risks related to loans, which is available for use even today, albeit in a basic form. To assist customers in deciding to provide credit, technology will examine past information depending on prior lending activities, debt, relationship status, financial position of clients, and much more. Artificial intelligence credit rating may decrease non-performing loans by up to 53% while also increasing income by 37%. Organizations would decrease risk and shorten judgement stages to days rather than weeks as a result of AI and machine learning.

Robo-Advisers

Customer support will gain greatly from the use of robot-advisors. Without human involvement, they computerised asset managing and customized product suggestions. Customer data regarding their current finances and ambitions is collected by AI/ML advisors, who then provide guidance and alter the selling strategy seamlessly. However, there are many arguments over the software's morality and efficiency, its need will continue to expand in the upcoming years. The newest Artificial technology systems can advise a customer, for example, beginning to save wealth now to finance for a student's future in 10 years, based on relationship status, earnings, and assets. (Dmitry, 2021)

Security

Since cyber-attacks get more complex and attack a wider range, cyber-security must be aware to anticipate risks and remove them. AI can assist with issues that humans are unable to address. Individual mistakes account 95% security problems and information leakage, according to stats.

Every year, overall rate of cyber-attacks is increasing. As per Experian, 55% of businesses claimed cybercrime in the previous year, with that number expected to rise to 60 percent by 2025. Forgery is frequent in the loan industry. Artificial Intelligence in finance enables users to detect security vulnerabilities and investigate possible options. It would be capable to examine paperwork for account creation, identify difficulties with user's accounts, and more.

How to Adapt ML and AI?

AI and ML in finance will become more technologically proficient and suited to business operations as technology evolves. When it comes to selecting technological innovations for the organisation, it's best to begin with one part, figure that out, and then to next. Examine your company operations, identify any issues, and start there. Consider that artificial technologies and machine learning are still developing technologies. These would be crucial in the coming time for any firm seeking to develop and gain leading position. (Forbes, 2021)

CHALLENGES- CLEAN DATA IS THE FOUNDATION FOR ML/AI

It is easier to discuss about such technology, although implementing these into practise could be difficult. Even before analysis could proceed, strong and efficient machine learning / artificial intelligence requires organised datasets. Consider it similar to memorizing the alphabet before learning to reading (Forbes, 2021).

Finance technologies are bringing on machine learning and artificial intelligence, however the finance sector must first address the severe data issue prior exploring Machine Learning / Artificial Intelligence. People who initially clean the dataset problem first will generate good data and their works becomes easier for future Unfortunately, effective implementation involves several steps, the most crucial of which is accurate and clear data (Forbes, 2021).

Throughout years, the finance sector has struggled with this issue. When it comes to dataset, there's an old expression that goes, "trash in, garbage out." The outcomes of machine learning and artificial intelligence are similar. Ones AI technology will produce negative or unexpected outcomes if users develop their model on poor dataset. It's like preparing for exams by using the incorrect notes (Forbes, 2021).

As a result, that very first step in any machine learning/artificial intelligence approach should be cleaning and the normalization of entire data to assure that the systems are consistently strong. Defining an aggregate connection is the most significant data normalisation choices a finance sector organisation will take. The second stage is to ensure that the dataset contains most of the necessary information for successfully training systems and finds the traits, outputs, or findings needed. This demands that our workforce thoroughly knows and understands the particular result or task that the artificial intelligence system is creating, as well as the dataset it needs. There are highly comprehensive datasets spanning numerous businesses of all sizes, economic factors, and social behaviour nowadays, but "subject matter expertise" (SMEs) are required to select the appropriate sets of data for the machine learning / artificial intelligence operations one is executing. The sooner SMEs are brought in, the further time and expense businesses could save (Forbes, 2021).

Ensuring information security is crucial once you've discovered and standardised the large datasets. This implies you'll need well predefined processes and regulations to guarantee that everyone in your company follows the exact data guidelines. Additionally, you'll really want a mechanism for "quality control" (QC) and certain amount of monitoring by people. Also, a significant use of artificial intelligence is the systematisation of information and quality control of documentation; robots can accomplish this much faster and more successfully as compared to people (Forbes, 2021).

Finally, the efficient use of machine learning and artificial intelligence tools might be a significant differentiator for finance sectors firms. These technologies enable the sector to streamline and automate back-office activities, as well as provide more focused consumer experience. In a summary, it may save operational expenses, improve cross-selling, and boost client acquisitions. An effective machine learning / artificial intelligence plan, on the other hand, necessitates a well-thought-out plan and clean datasets. Conventional banking organisations, fintechs, and the technological organisations that are supporting them, must concentrate on building Artificial Intelligence strategies for competing in the dynamically changing marketplace (Forbes, 2021).

Overcoming Barriers to AI Adoption in the Finance Industry

1. **Data silos:** Ml operations (MLOps) and data operations, similar to DevOps in developing applications, are now being utilized to distinguish data silos. The huge volumes of separated data financial institutions, on the other hand, make consistency and utility challenging.
2. **Various Stakeholders**: Several individuals participated in Artificial Intelligence programs are scientists, data analysts, and IT engineers, everyone having their individual opinions for technological tools and the way they function. Considering the enormous diversity of tools, systems, and Artificial Intelligence techniques, banking institutions struggle to build a consistent strategy that helps everybody (DqIndia, 2021).
3. **Handling present infrastructure**: Rigid infrastructure, shortage of standardisation, and evolving technology hinder both deployments and MLOps experts, demanding continual repacking and integrating throughout banking Technology processes (DqIndia, 2021).

4. **Myriad processes:** Data ingestion, evaluation, transition, verification, model building, recognition and tracking, and also logging and mentoring, put Information technology under a massive burden to incorporate a forward-looking datacentre or multi - cloud technique to adapt to changing scale of data science customers and procedures (DqIndia, 2021).

Such difficulty may hamper Acceptance of artificial intelligence at large volume, increasing the period among deployment and a satisfactory ROI. As an outcome, senior promoters and organization leaders may lack sight of the big picture and lose trust in the project.

Excellent Ways for Acquiring the Most from AI in Finance Industry

Segment based good practices are required by banking firms to handle a variety of business deployment challenges, including:

Data Architecture– Identifying and preserving validated and filtered information is necessary for Artificial Intelligence projects since good-quality information helps ML algorithms easy to operate, resulting in faster delivery (DqIndia, 2021).

Hybrid Cloud- Banking Institutions employ both on-premises and cloud - based services, thus a multi - cloud strategy is essential. In a number of IT scenarios, containers and Kubernetes methods are beneficial for handling Artificial intelligence and ML (DqIndia, 2021).

Infrastructure- Infra Acceptance must be outlooking in order to provide growth, productivity, faster provision, and information protection (DqIndia, 2021).

MLOps – Banking institutions might leverage corporate services that seek to working of Machine Learning and Artificial Intelligence by overcoming obstacles, integrating routines, offering data combination, and using the accessible tools and frameworks to improve deployment rate and solution usage (DqIndia, 2021).

Banking institutions can use AL and ML to reduce risk, enhance the client experience, and automate essential procedures by using database systems at scale. Banking Institutions, on either side, need to overcome significant challenges and implement best practises throughout their IT infrastructures to effectively transform from conventional to innovative.

The technological advancements are an unavoidable phenomenon and integrating them cohesively can give multiple benefits as discussed above, however for authorities such as SEBI, it becomes critical to regulate it in a manner that fair trade practices are ensured and an equitable environment can be created, giving equal opportunities to all stakeholders such as small investors while also complying with legal norms and regulations.

It is imperative that these challenges are seen as stepping-stones or as issues which must be resolved by investors, brokers, government and even regulatory bodies such as SEBI rather than reasons to develop skepticism and avoid them altogether. The Indian Capital market holds more than 2 trillion USD of wealth even without participation from several sectors of the Indian society and economy. Its development could help unlock value in several businesses of India and even serve as a boost to the GDP and development of the country in the long term.

FUTURE OUTLOOK

SEBI has plans to acquire software to control capital market related data on social media websites since they are used extensively for market manipulation (Tyagi, SEBI, 2020). They have also envisioned a 'data lake' which uses DA, AI and ML to store datasets in a raw and uncleaned manner to maintain a data bank for surveillance and mining purposes. This raw data will be maintained even after it is filtered and analysed (IBM, 2021).

Traders and brokers have shown enthusiasm in using and applying ML and DA techniques to find undervalued stocks and gain insight in decision making process by assessing risk, possible returns, identifying patterns and repetitions to develop automated models which have not given favourable results till now but hold a lot of promise as they are developed and become more sophisticated. Here is what all is expected to grow by using AI/ML in the finance sector:

Client Assistance

Chat-bots and virtual assistants have become increasingly popular. Businesses can utilize a wide range of global chatbot systems from several domains, but sector-specific software for banking institutions has been available. This technology can assist customers in quickly doing the necessary computations and evaluating their budgeting (IBM, 2021).

Furthermore, speech recognition enables banking institutions to provide assistance in the most comfortable manner possible. Banking institutions that provide rapid interactions and inquiring will draw customers from conventional banking that need their customers to get on financial platforms, hunt for main features, and research for the relevant data manually.

Enhanced Security Specifications

In the near future, credentials, user ids, and safety issues may become obsolete in the finance sector. Primarily in finance sector, security is crucial since most consumers prefer to get ones social-media profiles hacked than getting personal bank account details stolen.

As a result, the finance sector is most inclined to implement AI-powered security control to help that nothing can access their client's information (IBM, 2021).

AI, as earlier stated, can recognise strange and odd conduct. Banking institutions may be capable to increase new levels of safety or even seek alternative passcode with more effective ways like voice detection, face recognition, and biometric data (IBM, 2021).

Guidance

There are currently financing selling techniques using automation, but most of these don't use machine learning. The majority of the time, they are guideline methods. Automated systems, on the other hand, can provide personalized suggestions. For e.g., Virtual assistants can currently provide recommendations regarding portfolio modifications, and can further research numerous sites offering insurance assistance and assist customers in selecting an option that suits ones goals. Personalization has become more important in Artificial Intelligence apps, but tailored suggestions are no longer exclusively a human skill or expertise. (IBM, 2021)

CONCLUSION

The growth of technology is an unavoidable phenomenon and must be integrated in the future to maximize the output and efficiency of Valuable systems such as Capital Markets in India. We have seen historically that integrating technology reaps rewards such as electronic trading and dematerialisation by NSE. Hence regulators such as SEBI have shown a positive and integrative attitude with regards to technology in capital markets.

Conclusively, the plan for the future should be to leverage technological advancements and execute its application creatively to make the capital market flourish and act as a stimulus of recovery post COVID and also act as a springboard towards our dream of a 5 Trillion-dollar economy.

REFERENCES

Agarrwal, K. (2021, May 22). AI, machine learning help investors gain 'edge' while investing. *Money Control.* https://www.moneycontrol.com/news/business/markets/ai-machine-learning-help-investors-gain-edge-while-investing-6922331.html

Dolgorukov, D. (2021). How AI and ML Will Be Transforming Banking and Finance. *Finextra.* https://www.finextra.com/blogposting/19774/how-ai-and-ml-will-be-transforming-banking-and-finance

DqIndia. (2021). Overcoming the challenges in AI deployment for financial sector. *DqIndia.* https://www.dqindia.com/overcoming-challenges-ai-deployment-financial-sector/

IBM. (2021). Artificial Intelligence in Finance: Opportunities and Challenges *IBM.* https://community.ibm.com/community/user/datascience/blogs/stephen-crenshaw/2021/11/14/artificial-intelligence-in-finance-opportunities-a

Lappetito, C. (2021). AI And ML Can Transform Financial Services, But Industry Must Solve Data Problem First. *Forbes.* https://www.forbes.com/sites/forbesfinancecouncil/2021/10/13/ai-and-ml-can-transform-financial-services-but-industry-must-solve-data-problem-first/?sh=1eb612a96ea3

Research and Markets. (2018, June 18). Global Algorithmic Trading Market 2018-2022 with Citadel, Optiver, Tower Research Capital, Two Sigma Investments & Virtu Financial Dominating. *GlobeNewswire.* https://www.globenewswire.com/news-release/2018/06/18/1525672/0/en/Global-Algorithmic-Trading-Market-2018-2022-with-Citadel-Optiver-Tower-Research-Capital-Two-Sigma-Investments-Virtu-Financial-Dominating.html

Rout, D. (2021). *CEO Insights.* .CEO Insights. https://www.ceoinsightsindia.com

Tyagi, S. E. B. I. (2020, Jan 23). 7 Benefits of AI/ML in the Financial Services Industry.. *The Hindu Business Line.* https://www.thehindubusinessline.com/markets/social-media-key-tool-for-market-manipulation-ajay-tyagi/article30633275.ece

Vargas, R. (2021). 7 Benefits of AI/ML in the Financial Services Industry. *Encora.* https://www.encora.com/insights/7-benefits-of-ai/ml-in-the-financial-services-industry

Chapter 2
Blockchain and Smart Contracts for Secure and Sustainable Development

Sunil Kumar
AURO University, India

Rohit Singh
The Assam Royal Global University, India

ABSTRACT

Smart contracts play an important role of simplifying business and trade between the identified and anonymous parties without need of any intermediary to handle the transaction, as well as the intermediary's associated fees and time delays. A business can easily bring the transparency and build the trust of the customers by storing the encrypted records of transaction across participants. It also prevents hackers from breaking the integrity of the transaction because each record is connected on a distributed ledger, and if hackers want to alter any particular record, he/she would have to modify the entire chain for a single record. Therefore, a smart contract has huge potential to streamline and automate the business work across industries around the world. In this chapter, the authors will explore the potential of blockchain and smart contracts in the different aspects of business world, like supply chain, insurance, mortgage loans, financial settlements, and many more applications in the financial industry.

DOI: 10.4018/978-1-6684-4483-2.ch002

Copyright © 2023, IGI Global. Copying or distributing in print or electronic forms without written permission of IGI Global is prohibited.

INTRODUCTION

In the 21ˢᵗ century, we can see that technology is taking place in every aspect of our life. We know that every technology comes with some special characteristics and with a specific purpose, but privacy is a big threat in the technology world. So, we need such type of technology that can provide tamper-proof and highly secure transmission of data at a very low cost. In 1991, a conceptual framework was first put forwarded by a group of researchers which was initially intended for time-stamping digital documents such that backdating them will not be possible after creation. However, it was mostly unused until it was again stated by Satoshi Nakamoto the name behind the first blockchain, which is Bitcoin. Bitcoin is the first blockchain famous product which came into existence in 2009 (Nakamoto, 2008). As we have seen that in last decade, bitcoin has gain popularity, and the underlying technology became even more popular. Also in last few years, we have seen that cryptocurrency has gained the big attention in not only in the industry but also in the government of developed and developing countries. Nowadays, everyone wants to know that how this digital currency is growing so fast. Even some countries are not allowing as a legal currency because of some technical issues, but they are ready to accept the blockchain, which is known as the backbone of cryptocurrency. Blockchain is the backbone technology of all types of cryptocurrencies, maintained by a decentralized computer network. But it's not limited to that finance only, there are many opportunities in all domains of our life where we want to bring trust and transparency.

In this digital era, where every digital transaction is happening with the help of intermediaries, for every transaction a customer must not only have to trust on the third-party but also must pay some amount in some cases. So, we are bounded with the terms and conditions of our mediator for the authentication procedure and delay. The Blockchain technology has bring a transparency and security in the field of transaction of each type. In the Blockchain using the Smart contracts can be considered as an agreement which is basically simply computer logic stored and run when predetermined conditions are met and we use smart contracts to automate the execution of an agreement.

OVERVIEW OF BLOCKCHAIN TECHNOLOGY

Motivation

For humans, for thousands of years we have had the notion of currency and the notion of jobs. Before currency there was something else and it was even primitive that we used to hunt and eat, then sleep. On the next day, when wake up and feel hungry again hunt. It seems hunting was profitable, if hunt in group because if they hunt alone, it will not be very successful and profitable. Human-beings are intelligent beings, so they found that when they hunt in group, then they have better chance of hunt quickly. When someone in their group is sick and can't work for a month, you show some patience and lend some loan, it's not a written contract; it's an expectation. So, this type of incomplete contract came into the existence. If the borrower breaks that contract, that person will be called a cheat. Now, some authors have defined the trust as in a simple way that when a contract is not honoured, then trust is breached. Contract has basically two types: Complete and Incomplete. In the complete contract, we can list down all the terms and conditions, whereas in the incomplete contract only the expectation exist. Majority of the work that we do in the world is incomplete contract like eating the food in the restaurant or purchasing something from a shop because the owner handover the goods to the customer and wait for the payment. Things are different on the internet, where we can find that if music file or some digital content is delivered, and we don't pay. We might have seen that some businesses take the help of third party for the enforcement of their contract. For example, in some hotels or canteens, when someone is not making the payment after eating the foods, then some strong men will come as a enforcing agent to collect the amount.

In the similar way, in our current society and interactions that we have can easily found some examples of third-party. For example, Banks, shopping websites, credit rating agencies, payment gateway, certificate authority, social networking sites (Facebook, Linked-in or Instagram) and so on. If anyone from these well-known third parties start misbehaving with their customers. For example, if credit-rating agency become liar, then you will get the loan the without actual verification. Is there any guarantee that they are not producing our data to someone for their own benefit or for the money? Are they trusted third-party? We also know that certificate authority (CA) is very important component of our safe internet but we never check that it's installed in our web browser or not. CA is part of all online E-commerce transaction because it helps our browser to reach correct information. So, we can't fully trust on any third party. So, Blockchain is the technology that use the peer-to-peer (P2P) network and is considered an open ledger where all online transactions are recorded and everyone is allowed to connect, to send or verify transactions. It maintains the privacy, transparency and trust among the parties.

Definition

We can find many definitions of Blockchain on the internet. For the layman, Blockchain is a ledger that is maintaining the records; these records are known as blocks and are securely connected to each other. For a technical person, it's a digital system of maintaining records which records all transactions according to a set of rules or protocol to prevent unauthorized access and interference.

By (Zheng, 2016) Blockchain was defined as a technology that integrates decentralization, distributed computation, asymmetric encryption, timestamp, and consensus algorithm. It provides a distributed ledger to simplify account settlement procedure through encryption techniques and capable to manage a large amount of data through decentralization. It is also capable to increase data processing efficiency and offers data sharing function with the surety of data security. Hence, comparatively to traditional technologies, (Nguyen, 2016) discussed that blockchain technology is fortified with the powers of compatibility, sustainability, data sharing and interconnectivity. Blockchain have already shown their potential to reduce the costs and can bring major changes in all the field of our daily life. (Yu et al., 2018) discussed about the applications of blockchains has exposed a new period with wonderful opportunities, where the flora of business and race will need to be changed, specially it's transforming business model and captivating steps to apply in financial activities would be a strategic preparation for a sustainable development of corporations.

Key Benefits of Blockchain

(Simom, 2017) has explained the use of Blockchain as a decentralized ledger has designed a technological model for a payment substructure with the support of low costs and transparency, which is generating key impressions on worldwide financial market. Some key benefits are follows:

- Smart contracts can be created by using Blockchain, which rises the productivity of payments and transactions in the stock market. It provides cheaper and faster services as compared to other financial services, therefore now it's a well-established powerful tool that placed finance in accord.
- It has the potential of reducing the foreign exchange transactions fee, credit card transactions substantially. For example, it is assessed that $14 billion will be saved annually, equally one third of transaction fees. Capital requirements for banks can be reduced by $120 billion. Costs for remittances will fall approximately 1% compared to the global average of the "traditional channels" of 7.7%.
- Information is recorded automatically and can be easily monitored during the transaction processing that promote transparency and stop the financial crime such as money laundering.

- Digitization of records has reduced the follow-up process and save the paper. It also provides the protection and privacy against the tracking of customers like banks and other regulatory bodies.
- Boost-up the efficiency, execution speed and optimized the time for the completion of the transactions.

Blockchain Architecture and Components

(Chuen, 2015) has suggested that Blockchain is the collection of blocks and each block consists of the list of transactions (Tx) just like the conventional public ledger. Figure-1 has illustrated the example of a blockchain.

A block consists of two parts as shown in Figure-2, Block Header and Block Body. Block header includes the following components:

i) Block version: contains the set of block validation rules.
ii) Merkle tree root hash: store the hash value of all the transactions of the block.
iii) Timestamp: roves when and what has happened on the blockchain. It indicate current time(in seconds) since 1-Jan-1970.
iv) nBits: contains the target threshold.
v) Nonce: store a 4-byte value, starts with 0 and increase after every hash calculation.
vi) Parent block hash: store a 256-bit hash value that indicating to the previous block.

Whereas the block body store a transaction counter and number of transactions. Blockchain use the Digital signature mechanism to authenticate and validate the transactions.

Role of Merkle Tree in Transaction wrapping in a block?

A Merkle tree is a hierarchical data structure used in blockchain solutions such as Bitcoin for organizing transactions. It's a tree which is constructed by holding hash of transaction in the leaf node and root node is used to holds hash of all its child node as shown in Figure-3. Merkle-tree is tamper-proof data structure as if any intruder will try to temper at any level in the tree it would be difficult to change all the hashes of whole tree. It also maintains the integrity of the order of transactions. Merkle tree provides an efficient way to find & verify a transaction belongs to a block in just log(n) time. We can also find the use-cases of Merkle-tree in many popular database applications such as NoSQL databases- Cassandra, BitTorrent, Apache Wave etc.

Types of Blockchain

There are three types of blockchain as follows:

i.   Private Blockchain

It is also known as permissioned blockchain it is essential to take permission to join the blockchain network. All the transactions will be kept private and more centralized then public blockchain.

j.   Public Blockchain

In this type of blockchain permission is not required to join the network, therefore details of transaction available to anyone in the network. It is open source which allow everyone to be engaged as developers, users or miners and fully decentralized. Bitcoin is the best example of the public blockchain.

k.   Hybrid Blockchain

It is the combination of private and public blockchain. It helps the business person to have more transparency and security. Hybrid blockchain allows multi-chain concept of network.

To better understand all the features **Table-1** is given below.

Table 1. Types of Blockchain

Features	Private Blockchain	Public Blockchain	Hybrid/Consortium Blockchain
Decentralized	Partially	Fully	Partially
Consensus process (to read and write)	Needs permission	Permission less	Permission required
Controlling	Controlled by a single fully trusted organization.	Controlled by every mode in the network.	Controlled by a few predetermined nodes.
Consensus Algorithms used	PoET, RAFT, PBFT	PoW	PoET, RAFT, PBFT
Reward	No	Every node will be rewarded.	Can be rewarded
Defence Mechanism	Not required because it is permissioned	Byzantine Fault Tolerance(BFT)	BFT
Use cases	Good for organization blockchain because they required full control.	Almost every industry. Good for creating cryptocurrency	Effective in Banking, Finance, IOT, Supply chain.
Example	Ripple,Corda, Monax, Multichain	Bitcoin, Ethereum, Litecoin	XDC, Hyperledger

Blockchain Frameworks

A Blockchain framework provides a platform to give a simplified technical business solution that undergoes through problem definition, development and deployment of complex business problems. There are some famous blockchain frameworks:

1. Ethereum

Just like the Bitcoin, Ethereum is another mature blockchain platform available today that was founded by a 22-year-old Russian-Canadian boy, Vitalik Buterin. It's a public blockchain famous for its robust smart contract design philosophy, flexibility, and functionality. Ethereum is widely used in many industry use-cases like e-voting, land registration, stock trading, initial coin offering. The most attractive feature in ethereum framework is that it builds an abstract foundation layer to hide the complexities from the developers and provides a flexibility to different application to run on all ethereum nodes and all application that runs on it will have to pay a transaction fees to the miners to make a self-sustainable network.

2. Hyperledger Fabric

Hyperledger fabric is a permissioned distributed ledger technology(DLT) which enables developers to create an enterprise-level applications and to provide a feasible solution to many private sectors like real-state, finance, supply-chain, internet of things (IoT), Pharmaceuticals as well as Government sector such as Land-registry, Agriculture also. Walmart has successfully used the Hyperledger fabric in their food supply-chain to improve the transparency and build the trust of their customers. Another uses in hyperledger is done by Change Healthcare company to improving their insurance claim life cycle.

3. R3 Corda

Corda is an open-source peer-to-peer cloud-ready decentralized platform on which we can build highly scalable, secure private applications to build the trust of the customers by using the smart-contracts. Corda has proved by providing the best supports in the finance, healthcare, insurance, capital markets, energy, and government sector.

4. Ripple

Ripple is a peer-to-peer blockchain-based decentralized digital payment platform with its own cryptocurrency known as XRP that allows a seamless transfer of money in many forms either in currency like Dollars, Yen, Euros or any cryptocurrencies such as Bitcoin etc. As compared to bitcoin, it consumes less energy and time to confirm the transactions. Ripple transaction uses a consensus protocol to validate the account and transactions rather than PoW(Proof-of-Work) consensus system of bitcoin.

Table 2. Comparison of different blockchain frameworks features

	Bitcoin	Ethereum	Hyperledger Fabric	R3 Corda	Ripple
State	Stateless	Statefull	Stateful	Stateful	Stateless
Turning Support	No	Yes	Yes	Yes	No
Consensus	Proof-of-work	Proof-of-Work(PoW)	Pluggable framework	Pluggable framework	Problis Voting
Cryptocurrency	BTC	Ether	None	None	XRP
Industry focused	Financial	Cross-industry	Cross-industry	Cross-industry	Financial
Ledger Type	Permission less	Permission less	Permissioned	Permissioned	Permissioned
Smart Contract functionality	Yes	Yes	Yes	Yes	No

BLOCKCHAIN AND SMART CONTRACTS

Overview

Over a period of time Blockchain technology has gained growing curiosity from both academia and practitioners in a range of industries, including banking, insurance, trade, and medicine. It has potential in various industries, including in healthcare, financial applications, supply chains and the insurance industry.

Smart Contracts are the important and integral component of blockchain framework. In general, a smart contract is a simple computer program stored on a blockchain that is specifically designed to satisfy the predetermined requirements of the buyer and seller and it execute automatically when the terms and conditions of both buyer and seller are met.

A Smart contract facilitate the internet user to trade with having any intermediaries authorities or human intervention. It provides transparency, easy traceability of all the transactions in a trusted environment.

Life Cycle of Smart Contract: To ensure the integrity and implementation of the smart contracts, we have to relies of a distributed digital ledger i.e. blockchain technology. (Sillaber, 2017) explained the life cycle of smart contracts that consist of four following phases: creation, deployment, execution, and completion, which is depicted in Figure-4.

Key Benefits: There are several benefits of Smart Contract, which are given below:

Transparency and Trust

As there is no need to involve any third party between the sender and receiver, and because all the transactions will be encrypted before sharing to other participants, therefore all participants can have the trust on shared information and transparency also.

Efficiency, Accuracy, and Speed

Because smart contracts get executed automatically and digitally, once the required condition will met. No extra time will be spent that often required to verify if we do the same process manually.

Security

To prevent the records of transaction from hackers, all transactions will be encrypted to provide the confidentiality. Also, each block that consists of a record of transactions will be interconnected to maintain a consistency on a distributed ledger, therefore if a hacker tries to make a single change in any of block he would have to alter the entire chain of blocks.

No Intermediator

As Smart contract has removed the requirement of any intermediaries to handle transactions as well as their will be no associated time delays.

SMART CONTRACT AND BLOCKCHAIN APPLICATIONS

Use of smart contract in blockchain is not limited to financial sector only, it can be easily deployed on wide range of government and the private sectors as follows:

i)   Supply Chain Management(SCM)

Some reputed private manufacturing companies are start using the blockchain services in their supply chain management system to provide the transparency and trust to their customer.

ii)   Land registry

Government agencies are using Blockchain services to maintaining the records of land registries that provides the transparency and trust among the parties.

iii)   Farm insurance

Nowadays, some government and private insurance agencies are start using blockchain to providing transparency in farm insurance.

iv)   Digital Certificates

Blockchain is capable of providing protection and transparency to any type of digital certificates over the globe and some countries are now using blockchain in this area.

v)   Financial transaction

Mastercard® is a registered financial service company is now using blockchain to manage vast amount safely around the world. They are using public blockchain for this purpose.

vi)   Food industry

Walmart is well-known brand in the food industry, now they are start using blockchain services to track their food globally. Because of the assurance that they are providing to the customers, which makes one of most trusted companies in their domain.

vii) Healthcare

There is huge scope in the field of healthcare of blockchain. Companies in the developed countries like US, UK or Canada had employed blockchain technology to secure digital health records to patient. For example: UK based Medicalchain's blockchain is maintaininig the integrity of health records for establishing a single point of truth.

viii) E-commerce

With the help of blockchain key features, e-commerce industry are accepting it in their system to maintain the trust and transparency.

ix) Trading

According to (Singh, 2018) the trading it is necessary to keep all the transactions secure and private. With the help of blockchain decentralization and automation this work can be done easily. Japan finance services agency has allowed using blockchain as its core trading infrastructure and in 2015 Nasdaq had already allowed blockchain technology to record private securities transactions.

x) Transportation

FedEx® is the first shipping company who is blockchain technology to track their high value cargo products. Other transportation agencies are now start implementing blockchain in their system.

Key Challenges

Despite the great potential of blockchain, still there are some challenges, which limit the usage of blockchain. Some major challenges are as follows.

i) Scalability

In the digital era, transactions are increasing day by day and the blockchain can only process nearly seven transactions in a second. So, It can't manage the millions of transactions in real-life manner. Therefore, many efforts are proposed to address this scalability problem of blockchain.

ii) Privacy Leakage

(Kosba, 2016) has discussed how blockchain is maintaining massive amount of privacy by using public and private key and using the asymmetric cryptography but blockchain can't give the guarantee of transactions privacy because the values of all transactions and balances for each public key are publicly visible.

iii) Selfish Mining

According to (Eyal et al., 2014) blockchain is still susceptible to attacks of colluding with miners. He has shown that the blockchain network is vulnerable even if only small portion of the hashing power is used to cheat.

CONCLUSION

In this chapter, we have tried an attempt to synthesize and analyze the features, applications that make blockchain a sustainable and trust management framework. We have also covered some important area of our life where blockchain can provide better security, transparency and trust. Still there are many challenges and open issues with this new technology, but efforts are still working to mitigate these challenges and hopefully in the future, we will get a full proof version of blockchain technology for our sustainable development.

REFERENCES

Abideen, S. (2017). Blockchain E-Book. Cybrosys Technology.

Eyal, I., & Sirer, E. G. (2014). Majority is not enough: Bitcoin mining is vulnerable. In *Proceedings of International Conference on Financial Cryptography and Data Security*, (pp. 436– 454). IEEE.

Kosba, A., Miller, A., Shi, E., Wen, Z., & Papamanthou, C. (2016). Hawk: The blockchain model of cryptography and privacy-preserving smart contracts. in *Proceedings of IEE Symposium on Security and Privacy (SP)*, (pp. 839–858). IEEE.

Lee Kuo Chuen, D. (2015). *Handbook of Digital Currency*, (1st ed). Elsevier. http://EconPapers.repec.org/RePEceee:monogr:9780128021170

Nakamoto, S. (2008). Bitcoin: A peer-to-peer electronic cash system. *Bitcoin*.

Nguyen, Q. K. (2016). Blockchain - A Financial Technology for Future Sustainable Development. *3rd International Conference on Green Technology and Sustainable Development (GTSD),* (pp. 51-54). IEEE. 10.1109/GTSD.2016.22

Sillaber, C., & Waltl, B. (2017). Life Cycle of Smart Contracts in Blockchain Ecosystems. *Datenschutz Datensich, 41,* 497–500. doi:10.1007/s11623-017-0819-7

Simom, J. (2016). The End of Big Banks. *Project sandicate.*

Singh, S. S. (2018). How blockchain will change the way you trade in stock markets. *Economic Times.* https://economictimes.indiatimes.com/markets/stocks/news/how-blockchain-will-change-the-way-you-trade-in-stock-markets/articleshow/62161610.cms?from=mdr, 2018

Susan, A. (2016). 5 ways digital currencies will change the world. *World Economic Forum, Khoa Tran Trans.* Bitcoin Vietnam.

Yu, S., Lv, K., Shao, Z., Guo, Y., Zou, J., & Zhang, B. (2018). A High Performance Blockchain Platform for Intelligent Devices. *1st International Conference on Hot Information-Centric Networking (HotICN),* (pp.260-261). IEEE.. 10.1109/HOTICN.2018.8606017

Zheng, Z., Xie, S., Dai, H., Chen, X., & Wang, H. (2017). An Overview of Blockchain Technology: Architecture, Consensus, and Future Trends. *International Congress on Big Data (BigData Congress),* (pp.557-564). IEEE. 10.1109/BigDataCongress.2017.85

Chapter 3
Cryptocurrency and the Indian Monetary System

Ranjana R. Kamath
SHSS, Jain University (Deemed), India

Mahammad Habeeb
SHSS, Jain University (Deemed), India

ABSTRACT

"Change is the only constant," wrote the ancient Greek philosopher Heraclitus of Ephesus. And in today's world, one of the greatest changes is the changing nature of money. As the world embraces the ease in accessibility to high-speed internet services across all spectrums, the medium of exchange is transforming from fiat currency to virtual and cryptocurrencies. The exchange of cryptocurrency heavily revolves around speculation by professionals, and institutional investors dealing with large sums of money. The global adoption of cryptocurrency has increased over the last few years and has seen an 880% increase in year-to-year transactions in the last year, reflecting the increased acceptance in cryptocurrency usage in emerging markets. India ranks second in the overall crypto-adoption index ranking, backing the increased interest of Indian investors in the cryptocurrency markets. The major focus of this paper is regarding the next phase of transition into digital and cryptocurrency and its implications on monetary policies with a specific focus on the Indian monetary system.

DOI: 10.4018/978-1-6684-4483-2.ch003

Copyright © 2023, IGI Global. Copying or distributing in print or electronic forms without written permission of IGI Global is prohibited.

INTRODUCTION

In her book *Blockchain: Blueprint for a New Economy*, Melanie Swan goes into great detail on digital currency and its possible applications. Swan claims that developing 21st-century digital currencies contain three distinct components: the digital money itself (for example, Bitcoin), the transaction software, and the underlying ledger on which all transactions are recorded. The currency itself is a string of code at the "top level" of the digital currency stack. The code identifies the money object and contains cryptographic protections to safeguard individual users and the system as a whole from hackers. It's also conceivable that the currency's code contains extra information. When it comes to something with the word "digital" in its name, a strong technological foundation is required. As a result, even with digital currency, Blockchain introduced a new paradigm. A blockchain is a consensus system for creating an append-only log (a transaction ledger in the case of Bitcoin) that can subsequently be used to establish an auditable database (in Bitcoin, a record of who owns which coins). This database is built by a group of people who may or may not trust each other, and it is secured using encryption so that every entry can be audited and validated. The outcome is a real-time, consensus-based record of transactions with a wide range of possible uses, including non-currency value and data transfers. (The blockchain catalyst for change | VOX, CEPR Policy Portal, 2018). Apart from private cryptocurrencies, The Bank for International Settlements is working with a group of seven central banks (the Bank of Canada, the Bank of England, the Bank of Japan, the European Central Bank, the Federal Reserve, Sveriges Riksbank, and the Swiss National Bank) to investigate central bank digital currencies (CBDCs) for the general public ("general purpose" or "retail" CBDC). With this increased interest in the cryptocurrency markets, it's now up to the policymakers and regulatory authorities to look into the type of regulations that can be bought in place to protect consumer interests as well as provide an equal platform to cryptocurrency exchanges rather than prohibiting the use of virtual and cryptocurrencies by the financial institutions and entities regulated by the central bank of India. Another important challenge, in the long run, is whether cryptocurrency can be used as a means of transfer for everyday transactions. Many factors have influenced the increase in the use of cryptocurrencies over the past few months and this paper discusses these factors. Along with this, the paper also focuses on whether cryptocurrencies can penetrate deeper into the Indian markets and the kind of changes that need to be brought in place to aid this transition if it is going to take place shortly. The emergence of one of the first major cryptocurrencies, Bitcoin in 2009 led to a revolutionary change in the financial system. Bitcoin, defined as a peer-to-peer version of electronic cash that would allow online payments to be sent directly from one party to another without going through a financial institution (Nakamoto, 2008), was first introduced by Satoshi

Cryptocurrency and the Indian Monetary System

Nakomoto in the paper titled "Bitcoin: A Peer-to-Peer Electronic Cash System". This decentralized system has inspired the creation of many similar cryptocurrencies based on blockchain technology. Litecoin, ethereum, and Tether are some of the popularly mined cryptocurrencies in today's market.

Understanding the Technology Behind Cryptocurrencies

The underlying technology of such decentralized currencies is the DLT or the distributed ledger technology. DLT refers to the processes and related technologies that enable nodes in a network (or arrangement) to securely propose, validate, and record state changes (or updates) to a synchronized ledger that is distributed across the network's nodes. (Townsend, 2020). Thus the payment system does not require any central authority to oversee the transactions made through these secure networks. The DLT focuses on specific protocols and procedures that are set in place to ensure the security of these networks through cryptographic codes. Under the DLT system, the blockchain system is particularly used as the underlying technology for cryptocurrencies like Bitcoin. Blockchain uses cryptographic code and algorithms that need to be solved by miners to obtain access to the cryptocurrency. This process is also used to verify the ever-growing, append-only data structure that takes the form of a chain of so-called 'transaction blocks' – the blockchain – which serves the function of a ledger. (Krause et al., 2017).

The Current Financial System and the Disruptions Bought in by Cryptocurrencies

In the current financial system, the payments and transactions made by households and individuals are made through a payment gateway overseen and recorded by a central authority i.e. the central banks in a given banking system, and these intermediaries also charge a transaction process g fee. On the other hand, the use of DLT underlined cryptocurrency technology as a payments system eliminates the need for a financial intermediary. The role of financial institutions like banks comes down as all the transactions are recorded automatically in real-time on the ledger.

Proponents of the technology highlight its ability to transform financial services and markets by (i) reducing complexity; (ii) improving end-to-end processing speed and thus the decentralized availability of assets and funds; (iii) decreasing the need for reconciliation across multiple record-keeping infrastructures; (iv) increasing transparency and immutability in transaction record keeping; (v) improving network resilience through distributed data management; and (vi) reducing operational and financial risks (Mills et al., 2016). These factors have played a key role in promoting the use of cryptocurrencies.

Introduction of Cryptocurrency in the Indian Markets

In 2013 the launch of cryptocurrency exchange Unocoin provided an opportunity for traders in India to access the crypto market through bitcoin trading (Srivastav, 2021). However, the RBI in its press release on 24 December 2013, cautioned users against trading cryptocurrency. They highlighted the risk of using cryptocurrencies such as bitcoin due to their volatility, absence of any central authority overlooking the transactions, absence of any underlying assets backing cryptocurrencies, and risk due to hacking, loss of password, or malware attack (Reserve Bank of India, 2013). This did not deter people from investing in cryptocurrency and an estimated 1.5 crore people in India have actively invested in cryptocurrencies.

ANALYSIS OF CRYPTOCURRENCY IN THE INDIAN MARKETS

Since its introduction in 2013, interest in cryptocurrency has grown exponentially in India. Apart from Unocoin, there are over 350 cryptocurrency exchanges based in India (BI India Bureau, 2021), the volume of cryptocurrency transitions over these wallets has increased significantly since 2017.

As stated earlier, the RBI was not in favor of cryptocurrency since its introduction in India in 2013, and the central bank of India has continued to maintain this stance to date. In a circular dated 06 April 2018, the RBI issued a ban on dealing in virtual currencies, including bitcoin, and stated that "entities regulated by the Reserve Bank shall not deal in VCs or provide services for facilitating any person or entity in dealing with or settling VCs. Such services include maintaining accounts, registering, trading, settling, clearing, giving loans against virtual tokens, accepting them as collateral, opening accounts of exchanges dealing with them, and transfer/ receipt of money in accounts relating to purchase/ sale of VCs."(*Reserve Bank of India*, 2018). The Hon'ble Supreme Court of India overturned the circular dated 06 April 2018 based on a writ petition filed by the 'Internet and Mobile Association of India,' which represents the interests of the online and digital services industry, a few companies that run online crypto assets exchange platforms, their shareholders/ founders, and a few individual crypto-assets traders (*Writ Petition (Civil) No.528 of 2018 INTERNET AND MOBILE ASSOCIATION OF INDIA Petitioner Versus RESERVE BANK OF INDIA Respondent WITH Writ Petition (Civil) No.373 of 2018.*) This judgment proved crucial in the ability to run cryptocurrency exchanges in India and has paved the way for more individuals to register on cryptocurrency exchanges and deal in cryptocurrencies.

The March 2020 lockdowns due to the coronavirus pandemic also boosted the trade of cryptocurrency markets in India. Even as the Indian economy continued to struggle throughout the pandemic, the cryptocurrency markets were consistently resilient. The increase in the accessibility and availability of interaction in the global markets 24/7 and the added advantage of leisure due to the work from home scenario created an ideal environment for digital currency and financial market enthusiasts. In terms of the adoption of cryptocurrency, India ranked second in the overall crypto adoption index ranking. (*The 2021 Global Crypto Adoption Index, 2021*). A report by Finder suggests that bitcoin is the most popular cryptocurrency trading in India, followed by Ethereum, Ripple, Litecoin, and Bitcoin Cash amongst others. (*Cryptocurrency adoption rates*,2021.)

WazirX, one of the most popular cryptocurrency exchanges in India saw a trading volume of $152.69 million as of 25 August 2021. (WazirX Exchange, 2018). Over the last few months, the value of the cryptocurrency has hit record highs but subsequently corrected for their values.

Figure 1. Price history of Bitcoin(in USD) From 1 April 2021 to 31 August 2021
Source: Bitcoin Historical Data - Investing.com, 2021

Figure 2. Volume Traded history of Bitcoin (in Thousands) From 1 April 2021 to 31 August 2021
Source: Bitcoin Historical Data - Investing.com, 2021

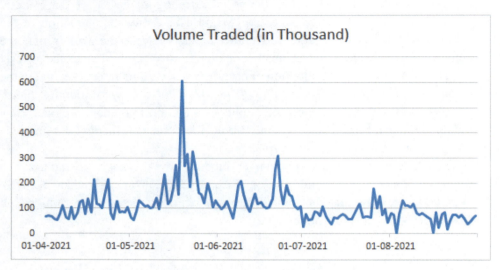

Figure 3. Price history of Ethereum (in USD) From 1 April 2021 to 31 August 2021
Source: Bitcoin Historical Data - Investing.com, 2021

Figure 4. Volume Traded history of Ethereum (in Millions) From 1 April 2021 to 31 August 2021
Source: Bitcoin Historical Data - Investing.com, 2021

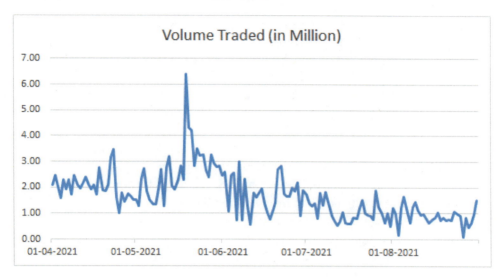

Figure 5. Personal Remittances received in India(in billions, current USD)
Source: (Personal remittances, received (current US$) - India \ Data, 2021)

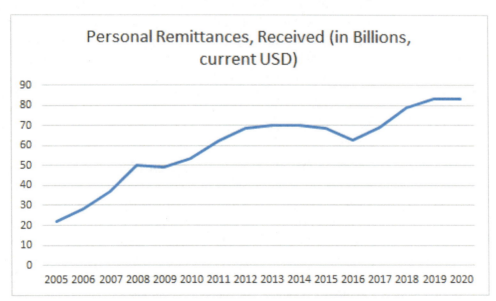

ROLE OF CRYPTOCURRENCY NETWORKS IN CROSS-BORDER TRANSACTIONS

Apart from acting as a source of investment, cryptocurrencies also act as a transfer of value for cross-border transactions and remittance inflows. India is deemed as the largest recipient of remittances in South Asia, receiving inward personal remittances worth $83.149 billion in 2020. (Data, 2021).

Cross-border transactions include B2B, B2P, P2B, and P2P payments. In India, beneficiaries can receive cross-border inward remittances through banking and postal channels. The International Financial System (IFS) platform of Universal Post Union (UPU) is generally used for the postal channel. Besides, there are two more channels for receiving inward remittances, viz. Rupee Drawing Arrangement (RDA) and Money Transfer Service Scheme (MTSS) are the most common arrangements under which the remittances are received into the country. (Reserve Bank of India, 2017). There are significant costs attached to these transactions due to the presence of banking intermediaries charging a certain fee for every cross-border transaction, the average cost being 5.4% (Data, 2011). These additional fees levied negatively impact the people depending on these remittances for their day-to-day activities and essentials. With the use of cryptocurrencies for such transactions, the costs are significantly bought down due to the absence of any intermediaries. According to recent surveys, the use of blockchain-based technology in cross-border transactions may reduce costs by up to 60%. (Flore, 2018). This also aids in preventing international fraud since cryptocurrency transactions take place in secure peer-to-peer networks. Apart from the costs, the time taken to make such transfers are reduced significantly.

However, due to a lack of awareness and access to cryptocurrency in significant regions of India, adopting cryptocurrencies as a form of remittance transfer has a modest disadvantage.

ANALYSIS OF THE INDIAN MONETARY POLICY

A monetary policy refers to a policy introduced by the central bank, the Reserve Bank of India in this case, to control monetary instruments under its purview. This responsibility of the RBI is mandated under the Reserve Bank of India Act, 1934.

The monetary policy framework in India aims at maintaining price stability while keeping in mind the growth objective, thereby maintaining sustainable growth. The amended RBI Act explicitly provides the legislative mandate to the Reserve Bank to operate the monetary policy framework of the country. The framework aims at setting the policy (repo) rate based on an assessment of the current and evolving macroeconomic situation, and modulation of liquidity conditions to anchor money market rates at or around the repo rate. Repo rate changes transmit through the money market to the entire financial system, which, in turn, influences aggregate demand – a key determinant of inflation and growth. (Reserve Bank of India, 2016). Apart from this, the RBI, in coordination with the Government of India, is the sole issuer of currency in India. They're responsible for the design, production, and supply of the banknotes. The Government of India is the issuing authority of coins and supplies coins to the Reserve Bank on demand. The Reserve Bank puts the coins into circulation on behalf of the Central Government.

CHALLENGES TO THE MONETARY SYSTEM IN THE AGE OF CRYPTOCURRENCY

As discussed in the monetary policy system of India, one of the roles of RBI is to keep a check on the inflation in the economy and base their decisions on changing interest rates in the future. This system currently considers only the fiat currency of India, the rupee. But the widespread adoption of any other private currency, i.e cryptocurrency, having a different exchange rate, will lead to complications in the monetary system. (IMF F&D Magazine, 2018).

Currently, cryptocurrencies are considered as a means of investment asset rather than a medium of exchange. As a speculative investment, cryptocurrencies are prone to bubbles. The collapse of a cryptocurrency bubble may have implications for the entire financial system of an economy. Central banks would then face a double risk: first to the stability of financial institutions they supervise, from the potentially unregulated cryptocurrency debt markets, and, second, to price stability, from the effects on the real economy of deleveraging and defaulting by an economic agent. (Cryptocurrencies and monetary policy, 2018)

CONCLUSION

Cryptocurrencies' future role and value remain very ambiguous, owing to outstanding concerns about their potential to serve as money effectively and efficiently, and disrupt existing money and payment systems. Cryptocurrencies, according to proponents, will become a common payment mechanism that will promote economic efficiency, privacy, and independence from centralized organizations and authorities. The World Bank continues to maintain that cryptocurrencies are nothing more than speculative assets. Policymakers around the world are still trying to understand the various aspects of cryptocurrency, analyzing the risks associated with the widespread application of cryptocurrency in the economy and central banks are working on introducing their own central bank digital currency (CBDC) with the underlying principles of cryptocurrency. The extent to which a central bank could or would wish to develop a blockchain-enabled payment system would very certainly be assessed against the fact that these government entities currently have reliable digital payment systems in place. Because of these factors, it's unclear what form CBDCs will take; they could have a variety of features and qualities. Considering the immense benefits as well as taking adequate precautions against the misuse of cryptocurrency, central banks, policymakers, and governments need to figure out a pathway for accommodating cryptocurrency in the economy.

REFERENCES

Benigno, P. (2019). *Monetary policy in a world of cryptocurrencies*. Voxeu.org. https://voxeu.org/article/monetary-policy-world-cryptocurrencies

BI India Bureau. (2021, July 28). Equalisation levy on crypto exchanges in India will not apply to investors, according to the Finance Minister. *Business Insider India*. https://www.businessinsider.in/cryptocurrency/news/the-indian-government-has-no-data-on-how-many-crypto-exchanges-and-investors-working-on-cryptocurrency/articleshow/84821709.cms#:~:text=In%20addition%20to%20exchanges%2C%20India,owned%20by%20crypto%20giant%20Binance

Bordo, M., & Levin, A. (2017). *Central Bank Digital Currency and the Future of Monetary Policy*. Hoover. https://www.hoover.org/sites/default/files/bordo-levin_bullets_for_hoover_may2017.pdf

Carstens, A. (2021). *Digital currencies and the future of the monetary system: Remarks by Agustín Carstens*. Bank for International Settlements. https://www.bis.org/speeches/sp210127.pdf

ChainAnlysis Team. (2021). *The 2021 Global Crypto Adoption Index*. Chainalysis.com. https://blog.chainalysis.com/reports/2021-global-crypto-adoption-index

Chiu, J., & Koeppl, T. V. (2017). The Economics of Cryptocurrencies Bitcoin and Beyond. *Electronic Journal*. doi:10.2139/ssrn.3048124

Claeys, A., Demertzis, M., & Efstathiou, K. (2018). *Cryptocurrencies and monetary policy*. ECON Committee. https://www.europarl.europa.eu/cmsdata/150000/BRUEGEL_FINAL%20publication.pdf

Coin Ranking. (2018). *WazirX Exchange*. Coinranking. https://coinranking.com/exchange/W9qIIHDJ_+wazirx

Cryptocurrency and the Indian Monetary System

Congressional Research Service. (2018). Cryptocurrency: The Economics of Money and Selected Policy Issues. *CRS Report.* https://fas.org/sgp/crs/misc/R45427.pdf

Economic Times. (2021, May 20). *Cryptocurrency has risen despite the pandemic & is expected to continue.* The Economic Times. https://economictimes.indiatimes.com/markets/cryptocurrency/cryptocurrency-has-risen-despite-the-pandemic-is-expected-to-continue/articleshow/82800680.cms?from=mdr

Finder. (n.d.). Cryptocurrency adoption rates. *Finder Crypto Report.* https://dvh1deh6tagwk.cloudfront.net/finder-us/wp-uploads/sites/5/2021/06/Crypto_Adoption_final-compressed-1.pdf

Flore, M. (2018). *How Blockchain-Based Technology Is Disrupting Migrants' Remittances: A Preliminary Assessment.* https://core.ac.uk/download/pdf/186490943.pdf

Gallo, A. (2021, May 25). *Central Bank Digital Currencies Will Fix Bad Policy.* Bloomberg. https://www.bloomberg.com/opinion/articles/2021-05-25/central-bank-digital-currencies-will-fix-bad-monetary-policy

Holtmeier, M., & Sandner, P. (2019). *The impact of crypto currencies on developing countries.* Frankfurt School Blockchain Center. http://explore-ip.com/2019_The-Impact-of-Crypto-Currencies-on-Developing-Countries.pdf

International Money Fund. (2018). *Central Bank Monetary Policy in the Age of Cryptocurrencies - IMF F&D Magazine, 55*(2). Imf.org. https://www.imf.org/external/pubs/ft/fandd/2018/06/central-bank-monetary-policy-and-cryptocurrencies/he.htm

Investing. (2021). *Bitcoin Historical Data.* Investing.com. https://www.investing.com/crypto/bitcoin/historical-data

Krause, S. K., Natarajan, H., & Gradstein, H. L. (2017). Distributed Ledger Technology (DLT) and Blockchain. In *The World Bank.* The World Bank., https://documents1.worldbank.org/curated/en/177911513714062215/pdf/122140-WP-PUBLIC-Distributed-Ledger-Technology-and-Blockchain-Fintech-Notes.pdf

Mills, D., Wang, K., Malone, B., Ravi, A., Marquardt, J., Chen, C., Badev, A., Brezinski, T., Fahy, L., Liao, K., Kargenian, V., Ellithorpe, M., Ng, W., & Baird, M. (2016). Distributed Ledger Technology in Payments, Clearing, and Settlement. *Finance and Economics Discussion Series, 2016*(095). doi:10.17016/FEDS.2016.095

Nakamoto, S. (2008). Bitcoin: a Peer-to-Peer Electronic Cash System. *Bitcoin.org.* https://bitcoin.org/bitcoin.pdf

NDTV Gadgets 360. (2021). *Cryptocurrency Prices in India Today (24th August 2021)*. NDTV Gadgets 360. https://gadgets.ndtv.com/finance/crypto-currency-price-in-india-inr-compare-bitcoin-ether-dogecoin-ripple-litecoin

PricewaterhouseCoopers. (2015). *Understanding the evolving cryptocurrency market: PwC*. PwC. https://www.pwc.com/us/en/industries/financial-services/library/cryptocurrency-evolution.html

Reserve Bank of India. (2013). *Press Releases*. Rbi.org.in. https://www.rbi.org.in/Scripts/BS_PressReleaseDisplay.aspx?prid=30247

Reserve Bank of India. (2016). *Function Wise Monetary*. Rbi.org.in. https://m.rbi.org.in/scripts/FS_Overview.aspx?fn=2752

Reserve Bank of India. (2017). *FAQs*. Rbi.org.in. https://m.rbi.org.in/scripts/FS_FAQs.aspx?Id=112&fn=5

Reserve Bank of India. (2018). *Notifications*. Rbi.org.in. https://www.rbi.org.in/scripts/FS_Notification.aspx?Id=11243&fn=2&Mode=0

Srivastav, S. (2021, June 29). *History of the cryptocurrency market in India*. CNBCTV18. https://www.cnbctv18.com/photos/cryptocurrency/history-of-the-cryptocurrency-market-in-india-9816081-5.htm

Statista. (2021). (2021). Most popular cryptocurrency apps India 2021. *Statista.* . https://www.statista.com/statistics/1209741/most-popular-cryptocurrency-wallets-india/

The World Bank. (2021). *Personal remittances received (current US$) - India* [Data set]. Worldbank.org. https://data.worldbank.org/indicator/BX.TRF.PWKR.CD.DT?locations=IN

Worldbank. (2011). *Average transaction cost of sending remittances to a specific country (%) - India* [Data set]. Worldbank.org. https://data.worldbank.org/indicator/SI.RMT.COST.IB.ZS?locations=IN

Writ Petition (Civil) No.528 of 2018 INTERNET AND MOBILE ASSOCIATION OF INDIA Petitioner Versus RESERVE BANK OF INDIA Respondent WITH Writ Petition (Civil) No.373 of 2018. https://main.sci.gov.in/supremecourt/2018/19230/19230_2018_4_1501_21151_Judgement_04-Mar-2020.pdf

Chapter 4

A Theoretical Perspective of Artificial Intelligence in Hostility of Cyber Threats in the Banking Sector

Diksha Verma
Chandigarh Group of Colleges, India

Pooja Kansra
Lovely Professional University, India

Sarabjit Kaur
Chandigarh Business School of Administration, India

ABSTRACT

With the progress of new know-how and technology, various cyber centers are utilized by illegal persons to augment cyber related crime. To alleviate this digital crime and cyber threats, artificial intelligence is being implemented by banks and financial institutions. A variety of avenues are offered by artificial intelligence techniques, which facilitate the banks to amplify affluence plus wealth. As per various literatures it has been observed that the expenses of cybercrime were around $ 450 million globally. Therefore, it becomes imperative to introduce certain security programs for guarding cyber threats in banking area. To battle and overcome hackers many banks are moving hands to employ artificial intelligence. Various kinds of cybercrimes are prohibited and recognized by AI-based fraud detection systems. However, execution and preservation of artificial intelligence consist of the high cost. After it, joblessness rate is also augmented by AI techniques. In this study various artificial intelligence techniques will be discussed along with their utilization and limitations.

DOI: 10.4018/978-1-6684-4483-2.ch004

Copyright © 2023, IGI Global. Copying or distributing in print or electronic forms without written permission of IGI Global is prohibited.

INTRODUCTION

Computers, digitalization, as well as transformation in the internet technologies have mounted to the level of growth and also affected the societies in different manner. It is quite unrealistic to envision any person without laptops or any electronic devices (Kaya et al., 2019). As an outcome of this, crime on the other hand is also budding for digital users. Number of large organization whether in public sector or in private sector are witnessing this threat as all are practicing computers and internet for their tasks (Bamrara et al., 2013). As digital banking, digital transactions, e-commerce is gaining recognition in the recent times, cyber threat term is also getting famous side by side (Gunjan et al., 2013). According to a report by Global Findex Database 2017, approximately 1.2 billion people have their accounts in banks. As the concept of digital India is approaching, majority of people (51 percent) are switching towards digitization and even many (26 percent) prefer e-banking rather than physical banking facility. With this extraordinary growth of digitalization in banking industry, cyber threats have become major issue for distress. Indian banking sector alone witnessed 22 percent cyber-attacks in the recent times. In India, cyber threats were identified in the year 1998 after the introduction of privatization of banking segment. Mostly, virus attacks, webpage hackings, theft or phishing etc. were the kind of threats witnessed at that time. A popular incident of cyber-attack on Union Bank of India was observed in May 2017. India has around 42 millions of cases for cyber-attacks and the number is increasing day by day causing financial losses to the to the general public as well (Acharya & Joshi, 2020). Globally these numbers are around 114 billion which costs around US $ 274 billion financially (Raghavan and Partibhan, 2014).

However, Artificial Intelligence (AI) is speedily gripping as the worldwide body. It basically deals with the thinking progression of the customers along with it contract with showing those systems through machines (like computers, robots, etc.). Conceptually, Artificial intelligence has been in existence since a long time. However, now various hasty developments have taken place in the area of Artificial intelligence and due to these evolutions, business organizations have started taking interest in AI. Still there is bewilderment about actual meaning of AI as it actually includes various groups of technologies which include big data analytics, machine learning, effective agents and extrapolative/regulatory analytics. Therefore, AI seems to be a complicated concept (Singh & Agarwal, 2019). However, from various reviews it has been identified that artificial intelligence is a distinctive technique which ultimately results in various utilities which are allied with human minds. Reasoning, learning, practicing inventiveness, brain storming, finding solutions for the problems etc. are the functions which are basically associated with artificial intelligence and a high quantity of structured as well as unstructured data is maintained by combination of both. Various algorithms, principles, processes, and problem definitions are basically used as an actionable approach for controlling individual human behavior (Soni, 2019).

LITERATURE BACKGROUND

The two interchangeably terms are cyber security and information security. Both the terms are considered for the inputs of human (Thakur et al., 2015). After the outbreak of COVID-19, there were various cases of forgery, malware harassment, false links all over the world and various cases of fake mails etc., that were enough for disbursement of cyber threats in the recent times (Khan et al., 2020). Of all the above cyber threats, the most common threat was Malware that basically exploited various exclusive technologies. Hence a system is required for cyber security (Jaccard & Nepal, 2014).

Cyber Security Threats in Banking Sector

There are various cyber security thefts which nowadays have become popular and are more in practice usually. Theft is one such threat which is very common among all. It is basically a practice of using someone else' monetary as well as private data without their awareness with the intention of illegitimate activities. When there is confidentiality contravene in a bank, that information of the customer is usually sold and purchased on the dark web by illegal organizations and other cybercriminals.

A relatively new type of cyber threat that has turned out to be in style nowadays is spoofing. Under this practice, hackers or attackers generate a site analogous to original bank's website. Sometimes customers assuming it as original website, share their valuable information. This information submitted by the customer on the counterfeit website is then hurriedly taken by hackers to be exploited or sold later somewhere.

Banks usually use third party tools like chatbots and customer relationship management software which are basically outsource companies providing services to banks. These outsourced companies might not be cyber secure and impact the bank and customers in one way or the other (Musthafa, 2021).

Another cyber threat existing these days is not to steal data but to change it. Changed data is parallel to the novel data and hence it creates difficulty in identifying any attack by hackers if it actually happened. Sometimes computers and mobile phones which are compromised by malware also cause a peril to computer-generated security of the bank. Sensitive data is shared and if customers have malware installed in their system that is even devoid of appropriate protection, it could attack the bank's networks.

ARTIFICIAL INTELLIGENCE IN BANKING SECTOR

Digital challenges, hyper-connected atmosphere, and antagonism has increased the requirement of up gradation and innovativeness for banking sector and thus artificial intelligence is one of the tools which has resulted in the task of re-imagination for the banks (Anbalagan, 2017). Recognition of fraud, anti- money laundering, humanoid Chatbot interfaces, elimination of human errors, risk management, log analysis, bogus emails etc. are various tasks performed by artificial intelligence in every field especially in banking sector (Meghani, 2020).

According to a survey, around 70 percent of the CEOs of different financial and banking sector organizations believe cyber security a threat to their business. Financial service industries are more affected by these cyber threats as compared to other business sectors. Therefore, it becomes imperative to develop a security program in order to reduce and even protect these cyber threats especially in banking sector. Thus, artificial intelligence is the path to be followed for achieving aforesaid target. Whenever banks try to congregate the data of customers, statistical analysis, regression, correlation, decision trees etc. are the tools used by banks which reduce the credit risk of customers for the banks as it provides various methods that help customers in repaying their loans. Artificial intelligence techniques are used by banks to alleviate the jeopardy of non-performing assets. The most appropriate withdrawal arrangement is chosen by banks with the surveillance of artificial intelligence (Soni, 2019).

AI Techniques used in Combating Cyber Threats in Banking Sector

Numerous types of techniques as part of Artificial intelligence which are used in combating cyber or digital threats in banking sector has been discussed further. For providing advancement in customer experiences and quality of service AI techniques are becoming trendy day by day. AI based chatbots are of the techniques used in banking sector. It endows with 24*7 services and provides accurate replies to the queries and doubts of the customers and ultimately fetches customers' attention for their services, optimize quality and inflate the branding value of banks in the industry.

Through omni channels, banking sector is providing more personalized services to their customers. Mobile applications which are taking aid of ML algorithms are competent to oversee the deeds and lifestyle of their service users which eventually improvising the eminence of service provided by bankers to their customers. Therefore, approximately 70 percent of the banks are in queue to amalgamate AI in mobile banking apps and step forward to cuddle the fair prospect of AI in banking industry.

Artificial intelligence in the banking sector can professionally execute facts compilation and analysis processes. Proven data sets are necessary for Artificial intelligence tools to evaluate the data. AI-powered mobile banking applications accumulate and generate an appropriate erudition practice for enhancing the general consumer know-how. Following a suitable investigation of the data, the consumer experience can turn out to be more personalized.

Utilizations of Artificial Intelligence in Banking Sector

Diminution in Operational expenses in addition to risk

The foremost advantage or merit of amalgamating artificial intelligence with the banking industry is AI. As banking sector has turned in to an innovative arena now, still it is challenged by human based processes that sometimes lead to delay in work or task and ultimately augment the operational costs. Robotic Process Automation software is a technique worn by banks as an element of artificial intelligence that eradicate much of the time concentrated and error prone work.

Enhanced Client Familiarity

New techniques involved in artificial intelligence have conquered the conservative troubles that customers used to countenance previously. Chatbots that provide 24*7 services to the end user exclusive of any superfluous endeavor has made customers increasingly contented with the banking issues. Along with this banks are also up to date about making aware about additional offerings and new services with latest benefits for their customers which is called upselling.

Better Fraud Revealing and Authoritarian Fulfillment

Owing to appliance of artificial intelligence it has turn out to be very effortless for the banks to discover deception and duplicated entries. Compliance of banking with artificial intelligence has lessened the probability of frauds and errors especially in financial sector. Banking is one of the most highly regulated sectors of the economy. Governments employ their regulatory power to make certain that banks have good enough risk profiles to evade large-scale evasions, as well as to make sure banking customers are not using banks to commit financial crimes and nowadays banks are opting AI virtual assistants to supervise dealings, to keep an eye on customer routines and habits, and audit and project information to a variety of acquiescence and regulatory organizations.

Better Advance and Credit Conclusions

With the assistance of artificial intelligence techniques banks are able to perform better in every task like deposits, giving loans etc. still sometimes bank witness little issues related to credit worthiness of their customers, credit score of their customers. AI based loan decision systems and machine learning algorithms keep a check on behaviors and prototype of the customers to conclude if a customer with inadequate credit in the past might in fact make a good quality credit score and a customer whose prototype might raise the odds of defaulting.

Artificial Intelligence for Portfolio Administration

Wealth and portfolio management can be done more effectively with artificial intelligence. AI aids those consumers who are unable to reach the banks often. On transacting funds through online banking applications, Artificial Intelligence technology, stimulates and forwards on the spot transaction message to the consumers. If any mistrustful deal generate, the AI machines instantaneously make the consumer alert. Hence, Artificial Intelligence make certain safe transactions and investments.

Artificial Intelligence for Threat Supervision

It is one of the noteworthy recompense of artificial intelligence accommodated effective banking services. For occasion, scrutiny of monetary standing, manuscript authentication, and providing loans are risk reluctant activities for bankers. The utilization of AI and mechanism erudition in banking can undertake this wisely.

Figure 1.
Source: Author's compiled model based on literature review

Limitations of Artificial Intelligence in Banking Sector

Up-and-coming knowledge is perilous owing to its pettiness and the inadequate moment they have been in act. The risks of using AI are accompanied by the fact that the system has embryonic so quickly. In accumulation to the advantages of using Artificial Intelligence in banking sector, the sector must also think of the following menace and confront:

Artificial Intelligence Biasness

As humans develop the models and algorithms to be used in Artificial intelligence techniques, therefore the odds of biasness and assumptions are always there. These ultimately lead to troubling results. This description of mechanism learning prejudice clarify the dissimilar kind of bias that can unintentionally have an effect on algorithms and the steps companies necessitate to acquire to abolish the errors.

Aptitude and Moral Values

Banking companies function beneath set of laws that necessitate them to describe clarification for their loan providing verdicts to probable customers. This makes it complicated to put into practice the tools and techniques of AI made through detailed learning neural networks, which work through delicate correlations amid thousands of variables that are classically unfathomable to the human mind.

Client Suspicion

In accumulation to fulfilling the rules and regulations, banking companies must be heedful of client conviction when using Artificial Intelligence tools. Chatbots one of the technologies valued for their expediency, will leads to loss of customer interest if they make error.

Cost

There is frequently an interval amid the time when algorithm is formed and when it is installed, just for the reason that it is excessively costly to use it. But even widely adopted algorithms can prove too valued to use beneficially.

Documentation Wadding

By using stolen details of the customers, attackers can achieve illicit right of entry to customer financial records using computerized login credentials. The stolen data then is used to barrage online portals of the banks sequentially to endeavor admittance to significant banking resources available online. There is an automatic system in which the attacker easily log in numerous passwords and usernames and then steal the data and sell further for his own purpose. Documentation Wadding is certainly a process that will definitely emerge and enlarge by the time passes and result in increase in data and account breaches for the coming years.

Cloud Bringer

With abundant of data existing on cloud, it has turned out to be consequently effortless for the hackers to attack the open reserves of information of bank customers and other clients of other sectors also. Pegasus was one of the software developed with such a characteristic to hijack the data available in abundance. Usually attackers called as APT 10 attacks and hacks the accounts of bank customers, whereas companies suppose their data and information is stored safely and protected.

Phishing Harassment

Phishing is an ordinary kind of virtual assault that's regularly steals the data of the bank customers together with login testimonial, debit and credit card numbers. But not long, there has been an augment in phishing assails basically objecting bankers. An assault can have distressing outcomes on a company — particularly a financial establishment like a bank. Phishing can be used to achieve traction in a set-up as a piece of a superior attack like an advanced persistent threat (APT) event. In this situation, a worker is in negotiation in order to find a way around for safety side, allocate malware within a clogged atmosphere, or expand honored contact to safe and protected data. Through admission to a banker's email account, assaulters can study and translate the private information of the bank, deliver emails on the behalf of bank, slash into the bankers' accounts and expand reach to inside credentials plus buyer monetary information resulting in loss of millions of currencies.

Malicious Software

This software basically encrypts the data of the bank customer and then makes it next to impossible for the bankers to access that data unless an amount of ransom is paid for the same. On March 2017, the WannaCry virus dispersed everywhere from end to end networks of Microsoft Windows devices, ultimately impacting thousands of systems badly and negatively which lastly ended with a sum of 327 payments amounting $130,700. Banks are the topmost target of cybercriminals for easy attacking purposes.

Figure 2.
Source: Author's compiled model based on literature review

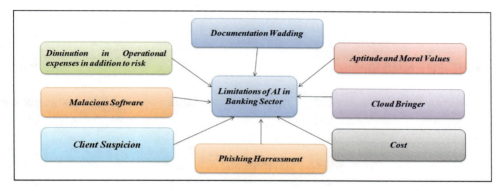

CONCLUSION

The banking sector has developed into stronger in tenure of enlargement, financial expansion also the figure of customers in the economic sector. These days, the new-fangled expertise and technologies are making certain that the prospect of banking will initiate more avenues and quality services to their customers with the innovative banking product and services. Banking sector also augmented the ease of access of an ordinary being to bank for his output and necessities. The conventional banking has developed and more and more banks are espousing new technologies like Artificial Intelligence, Cloud, and block chain to slash their working capital and get better competence. Though it is still in its emerging point, banks are still at cusp of an artificial intelligence rebellion. Up gradation in addition to growth in the Artificial Intelligence business will raise efficiency at an abridged price. The research clearly suggests that banks using artificial intelligence have certain limitations as well. Various threats existed in digital era has made it compulsory to implement Artificial intelligence in this field. Various AI techniques make it challenging for the cybercriminals to attack banking customer details effortlessly. Banks also uses artificial intelligence for human resources routine evaluation, Credit evaluation and portfolio analysis. As the probability of block chain technology is yet to be bring into being till then, AI techniques implementation is heading the Banking Sector in addition to it serving the customers for demanding quicker and effortless service for themselves. It is furthermore being used to meet authoritarian acquiescence, spotting of scam along with evaluating person's creditworthiness.

Conflict of Interest: The authors declare that they have no conflict of interest.
Ethical Approval: The present study is a critical review based, so it doesn't encompass any reports based on animals.
Funding: None

REFERENCES

Acharya, S., & Joshi, S. (2020). Impact of Cyber-Attacks on Banking Institutions in India: A Study of Safety Mechanisms and Preventive Measures. *Palarch's Journal of Archaeology of Egypt/Egyptology, 17*(6), 4656-4670.

Anbalagan, G. (2015). New Technological Changes in Indian Banking Sector. *International Journal of Scientific Research and Management*, 5(9), 7016–7021.

Bamrara, A., Bhatt, M., & Singh, G. (2013). Cyber Attacks and Defense Strategies in India: An Empirical Assessment of Banking Sector. *International Journal of Cyber Criminology*, 7(1), 49–61. doi:10.2139srn.2488413

Cocco, L., Marchesi, M., & Pinna, A. (2017). Banking on Blockchain: Costs Savings Thanks to the Blockchain Technology. *Future Internet*, 9(25), 1–20. doi:10.3390/fi9030025

Digalaki, E. (2019). The impact of artificial intelligence in the banking sector & how AI is being used in 2020. *Business Insider.* https://www.businessinsider.in/finance/news/the-impact-of-artificial-intelligence-in-the-banking-sector-how-ai-is-being-used 2020/articleshow/72860899.cms

Gunjan, V. K., Kumar, A., & Avdhanam, S. (2013, September 21-22). *A survey of cyber crime in India.* [Paper presentation]. 15th International Conference on Advanced Computing Technologies (ICACT), Rajampet, India. 10.1109/ICACT.2013.6710503

Jaccard, J. J., & Nepal, S. (2014). A survey of emerging threats in cybersecurity. *Journal of Computer and System Sciences*, 80(5), 973–993. doi:10.1016/j.jcss.2014.02.005

Kaya, O., & Schildbach, J. AG, D. B., & Schneider, S. (2019). Artificial intelligence in banking: A lever for profitability with limited implementation to date. *EU Monitors Global financial markets.https://*www.dbresearch.com/PROD/RPS_ENPROD/PROD0000000000495172/Artificial_intelligence_in_banking%3A_A_lever_for_pr.pdf?undefined&realload=VhsiDhBWr~jzgZ~OD9X1XXylwp5O2UH6Q/fscdzc1KSVG4FsZDR0MPXIR1rxXSk2

Khan, N. A., Brohi, S. N., & Zaman, N. (2020). Ten Deadly Cyber Security Threats Amid COVID-19 Pandemic. TechRxiv *Powered by IEEE. file:///C:/Users/DELL/Downloads/Ten%20Deadly%20Cyber%20Security%20Threats%20Amid%20COVID-19%20Pandemic.pdf*

Khurshid, A. (2020). Why Banks need artificial intelligence? *Wipro.* https://www.wipro.com/business-process/why-banks-need-artificial-intelligence/

Kunt, A.D., Klapper, L., Singer, D., Ansar, S., & Hess, J. (2017). *The Global Findex Database: Measuring Financial Inclusion and the Fintech Revolution.*World Bank Group. file:///C:/Users/DELL/Downloads/9781464812590.pdf

Kutub, T., Meikang, Q., Gai, K., & Ali, M. L. (2015, November, 3-5). *An Investigation on Cyber Security Threats and Security Model.* [Paper presentation]. IEEE 2nd International Conference on Cyber Security and Cloud Computing, New York, NY, USA. 10.1109/CSCloud.2015.71

Malali, A., & Gopalakrishnan, S. (2020). Application of Artificial Intelligence and Its Powered Technologies in the Indian Banking and Financial Industry: An Overview. *Journal of the Humanities and Social Sciences*, *25*(4), 55–60.

Meghani, K. (2020). Use of Artificial Intelligence and Blockchain in Banking Sector: A Study of Scheduled Commercial Banks in India. *Indian Journal of Applied Research*, *10*(8), 1–4.

Musthafa, M. (2021). Cyber Threats To The Banking Sector To Watch Out For. *Claysys.* https://www.claysys.com/blog/cyber-threats-to-the-banking-sector/

Raghvan, A. R., & Partibhan, L. (2014). The effect of cybercrime on a Bank's finances. *International Journal of Current Research and Academic Review*, *2*(2), 173–178.

Sabharwal, M. (2014). The use of Artificial Intelligence (AI) based technological applications by Indian Banks. *International Journal of Artificial Intelligence and Agent Technology*, *2*, 1–5.

Schmelzer, R., & Tucci, L. (June, 2021). The top 5 benefits of AI in banking and finance. *TechTarget.* https://searchenterpriseai.techtarget.com/feature/AI-in-banking-industry-brings-operational-improvements

Singh, S., & Aggarwal, L. (2019). *Pros and Cons of Artificial Intelligence in Banking Sector of India.* [Paper presentation]. 14th India-Japan International Conference on Economic and Industrial Growth through Recent Innovations and Advancement, Jaipur, India. https://link.springer.com/book/10.1007/978-981-16-6332-1?noAccess=true

Chapter 5
Role of Technology in Improving the Quality of Financial Advisory for Personal Financial Management

Niranjan Kulkarni
https://orcid.org/0000-0003-0467-6510
Vishwakarma University, India

Omvir Gautam
https://orcid.org/0000-0003-2505-936X
Vishwakarma University, India

Swapnil Pradeep Shah
FinoGlobin Financial Services Pvt. Ltd., India

ABSTRACT

Increased per capita income, improved life span, families changing from joint to nuclear ones, and absence of robust social security system; justify the need for a shift in management of personal finance for many. As a result of it, financial advisory is needed. This chapter tries to explore the relation between significance of technology in financial advisory with special reference to personal financial management. The study focuses on describing current use of technology, areas of improvements, and impact on quality of financial advice in personal financial management. The financial advisory field is also witnessing technology disruption with help of machine learning and artificial intelligence getting democratized in the hands of individuals. A lot of information is available at the fingertips, but the role of an advisor will always play a crucial role in achieving the objectives of financial inclusion, financial independence, financial maturity, and financial stability.

DOI: 10.4018/978-1-6684-4483-2.ch005

Copyright © 2023, IGI Global. Copying or distributing in print or electronic forms without written permission of IGI Global is prohibited.

INTRODUCTION

Need for Personal Financial Management

The financial services industry is being disrupted by technology, paving the way for a future characterised by customer-centric products and solutions. Established financial institutions will need to innovate quickly if they want to stay relevant in this new environment and the competitive challenges posed by upstart digital competitors (the FinTech). Understanding the future of financial services, sporting trends by reshaping the race against rivals, capitalizing on emerging opportunities, and building a winning strategy for turbulent times will all play an important role in thriving in a world of digital disruption.

As a part of this study, it is important to understand the need for financial planning. For financial freedom, personal financial management plays a significant role in improving the quality of life and psychological conditions. It is important that we plan for and manage money at every step of our life. Improper planning leads to lack of bondage, not knowing how to get off and of course sufficiently pay your bills. Life within pay checks turns out to be very stressful. Hence possessing the adequate personal financial management skills can help us manage our money well and ensure a brighter financial future. A person may be literate by the definition of literacy but it is important to know various facets of money, its psychological condition and various tools and techniques to improve the current financial state and then achieve desired goals.

Developing economies like India exhibit great financial performances which are reflected through share market indexes. This provided great opportunity for people to improve their financial position. But lack of knowledge, techniques & skill may lead to losing capital in the rush of catching the growth bus. Hence financial literacy and personal financial planning plays a very important role, leading to improved expectations from life. One needs to utilise, apply and improve the knowledge of personal finance to be more proficient.

Growing Size of Retail Investors in India

Increasing income levels, awareness and need about financial planning, retail investing has been on the rise even before current pandemic era. Lock down and working from home just gave a bit of more push for young investors to actively participate in various financial markets to explore, experience and examine their financial literacy. Government initiatives about financial inclusion also played leading role for this to happen. Although the contribution from retail investors is peanuts as compared to institutional investors, it is playing an important role in driving the need qualified and experienced financial advisors. There has been a major shift in the investment patterns which is visible especially post pandemic 2020 as pointed by *Mr. Dhiraj Relli, MD & CEO, HDFC Securities*. Investor managing money actively increased by an astonishing 14.2 million in FY21, with 12.25 million new accounts being opened on CDSL and 1.9 million in NSDL.

Need for Financial Advisory Services

There has basically been a development in the interest in financial planning in India for quite some time; for probably 15+ years. It takes time, skill, and effort for managing investments properly and making the right financial decisions. Busy business executives, start-up founders, working parents, and caretakers have a lot on their plate than actively looking at their finances. Finding time to do some research about financial questions, evaluating various options, and executing a decision take a toll of time. Hence, Do-It-Yourself (DIY) easily turns into no-one-does-it. Ability of a financial advisor makes him worth to keep the investor on track and proactively identify financial risks and opportunities. A wealth manager can help to qualify and quantify decision of investing.

The demand drivers such as higher disposable incomes, customized financial solutions and supply drivers such as new service providers in existing markets, new financial solutions and products, etc are leading to growth in the financial services industry in India. Various options such as mutual funds, pension funds, insurance companies, stock-brokers, wealth managers, financial advisory companies, and commercial banks- ranging from small domestic players to large multinational companies are emerging to serve diverse facets of investors. Government of India is also bringing various flagship schemes such *as Jan-Dhan Yojana* to *Jan-Suraksha Yojana* as a part of financial inclusion regime.

Increasing Role of Technology in Financial Advisory Services

Over the last decade the financial services sector has been renovated with the use of digital technologies which is commonly known as Fintech. To create robo – advisory platforms, big data and artificial intelligence (AI) have been leveraged which offer better investment advice with little human intervention that too in a cost effective manner. Although this is matter of concern for advisors, this is a new normal. The industry is evolving in such a way that clients will be offered a mix of traditional advice and robo-advice. Financial advisors and robot advisors will thus, co-exist.

Anyways, financial advisors have been using computer-based financial models for a while now, so robot-advisors will not create a direct threat to them. The aspect of human interaction between the advisor and the client play a pivoting role here.

Figure 1.
Adapted from https://www.ibef.org/industry/financial-services-india.aspx

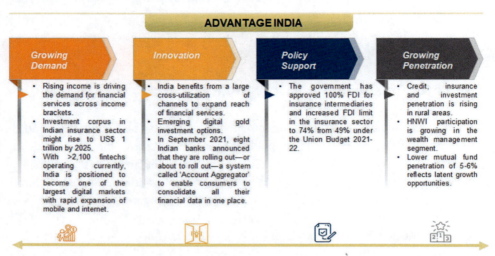

It is difficult to some extent for a technology to capture client's thoughts and emotions and hence a a true picture of his situation.

However, financial advisors do not have a choice. It is important to embrace technology or risk going out of business.

Once an advisor has gathered relevant information, both qualitative and quantitative, he can feed it into suitable technology tools that will throw up appropriate investment advice for the client and also aid in servicing the client on an ongoing basis. This will help advisors to enhance the value they offer to their clients, build on relationships with existing clients and also get more business.

Changing demographics will play a role in how advisors engage with their clients in the future and what types of advice they're able to offer at key life stages.

Rural Trend of Embracing Personal Finance

India is one of the largest and the fastest growing markets for digital consumers. With more than 700 million internet users in 2021 this is growing at a rapid speed. Although, this substantial growth of digital was clocked by consumers in the urban region, but with the government's push towards financial inclusion initiatives, rural India have also started embracing the digital economy. As per the TRAI report, rural internet subscribers account for more than 40% of the total internet subscribers in the country as of March 2021, increasing from about 32% in March 2017.

Despite the growing number of internet users in rural India, two factors – lack of infrastructure and awareness are limiting the penetration of technology. To overcome this, Indian government has launched the "Digital India" programme with an objective of improving digital infrastructure particularly in Rural India. Initiatives such as Bharatnet aimed at providing broadband access to more than 250,000 Gram Panchayats through optical fibre net. Common Service Centers (CSC) are established to provide services related to e-governance. Universal access to mobile is being given to increase the coverage among villages. Digitization of Post Offices is also initiated to enable improved access to savings and borrowings. To improve digital awareness, the Indian government launched 'Pradhan Mantri Gramin Digital Saksharta Abhiyan'. These initiatives by the government are expected to have a positive impact for the digitization of rural India.

REVIEW OF LITERATURE

Extensive literature review is conducted to understand the studies that have undergone in this subject matter. The literature review is done based on the timelines so as to make an opinion about the direction of research that has gone in evaluating the efficiency, efficacy and effectiveness of implementation of technology in improving the financial advisory services.

Growth in Personal Financial Management

Bashir, I., & Qureshi, I. H. (2022) the study is a systematic literature review of various publications & high impacting journals. The study revealed that financial wellbeing need to be understood in qualitative and quantitative manners separately. Financial wellbeing being a subjective concept, technology implementation plays vital role in increasing growth in personal financial management.

Ozturan, M et al. (2021) have revealed the readiness of finance industry to adopt technology to improve efficiency amid a raging pandemic. Issues arising from pandemic situation has led people to find alternate means of finances. As a result, digital transactions picked up at par with the increasing digitization of financial services.

India is a country with highest youth population. There is gender-wise difference in financial goals which demands a need for different approaches towards all the components of financial planning.

Goel, I., & Khanna, S. R. (2014) suggests that financial awareness equips the individual investors with the ability to know, monitor, and effectively use financial resources to enhance the well-being and economic security for the self, family, and one's business. This awareness can be built up more effectively with the help of technology. It is important to understand the role and scope of implementation of technology for upbringing the awareness about financial products, strategies and knowledge.

Mahapatra et al. (2017) describes that the term financial planning has been an area of research interest since few years. Cognitive factors in individuals' financial decisions are prevailing in financial planning. Impact of various cognitive factors in personal financial planning of the Indian households has been studied with reference to risk attitude, financial attitude and financial knowledge. Author has tried to exhibit aspects of personal financial planning decisions thereby highlighting the scope for need and constraint in the growth of personal financial planning.

Munohsamy, Thulasimani (2015) has observed that Financial experts agreeing to the fact that, the amount of knowledge on how to manage that money hasn't kept pace- not at all (Maura Fogarty, 2012). Taking charge of planning and managing finances and putting it into the practice is becoming more important. It is important to have consensus between financial advisors and the investors to work out the best plan. It is important to understand the readiness of the investor rather than the capabilities of the advisor.

Kwela H A (2015) has pointed out personal financial management education has focused on recommended practices believed to ensure long-term financial security but a very few people actually implement such practices. It is important to understand and experience the magic of compounding. Also the intent of investments matters a lot while playing a long term goal. Magic of compounding will improve the patience levels amongst the investors leading to staying long in the financial plan.

Murphy et al. (2010) have focused on personal financial planning attitudes of MBA students. The study also indicates that less than 13 percent have prepared a comprehensive personal financial plan. A perceived need of respondents is to feel that their financial planner will put their needs first. The hallmark of independence has been less dependence on financial planner. Over the period things start going wrong and then respondents were observed to look for financial planners.

Financial Advisory Services and Personal Financial Management

Khasanah & Irawati, (2022) state that how financial literacy is an important parameter for financial advisory services. Increase in the literacy levels should be the objective of financial advisory service providers. Financial Technology and Financial Attitude can be supplementary for increasing the participation and effective personal financial management. *Law, K. K., & Zuo, L. (2022)* this article throws light on the role of economic conditions on the composition of financial advisory services. Services during recessionary trend are more value adding as compared to inflationary trend. Economic conditions have an impact on shaping the types of financial advisors.

Kassem et al (2021) focuses on use of mobile technology as an important tool for portable and convenient financial advisory services. Especially people from farming backgrounds can take a great benefit of this device and use the advisory services for their benefit. It also mentions the fact that how farmers behave about the information at their disposal.

Palmie et al. (2020) stated that India has recently witnessed significant changes in its financial inclusion ecosystem. While financial inclusion is the point of entry to **lift** individuals **out of poverty**, the higher utilization of full range of financial services can alone serve as a path to the prosperity. It is also important to note that only the range of services will not suffice the purpose of financial inclusion. Veiga et al. (2019) in their research described the test of pre-existent scales to measure behaviours of personal financial management, purchasing impulsiveness & financial strain.

Results motivate the use of scales of the behavior of personal financial management in order to assess this trait of personal competence, supporting programs of financial education and marketing planning of the credit institutions. Bharucha (2019) explained that the purpose of this investigation is to examine which factors actually determine the level of personal financial literacy amongst the youth in India's financial capital city. It is equally important to understand the role of rural population in financial literacy. Availability of funds and application of funds need to go in tandem especially in rural areas. Saurabh et al. (2019) explained that the purpose of this investigation is to examine the impact of financial socialization & financial knowledge on financial satisfaction of a person with financial risk attitude as a mediator with special focus on the tier II city of India. Financial satisfaction plays an important role in planning and staying invested for a long run.

Begina et al. (2018) explained that empirically validated financial psychology tools have been created for use in the financial planning field. However, some financial planners are reluctant to integrate such tools into their work with clients because they fear that they are unqualified. The Klontz Money Script Revised Inventory (KMSI-R) has been empirically validated to recognize beliefs around money that might affect financial behaviors.

Mahapatra et al. (2017) studied that the term financial planning has been an area of research interest since few years. Investigations have underlined the impact of various cognitive factors in individuals' financial decisions. Behavioural finance has laid the foundation for the same and Financial Therapy will play crucial role to improve the results of investigations. It is important to set the purpose before starting with financial planning.

Asebedo (2016) presented a well-known & highly utilized conflict resolution framework from the mediation profession & exhibits how to apply this framework to money arguments. Klontz et al. (2016) stated that financial planners are uniquely positioned to offer the tools, knowledge, & processes to assist clients decrease their financial stress & thereby improve clients' psychological health, physical health, occupational functioning, & relationships. While presenting a new model for assisting clients, to achieve balanced & healthy financial lives- called integrated financial planning. It consolidates the interior, emotional aspects of finance with exterior financial knowledge & gives the advisor with an extended set of tools for working with clients to make & maintain financial health. It focuses on answering why than how. If the answer of why is clear then answers for how becomes more fruitful. Technology is making it easy, but for them who know why to use it. Xiao et al. (2016) explained that authoritative resource encapsulates the state of consumer finance research across disciplines for expert discoveries on—& strategies for enhancing—consumers' economic health. Consumer finance need to be understood from entirety to help needy consumers to take a help of it and abstain from overusing it. Delgadillo (2016) stated that albeit financial counselling has remained relatively stable throughout the long term, new changes are coming to the housing counselling industry, including the new certifications and requirements. Patel et al. (2016) studied that the expanding complexity of financial products makes it important for a person to seek experts' opinion in managing one's Personal finances.

Archuleta et al. (2011) explained what is generally meant when researchers & practitioners talk about financial planning and counselling as a field of study and practice. It also focuses on the process and theoretical underpinnings of financial planning and counselling. A review of the historical development of marriage & family therapy is also introduced. Lastly, a new emerging field of study, namely, financial therapy is presented.

Agarwal et al. (2010) in their research reported the findings about financial literacy & financial planning behavior based on the financial advisory program in India. Researchers find that the vast majority of respondents appear to be financially literate dependent on their answers to questions concerning interest rates (numeracy), inflation, & diversification/ risk. However, find variation across demographic & socioeconomic groups.

Financial Advisory Services and Role of Technology

Rose Jill et al (2021) focuses on the rapid change in financial structures and technologies. Traditional brick & mortar banking models are rapidly being disrupted. Purely digital start-up companies leverage technology and provide products or services to enhance the entire ecosystem.

Bharadwaj S (2021) from this paper it is revealed that the banking and financial sectors are among the top five applications for artificial intelligence across the globe. With India seeming to have woken up to the potential of AI, developments in the Indian artificial intelligence sector are covered in this paper.

PWC Financial Services Technology 2020 & Beyond (2020) this article mentions that that technology is affecting financial services in a multitude of ways. Financial institutions are looking for solutions from IT organizations to cope with the pace of changing personal financial planning. Fintech is growing to productise the financial planning process. Khan, Khurram Ajaz et al. (2020) this study sets out to solve a couple of research problems such as exploring the correlation between individuals' financial anxiety, financial advice, and EPS (electronic payment system use) initially and exploring the perceived differences among males and females, and to answer whether the gender inequality still prevalent amongst generation Z in India. Maximilian Palmié, et al (2020) this study focuses on disruptive innovations in the ecosystem. The study defines disruptive innovation ecosystems and illustrates the impact that the financial technology (FinTech) ecosystem has had on disrupting the financial services industry.

Mosteanu, N. R. (2020) in this report, it is revealed that the AI is the future for the finance industry. AI is making financial processes easier for the customers, it is very soon going to replace humans and provide faster and much more efficient solutions. It is equally important to understand the cognitive situation of the user to gage the worth of such decisions. Business Wire India (2019) sheds light on human often do not like to communicate to machines. Which is an important factor to take a financial decision. Hence improving customer satisfaction by improving AI capabilities will help in achieving the objective. Ayn, D. J. (2019) sheds light on Robo-advisors being the digital platforms that provide automated, algorithm-based financial planning services with little to no human supervision. Ashish Anantharaman, (2019) puts light on Artificial Intelligence (AI) is stirring up a lot of excitement among FinTech sector. AI has demonstrated potential to make the availability of financial services to everyone in a better, faster, and cheaper manner. Indian FinTech market is expected to grow at a CAGR of 22 percent over the next five years, with the transaction value crossing $73 billion by 2020 and counting.

Research Gap, Research Questions and Hypotheses

It is evident from the literature review that there is a need to evaluate the level of satisfaction of current technological applications in the field of Personal Financial Management (PFM) by the financial advisors, also various areas of improvement with respect to use of technology in the PFM and perceive whether the use of technology will impact quality of financial advice related to PFM. Based on which following research questions are developed.

RQ1- Are the current technological applications in the field of PFM by the financial advisors satisfactory?

RQ2- What are the areas of improvement in the use of technology?

RQ3- Will technology impact quality of financial advice related to personal financial management?

To test this, following hypothesis are developed.

H01: There is no relation of Current use of technology in personal financial advisory.

H02: There is no role of technology in financial advisory services.

H03: Use of technology will not impact quality of financial advice in personal financial management

METHODOLOGY

Population and Sample

Practising financial advisors across India were the population for the study. The Mint (2021, pg) reported that there are around 2000 certified financial planners in India. Their details were obtained from the Securities and Exchange Board of India (SEBI). A questionnaire was mailed to them. Reference to standard sample size tables like Krejcie and Morgan (1970) return a sample size of 322 for a population of 2000 at 95% confidence level and 5% confidence interval. A total of 356 responses were received meeting the sample size requirements. Ten senior financial advisors were interviewed personally.

Design of Questionnaire

A questionnaire was designed and hosted on Google Forms. It had the following sections:

Profile information
Section I – Current use of technology
Section II – Areas of improvement
Section III – Impact on quality of financial advice

Role of Technology in Improving the Quality of Financial Advisory for Financial Management

The sections were designed to collect information required to test the three hypotheses and consisted of ten statements each. Responses were sought on a 5-point Likert scale. Respondents were provided with a Don't Know filter (DK Filter) as suggested by Menold and Bogner (2016) by keeping Cannot Say as the first option in the response list.

The ten statements included under each of the three sections of the questionnaire are given in Table 1.

Table 1. Statements forming part of Section I of the questionnaire

Sr. No.	Statement	Strongly Agree (5)	Agree (4)	Cannot say (3)	Disagree (2)	Strongly Disagree (1)
I	**Current use of technology**					
1	Technology is reasonably used at planning stage for investors	5	4	3	2	1
2	Technology offers various scenarios for investors to seek their goals	5	4	3	2	1
3	Transactions with the clients are fully automated	5	4	3	2	1
4	An automated central client database is used	5	4	3	2	1
5	Technology offers us support to connect with major investment portals like moneycontrol.com	5	4	3	2	1
6	Technology offers us solutions for client portfolio manoeuvring	5	4	3	2	1
7	Technology has helped us improving communication with the clients	5	4	3	2	1
8	Clients get live updates on their portfolios	5	4	3	2	1
9	Settlement of transactions with clients is tech-driven	5	4	3	2	1
10	Technology has offered apps like investing in IPOs	5	4	3	2	1
II	**Areas of improvement**					
11	Providing different goal seek options to clients	5	4	3	2	1
12	Tracking portfolio history with return details	5	4	3	2	1
13	Tracking individual stock performance over a period of time	5	4	3	2	1

continues on following page

Table 1. Continued

Sr. No.	Statement	Strongly Agree (5)	Agree (4)	Cannot say (3)	Disagree (2)	Strongly Disagree (1)
14	Projecting scenarios for portfolios based on market projections	5	4	3	2	1
15	Projecting scenarios for individual stocks based on market projections	5	4	3	2	1
16	Providing risk assessment for investments	5	4	3	2	1
17	Mapping risk-return profiles for portfolios	5	4	3	2	1
18	Provision of updated market information	5	4	3	2	1
19	Secured gateways for executing transactions	5	4	3	2	1
20	Provision for details required for income tax capital gains calculations	5	4	3	2	1
III	**Impact on quality of advice**					
21	Technology will improve prescriptive analysis	5	4	3	2	1
22	Technology will improve predictive analysis	5	4	3	2	1
23	Technology will enhance scientific decision-making	5	4	3	2	1
24	Investment biases and prejudices on the part of investors will be reduced	5	4	3	2	1
25	Investment biases and prejudices on the part of advisors will be reduced	5	4	3	2	1
26	Real time data will improve timing of investment decisions	5	4	3	2	1
27	Objective and rational decisions will emerge	5	4	3	2	1
28	Investor confidence will increase	5	4	3	2	1
29	Investors would be well aware about the risks they are assuming	5	4	3	2	1
30	Investors would also be well aware about the returns they should expect	5	4	3	2	1

Methodology for Testing of Hypotheses

Scores for the all statements were averaged on the 5-point Likert scale. Applying these weights, a single average (of 356 respondents) percentage of agreement and disagreement was worked out for each of the all responses. These all averages were further averaged to calculate a single Likert scale aggregate agreement/disagreement percentage of the all statements. Maximum of the two (agreement/disagreement), that is, the sample mean responses, was then compared with a hypothesized 50% agreement/disagreement percentage connoting agreement/disagreement by chance to determine if the overall agreement/disagreement is statistically significant or not. A t-test was then applied to test the statistical significance at 95% confidence level by comparing the sample mean with hypothesized population mean taking into account the standard deviation of the sample. The null hypotheses were tested for rejection or otherwise based on the p-values. For instance, in case of Section I, first the responses were calculated for the ten individual statements and were averaged for the 356 respondents. The disagreement percentage (being higher of agreement/ disagreement) was compared with 50% disagreement connoting an event by chance. A t-test was used taking into account the standard deviation of the sample and based on the t-statistic and the resultant p-value, the first null hypothesis was tested.

Validity and Reliability of the Questionnaire

The questionnaire was tested for validity and reliability as under:

Test of validity –The hypotheses, hypotheses testing method, questionnaire etc. were validated by the experts in the field so as to ensure that the measurement was adequate and accurate in terms of the desired direction.

A check-list as prescribed by Brown et al. (2015) was applied for validation as under:

Table 2. Application of Brown et al. (2015) check-list for validation

Step No.	Step	Action
1	Establish Face Validity	The questionnaire has been validated for face validity by group of experts.
2	Clean Collected Data	As the data was collected through Google Forms using response options, no invalid data was collected.
3	Use Principal Components Analysis (PCA)	With barely three variables in the study, namely, current use of technology, areas of improvement, and impact on quality of financial advice, PCA was not applied.
4	Check Internal Consistency	This was done through Cronbach's Alpha

Source: Brown et al. (2015) check-list for validation

Test of reliability – Cronbach's Alpha and other tests were applied on the questionnaire and the results are summarized as under:

Table 3. Cronbach Alpha scores

Sr. No.	Section	Cronbach Alpha
1	Current use of technology	0.762
2	Areas of improvement	0.742
3	Impact on quality of advice	0.851
4	Entire questionnaire	0.767

As the Cronbach's alpha scores were more than 0.70, the questionnaire was considered as reliable.

DATA ANALYSIS AND INTERPRETATION

Descriptive Analysis

347 out of the 356 respondents were male while nine were female. 86 respondents were <30 years of age, 99 belonged to the age-group 30-39 years, 93 belonged to the age-group 40-49 years, and 78 were >=50 years of age. 36 respondents had work experience of <5 years, 98 respondents were from the work experience group of 5-10 years, and 222 respondents had work experience in excess of 10 years. 112 respondents reported an average client size of <100, 131 reported the same to be in the range of 100-200, whereas another 113 reported an average client size of >200. 311 out of the 356 respondents were running their business as proprietors, 42 were running it in the form of partnership firms and three were carrying it in the form of a company.

Inferential Analysis

Testing of the 1st hypothesis

H01: There is no relation of Current use of technology in personal financial advisory.

Plain count of responses to Section I is given below:

Role of Technology in Improving the Quality of Financial Advisory for Financial Management

Table 4. Plain count of responses (Frequency distribution)

Sr. No.	Statement	Strongly Agree	Agree	Cannot say	Disagree	Strongly Disagree	Total
1	Technology is reasonably used at planning stage for investors	81	20	5	225	25	356
2	Technology offers various scenarios for investors to seek their goals	93	19	2	209	33	356
3	Transactions with the clients are fully automated	88	28	1	209	30	356
4	An automated central client database is used	76	27	7	216	30	356
5	Technology offers us support to connect with major investment portals like moneycontrol.com	92	27	3	203	31	356
6	Technology offers us solutions for client portfolio manoeuvring	59	27	8	226	36	356
7	Technology has helped us improving communication with the clients	83	29	13	204	27	356
8	Clients get live updates on their portfolios	60	42	1	220	33	356
9	Settlement of transactions with clients is tech-driven	68	36	2	224	26	356
10	Technology has offered apps like investing in IPOs	52	33	11	222	38	356
11	Providing different goal seek options to clients	99	179	4	60	14	356
12	Tracking portfolio history with return details	120	177	4	42	13	356
13	Tracking individual stock performance over a period of time	115	175	4	47	15	356
14	Projecting scenarios for portfolios based on market projections	88	177	11	71	9	356
15	Projecting scenarios for individual stocks based on market projections	86	187	10	54	19	356
16	Providing risk assessment for investments	106	179	4	49	18	356
17	Mapping risk-return profiles for portfolios	113	176	1	49	17	356

continues on following page

Table 4. Continued

Sr. No.	Statement	Strongly Agree	Agree	Cannot say	Disagree	Strongly Disagree	Total
18	Provision of updated market information	109	168	5	54	20	356
19	Secured gateways for executing transactions	74	169	11	71	31	356
20	Provision for details required for income tax capital gains calculations	92	165	5	66	28	356
21	Technology will improve prescriptive analysis	99	179	4	59	15	356
22	Technology will improve predictive analysis	119	178	4	40	15	356
23	Technology will enhance scientific decision-making	115	175	4	43	19	356
24	Investment biases and prejudices on the part of investors will be reduced	88	177	11	65	15	356
25	Investment biases and prejudices on the part of advisors will be reduced	86	187	10	47	26	356
26	Real time data will improve timing of investment decisions	106	179	4	53	14	356
27	Objective and rational decisions will emerge	112	177	1	48	18	356
28	Investor confidence will increase	109	168	5	58	16	356
29	Investors would be well aware about the risks they are assuming	109	168	5	58	16	356
30	Investors would also be well aware about the returns they should expect	86	187	10	47	26	356

Responses by the 356 respondents to the statements of Section I of the questionnaire were averaged and were further averaged for the ten statements into a single disagreement percentage for the entire section.

Testing of 1st Hypothesis

H01: There is no relation of Current use of technology in personal financial advisory.

The average disagreement percentage was compared with a hypothesized mean of the population of 50% disagreement taking it as an event by chance and it was ascertained if the sample mean was statistically significant at 95% confidence level or not.

The hypothesis was tested by comparing sample mean (average awareness score for 356) with hypothesized population mean of 5 (being the mid-point of 0-10 score). The results showed that the sample mean ($\bar{x}$) was 61%. Same was compared with hypothesized population mean of 5.0. Standard deviation of the sample was 0.804. Taking the sample size of 356, the t-statistic was 2.55, p-value for which was <0.0001. Hence rejected.

Testing of 2nd Hypothesis

H02: There is no role of technology in financial advisory services.

Responses by the 356 respondents to the statements of Section II of the questionnaire were averaged and were further averaged for the ten statements into a single agreement percentage for the entire section.

The average agreement percentage was compared with a hypothesized mean of the population of 50% agreement taking it as an event by chance and it was ascertained if the sample mean was statistically significant at 95% confidence level or not.

This hypothesis was tested by comparing sample mean (average awareness score for 356) with hypothesized population mean of 5 (being the mid-point of 0-10 score). The results showed that the sample mean ($\bar{x}$) was 80%. Same was compared with hypothesized population mean of 5.0. Standard deviation of the sample was 0.924. Taking the sample size of 356, the t-statistic was 6.14, p-value for which was <0.0001. Hence rejected

Testing of 3rd Hypothesis

H03: Use of technology will not impact quality of financial advice in personal financial management

Responses by the 356 respondents to the statements of Section III of the questionnaire were averaged and were further averaged for the ten statements into a single agreement percentage for the entire section.

The average agreement percentage was compared with a hypothesized mean of the population of 50% agreement taking it as an event by chance and it was ascertained if the sample mean was statistically significant at 95% confidence level or not.

This hypothesis was tested by comparing sample mean (average awareness score for 356) with hypothesized population mean of 5 (being the mid-point of 0-10 score). The results showed that the sample mean ($\bar{x}$) was 81%. Same was compared with hypothesized population mean of 5.0. Standard deviation of the sample was 0.911. Taking the sample size of 356, the t-statistic was 6.48, p-value for which was <0.0001. Hence rejected

Discussion of Results

For section I, current use of technology, the average disagreement was found to be 61%. Technology is reasonably used at planning stage for investors was disagreed to the extent of 60%, Technology offers various scenarios for investors to seek their goals was disagreed by 57%, Transactions with the clients are fully automated by 57%, An automated central client database is used by 61%, Technology offers us support to connect with major investment portals like moneycontrol.com by 56%, Technology offers us solutions for client portfolio manoeuvring by 67%, Technology has helped us improving communication with the clients by 57%, Clients get live updates on their portfolios by 64%, Settlement of transactions with clients is tech-driven by 62%, and Technology has offered apps like investing in IPOs by 69%. In all the ten cases the disagreement was more than the agreement which was less than 50%. The standard deviation of responses in this section was 0.80393 with a maximum disagreement of 69% and the minimum disagreement being 56%.

For section II, areas of improvement, the average agreement was found to be 80%. Providing different goal seek options to clients as an improvement area was agreed to by 81% of the respondents, Tracking portfolio history with return details was agreed by 86%, Tracking individual stock performance over a period of time by 84%, Projecting scenarios for portfolios based on market projections by 80%, Projecting scenarios for individual stocks based on market projections by 80%, Providing risk assessment for investments by 82%, Mapping risk-return profiles for portfolios by 83%, Provision of updated market information by 80%, Secured gateways for executing transactions by 70% and Provision for details required for income tax capital gains calculations by 74%. In all the ten cases the agreement was more than the disagreement which was less than 50%. The standard deviation of responses in this section was 0.92411 with a maximum agreement of 86% and the minimum agreement being 70%.

For Section III, impact on quality of financial advice, the average agreement was found to be 81%. For the statement Technology will improve prescriptive analysis the agreement on the impact on quality was 81%, for Technology will improve predictive analysis by 86%, Technology will enhance scientific decision-making by 83%, Investment biases and prejudices on the part of investors will be reduced by 79%, Investment biases and prejudices on the part of advisors will be reduced by 78%, Real time data will improve timing of investment decisions by 83%, Objective and rational decisions will emerge by 83%, Investor confidence will increase by

Role of Technology in Improving the Quality of Financial Advisory for Financial Management

81%, Investors would be well aware about the risks they are assuming by 81%, and Investors would also be well aware about the returns they should expect by 78%. In all the ten cases the agreement was more than the disagreement which was less than 50%. The standard deviation of responses in this section was 0.91147 with a maximum agreement of 86% and the minimum agreement being 78%.

In sum, the ten interviews suggested that financial advisory field is witnessing technology disruption with help of machine learning and artificial intelligence getting democratised in the hands of individuals. A lot of information is available on the tips of fingers but the role of an advisor will always be crucial in achieving the objectives of financial inclusion, financial independence, financial maturity, and financial stability. The experts felt that while things like machine learning and artificial intelligence have vast potential in the field of personal financial management, its application as of now in India is at an early stage. It will take some time for both the investors and the advisors to adopt these advances in technology in practice. This is especially the case with financial advisors who are not operating in the metro places of the country.

CONCLUSION

Three conclusions clearly emerge. One, the current use of technology by the financial advisors is far from satisfactory. Use of technology falls short of expectations in various areas related to investments. Technology is not satisfactorily used in planning the investments. The same is the case when it comes to transacting with the clients. Technological gaps are observed in the interface with external contacts with sites like moneycontrol.com. There are barriers that are blocking the adoption of technology by both the investors and the financial advisors. This is quite a curious case and worth further investigation given the fact that technological advances are available. As stated Ashish Anantharaman, (2019), they need to be adopted and leveraged in practice. With rapid penetration of internet usage, the access to technology has improved in the recent years. Yet, in practice the actual utilization is lagging behind. The second conclusion is that there is a good scope for improvement which is agreed to by the financial advisors. This is a positive sign and it conveys a belief on the part of the advisors that there are benefits that are expected from the use of technology. The agreement to the improvement area indicate optimism on the part of the financial advisors. As pointed out by Abad-Segura et al (2021) the advisors see a role for technology in offering better management of stocks and portfolio. Moreover they can get a better idea of the risk-return profile associated with the investments. The advisors also see a potential for improvement by staying more updated with the latest market information. The third conclusion of the study is that technology is likely to have a profound impact on quality of financial advice in personal financial management. They see technology impacting quality by improving prescriptive and predictive analysis, and in moving towards scientific, objective and rational decision-making. They also see the scope to get rid of investment biases and prejudices. Impact on quality of financial advice through better assessment of risk and return is also envisaged.

Overall, there is a strong case for adoption of technology by the financial advisors in personal financial management. As suggested by the group of experts there is also a strong case for application of machine learning and artificial intelligence in the field of personal financial management. However, penetration of these technologies as of now is restricted to only select urban locations in the country.

Rural India is also an important part of the country's economy. But there is wide gap with respect to implementation of Financial Technology between urban and rural areas which mainly stems from two factors – lack of infrastructure and awareness. With the launch of Digital India program, the government of India is trying to bridge this gap and bring rural sector in mainstream financial technology. As discovered in the report by Mohanta, G., & Dash, A. (2022), the government introduced the Pradhan Mantri Jan Dhan Yojana (PMJDY) programme in 2014 aimed at making bank accounts accessible to all Indians. This programme has directly raised banking penetration in India, expanding the market for financial services sector in the country. Rapid financial inclusion of women is also observed under this program where, out of total savings accounts, there were overall 27% female accounts. However in 2019, under PMJDY, women accounts constitute 53% of the total Jan Dhan accounts.

Suggestions for further research include studies in the area of technology adoption by investors and the financial advisors. More research is desirable to study the reasons for lower rates of technology adoption despite proven benefits. Researchers can also look into ways for speedier application of machine learning and artificial intelligence in the field of personal financial management.

IMPLICATIONS

Findings of the study imply a few things for the financial advisors. One is that they have to improve the current levels of application of technology in personal financial management. Conscious efforts will have to be taken to step-up the application of technology in various dimensions of personal financial management. As mentioned in PWC Financial Services Technology 2020 & beyond (2020), they will have to take along with them the investors in this endeavour. Another implication of the findings is that there is fair degree of scope for improvement as seen by the financial advisors. This is a positive finding which spells out some optimism for the future despite poor current levels of application of technology. Another implication related to the finding is that the expectation of the investors of the quality of the financial advice is bound to increase in the future. As suggested by Nofie Iman et al (2020) they will expect much more quality advice from the advisors in the area of personal financial management as technology will bring about a paradigm change in the way the profession would be managed.

REFERENCES

Abad-Segura, E., González-Zamar, M.-D., Meneses, E., & Vázquez-Cano, E. (2020). Financial Technology: Review of Trends, Approaches and Management. *Mathematics.*, *8*, 951. doi:10.3390/math8060951

Agarwal, S., Amromin, G., Ben-David, I., Chomsisengphet, S., & Evanoff, D. (2010). Financial Literacy and Financial Planning: Evidence from India. *Journal of Housing Economics*, *27*. doi:10.2139srn.1728831

Alt, R., Beck, R., & Smits, M. T. (2018). FinTech and the transformation of the financial industry. *Electronic Markets*, *28*, 235–243. https://doi.org/10.1007/s12525-018-0310-9

Anantharaman, A. (2019). How artificial intelligence is enabling financial inclusion in India. *YourStory*. https://yourstory.com/2019/05/artificial-intelligence-enabling-financial-inclusion

Archuleta, K. L., Britt, S. L., & Klontz, B. T. (2016). Financial therapy. In *Handbook of consumer finance research* (pp. 73–82). Springer. https://link.springer.com/chapter/10.1007/978-3-319-28887-1_6

Archuleta, K. L., & Grable, J. E. (2011). The future of financial planning and counselling: An introduction to financial therapy. In *Financial planning and counselling scales* (pp. 33–59). Springer. https://link.springer.com/chapter/10.1007/978-1-4419-6908-8_3

Ariwala, P. (2019). 5 Ways ai is transforming the finance industry. *Maruti Techlabs*. https://marutitech.com/ways-ai-transforming-finance/

Asebedo, S. D. (2019). Psychosocial Attributes and Financial Self-Efficacy Among Older Adults. *Journal of Financial Therapy*, *10*(1), 2. doi:10.4148/1944-9771.1196

Ayn, D. J. (2019). Robo-advisors and Artificial Intelligence – Comparing 5 Current Apps. *Emerj*. https://emerj.com/ai-applicationcomparisons/robo-advisors-artificial-intelligencecomparing-5-current-apps/

Ayn, D. J. (2019). Robo-advisors and Artificial Intelligence –Comparing 5 Current Apps. *Emerj*.

Barik, R., & Sharma, P. (2019). Analysing the progress and prospects of financial inclusion in India. *Journal of Public Affairs*, *19*(4), e1948. https://onlinelibrary.wiley.com/doi/abs/10.1002/pa.1948

Bashir, I., & Qureshi, I. H. (2022). *A Systematic Literature Review on Personal Financial Well-Being: The Link to Key Sustainable Development Goals 2030*. FIIB Business Review. doi:10.1177/23197145221106862

Begina, & M. A, ., Hickingbottom, J., Luttrull, E. G., McCoy, M., & Klontz, B. (2018). Identify and Understand Clients' Money Scripts: A Framework for Using the KMSI-R. *Journal of Financial Planning*, *31*(3), 46–55.

Bharadwaj, R. (2019). AI in the Indian financial sector – current traction, opportunities and challenges. Retrieved from: https://emerj.com/ai-sector-overviews/ai-in-the-indian-financial-sectorcurrent-traction-opportunities-and-challenges/ on 28.12.2019

Bharadwaj, S., & Deka, S. (2021, December). Behavioural intention towards investment in cryptocurrency: an integration of Rogers' diffusion of innovation theory and the technology acceptance model. In Forum Scientiae Oeconomia, 9(4), 137-159.

Bharucha, J. P. (2019). Determinants of Financial Literacy Among Indian Youth. In P. Ordoñez de Pablos (Ed.), *Dynamic Perspectives on Globalization and Sustainable Business in Asia* (pp. 154–167). IGI Global. doi:10.4018/978-1-5225-7095-0.ch010

Bharucha, J. P. (2019). Determinants of financial literacy among Indian youth. In *Dynamic Perspectives on Globalization and Sustainable Business in Asia* (pp. 154–167). IGI Global. https://www.igi-global.com/chapter/determinants-of-financial-literacy-among-indian-youth/215111

Bhatia, A., Chandani, A., Atiq, R., Mehta, M., & Divekar, R. (2021). Artificial intelligence in financial services: a qualitative research to discover robo-advisory services. *Qualitative Research in Financial Markets, 13*(5), 632-654. doi:10.1108/QRFM-10-2020-0199

Bhatia, A., Chandani, A., & Chhateja, J. (2020). Robo advisory and its potential in addressing the behavioral biases of investors — A qualitative study in Indian context. *Journal of Behavioral and Experimental Finance, 25,* 100281, ISSN 2214-6350, doi:10.1016/j.jbef.2020.100281

Borate, N. (2021). India has just around 2,000 certified financial planners: Rajesh Krishnamoorthy. *Mint.* https://www.livemint.com/money/personal-finance/india-has-just-around-2-000-certified-financial-planners-rajesh-krishnamoorthy-11616600959703.html

Brown. (2015). Validation of the Intermountain patient perception of quality (PPQ) survey among survivors of an intensive care unit admission: A retrospective validation study Quality, performance, safety and outcomes. *BMC Health Services Research*, 15(1), 155.

Chandorkar, A., & Misra, K. (2019). How financial services industry in India is set for ai makeover. Retrieved from: https://www.financialexpress.com/industry/how-financial-services-industryin-india-is-set-for-ai-makeover/1723836/ on 26.12.2019.

Chatterjee, S., & Fan, L. (2021). Older Adults' Life Satisfaction: The Roles of Seeking Financial Advice and Personality Traits. *Journal of Financial Therapy*, 12(1), 4. https://doi.org/10.4148/1944-9771.1253

Das, S. C. (2016). Financial literacy among Indian millennial generation and their reflections on financial behaviour and attitude: An explanatory research. *The Indian Journal of Commerce*, 69(4). https://www.researchgate.net/publication/320009228_Financial_Literacy_among_Indian_Millennial_Generation_and_their_Reflections_on_Financial_Behaviour_and_Attitude_An_Explanatory_Research_By

Delgadillo, L. M. (2016). Financial Counseling and Financial Health. In J. Xiao (Ed.), *Handbook of Consumer Finance Research*. Springer. doi:10.1007/978-3-319-28887-1_7

Goel, I., & Khanna, S. R. (2014). Financial education as tool to achieve financial literacy. *ZENITH International Journal of Multidisciplinary Research*, 4(12), 73–81.

Iman, N. (2020). The rise and rise of financial technology: The good, the bad, and the verdict. *Cogent Business & Management*, 7(1), 1725309.

Iman, N. (2020) The rise and rise of financial technology: The good, the bad, and the verdict. *Cogent Business & Management,* 7(1). doi:10.1080/23311975.2020.1725309

Introduction to the FinTech Ecosystem Technology & Law 69 Department of Justice Journal of Federal Law and Practice 2021. (2021, March 8). HeinOnline; heinonline.org. https://heinonline.org/HOL/LandingPage?handle=hein.journals/usab69&div=36&id=&page=

Kassem, H. S., Alotaibi, B. A., Ghoneim, Y. A., & Diab, A. M. (2021). Mobile-based advisory services for sustainable agriculture: Assessing farmers' information behavior. *Information Development*, *37*(3), 483–495. https://doi.org/10.1177/0266666920967979

Kee, D. M. H., Syazwan, M. A., Rusydi, M. D., Anwar, M. A., Islah, M. H., Khan, Y. F., & Ganatra, V. (2021). Trust, Perceived Support and Organizational Citizenship Behavior Among Undergraduate Students in Universiti Sains Malaysia. [APJME]. *Asia Pacific Journal of Management and Education*, *4*(3), 49–60.

Khan, K. A., Akhtar, M. A., Dey, S. K., & Ibrahim, R. (2020). Financial Anxiety, Financial advice, and E-payment use: Relationship and perceived differences between males & females of Generation Z. *Journal of Critical Reviews,*. *7*(18). https://www.jcreview.com/index.php?mno=96289

Khasanah, U., & Irawati, Z. (2022, June 13). The Effect of Financial Literacy, Financial Attitude, and the Use of Financial Technology on the Financial Management of SMEs. *Atlantis Press*. https://www.atlantis-press.com/proceedings/icoebs-22/125975151

Klontz, B., Zutphen, N., & Fries, K. (2016). Financial Planner as Healer: Maximizing the Role of Financial Health Physician. *Journal of Financial Planning*, *29*, 52–59.

Krejcie, R. V., & Morgan, D. W. (1970). Determining sample size for research activities. *Educational and Psychological Measurement*, *30*(3), 607–610.

Kwela, H. A. (2015). *The effectiveness of the Personal Financial Management Programme on the well-being of employees in the Department of Rural Development and Land Reform in the Pietermaritzburg region* [Doctoral dissertation, University of Pretoria, South Africa].

Law, K. K., & Zuo, L. (2022). Public concern about immigration and customer complaints against minority financial advisors. *Management Science*, *68*(11), 8464–8482. doi:10.1287/mnsc.2021.4283

Law, K. & Zuo, L. (2022, June 1). How Does the Economy Shape the Financial Advisory Profession? *Management Science*. doi:10.1287/mnsc.2020.3655

Mahapatra, M., & De, A. (2017). A Study on Influence of Financial Cognition on Personal Financial Planning of Indian Households. *Academic Research Colloquium for Financial Planning and Related Disciplines*. https://ssrn.com/abstract=3040807 or doi:10.2139/ssrn.3040807

Menold, N., & Bogner, K. (2016). *Design of Rating Scales in Questionnaires (Version 2.0)*. doi:10.15465/gesis-sg_en_015

Mohanta, G., & Dash, A. (2022). Do financial consultants exert a moderating effect on savings behavior? A study on the Indian rural population. *Cogent Economics & Finance, 10*(1), 2131230.

Mosteanu, N. R. (2020). Artificial Intelligence and Cyber Security–A Shield against Cyberattack as a Risk Business Management Tool–Case of European Countries. *Quality-Access to Success, 21*(175).

Munohsamy, T. (2015). Personal. *Financial Management*.

Murphy, D., & Yetmar, S. (2010). Personal financial planning attitudes: A preliminary study of graduate students. *Management Research Review, 33*, 811–817. doi:10.1108/01409171011065617

Ozturan, M., Atasu, I., & Soydan, H. (2019). Assessment of blockchain technology readiness level of banking industry: Case of Turkey. *International Journal of Business Marketing and Management (IJBMM), 4*(12), 01-13.

Pal, A., Sharma, S. S., & Gupta, K. P. (2021). The Role of Analytics and Robo-Advisory in Investors' Financial Decisions and Risk Management: Review of Literature Post-Global Financial Crisis. [IJBAN]. *International Journal of Business Analytics, 8*(2), 46–62. https://doi.org/10.4018/IJBAN.2021040104

Palmie, M., Wincent, J., Parida, V., & Caglar, U. (2020). The evolution of the financial technology ecosystem: An introduction and agenda for future research on disruptive innovations in ecosystems. *Technological Forecasting and Social Change, 151*, 119779. doi:10.1016/j.techfore.2019.119779

Palmié, M., Wincent, J., Parida, V., & Caglar, U. The evolution of the financial technology ecosystem: An introduction and agenda for future research on disruptive innovations in ecosystems, Technological Forecasting and Social Change, Volume 151, 2020, 119779, ISSN 0040-1625, doi:10.1016/j.techfore.2019.119779

Patel, A. & Kumar, S. (2016). Awareness & Attitude Of Investors Regarding Personal Financial Planning. *Paripex-Indian Journal of Research, 5*(11).

Phimolsathien, T. (2021). Determinants of the use of financial technology (Fintech). In *Generation Y Utopía y Praxis Latinoamericana, 26*(2), Universidad del Zulia, Venezuela. https://www.redalyc.org/articulo.oa?id=27966514003

PwC. (2020). Financial services technology 2020 and beyond: embracing disruption. *PwC*. https://www. PwC. Com/gx/en/financial-services/assets/pdf/technology2020-and-beyond.Pdf.

Rose, J. W., Andrews, K., & Kenny, K. (2021). Introduction to the FinTech Ecosystem. *Dep't of Just. J. Fed. L. & Prac., 69*, 23.

Saurabh, K., & Nandan, T. (2019). Role of financial knowledge, financial socialisation and financial risk attitude in financial satisfaction of Indian individuals. *International Journal of Indian Culture and Business Management, Inderscience Enterprises Ltd, 18*(1), 104–122. doi:10.1504/IJICBM.2019.096925

Schwabe, G., & Matter, P. (2009). Why information technology is not being used for financial advisory. *17th European Conference on Information Systems,* 1524-1535. ECIS.

Singhvi, S. (2021). Understanding the Emerging Role and Importance of Robo-advisory: A Case Study Approach. In: Al Mawali N.R., Al Lawati A.M., S A. (eds) *Fourth Industrial Revolution and Business Dynamics*. Palgrave Macmillan. doi:10.1007/978-981-16-3250-1_3

Stars, D. (2019). 6 examples of ai in financial services. *DJangostars*. https://djangostars.com/blog/6-examples-ai-financial-services/

Thornton, G. (2020). Financial inclusion in rural India. *Grant Thornton*. https://www.vakrangee.in/pdf/reports_hub/financial-inclusion-in-rural-india-28-jan.pdf

Veiga, R. T., Avelar, C., Moura, L.C., & Higuchi, A. K. (2019). Validation of Scales to Research the Personal Financial Management. *Revista Brasileira de Gestão de Negócios, 21*(2), 332-348. doi:10.7819/rbgn.v21i2.3976

Chapter 6

Blockchain in the Healthcare Industry:
Process and Applications

Vedica Awasthi
iD https://orcid.org/0000-0003-0870-9682
Lovely Professional University, India

Pooja Kansra
Lovely Professional University, India

ABSTRACT

Blockchain was first conceptualized in 2008, but became all the rage with Bitcoin. Blockchain is a digital ledger that records the transactions, excluding any third party. It has many features like transparency, security, privacy, accuracy, reliability, and decentralization. In the present study, the process and applications of blockchain in healthcare, and how and where blockchain is helpful for the healthcare industry, are discussed. The study shows that blockchain helps in generating a private key for its use, which can be accessed by that key only, ensuring privacy and security. Blockchain can record and manage the data of patients, which improves doctor-patient interaction with accuracy. It can also keep track of any upcoming outbreak of disease by helping epidemiologists and can help in claiming health insurance, which is helpful for both parties, i.e., insurer and insured. Lastly, it can help trace and secure the medical supplies without any fraud or manipulation, which can increase the product lifecycle by protecting the rights.

DOI: 10.4018/978-1-6684-4483-2.ch006

Copyright © 2023, IGI Global. Copying or distributing in print or electronic forms without written permission of IGI Global is prohibited.

INTRODUCTION

Blockchain is a technology and architecture platform conceptualized by Satoshi Nakamoto in 2008 and launched as Bitcoin in 2009. In essence, it is a digital ledger that records the transactions, excluding any middlemen or brokers. Its unique decentralization structure ensures trust between two parties as it doesn't involve any third party (Nakamoto, 2008; Patel, 2019; Revanna, 2020). Blockchain works by storing information in recording ledgers distributed in a decentralized manner across all computing devices that are part of the blockchain infrastructure. Blockchain technology facilitates a decentralized atmosphere with no need for a central authority (Hölbl et al., 2018; Khezr et al., 2019; Singh, 2020). Transactions are both secure and reliable because of the use of cryptography. Blockchain technology in healthcare can change the whole scenario by increasing patient health data safety and confidentiality (Li et al., 2018; Wang & Song, 2018; Wong et al., 2018). Recently, blockchain technology has also been proved helpful to the medical insurance sector. It also helps identify the forged data due to its quality of transparency (Nugent et al., 2016; Arora and Nabi, 2022). There are many applications in blockchain healthcare and can improve mobile health applications by monitoring and accumulating Electronic Medical Records (EMRs) (Angraal et al., 2017; Griggs et al., 2018). Cryptocurrencies are just one example of blockchain technology (Hölbl et al., 2018). Regular electronic documentation of data structure depends on a central administrator who acts as a data caretaker. If anyone sneaks the caretaker, he can access the complete information undetectably for an indefinite period (Singh, 2020). Blockchain technology shifts to the determined transformation and rebellion. It is a chain of blocks having data and transparency of data between two parties despite the distance between them. Blockchain in healthcare assures to eradicate the threat of counterfeit medication that jeopardizes patients' worldwide (Khezr et al., 2019). At present, Blockchain technology is being used in healthcare for data management, keeping records, privacy and security of health records (El-Gazzar & Stendal, 2020).

Difference between Blockchain and Database

A database is a collection of information stored electronically on a computer system. It is designed to hold a large amount of information that can be accessed, filtered and manipulated quickly and easily accessed by the number of users at once. In contrast, blockchain collects information together in groups, also known as blocks that hold sets of information. Blockchain structures its data into blocks that are chained together. Another difference between blockchain and database is that blockchain works in a decentralized manner i.e., it does not involve any third party whereas, database works and stores data in centralized manner. Also, one can edit

Blockchain in the Healthcare Industry

the information stored in database, but in case of blockchain, once a block is added to the chain it cannot be either edited or removed.

LITERATURE REVIEW

The present section provides an overview on the various applications of blockchain in healthcare related to the present study through the review of various articles and literature carried out both at national and international level. The studies were mainly reviewed on the aspects of electronic medical records, security of data, insurance claims and medical supplies.

Table 1. Review of Literature Based on Different Applications of Blockchain in Healthcare

Sr. No.	Author (Year)	Electronic Medical Records	Security of Data	Insurance claims	Medical Supplies
1.	(Agbo et al., 2019)	✓	✓		
2.	(Cichosz et al., 2018)	✓			✓
3.	(Ehrenstein et al., 2019)	✓	✓		
4.	(Guo et al., 2018)	✓			
5.	(Hussein et al., 2018)	✓			
6.	(Kaur et al., 2018)	✓			
7.	(Kuckreja et al., 2021)			✓	
8.	(Li . et al., 2018)		✓		
9.	(Lowery, 2020)		✓		
10.	(Mishra, 2021)			✓	
11.	(Oberoi and Kansra, 2021)			✓	
12.	(Pandey et al., 2021).		✓		
13.	(Patel, V., 2019)	✓			
14.	(Roehrs et al., 2017)	✓			
15.	(Rudd and Beidas, 2020)		✓		
16.	(Senbekov et al., 2020).				✓
17.	(Shi et al., 2020)		✓		
18.	(Sun et al., 2020)	✓			
19.	(Thenmozhi et al., 2021)			✓	
20.	(Thomas, 2021)				✓
21.	(Usman et al., 2020)	✓			
22.	(Zhang et al., 2018)	✓			

Source: Based on Author's Compilation of Review

CHARACTERISTICS OF BLOCKCHAIN MODEL IN HEALTHCARE

1. **Decentralization:** There is no involvement of third party. (Agbo et al., 2019; Hussein et al., 2018; Kaur et al., 2018; Zhang et al., 2018; Sun et al., 2020; Usman et al., 2020; Hussein et al., 2021)
2. **Digital Ledger:** It is a digital recorder of transactions which distributes the data across the entire network. (Ratta et al., 2021)
3. **Transparency:** Blockchain provide full transparency as it is valid and auditable. (Saranya and Murugan, 2021)
4. **Accuracy:** Smart contracts are more accurate than the manual ones.
5. **Security:** Blockchain technology provides security of transactions and data with the help of cryptography.
6. **Privacy:** As there is no third party involved and the data is secured via cryptography so once a data is entered it can't be manipulated.

Figure 1. Characteristics of Blockchain Technology

Blockchain in the Healthcare Industry

Blockchain Model in Healthcare

Figure 2. Blockchain Model in Healthcare Industry

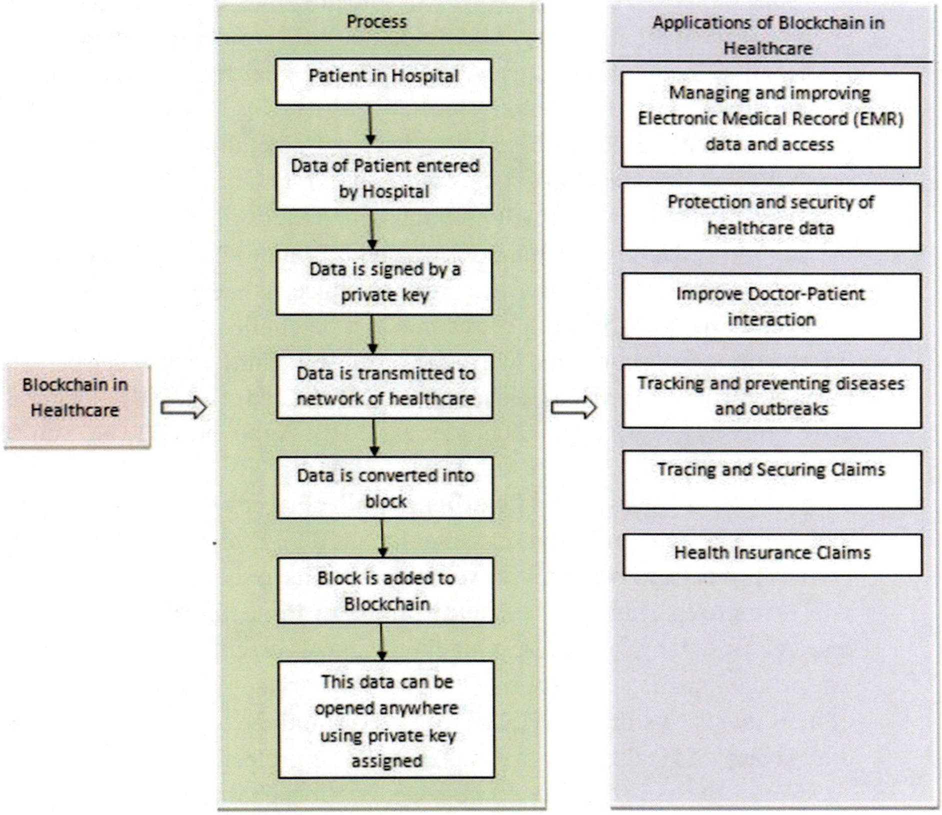

Process of Blockchain in Healthcare

The process of blockchain starts with the first steps, i.e., the patient went to the hospital for any checkup or treatment. After the checkup of the symptoms or having information regarding the disease, the second step will be entering the patient's data entered by the hospital or any health institution, in other words, a transaction is generated. After entering the data, a private key will be assigned for that transaction and the data will be transmitted to the healthcare network. Then the data will be converted into a block and that block will be added to a blockchain. That data can be accessed at any place with the help of internet but can only be accessed by the private key which was assigned which ensures safety and privacy.

APPLICATION OF BLOCKCHAIN IN HEALTHCARE

1. **Managing and improving Electronic Medical Record (EMR) data and access:** Electronic medical record (EMR) is an electronic description of a patient's medical records. An EMR includes the medical and treatment history of the patient (Garrett and Seidman, 2011). With the advancement in Information Technology in every field, the medical field has also opted for it. Ministry of Health & Family Welfare (MoH&FW, 2016) notified India's Electronic Health Record (EHR) Standards in September 2013. The standards were selected from the best existing and applied standards globally. It will help record patient data, which will help recognize the patient, his demographics, medications, diagnoses, laboratory tests, and symptoms (Roehrs et al., 2017; Ehrenstein et al., 2019). But the primary concerns are privacy and security of medical records. Sharing of records can be challenging to prevent as the information can be interfered with and exposed by a third party which blockchain technology can only solve (Cichosz et al., 2018; Guo et al., 2018; ; Kaur et al., 2018; Hussein et al., 2018; Zhang et al., 2018; Agbo et al., 2019; Sun et al., 2020; Usman et al., 2020).

2. **Protection and security of healthcare data:** Privacy is persistent regarding the future of health information technology (HIT). Ethical health research and privacy protections both provide valuable benefits to society. Health research is vital to improving human health and health care. Protecting patients involved in research from harm and preserving their rights is essential to ethical research. The primary justification for protecting personal privacy is to protect the interests of individuals (Institute of Medicine (US) Committee on Health Research and the Privacy of Health Information, 2009). The protection of data from cyber attackers is the main challenge for e-records. Blockchain technology provides a private key when a transaction is generated. Only with that private key can one access the data, which helps in privacy and security (Engelhardt, 2017; Agbo et al., 2019; Lowery, 2020; Rudd & Beidas, 2020; Shi et al., 2020; Pandey et al., 2021).

3. **Improve Doctor-Patient interaction:** The quality of healthcare services depends on the interaction between doctor and patient, which includes that how data is recorded, stored, shared and protected (Fan et al., 2018; TKEY, 2019). A slight mistake can be very costly for both parties. Blockchain has become the universal remedy to the problems that cause hindrances and distrust in doctor-patient interaction. The lack of compatibility can not only lead to medical inaccuracy but can also lead to administrative faults. Moreover, patients have to recall their medical history multiple times, which is very time-consuming as well as it can create confusion and misunderstanding because of partial

information (Vazirani et al., 2020). So if the history of medical records can be accessed, it can improve the doctor-patient interaction. Better information sharing between doctor-patient can provide accurate diagnoses, more effective treatment and overall improved ability of healthcare organizations to deliver cost-effective care (Sharma, 2017). So blockchain helps in improving doctor-patient interaction.

4. **Tracking and preventing diseases and outbreaks:** Epidemiologists face the challenge of gathering the data from which they can study and observe any epidemic, which is inevitable at any near time. Blockchain has the characteristic of decentralization, which means no need for a third party to be involved in amplifying the sense of security and reliability (Marbouh et al., 2020). Blockchain can help observe the health data by the local, national, and international health administrations such as the WHO (World Health Organization) in a much secure way. If any infectious or non-communicable disease patient is identified, it will be easy to share and diagnose the accurate data. Therefore, it can track and prevent diseases and any epidemic (Chang & Park, 2020; icommunity).

5. **Health insurance claims:** According to a report by FICCI, 2020, *"In India, while the private health insurance industry has been witnessing robust growth, with gross direct premium income underwritten by health insurance companies growing at 15% year-on-year to INR 449 billion for 2018-19, 2 the country is facing huge challenges in expanding the coverage owing to its massive 1.34 billion population and soaring healthcare needs."* In 2017, the gross premium of the global insurance industry was summed to be $ 4.8 trillion (Oberoi & Kansra, 2021; Oberoi & Kansra, 2022).Blockchain can help health insurance claims by increasing transparency in the claiming process, declining insurance claim frauds, and faster claim process. Blockchain has a facility to automate claims functions by verifying coverage between companies and reinsurers. It will not need any third party and hence will decrease cost. Also, blockchain will create transparency in the claiming process and help reduce fraud (Lounds, 2020; Kuckreja et al., 2021; Mishra, 2021). Whenever a patient gets treatment from the hospital, the data, i.e., cost occurred, will be saved to the back end of the server and shared with the insurance company for faster and transparent claims (Thenmozhi et al., 2021).

6. **Tracing and securing medical supplies:** Data from all over the world calculate approximately 6 percent of all health care spending is on blockchain technology (Clauson et al., 2018). Blockchain can also help in tracing and securing medical supplies and can present the check on costs with total transparency (Thomas, 2021). Blockchain can ensure that information is accurate, safe, transparent, and private (McNew, 2020; Senbekov et al., 2020). It will help in sharing

information with maintenance people, increasing the product lifecycle by protecting the rights. Also, it will assist in gathering the data of patient and device performance and reviewing it. Information can be protected from any kind of manipulation and falsification (Global Data Healthcare, 2021).

CONCLUSION

Blockchain technology is getting reasonable consideration from individuals and organizations of almost all extents. Blockchain technology is expected to redesign the healthcare network. Its decentralization feature and not involving the third party ensures trust and reliability. The procedure will be safe and crystal clear, and the quality will be amplified at a reasonable cost. Doctors can share the clinical data with other doctors for references with full safety and security. The patients have the right and to access the data and can decide who can have access to the data. There are many advantages of blockchain in healthcare industry, like it can help in managing and recording health data with transparency, security and privacy. It protects data from cyber attackers and builds trust between two parties as it does not involve any third party; also, it helps in improving the Doctor-Patient relation by providing accurate data as it is not possible to share the previous health data accurately by a patient. If doctor knows the accurate medical history of a patient, he can efficiently treat that patient. Blockchain can also prevent outbreaks of any disease as it helps the epidemiologists to keep a track of any new kind of disease occurred at any place via electronic health records. It can also help in health insurance claims without violation of any parties' rights with full transparency as both insurer and insured are secured by the blockchain technology and insurer will know whether insured is not a fraud. Blockchain can also help in tracing and securing medical supplies as it keeps the whole record of the supplies and it can share the information with related people for increasing its product life. Therefore, one can say that the blockchain is a technology that should be embedded in healthcare industry.

REFERENCES

Agbo, C. C., Mahmoud, Q. H., & Eklund, J. M. (2019). Blockchain technology in healthcare: a systematic review. In Healthcare, 7(2), p. 56.

Angraal, S., Krumholz, H. M., & Schulz, W. L. (2017). Blockchain technology: Applications in health care. *Circulation: Cardiovascular Quality and Outcomes*, *10*(9), e003800. doi:10.1161/CIRCOUTCOMES.117.003800 PMID:28912202

Blockchain in the Healthcare Industry

Arora, S., & Nabi, T. (2022). Blockchain Adoption in Banking Systems: A Boon or Bane? In Applications, Challenges, and Opportunities of Blockchain Technology in Banking and Insurance (pp. 19-42). IGI Global. doi:10.4018/978-1-6684-4133-6.ch002

Chang, M. C., & Park, D. (2020). How can blockchain help people in the event of pandemics such as the COVID-19? *Journal of Medical Systems*, *44*(5), 1–2. doi:10.100710916-020-01577-8 PMID:32300906

Chen, H. S., Jarrell, J. T., Carpenter, K. A., Cohen, D. S., & Huang, X. (2019). Blockchain in healthcare: A patient-centered model. *Biomedical Journal of Scientific & Technical Research*, *20*(3), 15017. PMID:31565696

Cichosz, S. L., Stausholm, M. N., Kronborg, T., Vestergaard, P., & Hejlesen, O. (2019). How to use blockchain for diabetes health care data and access management: An operational concept. *Journal of Diabetes Science and Technology*, *13*(2), 248–253. doi:10.1177/1932296818790281 PMID:30047789

Clauson, K. A., Breeden, E. A., Davidson, C., & Mackey, T. K. (2018). Leveraging Blockchain Technology to Enhance Supply Chain Management in Healthcare: An exploration of challenges and opportunities in the health supply chain. *Blockchain in healthcare today*.

Culinda. (2022). Medical Device Tracking on Blockchain. *Culinda*. https://www.culinda.io/wp-content/uploads/2020/10/Medical-devices-Blockchain.pdf

Ehrenstein, V., Kharrazi, H., & Lehmann, H. (2019). Obtaining Data From Electronic Health Records. In: Gliklich RE, Leavy MB, Dreyer NA, (eds.) *Tools and Technologies for Registry Interoperability, Registries for Evaluating Patient Outcomes: A User's Guide*, (3rd ed). Agency for Healthcare Research and Quality.https://www.ncbi.nlm.nih.gov/books/NBK551878/

El-Gazzar, R., & Stendal, K. (2020). Blockchain in health care: Hope or hype? *Journal of Medical Internet Research*, *22*(7), e17199. doi:10.2196/17199 PMID:32673219

Engelhardt, M. A. (2017). Hitching healthcare to the chain: An introduction to blockchain technology in the healthcare sector. *Technology Innovation Management Review*, *7*(10), 22–34. doi:10.22215/timreview/1111

Fan, K., Wang, S., Ren, Y., Li, H., & Yang, Y. (2018). Medblock: Efficient and secure medical data sharing via blockchain. *Journal of Medical Systems*, *42*(8), 1–11. doi:10.100710916-018-0993-7 PMID:29931655

FICCI. (2020). *Revamping India's health insurance sector with blockchain and smart contracts*. PwC. https://www.pwc.in/assets/pdfs/healthcare/revamping-indias-health-insurance-sector-with-blockchain-and-smart-contracts.pdf

Garrett, P., & Seidman, J. (2011) EMR vs EHR – What is the Difference? *Health IT*. https://www.healthit.gov/buzz-blog/electronic-health-and-medical-records/emr-vs-ehr-difference

Global Data Healthcare. (2021). *Blockchain's potential in the medical device and healthcare industries*. Medical device Network https://www.medicaldevice-network.com/comment/blockchain-medical-device-healthcare-industries/

Griggs, K. N., Ossipova, O., Kohlios, C. P., Baccarini, A. N., Howson, E. A., & Hayajneh, T. (2018). Healthcare blockchain system using smart contracts for secure automated remote patient monitoring. *Journal of Medical Systems*, *42*(7), 1–7. doi:10.100710916-018-0982-x PMID:29876661

Guo, R., Shi, H., Zhao, Q., & Zheng, D. (2018). Secure attribute-based signature scheme with multiple authorities for blockchain in electronic health records systems. *IEEE Access: Practical Innovations, Open Solutions*, *6*, 11676–11686. doi:10.1109/ACCESS.2018.2801266

Hölbl, M., Kompara, M., Kamišalić, A., & Nemec Zlatolas, L. (2018). A systematic review of the use of blockchain in healthcare. *Symmetry*, *10*(10), 470. doi:10.3390ym10100470

Hussein, A. F., ArunKumar, N., Ramirez-Gonzalez, G., Abdulhay, E., Tavares, J. M. R. S., & de Albuquerque, V. H. C. (2018). A medical records managing and securing blockchain based system supported by a genetic algorithm and discrete wavelet transform. *Cognitive Systems Research*, *52*, 1–11. doi:10.1016/j.cogsys.2018.05.004

Hussien, H. M., Yasin, S. M., Udzir, N. I., Ninggal, M. I. H., & Salman, S. (2021). Blockchain technology in the healthcare industry: Trends and opportunities. *Journal of Industrial Information Integration*, *22*, 100217. doi:10.1016/j.jii.2021.100217

icommunity. (2022). Blockchain technology for the prevention of pandemics such as the corona virus. *iCommunity*. https://icommunity.io/en/blockchain-technology-for-the-prevention-of-pandemics-such-as-the-coronavirus/

Institute of Medicine (US) Committee on Health Research and the Privacy of Health Information. (2009). The HIPAA Privacy Rule; Nass SJ, Levit LA, Gostin LO, (eds.), *Beyond the HIPAA Privacy Rule: Enhancing Privacy, Improving Health Through Research*. National Academies Press (US); https://www.ncbi.nlm.nih.gov/books/NBK9579/

Kaur, H., Alam, M. A., Jameel, R., Mourya, A. K., & Chang, V. (2018). A proposed solution and future direction for blockchain-based heterogeneous medicare data in cloud environment. *Journal of Medical Systems*, *42*(8), 1–11. doi:10.100710916-018-1007-5 PMID:29987560

Khezr, S., Moniruzzaman, M., Yassine, A., & Benlamri, R. (2019). Blockchain technology in healthcare: A comprehensive review and directions for future research. *Applied Sciences (Basel, Switzerland)*, *9*(9), 1736. doi:10.3390/app9091736

Kuckreja, J., Nigde, P., & Patil, P. (2021). Health Insurance Claim Using Blockchain. *International Research Journal of Engineering and Technology*, *8*(5), 2406–2409.

Li, H., Zhu, L., Shen, M., Gao, F., Tao, X., & Liu, S. (2018). Blockchain-based data preservation system for medical data. *Journal of Medical Systems*, *42*(8), 1–13. doi:10.100710916-018-0997-3 PMID:29956058

Lounds, M. (2020). Blockchain and its Implications for the Insurance Industry. *Munich Re*. https://www.munichre.com/us-life/en/perspectives/underwriting/blockchain-implications-insurance-industry.html

Lowery, C. (2020). What is digital health and what do I need to know about it? *Obstetrics and Gynecology Clinics*, *47*(2), 215–225. doi:10.1016/j.ogc.2020.02.011 PMID:32451013

Marbouh, D., Abbasi, T., Maasmi, F., Omar, I. A., Debe, M. S., Salah, K., Jayaraman, R., & Ellahham, S. (2020). Blockchain for COVID-19: Review, opportunities, and a trusted tracking system. *Arabian Journal for Science and Engineering*, *45*(12), 1–17. doi:10.100713369-020-04950-4 PMID:33072472

McNew, S. (2020). How Blockchain Can Solve Today's Medical Supply Chain Flaws And Improve Responses For Future Crises. *Forbes*. https://www.forbes.com/sites/forbesbusinessdevelopmentcouncil/2020/04/29/how-blockchain-can-solve-todays-medical-supply-chain-flaws-and-improve-responses-for-future-crises/?sh=1f475ee9750a

Ministry of Health & Family. (2016). Standards for India. *MOHFW*. https://main.mohfw.gov.in/sites/default/files/EMR-EHR_Standards_for_India_as_notified_by_MOHFW_2016_0.pdf

Mishra, A. S. S. (2021) Study on Blockchain-Based Healthcare Insurance Claim System. *Asian Conference on Innovation in Technology (ASIANCON)*, 1-4. IEEE. 10.1109/ASIANCON51346.2021.9544892

. Nakamoto, S. (2008). Bitcoin: A peer-to-peer electronic cash system. *Decentralized Business Review*.

Nugent, T., Upton, D., & Cimpoesu, M. (2016). Improving data transparency in clinical trials using blockchain smart contracts. *F1000 Research*, *5*, 5. doi:10.12688/f1000research.9756.1 PMID:28357041

Oberoi, S., & Kansra, P. (2021). Motivating Antecedents and Consequences of Blockchain Technology in the Insurance Industry. In *Blockchain Technology and Applications for Digital Marketing* (pp. 276–285). IGI Global. doi:10.4018/978-1-7998-8081-3.ch017

Oberoi, S., & Kansra, P. (2022). Blockchain Technology in the Insurance Industry. In Applications, Challenges, and Opportunities of Blockchain Technology in Banking and Insurance (pp. 160-172). IGI Global. doi:10.4018/978-1-6684-4133-6.ch009

Pandey, M., Agarwal, R., Shukla, S. K., & Verma, N. K. (2021). Security of Healthcare Data Using Blockchains. *Survey (London, England)*, 1–40.

Patel, V. (2019). A framework for secure and decentralized sharing of medical imaging data via blockchain consensus. *Health Informatics Journal*, *25*(4), 1398–1411. doi:10.1177/1460458218769699 PMID:29692204

Ratta, P., Kaur, A., Sharma, S., Shabaz, M., & Dhiman, G. (2021). Application of blockchain and internet of things in healthcare and medical sector: Applications, challenges, and future perspectives. *Journal of Food Quality*, *2021*(1), 1–20. doi:10.1155/2021/7608296

Revanna, N. (2020). Blockchain in Healthcare. *International Research Journal of Engineering and Technology.*, *7*(4), 3218–3224.

Roehrs, A., Da Costa, C. A., & da Rosa Righi, R. (2017). OmniPHR: A distributed architecture model to integrate personal health records. *Journal of Biomedical Informatics*, *71*, 70–81. doi:10.1016/j.jbi.2017.05.012 PMID:28545835

Rudd, B. N., & Beidas, R. S. (2020). Digital mental health: The answer to the global mental health crisis? *JMIR Mental Health*, *7*(6), e18472. doi:10.2196/18472 PMID:32484445

Saranya, R., & Murugan, A. (2021). A systematic review of enabling blockchain in healthcare system: Analysis, current status, challenges and future direction. *Materials Today: Proceedings*. doi:10.1016/j.matpr.2021.07.105

Senbekov, M., Saliev, T., Bukeyeva, Z., Almabayeva, A., Zhanaliyeva, M., Aitenova, N., Toishibekov, Y., & Fakhradiyev, I. (2020). The recent progress and applications of digital technologies in healthcare: A review. *International Journal of Telemedicine and Applications*, *2020*, 2020. doi:10.1155/2020/8830200 PMID:33343657

Sharma, U. (2017). *Blockchain in Healthcare Patient Benefits and more*. IBM. https://www.ibm.com/blogs/blockchain/2017/10/blockchain-in-healthcare-patient-benefits-and-more/

Shi, S., He, D., Li, L., Kumar, N., Khan, M. K., & Choo, K. K. R. (2020). Applications of blockchain in ensuring the security and privacy of electronic health record systems: A survey. *Computers & Security*, *97*, 101966. doi:10.1016/j.cose.2020.101966 PMID:32834254

Singh, M. H. (2020). A Study of Block Chain-Based Electronic HealthCare Record System. *International Journal of Advanced Research in Science & Technology*, *5*(5), 75–81.

Sun, J., Ren, L., Wang, S., & Yao, X. (2020). A blockchain-based framework for electronic medical records sharing with fine-grained access control. *PLoS One*, *15*(10), e0239946. doi:10.1371/journal.pone.0239946 PMID:33022027

Thenmozhi, M., Dhanalakshmi, R., Geetha, S., & Valli, R. (2021). Implementing blockchain technologies for health insurance claim processing in hospitals. *Materials Today: Proceedings*. doi:10.1016/j.matpr.2021.02.776

Thomas, D. L. (2021). Blockchain Applications in Healthcare. *News Medical Life Sciences* https://www.news-medical.net/health/Blockchain-Applications-in-Healthcare.aspx

Vazirani, A. A., O'Donoghue, O., Brindley, D., & Meinert, E. (2020). Blockchain vehicles for efficient medical record management. *NPJ Digital Medicine*, *3*(1), 1–5. doi:10.103841746-019-0211-0 PMID:31934645

Wang, H., & Song, Y. (2018). Secure cloud-based EHR system using attribute-based cryptosystem and blockchain. *Journal of Medical Systems*, *42*(8), 1–9. doi:10.100710916-018-0994-6 PMID:29974270

Wong, M. C., Yee, K. C., & Nøhr, C. (2018). Socio-technical considerations for the use of blockchain technology in healthcare. In *Building Continents of Knowledge in Oceans of Data: The Future of Co-Created eHealth* (pp. 636–640). IOS Press.

Zhang, P., White, J., Schmidt, D. C., Lenz, G., & Rosenbloom, S. T. (2018). FHIRChain: Applying blockchain to securely and scalably share clinical data. *Computational and Structural Biotechnology Journal*, *16*, 267–278. doi:10.1016/j.csbj.2018.07.004 PMID:30108685

Chapter 7

Does the Cryptocurrency Index Provide Diversification Opportunities With MSCI World Index and MSCI Emerging Markets Index?
Cryptocurrency and Portfolio Diversificaiton

Miklesh Prasad Yadav
Amity University, India

Sudhi Sharma
FIIB Delhi, India

Babita Parmar
https://orcid.org/0000-0001-8586-0250
CHRIST University (Deemed), India

ABSTRACT

The study is extending the ongoing discussion on Bitcoin as a diversification asset with the stock market. Some studies analysed cryptocurrencies as a diversification asset, and few challenged the same. During times of turbulence, it is crucial to gauge further diversification opportunities. Henceforth, the study revisits the opportunities of hedging and diversification with the crypto market from a broader perspective. The study captures the spillover from MSCI World Index and MSCI Emerging

DOI: 10.4018/978-1-6684-4483-2.ch007

Copyright © 2023, IGI Global. Copying or distributing in print or electronic forms without written permission of IGI Global is prohibited.

Markets Index to Bitwise 10 Crypto Index Fund (BITW). The study has contributed methodologically to the existing literature by applying DY with symmetric and asymmetric dynamic conditional volatility models. The results provide in-depth shreds of evidence that BITW is insulated, neither taking volatilities from other countries nor contributing to the volatilities of other countries. The study provides insight to policymakers and investors.

INTRODUCTION AND BACKGROUND OF THE STUDY

Financial integration accelerated the proficiencies of financial intermediaries and the financial markets of the countries (Jappelli et al., 2004). With the advent of liberalization and the initiation of foreign portfolio diversification, the scope of investment in emerging economies has increased. It has been captured by various studies that information spillovers observed from the US market, later transmitted to Asia Pacific markets because of the enormous portfolio inflows from the US (Kim, 2005). This transmission was significant during the financial crisis (Habiba et al., 2020). In the modern era, investors are concerned with portfolio diversification in world-class or non-conventional assets. Nowadays, studies are conducting on to identify diversification opportunities with alternative and non-conventional investments vehicles.

With the increase in technological innovations, virtual currencies are considered an emerging asset class for investment. In the 4th industrial revolution, the crypto market grew enormously and popularised as a digital financial asset for investment and diversification (Dyhrberg, 2016). Investors are fascinated to invest in cryptocurrencies because of the expectations to earn high returns. The global cryptocurrency market is estimated to grow at a CAGR of 56.4% over the forecasted period from 2019 to 2025 (Market Watch, 2021). The key factors leading to the rise in the cryptocurrency market include distributed or transparent ledger technology and the growth in venture capital investments. It is forecasted that popular digital currencies like Bitcoin, Litecoin, Ethereum, and many more will outshine and drive the market (Fortune Business Insights, 2020). The most dominated and highly traded cryptocurrency is Bitcoin, and it has reached an unprecedented height since its introduction in the year 2009. The price of Bitcoin was more than $60000 in April 2021, with a market capitalization of more than USD 1 Trillion (Statista, 2021).

The motivation that triggers the authors to take up this study depends on the fascination of the investors towards cryptocurrencies as an emerging or alternate asset class. The current research is another piece of contribution to the ongoing discussion on cryptocurrencies as a diversification asset. Few studies have analyzed cryptocurrencies as a diversification asset (Stensas et al. 2019, Kliber et al. 2019, Bouri et al. 2020, and Klein et al. 2018). Several studies have challenged the same (Shahzad et al. 2020, Wang et al. 2019, Susilo et al. 2020, and Naeem et al. 2020). During high volatile periods, it becomes crucial to gauge further the hedging and diversification opportunities. Henceforth, the study revisits diversification opportunities with the crypto market from a broader perspective. Studies based on diversification with digital currencies either based on Bitcoin or a few cryptocurrencies as a diversification asset, but the study examines the whole crypto market. Henceforth the study further strengthens the ongoing discussion and captures the crypto market, developed and developing markets. The study focuses on the identification of volatility transmission from developed and emerging markets to the crypto market.

The study examines the diversification opportunities in the Crypto market for investors investing in developed and emerging countries. Therefore, the study has contributed methodologically to the existing literature by applying Diebold and Yilmaz Spillover Index (2012) with other symmetric and asymmetric dynamic conditional volatility models. Thus, the current research contributes in scope as well as in methodology. The result provides in-depth evidence that BITW is an insulated index, and it is neither taking volatilities from other countries nor contributing to the volatility transmission of other countries. Moreover, BITW concluded as a diversification asset with MSCI Emerging Markets Index followed by MSCI World Index. The result of the study provides broader insight to policymakers and investors who are discussing the importance of an alternative technology-based asset.

The paper into various sections; the next part of the study is related to a literature review than research methodology and finally dedicated to empirical analysis. The study has applied statistical and econometric models. The analysis includes descriptive then followed by granger causality to find the causal relationship among the sample variables. To analyze the volatility transmissions and leverage effect, Dynamic Conditional Correlation Generalized Autoregressive Conditional Heteroscedasticity (DCC GARCH 1, 1); Dynamic Conditional Correlation Threshold Generalized Autoregressive Conditional Heteroscedasticity (DCC TGARCH 1, 1) and Dynamic Conditional Correlation Exponential Generalized Autoregressive Conditional Heteroscedasticity (DCC EGARCH 1, 1) have been applied respectively. Finally, to capture meticulous evidence of spillover Diebold and Yilmaz Spillover Index (2012) have been applied.

LITERATURE REVIEW

There are several studies done on Bitcoin as a diversification asset, and few studies challenged the same. It is an ongoing debate that cryptocurrency considers as a superior, safe, and diversified asset. The study further revisits the cryptomarket as a diversification asset while investing in the stock market during the pandemic. The study broadens the scope by capturing the whole crypto market and contributes methodologically by applying DY (Diebold & Yilmaz, 2012) with symmetric and asymmetric dynamic conditional volatility models. The literature review has been done under two sub-sections to identify the need for further analysis. The first section deals with the crypto market as a diversification asset with the stock market, followed by the crypto market as a diversification asset with other asset classes.

Section 1: Crypto market as a diversification asset with the Stock Market

Several research studies have been done on cryptocurrencies as a technology-based asset to find diversification opportunities. However, some of the studies challenged the same.

Studies that are in favor of cryptocurrencies as a hedge against the stock market. Qin et al. 2021, has captured the actively traded cryptocurrency that is Bitcoin acted as a safe investment during global uncertainty. The study has applied bootstrap rolling Granger causality tests and concluded that Bitcoin returns showed a positive causal impact of global economic policy uncertainty and thus acted as a hedge for investors. The very close study done by Bouri et al. 2020, identified diversification opportunities with various conventional and non-conventional assets with developed and emerging stock indices. The study had applied the Wavelet Coherency approach. It had concluded that all investment vehicles showed weak correlations with stocks. Finally, found that Bitcoin is a better diversification asset among all. In the same context, Mizerka et al. (2020) the study has applied the Bitcoin users graph to find the prominent bitcoin players. The research concluded that Bitcoin acts as a hedger with emerging markets but considers as a weak hedge against developing markets. Conlon, 2020 had contributed to the discussion in the context of the pandemic. Thus considered three major cryptocurrencies are Bitcoin, Tether, and Ethereum. Finally, it has been concluded with the application of value at risk (VaR) and conditional value at risk (CVAR) that Tether among them, considered as the safest investment with international markets. Xunfa et al. 2020 examined the dynamic causal relationship between the cryptocurrencies market and emerging stock markets. The study has applied the two causality techniques that are Granger Causality and Liang Causality analysis. The results of Granger initially captured no causality among the markets. However, Liang causality captures the short-term unidirectional causality from crypto to emerging markets. And long-term unidirectional volatility from the emerging to the crypto market. The study captured a few structural breakpoints and the dynamic causal relationships among them. The study concluded that both markets were independent at the initial period. But during violent market swings, both move unidirectionally. However, after drastic fluctuation, both markets tend to be stabilized and relatively become independent of each other. Another study that favors crypto as a safe investment with the stock market is Stensas et al. 2019, which applied DCC GARCH (1, 1) found that Bitcoin is a diversification or safe asset with seven developed and six developing markets. However, the study is limited to select countries and Bitcoin as a crypto asset. Kliber et al. 2019 has also studied Bitcoin as a diversification asset with five countries. The study has applied DCC GARCH (1, 1) and found shreds of evidence of hedging opportunity with a technology-based investment vehicle. However, few studies are finding Bitcoin as a resilient asset during times of vulnerability. Goodell et al. 2021 analyzed Bitcoin as a safer asset during pandemic times by applying Wavelet coherence. In the same context, Guo et al. 2021, Disli 2021, Su et al. 2020, Tiwari et al. 2021, and Bouri et al. 2017 have also captured Bitcoin as a safe investment during Global uncertainties.

On the other side, some studies contradict the ongoing debate that Cryptocurrencies as a safe investment with the stock market. Jiang et al. 2021 revisited relationships between cryptocurrencies and stock markets during the Covid-19 pandemic at different quantiles and frequencies. The study found a significant dependence among cryptocurrencies and representative stock indices. However, in most instances, it had found rarely any shreds of evidence of negative correlation. It indicates it cannot be considered as a hedge against the stock market. Goodell et al. 2021 has analyzed the impact of Covid -19 on the paired co-movements of six cryptocurrencies and Bitcoin futures with the VIX and 14 equity indices. The analysis revealed, during Covid-19, the co-movements between equity and cryptocurrencies gradually increased. Thus, no evidence of diversification opportunities through cryptocurrencies during the pandemic. Wang et al. 2019 had analyzed 30 international indices to examine cryptocurrencies as a hedge investment vehicle. Their findings revealed that cryptocurrencies cannot serve as a hedge but can act as a haven asset for some international indices for limited periods.

Section 2: Crypto market as a diversification with other Asset Class

Le et al. 2021 study demonstrated that during Covid-19 innovative assets like Bitcoin and Fintech index cannot be considered safe havens as they were the largest recipients of volatility spillovers. However, Gold is a better and more stable hedging instrument relatively Bitcoin. In contrast, Chemkha et al. 2021 had concluded Bitcoin as a superior asset class over yellow metal during the pandemic. Shahzad et al. 2020 had also captured yellow metal versus Bitcoin as a hedge against G7 countries. Susilo et al. 2020 studied the relationship between five cryptocurrencies, equity indices, and ishares - ETF MSCI World. The study concluded cryptocurrencies maximize the Sharpe ratio instead of hedging. Their study suggested that commodities prove to be a better hedge for Southeast Asia emerging markets. Trabelsi, 2018 captured the spillover effect among cryptocurrencies and other financial assets. It captured low evidence of spillover, and therefore, cryptocurrencies are weakly related to the global financial asset. However, a study conducted by Klein et al. 2018 found that Bitcoin has the lowest correlation with the MSCI EM50 index but a slight positive correlation with Gold, S&P 500, and MSCI World.

The above studies are on the ongoing debate on the Crypto market as a diversification asset. However, it is analyzed that majority of the studies are limited to Bitcoin. A Majority of the studies have applied Granger Causality and Dynamic conditional volatility models. The study is further considers the urgency of finding diversification opportunities during vulnerable economic times and revisits to find diversification opportunities with the Crypto market as a whole with more meticulous evidence. Henceforth the study widens the scope and contributes methodologically to the existing literature.

DATA AND ECONOMETRIC MODELS

Data

The study analyzes the whole cryptomarket to capture the diversification opportunities while investing in developed and emerging countries. The study has extended the ongoing discussion on a technology-based asset that is Bitcoin serves as a diversification and hedging asset with stock markets. To capture the crypto, emerging, and developed markets, the study has considered the respective proxies as Bitwise 10 Crypto Index Fund (BITW), Morgan Stanley Capital International Emerging Markets Index (MSCI Emerging Markets Index), and Morgan Stanley Capital International World Markets Index (MSCI World Index). The BITW tracks the Bitwise 10 Large Cap Crypto Index, a diversified index based on the market cap of cryptocurrencies. The index consisted of ten cryptos based on liquidity, custody, and other risks, subject to continuous rebalancing to ensure the same. It represents approximately 80% of the crypto market. Thus, it is considered an approximate proxy to represent the whole crypto market. MSCI Emerging Markets Index includes 27 emerging countries across five regions and captures more than 1300 large and mid-cap companies. The complete landscape of the emerging market has changed since 1988, and it has been coming up with a distinct asset class with a great fascination of institutional investors. The index is dynamic and subject to rebalancing to ensure the consistency of the objective based on economic development, size, liquidity, and market accessibility. The MSCI World Index is a representation of large and mid-cap equity performance across 23 developed market countries. The index captures approximately 85% of the free-float market capitalization in each country. Henceforth, both are the fair representation of emerging and developed markets, respectively. The study captures the spillover among them from 31st October 2016 to 31st August 2021. The daily adjusted closing prices had retrieved from Bloomberg and further converted into daily log returns. Daily log returns have been calculated by logarithmic differences of the closing prices two successive times that is, Rit = log (Pit / Pit-1). Where Ri, t log return at time t, and Pi, t–1 and Pi, t are two successive daily closing prices of ith exchanges.

Econometric Models

In this paper, a wide range of methods has been applied to analyze the volatility spillover among crypto and stock indices. The study employs the Granger causality test, the symmetric and asymmetric dynamic conditional correlation (DCC). The standardized DCC-GARCH (1,1) has been applied to check the symmetric dynamic linkages while DCC TGARCH (1,1) & DCC EGARCH (1,1) have been applied to check the asymmetric spillover among BITW, MSCI Emerging Market Index, and MSCI World Index. Further, to capture the more meticulous shreds of evidence of spillover, the Diebold and Yilmaz Spillover Index (2012) has been applied. The symmetric and asymmetric DCC have been applied to examine short and long-run spillover among constituent series while Diebold and Yilmaz (2012) are employed to investigate the total connectedness from one market to another (Yadav et al.,2020). The detailed elaboration of the models is discussed as below:

Symmetric and Asymmetric Dynamic Conditional Correlation

To examine the volatility spillover from MSCI Emerging Markets Index and MSCI World Index to BITW, the study has applied symmetrical and asymmetrical DCC-GARCH. For symmetrical DCC-GARCH, we have applied standard GARCH while Exponential GARCH and Threshold GARCH have been applied to capture the asymmetrical volatility. Generally, the volatility linkages among time series are captured through conditional correlation and conditional variances that are conditioned with time. Standard GARCH or Generalized GARCH is developed by Bollersleve 1986 in which conditional variance depends on its lags. It does not capture asymmetric and leverage effects. Hence, the study has applied E GARCH and T GARCH. E GARCH is computed on the logarithmic expression of the conditional variability. It is developed by Nelson (1991) to check the presence of leverage effect in the series. Similarly, T GARCH is another method to capture the asymmetrical effect developed by Zakoian (1994). It helps to examine the effect of good news and bad news in form of shocks in a positive and negative return. Engle (2002) has given Dynamic models to captures the dynamic correlations of returns of two variables under study. In the study, rt is the asset return consisting of vector n x 1, which can be depicted as rt = a+a1rt-1+εt. In this equation, "a" is constant, a1 is the coefficiet of lagged of return and εt = Ht(1/2) zt, in which Ht is the covariance matrix of assets return and zt is a vector n x 1 of independent and identically distributed (iid) of residuals. The model is estimated in two layers. Firstly, parameters of GARCH are determined and then the conditioal correlation is identified. This model is expressed as Ht= DtRtDt. Where, Ht is denoted as the estimator of conditional correlation. Dt may be expressed as diag (h1t1/2, ..., h1/2nt). Dt is conditional standard deviation which is n x n diagonal matrix and extracted from GARCH whereas Rt is the conditional correlation. Rt is presented as:

$$Rt = Qt*-1Qt\ Qt*-1 \tag{1}$$

This model is based on the logarithmic expression of conditional variability. The presence of leverage effect can be tested and this model enables to find out the best model, which captures the symmetries of the Indian stock market (Nelson 1991) and hence the following equation: $\ln(\sigma2\ t) = \omega + \beta1\ln(\sigma2\ t-1) + \alpha1\ \varepsilon t-1\ \sigma t-1 - -\pi 2 - \gamma\ \varepsilon t-1\ \sigma t-1$. (6) The left-hand side is the log of the conditional variance. The coefficient γ is known as the asymmetry or leverage term. The presence of leverage effects can be tested by the hypothesis that $\gamma < 0$. The impact is symmetric if $\gamma\ 0$.

Diebold and Yilmaz (2012) Spillover Index

To capture the flow of spillover meticulously Diebold and Yilmaz Spillover Index Method (2012) is applied, it's an extension of Diebold and Yilmaz (2009). Diebold and Yilmaz Index is based on a vector autoregressive (VAR) framework to check within and to and fro volatility transmissions. The index is developed by Diebold, F.X., and Yilmaz, K. (2012) to capture the cross volatilities and thus help to find the more refined diversification opportunities. It furnishes the magnitude and spillover direction in form of variance decomposition analysis (Pesaran, M.H. and Shin, Y.,1998). Indeed, existing spillover models consider the mean of the distribution and OLS to determine the VAR that undervalues the effects of spillover among variables. In this model, H-step forecast error variance decomposition can be accredited to the shocks for the variable as below:

$$\lambda_{il}(H) = \frac{\sigma_{ll}^{-1} \sum_{h=0}^{H-1} \left(e_i' A_h \Sigma e_l \right)^2}{\sum_{h=0}^{H-1} \left(e_i' A_h \Sigma A_h' e_l \right)} \tag{2}$$

The above equation å is termed as the estimated variance for the given error components of the vector autoregressive model, σ_{ij} signifies the standard deviation for the ith equation. The forecast error variance decomposition can be normalized following the sum of the following row:

$$(\Theta_H)_{j,k} = \frac{(\Theta_H)_{j,k}}{\sum_{k=1}^{n} (\Theta_H)_{j,k}}, \; with \; \sum_{k=1}^{n} (\tilde{\Theta}_H)_{j,k} = 1 \; and \; \sum_{k=1}^{n} (\tilde{\Theta}_H)_{j,k} = N \tag{3}$$

The cross variance of the variables helps to calculate total connectedness which is presented as the fraction of the H step ahead to forecast Yi because shocks to Yj. The shocks obtained by vector i from other vectors J are determined by directional connectedness and net connectedness is calculated differentiating the shocks obtained from others and shocks contributed to other markets or economies.

EMPIRICAL ANALYSIS

Results of Preliminary Analysis

The preliminary analysis had done through descriptive statistics shown in Table 1.1. The study reports the result of descriptive statistics on the log return of technology-based that is Crypto Index (BITW) and unconventional asset classes that are MSCI Emerging Markets Index and MSCI World Index. About the result, the maximum mean return realized from BITW (0.002) followed by MSCI Emerging Markets Index (0.001) and MSCI World Index (0.000). The maximum unconditional standard deviation has perceived on BITW (0.050) followed by MSCI Emerging Markets Index (0.010) and MSCI World Index (0.009). The results are in sync with the well-established theory that is higher the risk backed with high returns. But the volatility measured in descriptive is the traditional approach to assess the volatility, the unconventional time-varying volatility captured by time-varying conditional models. For the analysis of the same, the study is applying dynamic volatility models. The skewness of the time series of all markets is negatively skewed, reflecting the probability of getting a negative yield. The negative value of skewness of the MSCI World Index (-1.586) is higher than MSCI Emerging Markets Index (-0.717), followed by BITW (-0.026). It infers that the Crypto market has less probability of fetching than indices. It has been evident that kurtosis of all are showing more than the values of threshold level that is 3, which infer that the time series has a heavier tail than a normal distribution, and thus the series is leptokurtic. Finally, the result of the Jarque Berra test (JB Test) is concluding that all series are departing from normality. But the essential assumption is that the time series should be stationary. For this, Augmented Dickey-Fuller (ADF) test has been applied. Before applying the volatility model, there should be evidence of volatility clustering and the ARCH effect. Volatility clustering is captured by large changes are followed by large changes and small changes further are followed by small changes. The figure shown in 1.1 confirms the presence of volatility clustering. Similarly, the result obtained from the LM test confirms that there is an ARCH effect.

Further, the study applied the Granger causality test, Dynamic Conditional Correlation (DCC) volatility model, and Diebold and Yilmaz Spillover Index (2TheIn the results of the Granger causality test, it has observed the bidirectional causality among developed and emerging countries. The MSCI World Index return is a Granger cause of the MSCI Emerging Markets index at 0.01 significance level. The emerging markets return is a Granger cause of the developed countries index returns at the 0.05 significance level. However, there is no causality captured amongst BITW with MSCI Emerging market and MSCI World Index return. Henceforth from the preliminary analysis, it has been perceived that BITW is not affected by the volatility of the stock indices of both the MSCI Emerging Markets Index and MSCI World Index. These results are useful for those foreign portfolio investors who are looking for diversification to hedge their current position in emerging and developed indices. These results need to be validated further with the more sophisticated volatility models.

Result of DCC-MGARCH, DCC-T GARCH & DCC- E GARCH

The study presents the results obtained from both symmetric multivariate model (Dynamic Conditional Correlation- Generalized Autoregressive Conditional Heteroscedasticity, DCC-GARCH) and asymmetric multivariate models (Dynamic Conditional Correlation- T Generalized Autoregressive Conditional Heteroscedasticity, DCC-T GARCH & Dynamic Conditional Correlation- Exponential Generalized Autoregressive Conditional Heteroscedasticity, DCC-E GARCH) table 3. The models can capture both symmetric and asymmetric spillover from MSCI Emerging Markets Index and MSCI World Index to BITW.

Figure 1. Time Series Plot of Returns - Plot of Daily Returns of BITW, Plot of Daily Returns of MSCI Emerging Market Index and Plot of Daily Returns of MSCI World Index

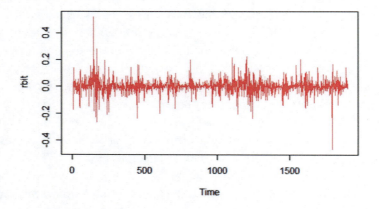

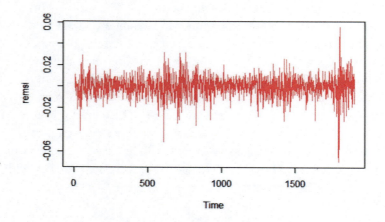

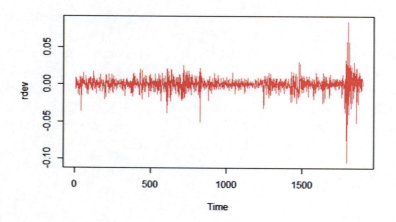

Table 1. Result of Descriptive Statistics

	R_BITW	R_MSCI Emerging	R_MSCI World
Nobs	1897	1897	1897
Minimum	-0.465	-0.069	-0.104
Maximum	0.521	0.056	0.084
Mean	0.002	0.001	0.000
Stdeviation	0.050	0.010	0.009
Skewness	-0.026	-0.717	-1.586
Kurtosis	13.620	5.993	26.964
JB Test	0.000***	0.000***	0.000***
ADF Test	0.01***	0.01***	0.01***
LM ARCH Test	0.0000***	0.0000***	0.0000***

Note: *5% significance level; **1% significance level and *** 0.01% significance level

Table 2. Results of Granger Causality Test

Null Hypothesis	Coefficient	Probability
R_BITW → R_MSCI Emerging	-2 1.1409	0.3198
R_MSCI Emerging → R_BITW	-2 2.3731	0.09347
R_BITW → R_MSCI World	-2 0.4298	0.6507
R_MSCI World → R_BITW	-2 2.812	0.06034
R_MSCI Emerging →R_MSCI World	-2 57.799	< 2.2e-16 ***
R_MSCI World→ R_MSCI Emerging	-2 3.5524	0.02885 *

Note: *5% significance level; **1% significance level and *** 0.01% significance level

Result of DCC-GARCH (1, 1)

The result of the DCC-GARCH model provides various parameters in terms of mean (μ), constant (ω), ARCH term (α), GARCH term (β), DCCα and DCCβ. The results of DCC-GARCH (1, 1) provide significant evidence of both short and long-term volatilities in all asset classes. However, the highest short-term (alpha 1) volatility is perceived in MSCI World Index (0.212), followed by BITW (0.160) and then by MSCI Emerging Markets Index (0.104). On the other hand, the highest long-term volatility (beta1) is perceived in MSCI Emerging Markets Index (0.867), followed by BITW (0.805) and then by MSCI World Index (0.763). The overall maximum time-varying volatility (alpha1+beta1) was captured in MSCI World Index (0.975), followed by MSCI Emerging Markets Index (0.971) and then by BITW (0.967).

The short-term and long-term volatility spillover from one asset class to another has been captured by dcca1 & dccb1, respectively. It has been evident that there is no significant short-term volatility transmitted from the MSCI Emerging Markets Index to BITW, whereas there is significant evidence of short-term volatility transmission perceived from the MSCI World Index to BITW. Therefore, there is an opportunity for portfolio diversification with BITW while investing in emerging countries. However, there is significant long-term volatility spillover perceived from both emerging and developed to BITW. The total volatility transmission (dcca1+dccb1) is maximum from MSCI World Index to BITW (0.966) compared to MSCI Emerging Markets Index to BITW (0.945). The results drawn from the bivariate GARCH model are important for the portfolio manager and hedge funds.

Table 3. Results DCC-MGARCH, DCC-T GARCH & DCC-EGARCH

RMSCI	Symmetric DCC		Assymetric – DCC T GARCH		Assymetric – DCC EGARCH	
	Estimate	p-value	Estimate	p-value	Estimate	p-value
Emerging to RBITW						
[remsi].mu	0.000	0.070	0.000	0.425	0.000	0.520
[remsi].omega	0.000	0.241	0.000	0.005	-0.236	0.000
[remsi].alpha1	0.104	0.000	0.003	0.736	-0.086	0.000
[remsi].beta1	0.867	0.000	0.917	0.000	0.975	0.000
[remsi].gamma1			0.108	0.000	0.123	0.000
[rbitw].mu	0.001	0.127	0.001	0.148	0.002	0.130
[rbitw].omega	0.000	0.014	0.000	0.016	-0.421	0.033
[rbitw].alpha1	0.160	0.001	0.154	0.001	-0.020	0.618
[rbitw].beta1	0.805	0.000	0.805	0.000	0.925	0.000
[rbitw].gamma1			0.012	0.842	0.304	0.000
[Joint]dcca1	0.013	0.138	0.014	0.109	0.013	0.141
[Joint]dccb1	0.931	0.000	0.932	0.000	0.929	0.000
World to RBIT						
[remsi].mu	0.001	0.000	0.000	0.005	0.000	0.007
[remsi].omega	0.000	0.365	0.000	0.420	-0.384	0.000
[remsi].alpha1	0.212	0.000	0.079	0.091	-0.141	0.000
[remsi].beta1	0.763	0.000	0.791	0.000	0.961	0.000
[remsi].gamma1			0.213	0.002	0.254	0.000
[rbitw].mu	0.001	0.128	0.001	0.146	0.002	0.128

continues on following page

Table 3. Continued

RMSCI	Symmetric DCC		Assymetric – DCC T GARCH		Assymetric – DCC EGARCH	
	Estimate	p-value	Estimate	p-value	Estimate	p-value
[rbitw].omega	0.000	0.014	0.000	0.016	-0.421	0.032
[rbitw].alpha1	0.160	0.001	0.154	0.001	-0.020	0.617
[rbitw].beta1	0.805	0.000	0.805	0.000	0.925	0.000
[rbitw].gamma1			0.012	0.841	0.304	0.000
[Joint]dcca1	0.018	0.050	0.018	0.036	0.019	0.040
[Joint]dccb1	0.947	0.000	0.947	0.000	0.947	0.000

Results of DCC T-GARCH & DCC- EGARCH

The study reports the result of DCC E-GARCH and T GARCH in table 3. The significance of ARCH and GARCH are similar to symmetrical GARCH in asymmetrical GARCH too, while gamma indicates the leverage effect. It is a condition when negative news is more prone to positive news. If gamma is negative and significant then it indicates that the magnitude of negative effect is high than positive news and vice-versa. The result of E-GARCH and T-GARCH is in a similar line with standard GARCH as ARCH and GARCH are significant which confirms the volatility persistence. The gamma in both models is significant but positive, which presents that positive shocks have a greater influence than negative news. The sum of alpha and beta is less than 1 in both asymmetrical GARCH indicating the decay in volatility persistence. Considering the volatility spillover from MSCI Emerging Markets Index to BITW derived from DCC E-GARCH and T-GARCH, there is no short-run volatility spillover (DCC a is more than 0.05) while there is long-run volatility spillover (DCC b is less than 0.05). There is both short-run and long-run volatility spillover from MSCI World Index to BITW as DCC a, and DCC b is significant.

Results of Diebold and Yilmaz (2012) Spillover Index

Further to strengthen the result of standalone volatilities and volatility spillover, Diebold &Yilmaz (2012) have applied. The results are encapsulated in table 1.4, in which off-diagonal values in the table indicate spillover effect across market while diagonal values are volatility within market/asset class. The term "From" refers to the spillover obtained from another market/asset class. "To" refers to the spillover contributed to another market/ asset class. The study captured interesting results from the application of the model that in the "From" column that is the spillover from others, MSCI Emerging Markets Index is shown maximum spillover transmission from others followed by MSCI World Index and lastly by BITW. Whereas, the row "To", captured the MSCI World Index shown maximum contribution in the volatility transmission followed by MSCI Emerging Markets Index and then BITW. Thus, Bitcoin is a resilient asset that is neither affected nor contributing to the volatility transmission. Henceforth, it could be considered as a diversification and hedging asset. The inference drawn is important for portfolio managers. The next row that is "GROSS", shows the openness of the sample asset/ indices that is the aggregation of spillover received and transmitted. The asset has a high "GROSS" value. It infers maximum openness in the asset/ index in terms of receiving and contributing spillover transmissions. Here, it has been observed that MSCI World Index has a high "GROSS" (22.67) followed by MSCI Emerging Markets Index (22.2) and then by BITW (1.02). Theoretically, the structural pattern is perceived in the result that the openness is high in MSCI World Index followed by MSCI Emerging Markets Index.

The "Net" shows a very crystal implication about "From" and "To" that captures the net effect of volatility transmission from others and contribution in the transmission to others volatilities. Positive net value reflects the volatility that has been transmitted from others comparatively greater than its contribution to others volatility. It has been taken from the results that the MSCI World Index has a negative value (-0.97) which reflects that the developed market is contributing greater in the transmission of volatilities particularly, in emerging countries. The results agree with the theory based on structural linkages. On the other hand, the net value of the MSCI Emerging Markets Index has a positive value (0.94) that signifies that emerging countries are affected more by the volatiles of others, particularly from the developed markets. The result further strengthened the inference drawn on structural linkages. Lastly, the BITW indicated a low positive value (0.04) that reflects meticulous insight into technology-based assets. It shows that it is least affected by the volatilities of others and mildly contributes to the volatilities of others. Hence, the technology-based asset can be considered as a diversification asset while investing in sample indices.

Lastly, referring to the off-diagonal values, it has been noticed that Bitcoin as a technology asset is highly volatile, and the results are in the consensus of descriptive statistics, followed by MSCI World Index and then by MSCI Emerging Markets Index. From the off-diagonal values that provide the cues of spillover transmission from one asset/ index to another. The study captured MSCI World Index contributed maximum spillover transmission to the MSCI Emerging Markets Index (34.29). It consistently strengthened the theory of structural linkages. Moreover, MSCI Emerging Markets Index shows volatility transmission to MSCI World Index (31.49). The results provide to and fro volatilities transmission among two indices. The volatility transmission from BITW to MSCI World Index and MSCI Emerging Markets Index are 1.07 and 0.42, respectively. On the other hand, MSCI Emerging Markets Index is contributing lesser the MSCI World Index in the volatility of BITW that is 0.41 and 1.17, respectively. It has been witnessed that BITW is an appropriate asset class for diversification in a given sample particularly with MSCI Emerging Markets Index and followed by MSCI World Index.

Table 4. Volatility Spillover among Bitcoin, EMSI Emerging and EMSI developed using Diebold-Yilmaz (2012)

	R_BITW	R_MSCI Emerging	R_MSCI World	FROM
R_BITW	**98.42**	0.41	1.17	0.53
R_MSCI Emerging	0.42	**65.30**	34.29	11.57
R_MSCI World	1.07	31.49	**67.45**	10.85
TO	0.49	10.63	11.82	22.95
GROSS	1.02	22.2	22.67	
NET	0.04	0.94	-0.97	

CONCLUSION

The study is extending the ongoing discussion on cryptocurrencies as a diversification asset with the stock market. Few studies have analyzed cryptocurrencies as a diversification asset (Stensas et al. 2019; Kliber et al. 2019; Bouri et al. 2020; Thomas et al. 2020). However, several studies have challenged the same (Shahzad et al. 2020; Naeem et al. 2020). The current research is further analyzing contradictory arguments and finds them crucial during vulnerable times. The majority of the literature is on either Bitcoin or a few Cryptocurrencies. The study considered the proxies of the whole crypto market (BITW), developed (MSCI Emerging Markets Index), and developing markets (MSCI World Index). Henceforth the study revisits the current argument with a broader perspective and contributes methodologically. The study has considered a wide range of methods and models. To find diversification opportunities started from preliminary analysis in the form of descriptive and Granger causality, followed by dynamic multivariate symmetric and asymmetric volatility models and Diebold Yilmaz (2012) have applied.

The study found from the preliminary analysis that the maximum return and risk captured in BITW followed by MSCI Emerging Markets Index and then by MSCI World Index. From the results of Granger Causality, it has been found that BITW is not affected by the volatility of the stock indices and is considered a haven investment.

Further, the results of the dynamic conditional models captured no significant short-term volatility transmissions from MSCI Emerging Markets Index to BITW. However, significant short-term evidence had found from the MSCI World Index to BITW. Henceforth, there is an opportunity for diversification with BITW while investing in MSCI Emerging Markets Index. However, there is significant long-term volatility spillover perceived from both emerging and developed to BITW. The results of the symmetric dynamic model have partially supported by the conclusions drawn from the causality model. The results of asymmetric volatility models provide no evidence of leverage effect. The conclusions drawn from dynamic volatility models were further strengthened by Diebold Yilmaz (2012).

Further, the study found cross volatility spillover from the results of the Diebold Yilmaz Spillover Index and captured interesting and in-depth results from the application of the model. It has been found that MSCI World Index shows maximum contribution in the volatility transmission followed by MSCI Emerging Markets Index, and followed by BITW. It has been concluded that BITW is a resilient asset. It is neither affected nor contributed to the volatility transmission. It has been found that MSCI World Index shows a high "GROSS" (22.67) followed by MSCI Emerging Markets Index (22.2) and then by BITW (1.02). Again the results are in the consensus of the previous inferences drawn for Bitcoin as a resilient asset. Moreover, it has been captured the net value of the MSCI World Index, MSCI Emerging Markets Index, and BITW are -0.97, 0.94, and 0.04, respectively. It infers that the developed market is contributing greater in the transmission of volatilities particularly, in emerging countries, and emerging countries are affected more by the volatiles of others, particularly from the developed markets. Lastly, Bitcoin is negligibly affected by the volatilities of others but, it is mildly contributing to the volatilities of others. It has been better to give rather than to receive (Diebold- Yilmaz, 2012). Henceforth, the technology-based asset could be considered as a diversification asset while investing in sample indices. The results also provide the to and fro volatilities transmission among the two indices. The volatility transmissions from BITW to MSCI World Index and MSCI Emerging Markets Index are 1.07 and 0.42, respectively. However, MSCI Emerging Markets Index is contributing lesser the MSCI World Index in the volatility of BITW that is 0.41 and 1.17, respectively. It has been witnessed that BITW could be considered as a strong diversification asset with emerging followed by developed markets. The results are in the consensus of Stensas et al. 2019; Kliber et al. 2019; Bouri et al. 2020; Thomas et al. 2020; Bouri et al. 2020, Qin et al. 2021.

The result of the study provides insight to policymakers and investors who are discussing the importance of an alternative technology-based asset.

FUTURE SCOPE OF STUDY

The study is limited to the Crypto market further provides scope to find diversification opportunities by including more technology-based and unconventional assets like Green funds, Energy funds, and Fintech.

REFERENCES

Alahmari, S. A. (2020). Predicting the price of cryptocurrency using support vector regression methods. *Journal of Mechanics of Continua and Mathematical Sciences*, *15*(4), 313–322. doi:10.26782/jmcms.2020.04.00023

Bouri, E., Gupta, R., Tiwari, A. K., & Roubaud, D. (2017). *Does Bitcoin hedge global uncertainty? Evidence from wavelet-based quantile-in-quantile regressions.* Finance. doi:10.1016/j.frl.2017.02.009

Bouri, E., Shahzad, S. J. H., & Roubaud, D. (2020). Cryptocurrencies as hedges and safe-havens for US equity sectors. *The Quarterly Review of Economics and Finance*, *75*, 294–307. doi:10.1016/j.qref.2019.05.001

Chemkha, R., BenSaïda, A., Ghorbel, A., & Tayachi, T. (2021). Hedge and safe haven properties during COVID-19: Evidence from Bitcoin and gold. *The Quarterly Review of Economics and Finance*.

Conlon, T., Corbet, S., & McGee, R. J. (2020). Are cryptocurrencies a safe haven for equity markets? An international perspective from the COVID-19 pandemic. *Research in International Business and Finance*, *54*, 101248. doi:10.1016/j.ribaf.2020.101248 PMID:34170988

Disli, M., Nagayev, R., Salim, K., Rizkiah, S. K., & Aysan, A. F. (2021). In search of safe haven assets during COVID-19 pandemic: An empirical analysis of different investor types. *Research in International Business and Finance*, *58*, 101461. doi:10.1016/j.ribaf.2021.101461

Dyhrberg, A. H. (2016). Bitcoin, gold and the dollar – A GARCH Volatility Analysis. *Finance Research Letters*, *16*, 85–92. doi:10.1016/j.frl.2015.10.008

Ferreira, P., Kristoufek, L., & Pereira, J.D.A.E. (2020). ADCCA and DMCA Correlations of Cryptocurrency Markets. *Physica A, 545*(C). . doi:10.1016/j.physa.2019.123803

Gkillas, K., & Katsiampa, P. (2018). An Application of Extreme Value Theory to Cryptocurrencies. *Economics Letters*, *164*, 109–111. doi:10.1016/j.econlet.2018.01.020

Goodell, J. W., & Goutte, S. (2021). Diversifying equity with cryptocurrencies during COVID-19. *International Review of Financial Analysis*, *76*, 101781. doi:10.1016/j.irfa.2021.101781

Guiso, L., Jappelli, T., Padula, M., & Pagano, M. (2004). Financial market Integration and Economic Growth in the EU. *Economic Policy*, *19*(40), 524–577. doi:10.1111/j.1468-0327.2004.00131.x

Guo, X., Lu, F., & Wei, Y. (2021). Capture the contagion network of bitcoin–Evidence from pre and mid-COVID-19. *Research in International Business and Finance*, *58*, 101484. doi:10.1016/j.ribaf.2021.101484 PMID:34518717

Habiba, U. E., Peilong, S., Zhang, W., & Hamid, K. (2020). International Stock Markets Integration and Dynamics of Volatility Spillover between the USA and South Asian Markets: Evidence from Global Financial Crisis. *Journal of Asia Business Studies*, *14*(5), 779–794. doi:10.1108/JABS-03-2019-0071

Jiang, Y., Lie, J., Wang, J., & Mu, J. (2021). Revisiting the roles of cryptocurrencies in stock markets: A quantile coherency perspective. *Economic Modelling*, *95*, 21–34. doi:10.1016/j.econmod.2020.12.002

Kim, S.-J. (2005). Information Leadership in the Advanced Asia–Pacific Stock Markets: Return, Volatility and Volume Information Spillovers from the US and Japan. *Journal of the Japanese and International Economies*, *19*(3), 338–365. doi:10.1016/j.jjie.2004.03.002

Klein, T., Thu, H. P., & Walther, T. (2018). Bitcoin is not the New Gold–A comparison of volatility, correlation, and portfolio performance. *International Review of Financial Analysis*, *59*, 105–116. doi:10.1016/j.irfa.2018.07.010

Kliber, A., Marszałek, P., Musiałkowska, I., & Świerczyńska, K. (2019). Bitcoin: Safe haven, hedge or diversifier? Perception of bitcoin in the context of a country's economic situation—A stochastic volatility approach. *Physica A*, *524*, 246–257. doi:10.1016/j.physa.2019.04.145

Le, L.-T., Yarovaya, L., & Nasir, M. A. (2021). Did COVID-19 change spillover patterns between Fintech and other asset classes? *Research in International Business and Finance*, *58*, 101441. doi:10.1016/j.ribaf.2021.101441 PMID:34518714

Mizerka, J., Stróżyńska-Szajek, A., & Mizerka, P. (2020). The role of Bitcoin on developed and emerging markets–on the basis of a Bitcoin users graph analysis. *Finance Research Letters*, *35*, 101489. doi:10.1016/j.frl.2020.101489

Naeem, M. A., Hasan, M., Arif, M., & Shahzad, S. J. H. (2020). Can bitcoin glitter more than gold for investment styles? *SAGE Open*, *10*(2). doi:10.1177/2158244020926508

Ødegård, A. T., & Volden, T. M. (2020). *Cryptocurrency entering uncharted territory: a combined deductive and inductive study into the mechanisms of institutional demand for cryptocurrencies and an examination of Bitcoin's safe haven capabilities* (Master's thesis).

Qin, M., Su, C. W., & Tao, R. (2021). BitCoin: A new basket for eggs? *Economic Modelling*, *94*, 896–907. doi:10.1016/j.econmod.2020.02.031

Shahzad, S. J. H., Bouri, E., Roubaud, D., Kristoufek, L., & Lucey, B. (2019). Is Bitcoin a better safe-haven investment than gold and commodities? *International Review of Financial Analysis*, *63*, 322–330. doi:10.1016/j.irfa.2019.01.002

Statista. (n.d.). Retrieved from https://www.statista.com/statistics/326707/bitcoin-price-index/

Stensas, A., Nygaard, M. F., Kyaw, K., & Treepongkaruna, S. (2019). Can Bitcoin be a diversifier, hedge or safe haven tool? *Cogent Economics and Finance*, *7*(1), 1593072. doi:10.1080/23322039.2019.1593072

Susilo, D., Wahyudi, S., Pangestuti, I. R. D., Nugroho, B. A., & Robiyanto, R. (2020). Cryptocurrencies: Hedging opportunities from domestic perspectives in Southeast Asia emerging markets. *SAGE Open*, *10*(4), 2158244020971609. doi:10.1177/2158244020971609

Trabelsi, N. (2018). Are there any volatility spill-over effects among cryptocurrencies and widely traded asset classes? *Journal of Risk and Financial Management*, *11*(4), 66. doi:10.3390/jrfm11040066

Wang, P., Zhang, W., Li, X., & Shen, D. (2019). Is cryptocurrency a hedge or a safe haven for international indices? A comprehensive and dynamic perspective. *Finance Research Letters*, *31*, 1–18. doi:10.1016/j.frl.2019.04.031

Wu, W., Tiwari, A. K., Gozgor, G., & Leping, H. (2021). Does Economic Policy Uncertainty Affect Cryptocurrency Markets? Evidence from Twitter-Based Uncertainty Measures. *Research in International Business and Finance*, *58*, 101478. doi:10.1016/j.ribaf.2021.101478

Xunfa, L. U., Liu, S. K., San Liang, X., Zhang, Z., & Hairong, C. U. I. (2020). The break point-dependent causality between the cryptocurrency and emerging stock markets. *Economic Computation and Economic Cybernetics Studies and Research*, *54*(4), 203–216. doi:10.24818/18423264/54.4.20.13

Chapter 8
Role of AI in the Inventory Management of Agri-Fresh Produce at HOPCOMS

Raghavendra A. N.
CHRIST University (Deemed), India

Amalanathan S.
https://orcid.org/0000-0002-2362-7645
CHRIST University (Deemed), India

ABSTRACT

Inventory management is vital for maintaining the efficiency of supply chain management. Fruits and vegetables being perishable in nature should involve inventory management to avoid wastage and loss in terms of over stocking and stock out situations. The present study focuses on the role of artificial intelligence (AI)-powered inventory management of fruits and vegetables at HOPCOMS, a cooperative society founded in Bangalore. In the road to satisfy the customers, it is necessary for the society to come up with different strategies to manage the inventories in which a retailer confronts overstock and stock out situation, affecting the profit of the society. Therefore, a study was conducted with the help of structured questionnaire among 122 retailers of HOPCOMS outlets in Bangalore. The results obtained from the study suggest that inventory valuation method positively influences AI-powered demand forecasting and customer order fulfillment, and AI-powered demand forecasting is positively related to customer order fulfillment.

DOI: 10.4018/978-1-6684-4483-2.ch008

Copyright © 2023, IGI Global. Copying or distributing in print or electronic forms without written permission of IGI Global is prohibited.

INTRODUCTION

Fruits and vegetables are loaded with nutrients, minerals, vitamins, carbohydrates, proteins and other health benefits contributing to the trend of leading a healthy lifestyle (Halder & Pati, (2011). Regardless of the increasing production and demand, the wastage caused in the commodities cannot be ignored. It is necessary to focus on different factors which affect the quality and freshness in fruits and vegetables. The presence of a large number of intermediaries and inefficient infrastructural facilities are to be concerned (Sandeep Sachdeva, 2013). One of the main characteristics of the perishable commodity is the 'life span'. Fruits and vegetables are restricted to limited shelf life and are expected to be consumed and traded within a particular period. Bhat et al., (2017) & Negi, (2014) highlights the characteristics of perishable commodities which includes temperature, moisture, and the environment. Fruits and Vegetables must be conserved accordingly, depending upon their characteristics to avoid any kind of wastage. To attain efficiency in time-dependent commodities it is significant to provide cold chain facilities to preserve the quality and freshness. Whilst, it is vital to provide cold chain facilities it is competence to follow 'direct marketing' in selling fruits and vegetables to consumer.

Time dependence in fruits and vegetables stipulated the need for an organized marketing system with efficient supply chain management in the process of reaching high-quality commodities to the customers. Therefore, the rise in demand for fruits and vegetable made way for new players in the Fruits and Vegetables market. To save the farmers from the hands of the middlemen, cooperative societies and private players came to the rescue. Karnataka one among the progressive states of India introduced HOPCOMS, a cooperative society under the guidance M. H. Marigowda intending to provide maximum share in consumer price for the farmers via promoting direct marketing (Chandrashekar, 2018). However, with the introduction of private players in the market, HOPCOMS needs to be flexible to the changing environment and upgrade itself to withstand the competition to retain the members in the society (Bharadwaj, 2015). Failing to use the potentiality efficiently, HOPCOMS was established with the need to being in a stronger management through a clear vision in the society (Kolady, Krishnamoorthy, & Narayanan, n.d. (2008).

The supply chain for the cooperative society of HOPCOMS which in turn acting as an intermediary to reach the commodity to the end users involves producer-farmers, retailers and customers. The society calls for high-quality fruits and vegetables from the producer-farmers wherein the retailers grade and sort the fruits and vegetables. The retailers are expected to sell the commodities procured from the procurement centers, to save themselves from penalty. Here, the penalty is subjected to a percentage loss of salary. As an effect, the retailers sell the left over commodities to bulk buyers such as hospitals, hotels, restaurants etc. However, due to limited cold storage facilities the retailer is given an exemption up to 3% (HOPCOMS, 2018).

Inventory management is vital for maintaining the efficiency of the supply chain management. Fruits and vegetables being perishable in nature should involve inventory management to avoid wastage and loss in terms of over stocking and stock out situations. The present study focuses on bringing in inventory management at HOPCOMS, a cooperative society. According to Sabir & Farooquie, (2017)& Sabir, (2016)managing and ordering inventory with a definite shelf life is a challenge for the retailers. Improper ordering decisions might result in stock out or overstock situation where the probability of wastage might increase. Whist, the retailers concentrate on stocking the commodities to satisfy the customers forgets to understand the actual demand for the particular commodity. Bhat et al., (2017) emphasize the perishable nature in fruits and vegetables which demands for effective inventory management as the customer choose to buy fresh and superiority commodities.

The retailer should be aware of such factors and must come up with strategies to balance the quality and freshness. One of the drawback to manage inventories is 'how much to order and when to order', Sharma, (2016)indicates that retailers are forecast driven and follow manual ordering wherein they stock the commodities based on their experience. Changing tastes and preference among customer should create awareness among retailers the need to understand the want before stocking up the commodities. The retailers at HOPCOMS have limited knowledge and experience in managing the inventories affecting the profit of the overall society. Therefore, the retailers must be demand driven rather than forecast driven to avoid overstocking and stock out situations. Mutually overstocking and stock out situation hinders the profit of society converging on the retailers to have a regular check to avoid such situations. Scarcity of attention and information on inventory management at HOPCOMS emphasized the need for the study. Further an attempt is made to study the role of artificial intelligence (AI) in the inventory management of agricultural produce of HOPCOMS in Bangalore.

LITERATURE REVIEW AND HYPOTHESIS DEVELOPMENT

The retailers are the vital part in the supply chain. Being the only person to come in contact with the customers the society looks up for the retailers. Rao, (2018) discovered that HOPCOMS lacks in providing training and capacity building to its members to increase the sales. Lack of training and knowledge among the retailers with respect to stocking of commodities in the outlets has resulted in overstocking and stock out situation. HOPCOMS having wide spread of retail outlets across the state should focus on retailing phase which comes under the direct contact with consumers. Customers are essential for the growth of the society, but having various marketing channels to choose from, the society should train and educate the retailers to sustain in the market(G. Nethravati, 2014). At the retailing phase, managing the inventories are a crucial part of the supply chain of fruits and vegetables. Inventory management is a necessity specifically for time-dependent commodities. The retailers must be aware while ordering and stocking the commodities in the outlet. Without much knowledge, the retailers in the road to satisfy the customers stock commodities resulting in overstocking and stock out situations(Baron, Berman, & Perry, 2010).

From the information collected on inventory management, the present study explains the variables which will be implemented for the study. The first variable considered is inventory evaluation method. Inventory evaluation method is necessary to determine the actual sales and the closing inventory value of the firm (Simeon & John, 2018). Choosing the appropriate evaluation method is vital. There exists the relationship between inventory management and the type of inventory evaluation method to manage the inventories. There exist different types of inventory valuation methods which includes FIFO, LIFO and weighted average methods (Gu, 2013). FIFO refers to sale of commodities which are procured first following the latter. Majority of studies suggests to implement FIFO for the valuation of time dependent commodities (Gu, 2013) & (Ionescu & Berger, 2018).

The next variable identified for the study is efficient infrastructural facilities. The commodities are restricted to a temperature and shelf life (Raha, 2018) for which efficient infrastructural facilities should be provided to maintain the quality until the expiration (Arivazhagan, Geetha, Parthasarathy, Weatherspoon, & Oehmke, 2012) through factor analysis identified different factors which would enhance the quality of perishable commodities namely method of transportation, number of distribution channels, cold storage facilities and, packaging. Murthy, Gajanana, Sudha, & Dakshinamoorthy, (2009) explored the wastage that occurred in the supply chain of fruits and vegetables at HOPCOMS. The Cooperative society lacks in providing efficient infrastructural and cold storage facilities which causes loss in terms of decaying, damaging, rottening and not so fresh commodities(Singh, Md, Zaman, & Meher, 2014). As a result, large quantity of fruits and vegetables are wasted affecting the profit of the society (Raha, 2018). Thus, HOPCOMS mainly dealing with perishable commodities should bring in cold storage facilities to enhance the life period (Balraj, 2016). Murthy et al., (2009) suggested the society to expand cold storage facilities to enhance the quality of fruits and vegetables to maintain their freshness and richness.

Optimal order policy is important for the good quality management of short shelf life commodities (Sabir & Farooquie, 2017). The next variable considered is optimal ordering policy. Ordering is the important part in managing the inventories; the retailers should have efficient knowledge on the demand before stocking the commodities at the retail outlets and purchases are supposed to be made when there is a requirement. The retailer's decision on the ordering policy provides a stand to manage the inventories and increase the profit (Sabir & Farooquie, 2018). In relation to this, (Naik, n.d.) stated the importance of marketing facilities in the society that ought to be implemented to gain its spot in the market. Unlike other private players, HOPCOMS fail to indulge in promotional activities like advertisements and discounts hindering the end users to purchase from the society. As an effect, it is necessary to initiate promotional activities to retain the existing and attract new customers by educating the need to consume fruits and vegetables to stay fit and to simultaneously increase sales. Contradicting to this, Krishna & Mokshapathy, (2013) revealed that the society does not concentrate on marketing the horticulture produce, acting as a boon for the society to grow and compete.

Customers are the vital element of any supply chain. The ultimate aim of the society is to satisfy the customers by fulfilling the orders (Sohail & Sheikkh, 2018). The last variable considered for the study is to fulfill customer's orders. The retailers play an important part in selling fruits and vegetables to the customers. In the aim to satisfy the customer, the retailers either end up overstocking the commodities than required or under stocking resulting in a stock out situation (Sabir & Farooquie, 2018). One of the conflicts that retailers face is how much to order and when to order in relation to this if the retailer gets a clear picture managing of inventory will be easier. Hence the retailers must take steps to retain the customers by managing inventories.

From the review constructed, the hypotheses for the study are developed to find the significance of among the variables. The hypotheses constructed for the study are as follows:

Lack of awareness regarding inventory valuation method will result in improper ordering decisions affecting the purchase planning, sales planning and product planning (Latha, 2017). Therefore, there exists a strong correlation between the choice of inventory method and ordering decisions(Simeon & John, 2018). The organization should examine the method of evaluating the inventories before arriving at a conclusion. In light of this, the first hypothesis considered for the study is the relationship between inventory valuation method and optimal order policy.

H1: Inventory valuation method is positively and significantly related to the Optimal Order Policy.

The next hypothesis is regarding the relationship between inventory valuation method and efficient infrastructural facilities. Here, the decision taken for ordering the inventories are based on the method of inventory evaluation (Chen, Hsueh, & Chang, 2009) and any wrong decision taken will result in holding inventories (Afolabi,

Onifade, & F, 2017). Fruits and vegetables are perishable in nature and are restricted to a temperature (Sabir & Farooquie, 2017; Sabir, 2016; Sabir & Farooquie, 2018). Infrastructural facilities are significant to maintain the freshness and quality of the holding inventories (Singh et al., 2014). Therefore, the next hypothesis is as follows:

H2: Inventory valuation method is significantly and positively related to efficient infrastructure facility.

The type of inventory method used to evaluate the commodities has an impact on fulfilling customer orders. Fruits and vegetables being time framed, the methods used to evaluate the inventories are FIFO, LIFO and weighted average methods (Gu, 2013). The main aim of any market is to store inventories to satisfy the customer (Sohail & Sheikkh, 2018). It is necessary for the firm to consider the correct evaluation method to plan the sales and increase customer satisfaction without holding inventories (Latha, 2017; Sabir, 2016; Sabir & Farooquie, 2017). The firm to avoid wastage and to attract the customers are expected to offer markdown (Sabir, 2016). In similar ways optimal order policy and efficient infrastructure facilities are required to retain the customers from choosing a different supplier. Based on this, the third hypothesis is framed as follows:

H3: Inventory valuation method is significantly and positively related to fulfilling customer orders

The ordering decision taken by the retailer during stocking the commodities strive to satisfy the demands of the customer (Sabir & Farooquie, 2017; Sabir, 2016; Sabir & Farooquie, 2018). A clear view on the actual demand of the commodities will save the retailer from overstocking and stock out situations. The decision he takes provides a stand to survive in the competitive market (Shah, 2014). The retailers are expected to prevent under stocking by understanding the actual demand and needs of the end user. Consequently, there exists a need to check the relationship between ordering decisions and fulfilling customer orders (Sabir & Farooquie, 2017). Hence, the fourth hypothesis considered for the study is:

H4: Optimal order policy is significantly and positively related to fulfilling customer orders

Perishable commodities demand efficient infrastructural facilities to maintain the freshness and quality (Gundewadi et al., 2013). The demand of the customer is volatile (Christopher, 2000) and it is the duty of the retailer to satisfy any such unpredictable need especially for commodities which are seasonal. Most legacy inventory management systems lack channel-specificity failing to forecast customer demand patterns. In this context, artificial intelligence (AI) powered demand forecasting will come to the rescue of marketers (AI in Inventory Management: Putting AI to work to optimize inventory, 2021). Therefore, to verify the relationship between AI powered demand forecasting and fulfilling customer orders, the last hypothesis is stated as follows:

H5: AI powered Demand Forecasting is significantly and positively related to fulfilling customer orders

The hypotheses stated for the research study are shown in the form of a conceptual model in Figure 1.

Figure 1. Hypothetical model for the study

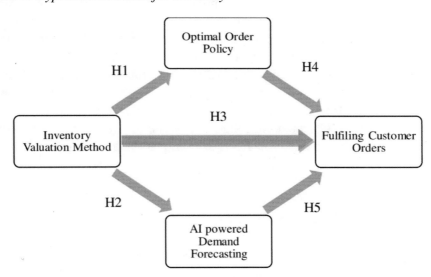

RATIONALE OF THE STUDY

The 'retailing phase' of HOPCOMS requires attention to overcome wastage and loss of inventories to escalate the quality and returns. Therefore, it is vital to understand the importance of inventory management for perishable commodities being sold in the outlets due to their restricted shelf life. In the process of satisfying the consumers of HOPCOMS, the retailing phase has taken up measures at the cost of its return. As a result, the retailer confronts overstock and stock out situation, affecting the profit of the society. An AI-powered autonomous inventory solution is a smart alternative helping retailers and hospitality companies to auto-detect and proactively avoid inventory scarcity issues or solve them. There is a lack of study accessible to the problems faced by retailers in managing the inventories through AI powered systems, and thus, this study helps to fill in the gap (AI in Inventory Management: Putting AI to work to optimize inventory, 2021). Therefore, it is vital to draw importance on evaluating the inventories with the most appropriate method to foster the growth of HOPCOMS.

RESEARCH METHODOLOGY

A descriptive study was carried out to seek an answer in respect to the problems related to inventory management at HOPCOMS, a cooperative society in Bangalore. The respondents included are the retailers, who come in direct contact with the customers. Subsequently, with sufficient reviews supporting the study, a questionnaire survey was carried out through convenience sampling in English and Kannada language to ensure more convenience for the retailers while providing the information. Structured questionnaire was distributed to 265 HOPCOMS retailers in the Bangalore Urban and Rural districts. Responses were received from 122 retailers attributing to a response rate of 46%. The study was conducted during July 2020 and November 2020. Statistical results including reliability analysis, item statistics and hypotheses testing of the study derived through Structural Equation Modeling (SEM) were done using SPSS version 21 and SPSS AMOS software.

RESULTS AND DISCUSSION

The retailer's demographic details are presented in Table1, which includes age group, experience, and, the distance of the procurement center from the retail outlet. According to the survey conducted, majority of the retailers belonged to the age group of 20-29 years with 28 percent; however, there were 15 percent respondents from 30-39 years of age group. Whilst, the highest experience of the retailer worked for HOPCOMS varied from 6- 10 years with 41 percent only 2 percent of the retailers had an experience above 15 years. The distance of the procurement center from the retail outlets was between 1-20 kilometers for majority of the retailers and only 8 percent of the retail outlets were situated beyond 60 kilometers.

Role of AI in the Inventory Management of Agri-Fresh Produce at HOPCOMS

Table 1. Demographic Details of the respondents

Variable		No. of respondents	Percentage
Age (years)	Less than 20 years	26	21
	20-29 years	34	28
	30 - 39 years	18	15
	40 - 49 years	22	18
	Above 49 years	22	18
Total		**122**	**100**
Experience (years)	Less than 1 year	36	29
	1-5 years	21	17
	6 - 10 years	50	41
	11 -15 years	13	11
	more than 15 years	2	2
Total		**122**	**100**
Distance of the procurement Centre	Less than 1Km	36	29
	1 Km-20Km	40	33
	21Km-40Km	18	15
	41Km-60Km	18	15
	More than 60Km	10	8
Total		**122**	**100**

Table 2 shows the quantity of commodity procured by the retailers from the procurement center to their respective outlets. Where, 29 percent of retailers procured 5 – 50 quintals of fruits and vegetables per week limiting to 9 percent who procured more than 200 quintals based on the demand.

Table 2. Quantity of fruits and vegetables procured by the retailers

Quantity procured	No of respondents	Percentage
5-50 Quintals	35	29
51-100 Quintals	33	26
101-150 Quintals	13	19
151-200 Quintals	21	17
More than 200 Quintals	10	9
Total	**122**	**100**

In order to establish the validity of the instrument used in this study, Confirmatory Factor Analysis (CFA) was performed and results indicate satisfactory validity. Cronbach Alpha of all 20 items used in the research study was found to be 0.899 (Table 3) which is far above the acceptable value of 0.7. This shows that the data collected is more reliable and suitable for further statistical analysis. The table 4 gives item statistics of all 20 items along with their description. Table 5 provides the details of Cronbach alpha for the four variables – *INVM - Inventory Valuation Methods, OOP – Optimal Order Policy, ADF – AI powered Demand Forecasting, COF – Fulfilling Customer Orders* taken individually. All the values in the table are above the acceptable value 0.7.

Table 3. Reliability Statistics of all 20 items

Cronbach's Alpha	N of Items
.899	20

Source: SPSS V.21 Output

Table 6 shows the correlation analysis for the variables included in the present study. As shown only three variables reached the significance level of $p < 0.01$

In order to test the hypotheses, structural equation modeling (SEM) using AMOS V21 was used. Figure 2 shows the standardized regression weights for the proposed model.

Table 7 presents the results of the hypothetical framework along with crucial ratios and the status of the hypotheses tested.

As shown in the SEM results, inventory valuation method and optimal order policy are not having a significant relationship. As an effect, the retailers do not consider the valuation methods before placing the orders from the procurement centers. The results also highlighted the relationship between optimal order policy and customer order fulfillment which was not positively significant and hence did not support the hypothesis.

However, inventory valuation method was found to be positively significant in relation to AI powered Demand Forecasting and customer order fulfillment. Results also proved the relationship between AI powered Demand Forecasting and customer order fulfillment to be positive and significant supporting the hypothesis.

Role of AI in the Inventory Management of Agri-Fresh Produce at HOPCOMS

Table 4. Confirmatory Factor Analysis (CFA)

Variables	Descriptions	Loadings	t value
INVM1	HOPCOMS is using the most effective method to calculate the required inventory on a daily basis.	.718	Fixed
INVM2	FIFO (first in first out) and LIFO (last in first out) inventory valuation methods are used by retailers of HOPCOMS.	.758	9.13
INVM3	We provide timely assistance on information, price about fruits and vegetables.	.737	10.45
INVM4	Measures are undertaken to avoid under stocking, overstocking and out of stock situation of fruits and vegetables at the retail outlets.	.685	11.28
INVM5	The retail outlets follow the ethical standard set up by HOPCOMS	.817	10.56
OOP1	To avoid stock out situation, fruits and vegetables are overstocked.	.760	Fixed
OOP2	We foresee the customer's expectation.	.630	11.56
OOP3	We exchange honest communication with customers	.792	11.29
OOP4	We maintain frequent contact with customers.	.686	10.49
ADF1	The retail outlet AI powered demand forecasting for wide variety of Fruits and Vegetables.	.700	Fixed
ADF2	AI integrated sorting and grading is followed strictly by the procurement center of HOPCOMS.	.791	10.32
ADF3	Modern AI powered techniques are used for the weighing and billing of F&V	.808	10.67
ADF4	Cold storage and warehouse facilities are provided at the procurement centers of HOPCOMS are managed through AI algorithms	.756	11.39
ADF5	HOPCOMS transportation facilities to transfer fruits and vegetables from the production point to procurement centers are AI integrated.	.703	11.2
COF1	Promotional activities such as advertisements, discounts are provided to customers	.834	Fixed
COF2	The attitude of the retailers influence the purchase of fruits and vegetables at HOPCOMS	.806	10.29
COF3	Easy to access the retail outlets of HOPCOMS	.818	11.02
COF4	Discounts and offers on fruits and vegetables are provided during festive seasons.	.774	11.37
COF5	You are allowed to render suggestion to increase the quality and quantity depending upon the demand.	.732	11.25
COF6	The retailer does not indulge in any kind of malpractices during the weighing and pricing of Fruits and Vegetables.	.849	10.93

Table 5. Cronbach Alpha for each of the four variables

Sl. No.	Variable Name	N	No. of items	Cronbach α
1	Inventory Valuation Methods	22	5	0.890
2	Fulfilling customer orders	22	4	0.701
3	Optimal order policy	22	5	0.738
4	AI powered Demand Forecasting	22	6	0.849

Source: SPSS V.21 Output

Table 6. Mean, Standard Deviation and Correlation

Variables	Mean	S.D.	1	2	3	4
1) Inventory Valuation Methods	2.969	0.936	1			
2) Fulfilling customer orders	3.604	0.692	.740**	1		
3) Optimal order policy	3.286	0.806	-.004	-.028	1	
4) AI powered Demand Forecasting	3.253	0.832	.666**	.761**	.115**	1

Figure 2. SEM Model

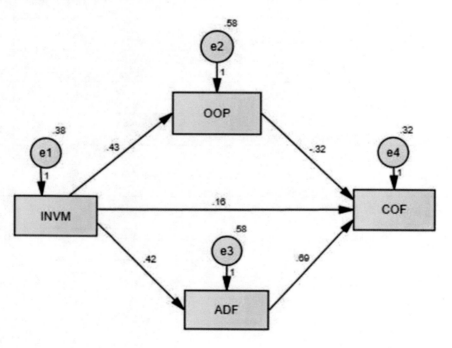

Role of AI in the Inventory Management of Agri-Fresh Produce at HOPCOMS

Table 7. SEM Results

Hypothesis	Standardized Coefficient	S.E.	C.R.	P	Conclusion
H1: INV → OOP	-0.003	0.067	-0.043	0.966	Not Supported
H2: INV → ADF	0.573	0.058	9.857	***	Supported
H3: INV → COF	0.362	0.061	5.966	***	Supported
H4: OOP → COF	-0.101	0.061	-1.653	0.098	Not Supported
H5: ADF → COF	0.516	0.071	7.316	***	Supported
$\chi2/d.f. = 3.087/1=3.087$; CFI= .990; IFI= .990; TLI= .940; RMSEA= .031					

*** $p < 0.001$

INV – Inventory Valuation Methods, OOP – Optimal Order Policy, ADF – AI powered Demand Forecasting, COF – Fulfilling Customer Orders

MANAGERIAL IMPLICATIONS

Inventory management is a crucial part in attaining the efficiency in supply chain management. Fruits and vegetables are time dependent and perishable in nature. Customers prefer to buy the commodities which are high in quality and freshness. Therefore, the retailer should ensure to fulfill the demand of the customers. One of the drawbacks of HOPCOMS is the infrastructural facilities. Seasonal fruits and vegetables depend on cold storage facilities. Being the state undertaking the government should sneak in to provide the required cold storage facilities to increase the sale in the competitive environment. Limited access to cold storage facilities results in decaying, rottening and shrinking of commodities affecting the profit of the society.

The ordering decision of the retailer plays a vital role as the commodities are procured on a daily basis. Depending upon the previous knowledge on sales they purchase the commodities to stock at the outlets. Without the actual consideration of the demand from the customer the procured commodities would result in overstocking or under stocking. Implementing inventory valuation methods would provide the retailers on the actual details and demand of the commodities required by the customers. The time dependency in fruits and vegetables recommends FIFO to evaluate the actual demand and to stock the commodity. FIFO increases the profit by selling the commodities procured first and selling the latter in the current price of the market.

Besides, the retailer should promote the commodities to increase sales. They should offer promotional activities such as discounts to sell the commodities in order to avoid loss. Overall the inventory management will impact the supply chain of HOPCOMS by decreasing wastage and loss.

CONCLUSION

The present study emphasizes to fill in the gap of inventory management at HOPCOMS by addressing different issues which affected the quality and freshness of fruits and vegetables at the retail outlets. The results obtained from the study suggest that inventory valuation method positively influences AI powered Demand Forecasting and, customer order fulfillment and, AI powered Demand Forecasting are positively related to customer order fulfillment. The type of valuation method implemented by the society should be clear and according to the characteristics of goods. Inventory valuation methods depict the actual demand and the quantity of fruits and vegetables to be procured in relation to the cold storage facilities to maintain the freshness and quality until the commodities reach the customers. Besides, an appropriate inventory evaluation method calculates the actual demand satisfying the customers. AI powered Demand Forecasting is a necessity for perishable commodities as it maintains the life span. Seasonal fruits require cold storage facilities. To satisfy the customers, the society should concentrate more on AI powered Demand Forecasting to increase customer orders.

These findings imply that inventory management can be attained through calculating the actual demand through appropriate methods using AI powered Demand Forecasting with the aim to satisfy the customer by fulfilling the orders and increasing the sales. The results also indicate that the retailers are aware of the importance of the cold storage facilities and the significant role in maintaining the freshness. Practicing AI powered Demand Forecasting as part of inventory management at the retail outlet of HOPCOMS is a significant driver for increasing customer satisfaction.

REFERENCES

Afolabi, O. J., & Onifade, M. K., & F, O. O. (2017). *Evaluation of the Role of Inventory Management in Logistics Chain of an Organisation* . doi:10.1515/logi-2017-0011

Arivazhagan, R., Geetha, P., Parthasarathy, R., Weatherspoon, D. D., & Oehmke, J. F. (2012). Analysis of Sources of Fruit Wastages in Retail outlets in Chennai, Tamilnadu, India. Academic Press.

Balraj, N. (2016). Issues and Challenges in the Supply Chain of Fruits & Vegetables Sector in India: A Review. *Splint International Journal of Professionals*, *3*(8), 113–118. doi:10.5121/ijmvsc.2015.6205

Baron, O., Berman, O., & Perry, D. (2010). Continuous review inventory models for perishable items ordered in batches. *Mathematical Methods of Operations Research, 72*(2), 217–247. doi:10.100700186-010-0318-1

Bharadwaj, K. V. (2015, january 27). Retrieved from The Hindu: https://www.thehindu.com/news/cities/bangalore/the-rise-and-fall-of-hopcoms/article6826063.ece

Bhat, S. A., Khan, F. A., & Narayan, S. (2017). *Storage Methods for Fruits and Vegetables*. Retrieved from https://www.researchgate.net/publication/317014767_Storage_Methods_for_Fruits_and_Vegetables

Chandrashekar, H. M. (2018). *Farmers Participatory Approach towards Role of the HOPCOMS Development of Agribusiness Management in Karnataka*. Academic Press.

Chen, H.-K., Hsueh, C.-F., & Chang, M.-S. (2009). Production scheduling and vehicle routing with time windows for perishable food products. *Computers & Operations Research, 36*(7), 2311–2319. doi:10.1016/j.cor.2008.09.010

Christopher, M. (2000). The Agile Supply Chain. *Industrial Marketing Management, 29*(1), 37–44. doi:10.1016/S0019-8501(99)00110-8

Gu, S. (2013). *Research and Analysis on Issued Inventory Valuation Methods of Enterprises*. Academic Press.

Gundewadi, B. B., Storage, K. C., Campus, R., Shivajinagar, N., Maharashtra, S., & West, S. (2013). *Role and Performance of Cold Storages in Indian Agriculture*. Academic Press.

Halder, P., & Pati, S. (2011). A need for paradigm shift to improve supply chain management of fruits & Vegetables in India. *Asian Journal of Agriculture and Rural Development, 1*(1), 1–21. http://search.proquest.com/docview/1416221058?accountid=13771

HOPCOMS. (2018). *HOPCOMS Report*. HOPCOMS.

Hypersonix. (2021). *AI in Inventory Management: Putting AI to work to optimize inventory*. https://hypersonix.ai/resources/blog/ai-in-inventory-management/

Ionescu, L., & Berger, G. (2018). Applied Analysis of the Impact of Inventory Valuation Methods on the Financial Situation and Financial Performance. *Applied Analysis of the Impact of Inventory Valuation Methods on the Financial Situation and Financial Performance., 9*(1), 67–76. doi:10.2478/vjes-2018-0007

Kolady, D., Krishnamoorthy, S., & Narayanan, S. (2008). *Small-scale producers in modern agrifood markets Marketing cooperatives in a new retail context : A case study of HOPCOMS*. Academic Press.

Krishna, K. M., & Mokshapathy, S. (2013). Performance and Prospects of HOPCOMS in Karnataka—A Direct Link between Farmers and Consumers. *International Journal of Research in Commerce, Economics and Management, 3*(2), 114–117. http://search.proquest.com/docview/1373419092?accountid=13042%5Cnhttp://oxfordsfx.hosted.exlibrisgroup.com/oxford?url_ver=Z39.88-2004&rft_val_fmt=info:ofi/fmt:kev:mtx:journal&genre=article&sid=ProQ:ProQ:econlitshell&atitle=Performance+and+Prospects+of+HOP

Latha, L. (2017). Inventory valuation methods in Indian manufacturing sector SMES - an empirical study. *Abhinav National Monthly Refereed Journal of Research, 6*(12).

Murthy, D. S., Gajanana, T. M., Sudha, M., & Dakshinamoorthy, V. (2009). *Marketing and Post-Harvest Losses in Fruits : Its Implications on Availability and Economy*. Academic Press.

Naik, D. S. (n.d.). Survey of Hopcoms Employees In Karnataka. *Introduction. Research Methodology, 2*(12), 249–257.

Negi, S. (2014). Supply Chain Efficiency: An Insight from Fruits and Vegetables Sector in India. *Journal of Operations and Supply Chain Management, 7*(2), 154. doi:10.12660/joscmv7n2p154-167

Negi, S., & Anand, N. (2015). Issues And Challenges In The Supply Chain Of Fruits & Vegetables Sector In India. *RE:view, 6*(2), 47–62. Advance online publication. doi:10.5121/ijmvsc.2015.6205

Nethravathi, K. G. A. T. O. (2014). *Analysis of consumer's preferences in purchasing fruits and vegetables across selected marketing organizations in Bangalore rural and urban districts*. Academic Press.

RahaR. (2018, September 4). https://thesoftcopy.in/2018/09/04/lack-of-cold-storage-facility-hinders-hopcoms-profit/

Rao, N. H. (2018). *A framework for implementing information and communication technologies in agricultural development in India*. doi:10.1016/j.techfore.2006.02.002

Sabir, L. B. (2016). Managing Fruits And Vegetables Inventory : A Study Of Retail. *SAJMMR*.

Sabir, L., & Farooquie, J. A. (2017). Effect of Different Dimensions of Inventory Management of Fruits and Vegetables on Profitability of Retail Stores : An Empirical Study. *Sage (Atlanta, Ga.)*, *19*(1), 99–110. doi:10.1177/0972150917713278

Sabir, L., & Farooquie, J. A. (2018). Effect of Different Dimensions of Inventory Management of Fruits and Vegetables on Profitability of Retail Stores: An Empirical Study. *Global Business Review*, *19*(1), 99–110. doi:10.1177/0972150917713278

Sandeep Sachdeva, T. R. (2013). Increasing Fruit and Vegetable Consumption: Challenges and Opportunities. *Indian Journal of Community Medicine*, *38*(4), 192–197. doi:10.4103/0970-0218.120146 PMID:24302818

Shah, N. H. (2014). *Ordering Policy For Inventory Management When Demand Is Stock- Dependent And A Temporary Price Discount*. Academic Press.

Sharma, P. K. (2016). Perishable inventory systems: A literature review since 2006. *International Journal of Applied Research*, *2*(9), 150–155.

Simeon, E. D., & John, O. (2018). Implication of Choice of Inventory Valuation Methods on Profit. *Tax and Closing Inventory.*, *3*(07), 1639–1645. doi:10.31142/afmj/v3i7.05

Singh, V., Md, H., Zaman, P., & Meher, J. (2014). Postharvest Technology of Fruits and Vegetables. *An Overview.*, *02*(02), 124–135.

Sohail, N., & Sheikkh, T. H. (2018). *A Study of Inventory Management System Case Study*. Academic Press.

Chapter 9
Emergence of Crypto Currency and the Digital Financial Landscape:
A Critique

Nidhi U. Argade
Faculty of Commerce, The Maharaja Sayajirao University of Baroda, Vadodara, India

Parag Shukla
iD https://orcid.org/0000-0002-7014-163X
Faculty of Commerce, The Maharaja Sayajirao University of Baroda, Vadodara, India

Madhvendra Pratap Singh
iD https://orcid.org/0000-0002-2573-791X
Management Institute, Kamla Nehru Institute of Physical and Social Sciences, India

ABSTRACT

The reality of the new normal induced by the pandemic has resulted in a radical transformation of the financial sector, where it is undergoing a dramatic digital change. With this backdrop, the purpose of this study is conceptualizing the role of crypto currencies and the effects on the digital financial (DiFi) landscape in India and worldwide. It has led to disruptive technological innovation and accelerated change in the financial system. In this light, the present study attempts to highlight the different digital initiatives undertaken by various developed and developing countries

DOI: 10.4018/978-1-6684-4483-2.ch009

Copyright © 2023, IGI Global. Copying or distributing in print or electronic forms without written permission of IGI Global is prohibited.

and the pros and cons associated with the same. This research study shall serve as a primer to demonstrate the effects of use of digitalization and technology-enabled initiatives for crypto currencies and is also aimed to encapsulate the restraining and facilitating forces that drive adoption of digital financial models and the hybrid role of government as we usher in the new financial landscape.

In real world, cash allows parties to exchange currency with some sort of central authority. Earlier, there was no electronic equivalent to this exchange. In 1982 David Chaum proposed anonymous electronic cash based system on blind signatures, and in 1990 he founded DigiCash as an electronic cash company. In the year 1997 and 1998 this DigiCash and the banks who had implemented electronic cash systems became bankrupt and thus between 1998 and 2008 there were no implementations of electronic cash. Virtual currencies have become a global phenomenon known to most people. Crypto currency is a digital asset which as a medium of exchange for buying or selling. Unlike traditional currency which were backed by gold or silver; A Crypto currency is a digital currency produced by a public network, rather than any government, that uses cryptography to make sure payments are sent and received safely. In recent years Crypto currencies has seen popularity due to their decentralised distribution, peer-to-peer protocols. Under centralized system governments or banks issues new currency whereas crypto currency when created is known from the beginning to the public thereby protecting it from political influences. Cryptography helps to secure a transaction. Transactions are recorded in a public ledger and then the minor verifies and secures the transactions in exchange of certain amount of crypto currency and thus new currencies are added to the system.

There were more than 1600 Crypto currencies available over the internet as of 19th August 2018 and growing. New crypto currency can be created any time. In recent years some major currencies such as Bit coin, Etherum, Bit coin cash, Litecoin and Ripple has emerged as a fascinating phenomenon in the financial markets because of their large market capitalization. Bit coin; the largest decentralized Crypto currency was created in 2009 and since then numerous other named as "altcoins" have been created. They are also associated with controversy ever since popularity, accompanied by increased public interest, reached high levels. As of 15 December 2018, total Crypto currencies market capitalization is $100bn and larger than GDP of 127 countries.

The reality of the new normal induced by the pandemic has resulted in a radical transformation of the financial sector, where it is undergoing a dramatic digital change. With this backdrop, the purpose of this study is conceptualizing the role of crypto currencies and the effects on the Digital financial [DiFi] landscape in India and Worldwide. It has led to disruptive technological innovation, and accelerated change in the financial system. The emergence of Digital Finance fuelled by crypto currency also calls for caution as there is a dire need to create a facilitative framework for creation of official digital currency to be issued by the Reserve Bank of India [RBI]. The risk elements and the technology of crypto currency led by Private companies also is a matter of concern. In this light, the present study attempts to highlight the different digital initiatives undertaken by various developed and developing countries and the pros and cons associated with the same.

This research study shall serve as a primer to demonstrate the effects of use of digitalization and technology enabled initiatives for crypto currencies and is also aimed to encapsulate the restraining and facilitating forces that drive adoption of digital financial models and the hybrid role of government as we usher in the new financial landscape.

INTRODUCTION: OVERVIEW OF CRYPTOCURRENCY

As rightly said by Stewart Brand, 'Once a new technology rolls over you, if you are not the part of steamroller, you are part of the road'. Till last decade, cash permits businesses to exchange currency with a central authority in the physical world, and there was no technological equivalent to this trade previously. David Chaum presented an anonymous electronic cash system based on blind signatures in 1982, he established DigiCash as an electronic cash corporation in 1990. Between 1997 and 1998, DigiCash and the banks that had developed electronic currency systems went bankrupt, thus, no electronic cash systems were implemented between 1998 and 2008. On October 30, 2008, a man who called himself, Satoshi Nakamoto, has published a paper titled "Bitcoin", which is aPeer to Peer Electronic Cash System, detailing a digital money named "Bitcoin" (A peer-to-peer electronic cash system,). Electronic cash is the payment system, which will allow internet payments to be transmitted directly from one person to another without an intervention of intermediary or banking system as it is fully peer to peer. The Bitcoin network was started on January 3rd, 2009, at a price of $0.0008 per Bitcoin, which has increased to $42,500 per Bitcoin in January 2022 (Best, 2022).

Digital currencies were unknown outside of the online video gaming world only a few years ago, but they are now widely used (Themistocleous et al., 2020a). Virtual currencies have become a worldwide phenomenon that most people are aware of. Unlike traditional currency, which is backed by gold or silver, cryptocurrency is a digital currency created by a public network rather than a government, and it uses encryption to ensure that payments are issued and received securely. From a

Emergence of Crypto Currency and the Digital Financial Landscape

technological standpoint, cryptocurrency is defined as a "kind of digital currency that uses cryptography to create and maintain the currency, usually in conjunction with a proof-of-work method." Governments or banks issue new currency under a centralised system, whereas cryptocurrency is known to the public from the start, insulating it from political interference. These transactions are much secured, Cryptography aids security to these transactions. Transactions are recorded in a public ledger and the minor verifies and secures them in exchange for a specific amount of bitcoin, allowing for the addition of new currencies to the system. The creation and validation of transfer of said money is done thorough a decentralised network of computer nodes which is of peer-to-peer, that are in sync and are part of main network. Ametrano (Ametrano, 2016) provides a more practical definition, cryptocurrency "can be exchanged immediately and securely between any two parties, using Internet infrastructure and cryptographic security, without the need for a trusted third party, the worth isn't guaranteed by any government or institution." Wiatr (Wiatr, 2014) also defines the cryptocurrency as "a modern digital means of trade."

The majority of cryptocurrencies were created in order to provide new units of currency with a finite total value. Cryptocurrencies have grown in popularity in recent years as a result of its decentralised distribution and peer-to-peer protocols. As of November 21, 2021, there were more than 10,000 Cryptocurrencies available around the world, and the number is growing (Investopedia, n.d.). At any time, a new cryptocurrency can be generated. Because of their high market capitalization, prominent currencies such as Bitcoin, Etherum, Bitcoin cash, Litecoin, and Ripple have emerged as fascinating phenomena in the financial markets in recent years. Bitcoin, the world's largest decentralised cryptocurrency, was launched in 2009, and since then, a slew of other cryptocurrencies known as "altcoins" have emerged. They've also been linked to controversy as their popularity soared, accompanied by a surge in public attention.

To summarise, we basically follow Spenkelink's (Spenkelink, 2014) lead and discover four key properties of cryptocurrencies. To begin with, Bitcoin operates on a decentralised network, which means it is unaffected by external regulations. It employs a robust peer-to-peer strategy which ensures that money is transferred directly from one party to another, whichever the type of transaction is - B2B, B2C, or C2C. Bitcoin makes advantage of public network of internet, it is faster, efficient, and provides scalability. It relies on public-key cryptography for ensuring the security of financial transactions. The Bitcoin was introduced as the first digital money in 2009 and rapidly became a global sensation, many cryptocurrencies began to expand after it. There are hundreds of alternatives to Bitcoin, each with its own set of advantages. For instance, Litecoin uses scrypt encryption and claims to be four times faster than Bitcoin in terms of transaction speed, making it a viable option for high-speed applications like financial trading.

The so-called Altcoins could be regarded 'forks' of either Bitcoin or Litecoin because they use the same type of algorithms. Feathercoin, ChinaCoin, and Dogecoin are just a few examples. Even though Bitcoins can theoretically be mined (produced by anybody), the Bitcoin system provides certain features that are needed for genuine (fiat) currencies. First, bitcoins are scares – limited to 21 million and that keeps inflation low. Second, it uses public and private keys to ensure the highest level of security. After registering as a Bitcoin provider, a person receives a digital Cryptocurrencies as a Disruption wallet identifying a number or ID which will be displayed in public as a person transfers Bitcoin. The blockchain keeps track of all previous transactions. Third, Bitcoin transfer is very simple, only a mobile Bitcoin app or wallet and the required amount of Bitcoins, which you may obtain via a Bitcoin exchange or an ATM, is what is required. Regardless of distance, the transmission takes very less time, only a few minutes.

Along with all these advantages of cryptocurrency, due to its modern technology, there are some very basic and inherent limitations as well as concerns about it. Although the blockchain technology that underpins cyber money is promising, most cryptos have no intrinsic value. Their current worth is based on the presumption that someone else will be willing to pay a higher price for it in the future. Meanwhile, the Indian government has no intentions to regulate or develop the cryptocurrency industry; instead, they intend to introduce a bill on controlled currency and a Digital Currency Central Bank (CBDT). It will be implemented by modifying the RBI Act 1934 to broaden the scope of bank notes to include digital currency supported by the country's central bank. Aside from the other advantages, it will be free of the volatility that is commonly associated with private cryptocurrencies. The most serious concern to the government must be that, in the absence of regulation, the crypto world will devolve into the Wild West, with cryptos serving as conduits for unlawful activities such as drug trafficking, money laundering, terrorism financing, and so on. Recognizing cryptos as an asset class and regulating them, on the other hand, will allow the government to monitor trading activity, tax investors' capital gains, and enforce certain transparency and code of behaviour norms. Diem, a stable coin proposed by Facebook, is connected to dollars, but its backing is opaque and falls short of regulatory regulations. Cryptocurrencies may be referred to as currencies, but they are unsuitable for any of money's three functions: store of value, unit of account, or medium of exchange. They are assets that have no intrinsic worth and do not pay dividends; instead, the asset's return is determined by the willingness of others to retain it, which increases its value. They are inappropriate as a medium of exchange due to their volatility.

The present chapter tries to highlight important features of cryptocurrency, various concerns related to it as well as highlights the blockchain technology, which is a backbone of these cryptocurrencies

Significance/Relevance of the Study

Typically, after the initial technology trigger and peak of (inflated) expectations by enthusiasts and visionaries, pragmatists will now need to deliver real applications based on crypto currencies and turn those into a profitable business. That may not be easy .As a first question, what key challenges need to be addressed before crypto currencies can achieve widespread consumer adoption. Here are five specific issues that make our proposed research study more significant and relevant

i.   Trust in service providers.
ii.   *Price stability.*
iii. *Technology performance.*
iv.   *Clear regulation.*
v.   *Compelling benefits.*

With these obvious underlying issues, there is one another important element that is related with risk and regulation.

A key question is when and how crypto currencies service providers will be regulated. Whereas some of the original proponents of Bit coin expressed 'libertarian' views and were principally against the intervention of any central authority, many crypto currency service providers and interest groups are now seeking to understand the regulatory environment better and to lobby and advocate for what they believe are appropriate forms of regulation. Several Bit coin service providers have hired Chief Compliance Officers, and sought to professionals for their services further in the knowledge that consumer confidence and risk management are vital if they wish to achieve broad adoption and commercial success. At the same time, the understanding of risks around crypto currencies is evolving and increasingly documented. In this research paper, an attempt shall also be made to study the same.

REVIEW OF LITERATURE

Bitcoin as Cryptocurrency

Raymaekers (2014) concentrated on Bitcoin as a means of payment. The goal of the study was to highlight important obstacles, substantial risks, killer apps, and fundamental crypto currency issues. In the short term, Bitcoin may not be able to replace traditional payment systems, but banks should keep an eye on its underlying technology as a potential generic new means to transmit ownership of wealth, according to the paper. Baur (2015), in one of the first publications, looked at digital currency as a potentially disruptive payment method, with a focus on Bitcoin. In an in-depth interview with 13 people from three different groups, determinants such as usability, utility, and subjective standards responsible for making Bitcoin a game changer are discussed. The findings show that perceived ease of use is poor, and perceived usefulness varies depending on who is involved. Ram(2018) has tried to determine whether Bitcoin can become unique and distinct class of asset or not. This will provide an insight into the use of Bitcoin as an option of diversification and investment by individuals. The analysis reveals that the Bitcoin presents unique attributes. The Bitcoin has numerous opportunities for investment and sufficient market capitalisation.

Blockchain is a Distributed Ledger Technology

Fanning and Centers (2016) have presented fundamental information regarding the blockchain, which is the foundation of bitcoin. They explained blocks, mining, cryptocurrencies, blockchain, and its impact on the financial services business in their piece.

Sapczyski (2019) attempted to answer the question of whether new technologies such as blockchain, which are gaining traction in numerous areas of public life, are safe for consumers and have an impact on national legislation. Joo, Nishikawa, and Dandpani (2019) attempted to identify the use and limitations of blockchain technology in finance in general, as well as sectors where the technology could have a greater impact on payment systems. Majuri (2019) used blockchain technology to suggest an Ethereum-based solution for overcoming economic stagnation in low-income communities. The study contributes to studies in the area of local currency systems and the use of blockchain technology to improve system efficiency. Tang et al. (2019) attempted to build a conceptual framework for dividing the study of blockchain ethics into three levels: micro-level (blockchain technology stack), meso-level (blockchain applications), and macro-level (blockchain governance) (blockchain implications for institutions and society). For each aspect, the fundamental principles and key ethical implications are thoroughly examined. The researchers want to raise awareness about the ethical challenges surrounding blockchain technology while also laying the groundwork for future research in the field. The researchers Jayawardhana and Colombage (2020) looked at how blockchain technology can be used to solve sustainability issues. They focused their qualitative research on two dimensions of sustainability: accountability and governance, as well as their relationship with blockchain and cryptocurrency. They came up with a definition that connected blockchain, cryptocurrency, and long-term sustainability.

Ease of Use

By incorporating control, intrinsic motivation, and emotions into the Technology Acceptance Model, Venketash (2000) created and tested an anchoring and adjustment-based theoretical model of the determinants of system-specific perceived ease of use. Over the course of three months, he tested the model on 246 employees to see how easy it is to use a computer. Alqaryouti et al (2020) attempted to establish a link between bitcoin use and consumers' perceived benefits and behaviour. Using the Technology Acceptance Model, they looked at three factors: ease of use, perceived advantages, and usage behaviour. They discovered a positive association between ease of use and usage of cryptocurrencies, but no significant relationship between perceived benefits and usage.

What is Cryptocurrency?

In one of the first research articles on cryptocurrency, Acuna and Pullas (2016) attempted to shed light on four aspects of the cryptocurrency: determining the correct definition, the role of the internet in the process, the link of digital currency with e-commerce, and regulatory issues. Reza (2018) has emphasised expert countermeasures and efforts to clarify how current cryptology functioned in usage around the world by utilising bitcoin as the primary example in his paper. Lipton, Hardjono, and Pentland (2018) provided a feasible mechanism for constructing a transaction-oriented cryptocurrency backed by an asset. They have created DTC by combining fresh technical advancements with well-established hedging approaches (Digital Trade Coin).They concluded that DTCs can serve as a crucial counterbalance to fiat currencies and, when fully developed, can play the role of a supranational currency promoting international business and allowing groups of tiny countries to construct their own viable currencies. Yuneline (2019) examined the nature of cryptocurrencies in terms of money features, legal perspectives, economic perspectives, and Sharia perspectives. Majumder, Routh, and Singha (2019) investigated a very different yet important aspect of cryptocurrencies, namely cryptocurrency's connection to terrorism financing. The study found that the bitcoin economy has grown so popular around the world that it has spawned an alternative virtual economy outside of national or regional rules. It was discovered using the vector error correction model (VECM) that there is a statistically significant long-run relationship between terrorist incidents and bitcoin transaction/ circulation in a panel of 12 nations from 2010 to 2016. However, there is widespread concern about its business practises and potential ties to terrorism financing. Over a seven-year period, Othman, Alhabshi, and Haron (2019) investigated the effect of symmetric and asymmetric information on the volatility structure of bitcoin currency daily market returns using several GARCH family models. Because the parameters of ARCH (a), GARCH (b) in the conditional variance equation are statistically significant at the 1% level in all GARCH models, the results show that symmetric information affects the bitcoin market return linearly. Capar (2020) investigates and debates the usage of cryptocurrency and transactions in the medical tourism industry. The usage of cryptocurrencies and transactions, which are highly new and up-to-date, in the field of medical tourism, which has a high value-added and is still a relatively new field, demonstrates that it is both a technology-intensive and labour-intensive sector. The findings of this study are said to have sparked a debate among healthcare institutions and states that provide medical tourism services about whether or not to use cryptocurrency in their operations. It is reasonable to assume that the usage of bitcoin and transactions, as well as other significant variables, will henceforth be among the selection criteria for potential medical tourists.

Study Design/Methodology/Approach

The study will make use of documentary review method to present meaningful insights from multiple countries regarding aspects of technology invasion in the financial sector keeping in mind the crypto currencies and digital finance with an attempt to evolve a multi-stakeholder perspective keeping in mind all beneficiaries of the same.

These aspects shall be covered in our study to delineate the merits and demerits of technology intervention in the financial sector. Further, an attempt shall be also made to address the critical questions as follows:

- Role of Technology for Crypto currency trading? Enabling role or restraining role
- Is the emergence of digital finance becoming investor-centric or technology centric?
- Do digitalization initiatives enhance the financial literacy or lead to chaos?
- What is the role of the stakeholders when it comes to the aspect of governance of digital technologies in finance?
- How effective and safe is the use of AI/ML and other digitalization initiatives in protecting the interests of the investors?

Concerns

In 2017, Facebook announced an issue of cryptocurrency named 'Libra' which was renamed as Diem backed by reserved asset such as US dollar. The backup of Diem together with several billion users of Facebook will give clout to it to pull payment

Emergence of Crypto Currency and the Digital Financial Landscape

away from domestic currencies into its own Diem will undermine the sovereignty of central banks.The reserve backing will potentially give stable coin the gravitas to pull the transactions away from the national currency into its own medium, putting the central bank out of the loop on economic activity. The central bank in turn will loose its ability to set the interest rate, calibrate the money supply and control inflation. The another worrisome situation is the most of the stable coins are likely to be pegged to the dollar, the dominant reserve currency. The US might actually see that as an advantage as it will strengthen the reach of the dollar and therefore be disinclined to regulate them. In such a scenario, what will prevent such stable coins, operating beyond regulatory gaze, to delink from the reserve peg, become independent creators of money and dent the domestic policy of the emerging and developing country? Managing the capital account consistent with their inflation target is already a complex challenge for the central banks of emerging economies like RBI. In this situation, capital flight via crypto will exacerbate that challenge. an investor may put domestic money in crypto and exit out of it abroad in a hard currency, China have reported to loss as much as $80 billion via cryptos before they banned them in September.

The value of Bitcoin fluctuated between $1000 in 2017 and close to $70,000 more recently, this volatility in the value of crypto can cause financial instability. When exposed to such instability banks become vulnerable, of course the volume of transaction is small but looking at the explosive rate of growth in trade of crypto, this is a matter of concern. The shared worry for the government and RBI is potential loss of seigniorage revenue. When the RBI buys assets, such as government securities, it pays for them by printing currency – in effect creating money out of thin air. The returns RBI earns on the assets so brought consists its seigniorage revenues which eventually accrue to the government. Crypto can eat this revenue by rendering money supply itself a less potent policy instrument. Cryptos may be called currencies but they do not perform any of three functions of money – they are unsuitable as medium of exchange due to their volatility; they do not have fundamental value and store value. It is a matter of concern for government and central banks if the crypto investment moved from niche play among small set of informed investors to ill-informed investors, attracted by possibility of quick money riding intraday volatility have to be protected not only for their sake but also for wider financial instability repercussions. Sharp fluctuations in value can create spill overs for the financial system. Domestic money may lose some value due to inflation but crypto can crash.

A broad exit from the domestic currency reduces the monetary base and the effectiveness of monetary policy. Seigniorage revenue falls for the government . a decentralised and dispersed money supply would not cater and respond the need of domestic cycle. Since the benefits of issuing it would go to the private players, they would not be used to create public goods. The exchanges are only intermediaries and regulating cryptos is not sufficient, the technology itself id based on distributed ledger. The primary issuance of crypto is in the hands of anonymous people within a very opaque structure. Though this is the USP of crypto but is it possible to regulate such person or system? Again whom will the regulator proceed in the event there is disruption or loss to the investor? In absence of any regulations related to cryptocurrency, the biggest threat from Government's perspective might be, cryptos becoming conduits for illegal activities like money loundering, drug trafficking, financing of terrorism and defrauding of gullible investors. On the other hand, recognising cryptos an asset class and regulating them will allow the government to monitor the trading activity, tax the capital gains of the investors and enforce some standards of transparency and code of conduct.

As our Hon'ble Prime Minister Shri Narendra Modi said while inaugurating Infinity Forum, 2021, 'Now it's time to convert these fintech initiatives into a fintech the introduction of CBDTrevolution. A revolution that helps to achieve financial empowerment of every single citizen of the country. The introduction of a CBDT has the potential to provide significant benefits, such as reduced dependence of cash, higher seigniorage due to lower transaction cost, and reduced settlement risk. The introduction of a CBDT would possibly lead to a more robust, efficient, trusted, regulated and legal tender based payment option. In India, the Garg committee came out with the proposal of banning all private crypto currency with few exceptions. Now the question here is there are more than 6000 cryptos across the world and in India two or three are more popular. On what basis will the government make exception of allow certain specific cryptos?

Blockchain Technology and Crypto

The concept of acquiring peer-to-peer network is the first and basic step for operation of blockchain. Computer networks with a decentralised and distributed architecture are referred to as peer-to-peer (P2P). This means that each computer and device on the network has a unique share. There is no centralised administrator, therefore all network connections i.e. hosts have equal rights. The hosts communicate among each other about availability of all the data as well as resources in the P2P network without using a centralized server as mentioned the main aim of this network is to allow network devices to directly network with each other. On the internet, P2P networks are used to send and receive files, by sending and receiving data at the same time by the hosts. This technology provides significant advantage through decentralisation and involvement of all users in the process of transaction authentication. These users have democratically sanctioned a given activity without any control or monitoring from centralised server. A key characteristic of this technology is that it uses multiple

Emergence of Crypto Currency and the Digital Financial Landscape

decentralised sites at the same time to download material in chunks rather than a single central location.

The so-called Distributed Ledger Technology is also worth considering (DLT). It is a database or information record that is spread over a network. DLT access might be granted or denied. Blockchain is a collection of data from computers connected by a peer-to-peer network and is one of the numerous types of distributed registry. Unlike Bitcoin, blockchain technology can store a variety of data types (not only related to exchange and payments).In this, transfer of data via the network in an encrypted format, allowing the transaction to be safe. The existing set is expanded by the host for additional information during occurrence of new transaction, its accuracy against existing agreed standards must be evaluated by the other verifying hosts before adding it to a block. Each block has a unique identifier for the previous block's (hash), which binds the blocks together in a sequence. The following are some of the key features of blockchain technology (Finanse., 2018):

- acceptance of agreements based on the consent of all network members who validate the accuracy of the data;
- Protection of cryptographic transaction– the blocks are added in the sequence after verifying it with agreed standards by existing hosts. This simply means that it is not possible to change or erase these records or information recorded in a particular block without changing its hash. Because the blockchain is decentralised, it will continue to function even if a portion of the network fails.
- a chronological record containing dates and times;
- all data is digitally saved.

A system of distributed register stated above has a number of advantages. Network functionality is kept even when individual joints fail, unlike centralised systems. In absence of middleman in this P2P transaction, people don't have to check the credibility of anybody, which increases transaction trust and security. What is required is trust of user in a system as a whole. The security of data is also enhanced by removal of intermediaries. External entities obtaining personal data is now a security risk; but, with blockchain, even if any data is received by third parties it may become obsolete, which strengthens the security of users. Blockchain technology is being used in a wide range of industries for a variety of applications. The financial sector, on the other hand, is the most common usage of blockchain technology. Because they are subject to the oversight and intermediation of multiple entities, traditional financial settlements are highly formalised and constrained. Various centralised authorities and institutions control the traditional financial transactions as well as settlements, which make them limited and formalised. The most popular and well known application of blockchain these days is Cryptocurrencies but the significant reason of their popularity is originated from the above fact of traditional financial transactions.

Blocks are manufactured by so-called miners in the case of Bitcoin, who are paid in Bitcoins or other cryptocurrencies like Ethereum for validating the blocks. To validate the blocks, the miners employ excavators, which are special computing devices. "Cryptocurrency mining" is the term for the entire process. The Bitcoin example highlights how the blockchain principle can change the way money is exchanged. Significant number of processes will be replaced in near future by Blockchain technology in the banking sector, dramatically enhancing the payment process. Credit card payments take few hours but with blockchain these payments may be settled in real time using the universal ledger adjustment and thus, the wait of few hours is also not required now (Glaser, 2017). Blockchain executes the transactions and contracts automatically in secure, cost effective as well as transparent manner, therefore it has an ability to change the entire process of traditional transactions (Fairfield, 2014). N. Szabo has proposed the concept of "intelligent contracts" it combines computer protocols with user interfaces to carry out contract conditions (Szabo, 1997).Because of the blockchain system's capacity to create intelligent contracts more quickly utilising blocks, they are becoming more popular. According to the author, a unique method like this could eliminate the need for lawyers and banks to be involved in the asset agreement contracting process. Intelligent contracts can be used to handle both tangible and intangible asset ownership (Fairfield, 2014).

Ethereum, a decentralised system proposed by Buterin, is an exemplary example of blockchain technology that treats intelligent contracts in the model manner outlined above (Szabo, 1997). Ethereum is a fork of the Bitcoin blockchain that allows for a larger range of uses. According to Fairfield, blockchain technology enables contracts to be established using cryptography without the involvement of third parties such as a notary public, Ethereum, Buterin's decentralised system, is an exceptional example of blockchain technology that treats intelligent contracts in the model manner stated above (Szabo, 1997). Ethereum is a Bitcoin derivative that enables for a wider range of applications. According to Fairfield, blockchain technology allows contracts to be made using cryptography without the use of third parties such as a notary public, which was traditionally essential to build trust. Cryptography allows people all over the world to trust one another and share many types of resources through peer-to-peer networks over the Internet. Which was previously necessary to create trust Cryptography allows people all over the world to trust one another and share many types of resources through peer-to-peer networks over the Internet. M. Crosby distinguishes between financial and non-financial blockchain applications, both of which, in his opinion, have the potential to change the character of financial transactions and have an impact on a variety of other parts of daily life. Imogen Heap,

Emergence of Crypto Currency and the Digital Financial Landscape

a British singer, sells all of her songs via blockchain (Buterin, 2014). Blockchain technology, on the other hand, has a wide range of uses. However, because of the lack of management and monitoring provided by a public trust authority, the greatest impact is expected to be felt in regions that have traditionally relied on third-party services. According to M Atzori, blockchain has the capacity to reshape politics and society as a whole (Crosby et al., 2016).

If societies begin to be managed and safeguarded through decentralised platforms, many institutional functions may become outdated. According to M. Atzori, decentralisation of government services via certified blockchain blocks is both conceivable and desirable because it might significantly improve the operation of public administration (Crosby et al., 2016). Societal transformation is crucial in developing countries. Wealth can be better secured using blockchain. When the local government tries to expropriate landowners in the third world, proving ownership can be challenging. Combining land tenures with blockchain technology can alleviate these existential problems. However, as F. Glaser points out, the interplay between the digital and physical worlds could be a weak link, eroding the digital trust that the blockchain system has built up (Glaser, 2017). The scientific community is still debating whether blockchain-based cryptocurrencies can fulfil the same functions as traditional money. According to W. J. Luther and L.H. White, cryptocurrencies are rarely used as a means of exchange (Luther & White, 2014). On the other hand, F. Glaser provides empirical evidence that Bitcoin is used as a speculative asset (Crosby et al., 2016). If entrepreneurs adopted cryptocurrencies as a replacement for traditional money, buying and selling assets would become much easier.

As a result, blockchain has the potential to revolutionise how people pay for things in the real world. When acquiring a property, for example, home purchasers now incur considerable transaction charges. According to Goldman Sachs, by reducing errors and human labour, blockchain can cut insurance prices and save $ 2-4 billion in the United States. While IT specialists focus on the technical and cryptographic challenges faced by blockchain, IT engineering systems and other disciplines researchers explore market design, trust, and privacy problems, as well as how to adapt and deploy the new technology to best serve society. Additionally, this game-changing innovation has the ability to disrupt and develop new business models, even influencing whole industries. As a result, studies are being conducted on the intersection of business models, technology, and markets. The blockchain technology is always being improved, demonstrating the system's efficacy and usability. For digital ecosystems, new architectural components and a framework for implicational analysis of blockchain systems have just been introduced (Crosby et al., 2016). As previously said, cryptocurrencies are riddled with controversy since they bypass traditional financial systems such as banks and financial institutions, which provide cash and non-cash transactions. These institutions feel that cryptocurrencies offer

Emergence of Crypto Currency and the Digital Financial Landscape

a danger of losing money because they rely on turnover to generate revenue. The same can be said for states that can lose money as a result of traditional transaction taxes. Another crucial legal consideration is the anonymity of transactions and the absence of control over cash flow that results from the lack of a single issuer and intermediary capable of collecting data on individual capital movements.

The lack of supervision or control over the entire process by participating entities with even a modest ability to alter and manage the process is referred to as "anonymity." There are only a few regulations that govern how activities are monitored and modified when it comes to blockchain technology. Despite the fact that it is required by law for organisations to register their participation in turnover, there is no certainty that all firms will comply with this requirement and that transactions will be accessible. As a result, it is controversial whether such a system is secure for both states and people from a legal aspect. In many countries, several government entities actively fight the legality of such solutions. On the other hand, because of the inability to reach the source, i.e., the firm providing the services, prohibiting actions related to the movement of cryptocurrency would be extremely difficult. Only the service provider who has registered as an entrepreneur to legitimise his business can be identified. Governments and central banks that manage money markets in their respective countries as part of their monetary policies are also at risk. Governments are concerned about these vulnerabilities because cryptocurrencies can be used to launder money or fund illegal activities. Many areas of law, including financial law, commercial law, banking law, economic law, civil and criminal law, are affected by cryptocurrency turnover. Legislators all over the world are attempting to adjust to the new reality that has emerged as a result of the increasing popularity of block chain technology.

TECHNOLOGY LED DISRUPTION IN CRYPTO CURRENCIES AND DECENTRALIZED FINANCE [DEFI]- AN INTERFACE

In the following section, the authors have made an attempt to briefly highlight the technological breakthroughs in emergence of crypto currencies and Digital finance that has changed the financial landscape of India and rest of the world.

The rapid growth of the crypto ecosystem presents new opportunities. Technological innovation is ushering in a new era that makes payments and other financial services cheaper, faster, more accessible, and allows them to flow across borders swiftly. Crypto asset technologies have potential as a tool for faster and cheaper cross-border payments. Bank deposits can be transformed to stablecoins that allow instant access to a vast array of financial products from digital platforms and

Emergence of Crypto Currency and the Digital Financial Landscape

allow instant currency conversion. Decentralized finance could become a platform for more innovative, inclusive, and transparent financial services

Crypto currency represents the beginning of a new phase of technology-driven markets that have the potential to disrupt conventional market strategies, longstanding business practices and established regulatory perspectives that results in to the benefit of consumers and broader macroeconomic efficiency. Crypto currencies carry groundbreaking potential to allow consumers access to a global payment system that denotes notion of 'anywhere and anytime' in which participation is restricted only by access to technology, rather than by factors such as having a credit history or a bank account. Crypto currencies and block chains have given rise to a new constellation of "decentralized finance" or DeFi businesses and projects. DeFi aims to offer people access to financial services—borrowing, lending, and trading—without the need for legacy institutions such as banks and brokerages, which often take large commissions and other fees. Instead, "smart contracts" automatically execute transactions when certain conditions are met. DeFi is surging in popularity, with investors pouring tens of billions of dollars into the sector. Cryptocurrencies have also given rise to a new set of challenges for governments to contend with. The anonymity and portability of crypto currencies make them appealing to bad actors such as criminal groups, terrorist organizations, and rogue states. There are also uncertainties about the regulatory treatment of emerging financial technologies. In addition, crypto mining can require enormous amounts of electricity, which has led to concerns about its environmental effects. Meanwhile, the rise of DeFi and crypto payments has raised questions about consumer protection, market volatility, and the ability of central banks to carry out monetary policy. The rapid rise of crypto currencies and DeFi enterprises means that billions of dollars in transactions are now taking place in a relatively unregulated sector, raising concerns about fraud, tax evasion, and cybersecurity, as well as broader financial stability. If crypto currencies become a dominant form of global payments, they could limit the ability of central banks, particularly those in smaller countries, to set monetary policy through control of the money supply.

Given this backdrop, the technological forefront is a matter of great concern with crypto currencies.

The Major Trends Dominated Cryptocurrency in Recent Times

The highlight of 2021 was the adoption and acceptance of cryptocurrencies and related schemes among uses full stop Unicorn Rush this year, two Crypto start-ups - CoinDCX and CoinSwitchKuber - made a surprising entry with a billion dollar valuations. with industry estimates of 15 to 20 million Crypto users in the country and total assets over $ 6 billion, government stands on cryptocurrencies has noticeably

Emergence of Crypto Currency and the Digital Financial Landscape

softened. regulatory uncertainty persists, even as the latest reports suggest that the Crypto bill won't be tabled in the winter session of parliament. the regulatory uncertainty notwithstanding the Crypto ecosystem seems poised to grow further in the year ahead. the number of Crypto users in the country has grown at least 10 fold in the last one year. There is no reason why we should not grow 10XAgain in 2022 The biggest Crypto craze this year has been around NFTs (non-fungible token) with Bollywood icons like Amitabh Bachchan and Salman Khan launching their virtual collectibles. Interestingly, it's not only start-ups such as totality corp, NFTically, KoinArth and Bollycoin data entering the space - companies like MG Motors are also looking to leverage the trend. Totality Corp, a Web Gaming firm, is going a step further and building label NFTs based on Indian mythological characters. Cryptography, code and digital assets are challenging our conventional notions of everything from technology and money, to law and institutions, Web2 is broken. in web 3 and DeFi, a new internet and a new financial systems is being built. thousands of new founders can leverage this opportunity and create a decentralized web3 that will take shape within the next 4 to 5 years

The original Crypto currency held its crown as the biggest and most well-known token though not without a host of challenges biting at its heels. Bitcoin sold over one 20% from January 12 other than record of almost $65,000 April. fuelling it was Tsunami of cash from institutional investors growing acceptance by major corporations such as Tesla and MasterCard and an increasing embrace by Wall Street banks. spurring investor interest Where's Bitcoins purported inflation proof qualities - it has a capped supply- as record-breaking stimulus packages fuelled rising prices. yet the token stayed volatile, it slumped 35% in May before soaring to a new all time high of 69000 dollar in November. even as Bitcoin remained the go Tu To for investors dipping their toes into Crypto a panoply of new -some would say a joke- tokens entered the sector. Memecoins - a loose collection of coins ranging from Dogecoin and Shibalnu to Squid game that have their roots in web culture - often have little practical use. Degacoin, launch in 2013 as a bitcoin spinoff, soared over 12000% to an all-time high in May before slumping almost 80% by mid December. The Memecoin phenomenon was linked to the' 'wallstreet bets' movement, where retail traders coordinated online to pile into stock searches game stop corp, squeezing hedge funds short positions. as money poured into Crypto, regulator fretted over what they so as its potential to enable money laundering and threaten Global financial stability. long sceptical of Crypto Watch Dogs called for more powers over the sector, with some warning consumers over volatility. when Beijing placed curbs on Crypto in May, Bitcoin tanked almost 50%, dragging the wider market down with it.

Emergence of Crypto Currency and the Digital Financial Landscape

DISCUSSION

Cryptocurrency has been touted for its potential to usher in a new era of financial inclusion and simplified financial services infrastructure globally. To date, however, its high profile has derived more from its status as a potential store of value than as a means of financial exchange. That disconnect is now evolving rapidly with both monetary authorities and private institutions issuing stabilized cryptocurrencies as viable, mainstream payments vehicles. Concurrently, multiple private, stabilized cryptocurrencies—commonly known as stablecoins—have emerged outside of statesponsored channels, as part of efforts designed to enhance liquidity and simplify settlement across the growing crypto ecosystem.

Although the endgame of this extensive activity that spans agile fintechs, deep-pocketed incumbents, and (mostly government-appointed) central banks remains far from certain, the potential for significant disruption of established financial processes is clear. Against this backdrop in this chapter the authors' have made an attempt to offer a fact-based primer on the universe of collateralized cryptocurrency, an overview of several possible future scenarios including potential benefits and obstacles, and near-term actions that participants in today's financial ecosystem may consider in order to position themselves. Various public statements indicate that central banks envision CBDCs as more than simply a digital-native version of traditional notes and coins. Beyond addressing the challenge of greater financial inclusion, some governments view CBDCs as programmable money—vehicles for monetary and social policy that could restrict their use to basic necessities, specific locations, or defined periods of time.

Implementing such functionality will be a complex and multilayered undertaking. Meanwhile, central banks face the challenge of introducing a timely CBDC model at least on par with digital offerings of private-sector innovators in order to establish credibility with such efforts and achieve adoption. The current state of financial infrastructure in India will play a key role in determining the speed and extent of adoption of CBDCs, stablecoins, or non-stabilized cryptocurrencies. Those with limited present-day capabilities are prime candidates for a "leapfrog" event, similar to the rapid emergence of M-Pesa as a payments vehicle in sub-Saharan Africa or Alipay in China. In developed economies with existing real-time payments rails, the near-term incremental benefits of reduced (even instantaneous) settlement time from CBDCs may be somewhat muted if financial institutions are reluctant to invest in the necessary additional infrastructure. In these instances, distinct benefits of stablecoins (such as their ability to engage with smart contracts) may prove to be a more compelling and defensible use case over the longer term, depending on the exact CBDC implementation. Residents of countries with sovereign currencies lacking historical stability have been among the most active adopters of cryptocurrencies as a means of exchange, especially where they are perceived as less risky than the available alternatives. Along with the potential for digital currencies to foster financial inclusion for citizens lacking access to traditional banking services (utilizing a universal digital wallet instead of a traditional fiat account), such an environment could serve as an indicator for a market primed for a potential leapfrog event.

Policy Imperatives

Many governments initially took a hands-off approach to cryptocurrencies, but their rapid ascent and evolution, coupled with the rise of DeFi, has forced regulators to begin crafting rules for the emerging sector, a process that could take years. Regulations vary widely around the world, with some governments embracing cryptocurrencies and others banning them outright. The challenge for regulators is to develop rules that limit traditional financial risks without stifling innovation. Robust and globally consistent standards are needed to mitigate financial stability risks. Where standards have not yet been developed, regulators need to use existing tools to control risk and implement a flexible framework for crypto assets. The growing systemic implications of crypto assets may indeed warrant immediate regulatory action in some countries. Regulators must use existing measures and international standards by focusing on areas of acute risk, such as wallets, exchanges, and financial institutions' exposures. Authorities should ensure that the regulatory framework is flexible enough to be adjusted in the future, in line with forthcoming international standards. Interim measures should be taken, including clear consumer warnings and investor education programs, especially where crypto adoption has been fast, such as in some emerging market and developing economies. National regulators should enhance cross-border coordination of supervision and enforcement actions. For example, because it is difficult to implement and enforce an adequate regulatory framework, some authorities have taken strong actions, such as banning unregulated crypto asset activities. Although bans can have a direct impact on the business of crypto exchanges, individuals are still likely to be able to trade and exchange crypto assets by alternative means. Therefore, jurisdictions should actively coordinate with the relevant authorities and international standard-setting bodies to maximize the effectiveness of their enforcement actions and minimize regulatory arbitrage. Greater cross-border collaboration can enhance enforcement actions, but the resources needed for such enforcement may present a greater challenge for emerging market and developing economies. Swiftly tackling data gaps is central to inform policy decisions. Greater data standardization can lead to better oversight of new developments and a more accurate understanding of risks and can support proportionate regulation of crypto asset markets. In that regard, an international agreement on common minimum principles for data should be developed. A globally consistent taxonomy

Emergence of Crypto Currency and the Digital Financial Landscape

can help data standardization and cooperation. There is also scope for international coordination on compilation and sharing of data sources from private companies for regulatory and public policy purposes. Fintech innovation, including the crypto ecosystem, has the potential to improve fundamental aspects of the macro economy with better financial services and greater financial inclusion, especially in emerging market and developing economies. Policymakers need to balance enabling financial innovation and reinforcing competition and the commitment to open, free, and contestable markets, on one hand, against challenges to financial integrity, consumer protection, and financial stability. As a first step, regulators and supervisors need to be able to monitor rapid developments and the risks they create. Depending on country circumstances, various forms of crypto assets may be adopted, and their economic functions may vary. Different countries have different policy priorities arising from the degree of crypto adoption and their existing vulnerabilities. Risks to financial integrity are high from crypto assets operating on anonymous platforms, but they may be addressable for some stablecoins.

UNCERTAIN LANDSCAPE: THE WAY FORWARD

Clearly these technological considerations, regulatory actions, and market dynamics carry major systemic implications for banking and the payments industry. Sheer regulation is highly unlikely to suppress the demand for digital currencies, and innovators will continue to push the envelope by developing new uses and distribution models satisfying both demand and legislative requirements. Most likely there will be some form of coexistence. Within this continuum we may see flavors determined by geography, by market incumbency among private institutions, or by sector. Although the market is far too nascent to confidently predict outcomes, constituents from all corners of the payments ecosystem can take valuable steps to position themselves for the inevitable changes on the horizon. The policy imperatives shall delve around: Providers of financial services infrastructure should continually monitor the suitability of their design choices for future interoperability with digital currencies. Retail banks, merchants, and payment service providers might consider the level of infrastructure investment likely needed for successful implementation of crypto currencies.The impact of CBDCs on private-sector banks likely depends on the speed of their adoption. The task for government, central banks, and regulators is somewhat more straightforward: to some extent, their decisions will dictate the moves of other parties, although any traction demonstrated by in-market stablecoin solutions will necessarily factor into central bankers' approaches.

Emergence of Crypto Currency and the Digital Financial Landscape

With the relative disparate needs of the various groups that are or might utilize the various forms of cryptocurrency, it is clear that no currency will meet the relative demands for all. As acknowledgement and acceptance of cryptocurrencies' feasibility increases demand from various groups, they are likely to flourish in existing and emerging markets – though it is unlikely that a single currency will be able to meet the demands of all the groups that would use it. This will likely result in the creation of new cryptocurrencies or adjustments to existing ones to give their targeted groups the satisfaction and confidence needed to move forward. The dynamics involved in these developments will determine if the market is flexible enough to meet these needs and the volatility that would come with them. In moving forward; cryptocurrency is still in preliminary stages of development and adoption, giving rise to other challenges that have yet to be fully addressed or answered. There are many questions related to regulations and governance of cryptocurrencies for traditional markets. For example, within the current cryptocurrency taxing structure, are property or capital gains taxes appropriate for a currency? When used for transactions, should sales taxes be applied and how would they be incorporated? Additionally, while smart contracts eliminate intermediaries by setting payment conditions into code in the block chain, what sorts of risks could arise from vulnerabilities in contract code or unanticipated conditions? With no knowledge of the identities of the parties involved, how would an institution that used cryptocurrency be able to mitigate flaws in the contracts exploited by malicious actors? How would funds be recovered, or would they be? These sorts of questions will continue to surface as cryptocurrency tries to prove its validity in traditional markets and for institutions; an area that will require further examination. However, the developments that have progressed thus far show that cryptocurrency will continue having a growing presence, requiring governments, institutions and consumers to prepare to incorporate it into future.

The future of cryptocurrency in India appears on certain but that has not deterred young Indians from embracing the so-called fourth industrial revolution world, where interconnectivity and smart automation much of it relying on blockchain technology, drive human civilization. Reserve Bank of India governor has repeatedly warned of macroeconomic instability and even serious consequences if cryptocurrencies turn mainstream. the country's Monetary Authority wants a China like total ban on Crypto, not even allowing this currencies to be treated as Investments. India now has the highest number of cryptocurrency investors in the world. and experts say that despite the prevailing uncertainty, Crypto will continue to grow in the country.

Emergence of Crypto Currency and the Digital Financial Landscape

REFERENCES

A peer-to-peer electronic cash system. (n.d.). Retrieved December 13, 2022, from https://bitcoin.org/en/bitcoin-paper

Alqaryouti, O., Siyam, N., Alkashri, Z., & Shaalan, K. (2020a). Cryptocurrency Usage Impact on Perceived Benefits and Users' Behaviour. In M. Themistocleous & M. Papadaki (Eds.), *Information Systems. EMCIS 2019. Lecture Notes in Business Information Processing* (Vol. 381). Springer. doi:10.1007/978-3-030-44322-1_10

Alqaryouti, O., Siyam, N., Alkashri, Z., & Shaalan, K. (2020b). Users' knowledge and motivation on using cryptocurrency. *Information Systems Lecture Notes in Business Information Processing*, *381*, 113–122. doi:10.1007/978-3-030-44322-1_9

AmetranoF. M. (2016). Hayek money: The cryptocurrency price stability solution. *Social Science Research Network*.

Atzori, M. (2015). *Blockchain technology and decentralized governance: Is the state still necessary?* Working Paper. Available at: http://nzz-filesprod.s3-website-eu-west1.amazonaws.com/files/9/3/1/blockchain+Is+the+State+Still+Necessary_1.18 689931.pdf

Baur, A. W., Bühler, J., Bick, M., & Bonorden, C. S. (2015). Cryptocurrencies as a Disruption? Empirical Findings on User Adoption and Future Potential of Bitcoin and Co. In Lecture Notes in Computer Science: Vol. 9373. *Open and Big Data Management and Innovation. I3E 2015*. Springer. doi:10.1007/978-3-319-25013-7_6

Best, R. (2022, December 13). *Bitcoin price history Apr 2013 - Dec 12, 2022*. Retrieved December 13, 2022, from https://www.statista.com/statistics/326707/bitcoin-price-index/

ButerinV. (2014). A next-generation smart contract and decentralized application platform. Available at: https://www.intgovforum.org/cms/wks2015/uploads/proposal_background_pa per/SSRN-id2580664.pdf\

Çapar, H. (2021). Using cryptocurrencies and transactions in medical tourism. *Journal of Economic and Administrative Sciences*, *37*(4), 677–693. doi:10.1108/JEAS-07-2019-0080

Crosby, M., Pattanayak, P., Verma, S., & Kalyanaraman, V. (2016). *Blockchain technology: Beyond Bitcoin*. Applied Innovation Review. Available at https://j2-capital.com/wp-content/uploads/2017/11/AIR2016-Blockchain.pdf

Fairfield, J. (2014). *Smart contracts, Bitcoin bots, and consumer protection*. https://scholarlycommons.law.wlu.edu/cgi/viewcontent.cgi?article=1003&context=wlulr-online

Fanning, K., & Centers, D. (2016). Blockchain and its coming impact on Financial Services. *Journal of Corporate Accounting & Finance, 27*(August), 53–57. Advance online publication. doi:10.1002/jcaf.22179

Finanse. (2018). *Portal Podatkowy*. Available at: https://www.finanse.mf.gov.pl/c/document_library/get_file?uuid=589b1960-46fd-41f2-bf17-4adf96ae2e13&groupId=764034

Glaser, F. (2017). Pervasive decentralisation of digital infrastructures: a framework for blockchain enabled system and use case analysis. In *50th Hawaii International Conference on System Sciences*. HICSS. Available at: https://pdfs.semanticscholar.org/859d/0535e16095f274df4d69df54954b21258a13.pdf

Hashemi Joo, M., Nishikawa, Y., & Dandapani, K. (2020). Cryptocurrency, a successful application of blockchain technology. *Managerial Finance, 46*(6), 715–733. doi:10.1108/MF-09-2018-0451

Investopedia. (n.d.). https://www.investopedia.com/tech/most-important-cryptocurrencies-other-than-bitcoin/#:text=One%20reason%20for%20this%20is,communities%20of%20backers%20and%20investors

Jayawardhana, A., & Colombage, S. (2020). Does Blockchain Technology Drive Sustainability? An Exploratory Review. In Governance and Sustainability. Emerald Publishing Limited. doi:10.1108/S2043-052320200000015002

Lipton, A., Hardjono, T., & Pentland, A. (2018). Digital Trade Coin: Towards more stable digital currency. *Royal Society Open Science, 5*(7), 180155. doi:10.1098/rsos.180155 PMID:30109071

Luther, W., & White, L. (2014). *Can Bitcoin become a major currency?* Working Paper. Available at: http://bahler.co/wpcontent/uploads/2016/11/Can-Bitcoin-Become-a-Major-Currency.pdf

Majumder, A., Routh, M., & Singha, D. (2019). A Conceptual Study on the Emergence of Cryptocurrency Economy and Its Nexus with Terrorism Financing. In The Impact of Global Terrorism on Economic and Political Development. Emerald Publishing Limited. doi:10.1108/978-1-78769-919-920191012

Majuri, Y. (2019). Overcoming economic stagnation in low-income communities with programmable money. *The Journal of Risk Finance*, *20*(5), 594–610. doi:10.1108/JRF-08-2019-0145

Othman, A. H. A., Alhabshi, S. M., & Haron, R. (2019). The effect of symmetric and asymmetric information on volatility structure of crypto-currency markets: A case study of bitcoin currency. *Journal of Financial Economic Policy*, *11*(3), 432–450. doi:10.1108/JFEP-10-2018-0147

Ram, A. J. (2019). Bitcoin as a new asset class. *Meditari Accountancy Research*, *27*(1), 147–168. doi:10.1108/MEDAR-11-2017-0241

Raymaekers, W. (2015, March 1). Cryptocurrency Bitcoin: Disruption, challenges and opportunities. *Journal of Payments Strategy & Systems, 9*(1).

Reza, T. (2018). A Study on Digital Currency: The Safety of Future Money. *JurnalTransparansi*, *1*(1), 134–139. doi:10.31334/trans.v1i1.145

Słapczyński, T. (2019). Blockchain Technology and Cryptocurrencies – legal and tax aspects. *ASEJ - Scientific Journal of Bielsko-Biala School of Finance and Law*, *23*(1). doi:10.5604/01.3001.0013.2653

Spenkelink, H. (2014). *The adoption process of cryptocurrencies. Identifying factors that influence the adoption of cryptocurrencies from a multiple stakeholder perspective*. Google Scholar.

Szabo, N. (1997). *Smart contracts: Formalizing and securing relationships on public networks*. Available at: https://firstmonday.org/article/view/548

Tang, Y., Xiong, J., Becerril-Arreola, R., & Iyer, L. (2020). Ethics of blockchain: A framework of technology, applications, impacts, and research directions. *Information Technology & People*, *33*(2), 602–632. doi:10.1108/ITP-10-2018-0491

Venkatesh, V. (2000). Determinants of Perceived Ease of Use: Integrating Control, Intrinsic Motivation, and Emotion into the Technology Acceptance Model. *Information Systems Research*, *11*(4), 342–365. doi:10.1287/isre.11.4.342.11872

Wiatr, M. (2014). *Bitcoin as a Modern Financial Instrument*. https://rep.polessu.by/bitstream/123456789/5570/1/30.pdf

Yuneline, M. H. (2019). Analysis of cryptocurrency's characteristics in four perspectives. *Journal of Asian Business and Economic Studies*, *26*(2), 206–219. doi:10.1108/JABES-12-2018-0107

Chapter 10
The Exploratory Study of Machine Learning on Applications, Challenges, and Uses in the Financial Sector

Tripti Pal
RATM, India

ABSTRACT

Artificial intelligence (AI) and machine learning (ML) have become essentials part of our lives by having their applications in various fields. Artificial intelligence is a technology that allows a machine to behave like a human. Machine learning is a subdivision of artificial intelligence that helps a machine to automatically learn from past data with more accurate predicting outcomes. In today's life, especially during the COVID-19 pandemic, our lives run online and almost all work is done online like office work, education, shopping, medical facilities, etc., as are so many cases where machine learning is used in the finance sector like financial monitoring, making investment predictions, process automation, secure transactions, risk management, financial advisory, customer data management, decision making, business analysis, and customer service-level improvement.

INTRODUCTION

In today's epoch of digitization, staying modernize on technological advancements is a compulsory for businesses to both outsmart the competition and achieve belonging business growth.

DOI: 10.4018/978-1-6684-4483-2.ch010

Copyright © 2023, IGI Global. Copying or distributing in print or electronic forms without written permission of IGI Global is prohibited.

The Exploratory Study of Machine Learning on Applications, Challenges, and Uses

Machine Learning in finance sector is now become a key factor for some financial services and applications for evaluating risk factor, calculating credit score for approving loan and credit card, decision making, managing assets and prediction of data when large volume of data is store in to the computer system (Murugesan & Manohar, 2019) Machine Learning algorithms are used to detect and prevent fraud, predict approaching opportunities, automated trading activities, (Milojević and Redzepagic, 2021) study business cases, portfolio management and provide financial advisory services to investors. This study extracts the factors, which will help the researchers to promote the Machine Learning in Financial sectors.

Figure 1. Introduction to Machine Learning.
Source: - htttps://data-flair.training/blogs/machine-learning-tutorial

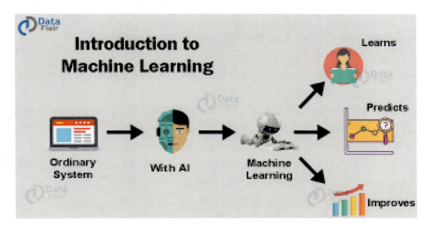

Nowadays, the finance industry, including the banks, trading, and Intec firms, are speedy use machine algorithms into their operations to automate time-consuming, mundane processes, and offering a far more streamlined process, reduced risks and personalized customer experience (Milojević and Redzepagic, 2021).

LITERATURE REVIEWS

This study Examine what is the impact of AI in banking sector & the application of AI that is used in baking sector. In this study they provides some reports for payment research. Business Insider Intelligence identifies the main three channel where banks use AI application to save cost at front offices, middle office, and back office. We also discuss the winning AI strategies used by financial institutions so far, and provide recommendations for how banks can best approach an AI-enabled digital transformation.

This study analyses now Indian banks uses the AI applications in term of customers satisfaction, digitisation process, fraud detection, fraud prevention, and the most important to provide privacy and security of data. They gives some examples of chatbot Application by banks like SIA by State Bank of India, Eva by HDFC and iPal by ICICI. Now banks uses the new business models with AI algorithms into systematic plans for analytics and for better customer satisfaction.

The study by Kou, G., Chao, X. Analyses that financial systemic risk has become a big problem to financial sector and market. So many machine learning algorithms have been developed to detect, find out, identify and prevent the risk in financial sector These algorithms provides some automated method that calculate the risk factor with high accuracy

How Does Machine Learning work in Finance?

Machine Learning works by find out significant data from raw sets of data and provides accurate results. This information is then used to solve complex and data-rich problems that are critical to the banking & finance sector (Milojević and Redzepagic, 2021)

Further, these machine learning algorithms are equipped to learn from data, processes, and techniques used to detect fraud, automate trading activities, and provide financial advisory services to investors (Donepudi, 2017).

Why Use Machine Learning in Finance?

Bring down operational costs because of process automation.
Upgrade revenues due to better productivity and improved user experiences.
Better compliance and reinforced security.

CHALLENGES FACED BY FINANCE COMPANIES WHILE IMPLEMENTING MACHINE LEARNING SOLUTIONS

Machine Learning is a key technology that more than 50% of businesses are at present used or planning to use (Donepudi, 2017). However, while implementing Machine Learning solutions, your business is likely to look at the positive side of things but there are multiple Machine Learning challenges encounter as discussed below ---

Lack of Understanding About Business KPIs

Finance industry want to deploy this great technology, but due to unrealistic expectations and lack of clarity on how AI and Machine Learning works, they often fail in this aspect (Milojević and Redzepagic, 2021). This could be due to a lack of experience as it is a newly appear sector or simply a more slim line staff body with no devoted department. So, the market is exceptionally competitive.

The High Cost of R&D

Financial services companies generally faced problems with data management having explode piece of data stored at different place such as reporting software, regional data hubs, CRMs, and so on (ALEXANDRE, M. (2021).). Prepare this data for data science projects is both time consuming and an expensive task for companies.

Lack of Machine Learning Experts

While developers are present in the Machine Learning journey, but a lack of skilled and developed ML experts yet rest the biggest Machine Learning challenges (Alexandre et al, 2021). You might not be capable to catch developers who can solve your problems.

Expensive Deployment

Mostly Machine Learning problem is the expensive deployment in the Business. Machine Learning implementation requires data scientists, project managers, and developers with skill technical expertise (Y, S. (2021)) .It is difficult to hire skilled experts at an affordable price. On the other hand, since Machine Learning algorithms work with big supply of data, these are additional infrastructure demands for implements. Without the proper infrastructure, testing becomes difficult.

MACHINE LEARNING USE CASES IN FINANCE

Here are a few use cases where machine learning algorithms can be/are being used in the finance sector.

Figure 2. Machine Learning Applications in Finance.
Source: - https://data-flair.training/blogs/machine-learning-in-finance/

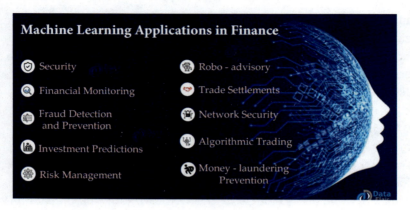

Process Automation

Process automation, is one of the most exciting technologies in the business world. Machine Learning provide finance companies to complete replacement manual work by Robotic Process Automation (RPA) for enhanced business productivity. RPA used to improve customer experience by adding chatbots as an additional interface for customers like SIA by State Bank of India, Eva by HDFC and iPal by ICICI (Balakrishna, D. R. (2020) Banking on AI). Chatbot, paperwork automation, and employee training are some common examples of process automation in finance using machine learning. This enables finance companies to enhance their customer experience, decrease costs, and expand their services (Donepudi, 2017). This process easily collect & access the data, interpret result, follow and recognize the patterns. This data or past data used for customer support system. It also learns from past experiences and uses for sharp analytics and forecast to timeline how tasks are completed

Secure Transactions

Machine Learning algorithms are superb to find out transactional frauds by examine millions of data points that not catch by humans. It also helps to find out many security points such as analysing documentation for account registration, detect issues with in account and more (Y, S. (2021)). Machine learning solution can also scan analyse millions of times and regulation content including legal documentation, guidance legal case, commentary to spot applicable requirements much more. Further, ML help to catch rejections and improve the precision of real-time approvals. These models are design behalf of client's behaviour on the internet and transaction history (Sadgali et al, 2019). Machine learning algorithms are very fast to assess these transaction with high accuracy. This speed helps to prevent frauds in real-time. This also help to find out doubtful account holder or person with high precision and prevent them in real time rather than the crime has been done.

According to a research, for almost every $1 lost to fraud, the recovery costs borne by financial institutions are close to $2.92.

Credit card fraud detection is the one of the best application of ML in bank. Tracking IP addresses of doubtful person from which a financial transaction done, help prevent fraud with discount coupons as well as identify fraudulent intentions.

Fraud Detection and Prevention

Machine learning algorithms are capable to analyse thousands of data points in real time and flag any suspicious of fraudulent transactions (Sadgali et al, 2019) thus stopping many fraudulent client in the process. The fraud detection tools can analyse client behaviours, track to allocation and determine purchasing habits therefore they can quickly detect any unusual activities (S, F., & M, R. (2021)). It also used to detect anomaly in spanning behaviour thus preventing step. Machine learning driven fraud analytic can process customer account transaction and even join special data to spot pattern that seems unrelated and simply go a notice by human data analytic. Machine learning based software that help banks to access perdition bar to immediately analyse countless fact that save cost and making the processes much faster.

Fraud is enormous problem for banking and financial services companies and it accounts for billions of dollars in losses each year (Sadgali et al, 2019). That's why one of the top reasons to introduce machine learning in finance. Losses experience by financial industry on all credit, debit, and prepaid general purpose and private label payment cards issued globally amounted to £16.74 billion ($21.84 billion) in 2015, according to a Bloomberg report.

The old Fraud detection systems were designed based on a set of rules & regulation which could be easily break down by cheater. So, today most of the industries purchase machine learning algorithm to prevent fraudulent financial transactions.

A global payment system Payoneer provides financial services and online money transfers worldwide. Accordingly, the company's customer database is estimated in millions. Since the company is a registered MasterCard provider worldwide, transaction security would fail without ML use cases in banking.

Machine learning has a potential to uncover money laundering activities by analyse transfer details about the money being mode, source, destination and the nature of via transfer along with the relationship of sender to the bank

Investment Predictions

The fact that Trading services using ML technology to understand Advanced Market. With the help of machine learning the fund manager predict market changes earlier than tradition investment models (Alexandre et al, 2021). ML technology assist to trading companies to maximize their investing opportunities with smart algorithms that know what is right time to buy and sell a stock (Song, X. H. (2014)). Even now the effective investing software help the user to place a preprogramed command on stock when it reaches a highest price or sell it the per-share price drops below a certain figure. It also predict the data based on automated analysis of market trade. But, if you think that with investment prediction your risk will be minimized, then it is never happening.

The most popular companies like JPMorgan, Bank of America, and Morgan Stanley have developed automated investment advisors that run on machine learning to enhance their bottom line. But, with that think that your risk will be minimized, then it is never happened.

Portfolio Management – Robo-Advisors

A portfolio is a collection of investment tools like bonds, shares, mutual funds, stock, cash and so on according to the person income, budget, time frame, risk tolerance power.

Portfolio management is an automated financial advice to individual's investor as per their income, budget, age and risk tolerance power (Kou et al, 2019). Portfolio management is the combination of basic three elements: investing time, changes in investments, and ability to undertake risk. Portfolio management is the art and science of suggesting the best and unique investment policy based on their financial situation with minimum risk.

Robo-Advisor are very common application of ML in finance domain. The application uses algorithms and statistics to automatically allocate, (Sadgali et al, 2019) establish, manage the investment of clients and optimize the clients' assets in real time market(ALEXANDRE, M. (2021).) AI power tool can help traders streamline the account opening

process and advise them on scaling their portfolio This could include financial plan, advising of plan home purchaser, retirement, protection need, asset planning etc. ML can used to optimize trade according to price and from which channel process to payment more quickly.

These services are cheaper than human financial advisor. Robo-advisors needed low account minimums.

Process Optimization

This aim to reduce operation cost and drive profitably in both front and backend activities such as:-

Claims Processing

Using artificial intelligence NLP we can analyse large volume of data about policy holder, their activities, habits etch in order to offer a more customized product in real time.

Mortgage Processing

NLP can be used to automatically read and understand documents that involve in loan and mortgage processing.

Customer Services

Custom built intelligent chatbots can be used to streamline TDS customer service processes to automatic solve simple customer request and prioritise other ticket based on sentiment for routing to the right things.

Operations Cost Reduction

Machine learning Algorithms handle large quantity of data thus increasing efficiency, accuracy and speed of mathematical calculation resulting in reduced operation cost.

Credit Decisioning

Through AI banks can capture data by analyse mobile phone activities, social media uses etc. to capture a more accurate assessment for credit worthiness (Alexandre et al, 2021) this will result faster and cheaper credit scoring and ultimately may quality loan assessment accessible to large number of people.(Farheen, S. and Raghuwanshi, M., 2021) It is also used to analyse large amount of financial or nonfinancial data using trend machine learning to predict credit defaulter with great accuracy than tradition method.

Trading and Wealth Management

Banks Increasingly using ML algorithms to derive new trading & investment strategies. They can analyse massive of data much quickly and perdition made by algorithms are much more accurate because they can analyse lots of historical data(S, F., & M, R. (2021)). It can also analyse specific investor long term and short term goal to provide recommendation on behalf of strong portfolio. Trading AI tact to_predict power of data helps to find spot new trends and potentially profitable trends the outside of human cup of understanding also helps for spot new signals of price movement to make more rapid trading decision (Alexandre et al, 2021). ML algorithms can provide a fast analyse of both structure and unstructured data related to stock market which capable to quick decision making.

Marketing and Customer Services

Using various machine learning solutions such as sentiment analysis, keyword matching, event extraction etc (Kou et al, 2019). We can answer question such a how can I keep my customer happy, what are people saying about me, who is interested in my product and what happen with my computer.

CONCLUSION

Machine Learning & AI Application in financial sector has become an important tool in the present era. ML algorithms are more accurate more efficient & more effective. They over take the financial sector we cannot do anything without them because they provide automation in all process & accuracy in calculation. ML & AL provide a new way to fulfil customer demands, who wants a smart, safe, convenient & effective process to save, spend & invest their money with all update on a single click. ML algorithm prevent fraud detect fraud find credit score, risk factor etc. So this technology become the essential part of financial sector in this modern era.

REFERENCES

Alexandre, M., Silva, T. C., Connaughton, C., & Rodrigues, F. A. (2021). The drivers of systemic risk in financial networks: A data-driven machine learning analysis. *Chaos, Solitons, and Fractals, 153*, 111588.

Donepudi, P. K. (2017). Machine learning and artificial intelligence in banking. *Engineering International*, *5*(2), 83–86. doi:10.18034/ei.v5i2.490

Kou, G., Chao, X., Peng, Y., Alsaadi, F. E., & Herrera-Viedma, E. (2019). Machine learning methods for systemic risk analysis in financial sectors. *Technological and Economic Development of Economy*, *25*(5), 716–742. doi:10.3846/tede.2019.8740

Milojević, N., & Redzepagic, S. (2021). Prospects of artificial intelligence and machine learning application in banking risk management. *Journal of Central Banking Theory and Practice*, *10*(3), 41–57. doi:10.2478/jcbtp-2021-0023

Murugesan, R., & Manohar, V. (2019). AI in Financial Sector–A Driver to Financial Literacy. *Shanlax International Jou*, 66-70.

S, F., & M, R. (2021). Performance of Machine Learning Techniques in the Prevention of Financial Frauds. *International Journal of Computer Sciences and Engineering*, 27-29.

Sadgali, I., Sael, N., & Benabbou, F. (2019). Performance of machine learning techniques in the detection of financial frauds. *Procedia Computer Science*, *148*, 45–54. doi:10.1016/j.procs.2019.01.007

Song, X. H., Hu, Z.-H., Du, J.-G., & Sheng, Z.-H. (2014). Application of Machine Learning Methods to Risk Assessment of Financial Statement Fraud. *Journal of Forecasting*, *33*(8), 611–626. doi:10.1002/for.2294

Y, S. (2021). Machine Learning Applied in the Financial Industry. *Financial Forum*, 239.

Chapter 11

Transforming Retail Markets Through IoT and AI–Enabled Architecture to Identify COVID–19 Shoppers

Mohan N.
CMR Institute of Technology, India

Sanjeev Kumar Thalari
CMR Institute of Technology, India

ABSTRACT

The novel corona virus disease (COVID-19) is a pandemic, and quarantines are helping to stop it. However, defections of confined individuals around the world are causing considerable concern. This study examines the impact of artificial intelligence methods in the retail business utilizing a qualitative concept research approach. It's encouraging to see the retail sector steadily getting back on track following the impact of COVID-19. This hand band device will easily find the COVID-19 affected. Persons are identified by a 5-metre radius, and they are warned by vibrating. Finally, this chapter provides a conceptual framework for speeding up the struggle to prevent the spread of COVID-19 in India by combining IoT and AI technologies used to combat COVID-19 outbreaks around the world. Business decision-makers and managers should prepare their organizations and workers for the upcoming market shifts based on the findings of this research.

DOI: 10.4018/978-1-6684-4483-2.ch011

Copyright © 2023, IGI Global. Copying or distributing in print or electronic forms without written permission of IGI Global is prohibited.

Transforming Retail Markets Through IoT and AI-Enabled Architecture

INTRODUCTION

The Corona virus (COVID-19) epidemic was initially discovered in late December 2019 in Wuhan, China, and the World Health Organization (WHO) proclaimed it a global pandemic in March 2020. The real innovation in dealing with the pandemic came on the backend, as high-end Artificial Intelligence algorithms delivered advice to new and existing consumers. Artificial Intelligence is pervasive in our lives, despite the fact that many people are ignorant of it. AI has the potential to make significant improvements. It always starts with a consideration of what clients want out of their buying experience. Data collection, data transfer, data analytics, and data storage are the four major functional components of IoT. Data can be collected using sensors that have been installed .end-user mobile hardware, such as phones, robotics, and health monitors, have sensors. Transferring collected data to a central cloud server for data analytics and decision-making, such as if equipment maintenance is required to avoid an unknown future malfunction or a patient check-up is required [6–8]. The deployment of IoT systems in the medical industry took the shape of smart sensors, medical equipment, big data, cloud computing, telemedicine, clinical information systems, and a variety of other types of applications. In order to combat COVID-19, IoT technologies in the healthcare industry can be used for a variety of objectives depending on their application, such as remote patient monitoring, contact network tracking, and hand wash monitoring sensor-based devices. Because of the large and diversified datasets acquired through various data collection techniques, further integrating IoT applications in the retail sector, particularly during the COVID-19 epidemic, promises a faster, more accurate reaction and a better overall healthcare service. This paper presents the results of an exploratory study using a Conceptual quantitative Research methodology, based on AI & IoT Hybrid technology and a location intelligence solution provider for IoT the companies providing Low-Power WAN networking solutions, are launching several solutions to tackle the Covid-19 pandemic at different stages, using various geolocate.

This article covers the most important components of AI and IoT, as well as the methodology employed, the analysis and discussion of the research findings, and the study's conclusions.

The Importance of AI and IoT in the Retail Sector

Covid-19 is brutally transforming everyday businesses into futuristic supermarkets. With disrupted supply chains, they must accommodate all new grocery shopping behaviours, from panic buying to delivery and pickup alternatives. Grocery stores are reacting in different ways. Some are reducing the quantity of things they sell, some are bypassing wholesalers and directly contacting product producers, and yet others are giving their physical storefronts a total digital makeover. Voice recognition, image identification, and handwriting suggestions, all of which are available on today's smartphones are examples of AI in people's and businesses' daily lives. According to Kietzmann, Paschen, and Treen (2018), there are highly valuable AI systems for marketers in order to increase understanding of consumer decision-making, regardless of the course of action taken, AI retail solutions will greatly improve retail operations.

Artificial Intelligence

Computerized systems that capture data to fulfil duties of intelligent individuals in order to enhance their odds of success, according to Russell and Norvig (2016) Strong AI (Artificial General Intelligence) refers to a machine that possesses consciousness and a mind, as well as intelligence in multiple areas. Narrow AI (weak AI) concentrates on specialised tasks (autonomous automobiles are derived from Narrow AI) Furthermore, some authors speculate that computers may be superior or smarter than humans, resulting in a new AI term known as Artificial Super Intelligence, however this is yet speculative.

According to Rosenberg (2018), based on the Constellation study, Artificial Intelligence will be worth over 100 billion euros per year in 2025, compared to only 2 billion in 2015. The marketing industry will not be an exception, with increased AI investment The authors Chui, et al. (2018) discovered that marketing and sales, supply chain management, and production have the biggest impact on the potential value of AI use, based on McKinsey & Company's examination of more than 400 AI use cases in 19 industries and 9 business functions.

AI assists retailers in analysing client data and altering customer interactions. Furthermore, AI aids in the prediction of product demand, allowing retailers to better manage inventories and ensure that in-demand items are always available. The paper presents examples to show how using consumer data to modify promotions, such as daily offer customisation, can result in a significant boost in sales.

Internet of Things in Retail

The Internet of Things (IoT) in retail is a network of connected devices that work together to reduce the strain in retail environments and assist retailers digitise and optimise their brick-and-mortar establishments. Because of their capacity to track inventory in real time and increase engagement through gadgets like interactive smart mirrors, connected devices can make operations more efficient, allowing customers to have a better retail experience.

The most significant benefit of implementing IoT in the retail industry is that logistics and supply chains become more manageable. Inventory is tracked in real time with smart shelves and Radio Frequency Identification tags, so something being out of stock is nearly impossible. Retailers have a greater understanding of what is going on in the store. Interactive kiosks, tablets for salespeople, digital signage, mobile point of sale, and other innovations have all added to a retailer's expertise, resulting in a better in-store experience for customers.

There are many more possibilities that IoT can provide that have yet to be discovered. Self-checkout counters and virtual shelves have already made their way into a number of stores on a trial basis, and retailers intend to make the most of these features to improve the shopping experience and their own capabilities.

There are four fields that would benefit from the combined usage of IoT and AI

Inventory Control in Stores

Inventory may be tracked in real time, reducing the chances of things running out of stock. Predictive analysis can assist businesses in stocking up on things that are in high demand among customers and reducing the amount of useless merchandise in their stores. Inventory planning, tracking, stocking, and forecasting will all benefit from data insights.

Logistics and Supply Chain

With the help of AI-supplied data, IoT-driven solutions may help automate and improve the whole logistics and supply chain. When items approach a pre-determined lower limit, an ideal supply chain management system will automatically arrange them. It will be able to successfully control demand spikes caused by unforeseen circumstances.

Shopping With a Personal Touch

Retailers can leverage data obtained through AI and IoT to personalize ad promotions, provide product recommendations, and create digital signage content, among other things. Customers' tones may also be detected by the technology, which allows it to determine the best method to respond to their comments, questions, and complaints.

Optimization of Costs

It's impossible to create an ideal shop environment if the pricing aren't competitive. Data acquired from AI systems and a connected network of devices might be used to help determine when to lower commodity prices and when to raise them, based on demand and availability.

AI and IoT are developing technologies that have been used by a number of global retail behemoths. Amazon and Walmart have already begun to deploy them in their retail stores, and the effects are visible to the public. Amazon is developing a new technology for its grocery stores that will utilise artificial intelligence to provide customers with a checkout-free experience. while Walmart is working on introducing a smart shopping cart that helps buyers navigate around the stores and select what they want to buy from the smart shelves.

METHODOLOGY

This work is a descriptive and exploratory investigation of a single notion. The research methodology is qualitative and, most importantly, descriptive. This study attentive on the viewpoint of public who work with Hybrid AI & IoT Tech bees, built on the framework of AI & IoT Technology tackles useful in publicizing, offered in opinions sage, even if clients constantly undertake themselves as vital and organizing facts in investigation, due to their continuous association with them.

Because this is an experimental and descriptive study, the goal is to learn about the tactics of firms that utilise AI, the benefits, the hurdles, the ethical considerations, and the financial impact of these activities.

Research Objectives

The results of the investigation were favourable.

1. To learn about retailers' methods for reducing Covid -19 afflicted customers using IoT and AI.
2. To be aware of the benefits and problems those are provided, as well as the ethical issues and the financial impact of IoT devices and AI on businesses.
3. To understand the significance of how this IoT Device will deduct Covid afflicted shoppers, preventing them from entering the store and spreading the virus...
4. This research will help companies support and execute successful IoT and AI technology in order to save lives.

Changes in Retail Operations

A pandemic is defined as "the worldwide spread of a novel illness "by the World Health Organization (WHO). A pandemic is defined as "an epidemic that occurs worldwide, or over a huge area, crosses international borders, and usually affects a large number of people"

The WHO declared the outbreak of new corona virus disease "(n CoV or COVID-19 or SARS-CoV-2) a pandemic on March 11, 2020" with more than 2.1 million confirmed infections, 135 thousand confirmed deaths, and spread throughout 213 nations, areas, or territories as of April 21, 2020 5:00 PM Indian standard time. Several COVID-19-related studies, including used an exponential growth function to numerically estimate the number of infections. If precautions such as quarantine and isolation of infected or exposed people are not taken, an outbreak of coronavirus infections could ensue.

Figure 1. System architecture of the IoT-Q-Band system

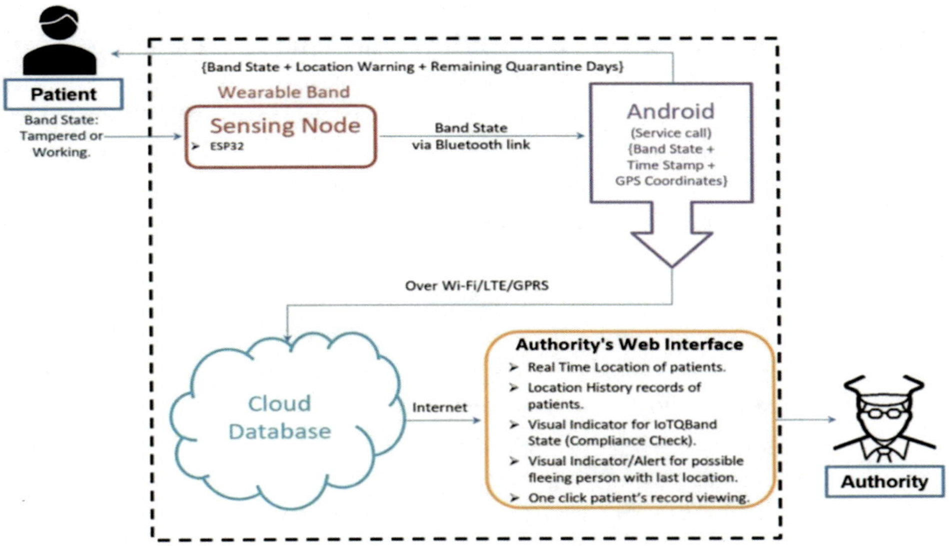

Quarantine (along with isolation and social distancing) plays an important role in limiting the spread of infections as defined by the WHO which is defined as "the restriction of activities of or separation of persons who are not ill but may be exposed to an infectious agent or disease, to monitor their symptoms and ensure the early detection of cases." When isolation procedures are implemented initial in a disease outbreak, the disease spreads slower and the peak of an epidemic in a country is delayed.

COVID-19 positive patients are primarily tracked using smartphone applications, such as Aarogya Setu. This has been working on the concept of crowdsourcing from April 21,2020. The functionality of notifications to nearby users is limited, according to user reviews, because it presupposes that everyone with a smartphone has this app installed.

Users have also expressed worries regarding the validity of data entered into the app, implying the need for a verification or approval authority. Though mobile app-based tracking appears to be insufficient, a visual indicator-based tracking approach. As a result, none of the two techniques discussed appear to perform effectively in detecting Covid effected shoppers in supermarkets subjects in a timely manner, and they also breach the subjects' privacy in some way. According to various healthcare research, such as the use of a wearable device makes a patient more compliant to medical routines and limits; consequently, a wearable band would be an appropriate solution in this scenario.

As a result, we created a wearable band that, when combined with a smartphone app, can detect and monitor absconding quarantine subjects in real time. This wearable band is only meant to be used in retail malls for the duration of the shopping period, after which they must return to the retail customer case disc, where they will sanitise the device and charge it for the next use. Concerned CSD team are authorities to have control of the tracking system and are responsible for the initial subject registration, reducing privacy concerns and ensuring the legitimacy of the data.

The tracking technology creates real-time notifications and helps authorities to spot the Covid Effected Patents entering the store for buying in real-time by using GPS-based geofencing. During active shopping mode, the mobile app also detects any disembarkation or tampering with the wearable band. We made our prototype as simple as possible so that it required less maintenance. Keeping in mind the health and wealth of those who have been exposed to a COVID-19 positive patient, we have chosen wearable band components that help to detect COVID-19 positive patients from a distance of 5 metres and warns people who are wearing the band via messaging and vibration. Because the reuse of tainted devices is typically prevented in epidemic settings,

Figure 2. Monitoring Mechanism

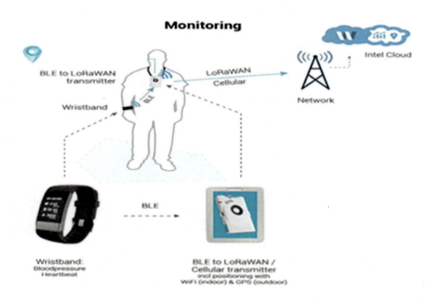

Figure 3. Data Flow Diagram of IoT Band System

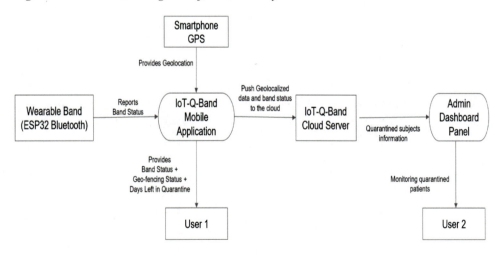

Software and Applications

Data Collection: The IoT generates vast amounts of data: from sensors attached to machine parts or environment sensors. The data collection software are used to filter, secure and measure this huge amount of data, but it's also used in distributing the data to various devices. That means the IoT is a significant driver of big-data analytics projects because it allows companies to create vast data sets and analyse them.

Device Integration: This software ensures that devices are able to bind and connect to networks establishing information sharing. A stable cooperation and communication is ensured between multiple devices

Real-Time Analytics: IoT analytics is performed by running data analysis software or procedures to the various types of IoT data. Using IoT analytics, valuable information can be extracted from massive data collections that can then be used to improve on procedures, applications, business processes, and production, while allowing automation and increasing the productivity.

Application and Process Extension: These applications are key component of any IoT system, as they extend the reach of existing systems and software to allow a wider, more effective system. They are able to integrate predefined devices for specific purposes. These software support improved productivity and more accurate data collection.

OVERVIEW OF THE SYSTEM

The architecture of the IoT-Q-Band system is shown. We took care to create the wearable band with as few components as possible so that it can run for a long time, and we re-used several smartphone features, such as internet and GPS access, because the wearable band is powered by a battery and should be lightweight for comfortable wear (like our previous work). A quarantine subject wears the wearable band on their hand, arm, or leg, which is wirelessly connected to the mobile application via a Bluetooth link.

The band's processing unit (ESP32) detects whether the band has been tampered with at regular intervals. After sensing, the band sends a status update (a byte of data) to the mobile app every two minutes. Only the concerned retail authorities will register the subject to the IoT-Q-Band system, and they will be responsible for determining the duration of the quarantine and authenticating the information. The authority's supervisory role eliminates the risk of harmful data entering the tracking system while also protecting the privacy of quarantine subjects. Along with the personal information, the GPS coordinates of the quarantine location are also saved throughout the registration process.

The mobile application demonstrations whether the wearable band is operating or has been tampered with, whether the subject is within a 50-meter radius (geo-fencing) of the registered quarantine location, and how much time is left in the quarantine. Following the early issue's record-keeping in the mobile application sends a JavaScript Object Notation (JSON) packet to the cloud server at regular intervals of two minutes, containing information about the wearable band's state (tampered or working), timestamp, and GPS coordinates (longitude and latitude). A designated individual can keep track of each quarantine case via a web interface that pulls up all active cases and displays them in a legible format. The data flow starts with the wearable band and ends with the one-to-one care web interface (admin dashboard panel) is represented.

Specifications for Implementation and Design

IoT architecture consists of different layers of supporting technologies that rely on each other for the scalability, modularity and configuration of IoT deployment in different scenarios. The functionality of each layer is briefly described below.

Smart Device/Sensor Layer

The lowest layer is made up of smart objects integrated with sensors. These devices consist of a variety of modules such as energy modules, power management modules, RF modules, and sensing modules. Most sensors require connectivity to the sensor gateways. This can be in the form of a Local Area Network (Ethernet and Wi-Fi connections) or Personal Area Network (ZigBee, Bluetooth and Ultra Wideband).

For sensors that do not require connectivity to sensor aggregators, their connectivity to backend servers/applications can be provided using Wide Area Network such as (GSM, GPRS and LTE). Sensors that use low power and low data rate connectivity, they typically form networks commonly known as wireless sensor networks. The WSNs are gaining popularity due to the fact that they are able to accommodate far more sensor nodes while retaining battery life and covering extended areas.

Gateways and Networks

Due to the large amount of data that is being produced by the sensors, a robust and high performance wired / wireless network infrastructure for efficient transport is required. Current networks, often tied with very different protocols, have been used to support machine-to-machine networks and their respective applications, but a wider range of IoT services and applications needs to be served such as high speed transactional services, context-aware applications. Multiple networks with various technologies and access protocols need to work with each other in a very heterogeneous configuration. These networks can be in the form of a private, public or hybrid models and are built to support the communication requirements for latency, bandwidth or security.

Management Service Layer

The management service renders the processing of information possible through analytics, security controls, process modeling and management of devices. One of the important features of the management service layer is the business and process rule engines. IoT is providing information in the form of events or contextual data (e.g. temperature of goods, current location, traffic data). Some of these events require response to the immediate situations (e.g. reacting to emergencies on patient's health conditions) while others require filtering or routing to post-processing systems (e.g. capturing of periodic sensory data). The rule engines support the formulation of decision logics and trigger interactive and automated processes to enable a more responsive IOT system. Various analytics tools are used to extract relevant information from massive amount of raw data and to be processed at a much faster rate. With data management in the management service layer, information can be accessed, integrated and controlled. Higher layer applications can be shielded from the need to process unnecessary data and reduce the risk of privacy disclosure of the data source.

Application Layer

The layers of the IoT architecture are of course based on the 2 basic components: hardware and software. IoT Hardware includes a wide range of devices such as devices for routing, bridges, sensors etc. These IoT devices manage key tasks and functions such as system activation, security, action specifications, communication, and detection of support- specific goals and actions. IoT Hardware components can vary from low to high power boards.

IoT Software

The most popular operating systems used in IoT are Linux or UNIX-like OSs like Ubuntu Core or Android. The programming languages on which IoT works uses very common programming languages like C++ or Java, but IoT software encompasses a wide range of software and programming languages. Keeping up with the development of big data related technologies, Python is one of the newer contenders to the role of most used programming language in IoT.

Transforming Retail Markets Through IoT and AI-Enabled Architecture

IoT System in the Analysis of Covid 19 Patients in Retail Malls:

In the midst of the Corona Virus pandemic, we designed the specifications of a system capable of detecting Corona Virus patients using an IoT system

The IoT system has multiple benefits in telemedicine: prevention and first aid for people who are susceptible to heart attacks, monitoring for epileptic seizures, monitoring for people suffering from alcoholism, screening for Covid patients 19 to name a few of the worst situations.

Figure 4. IoT System in Corona Virus Pandemic Situation

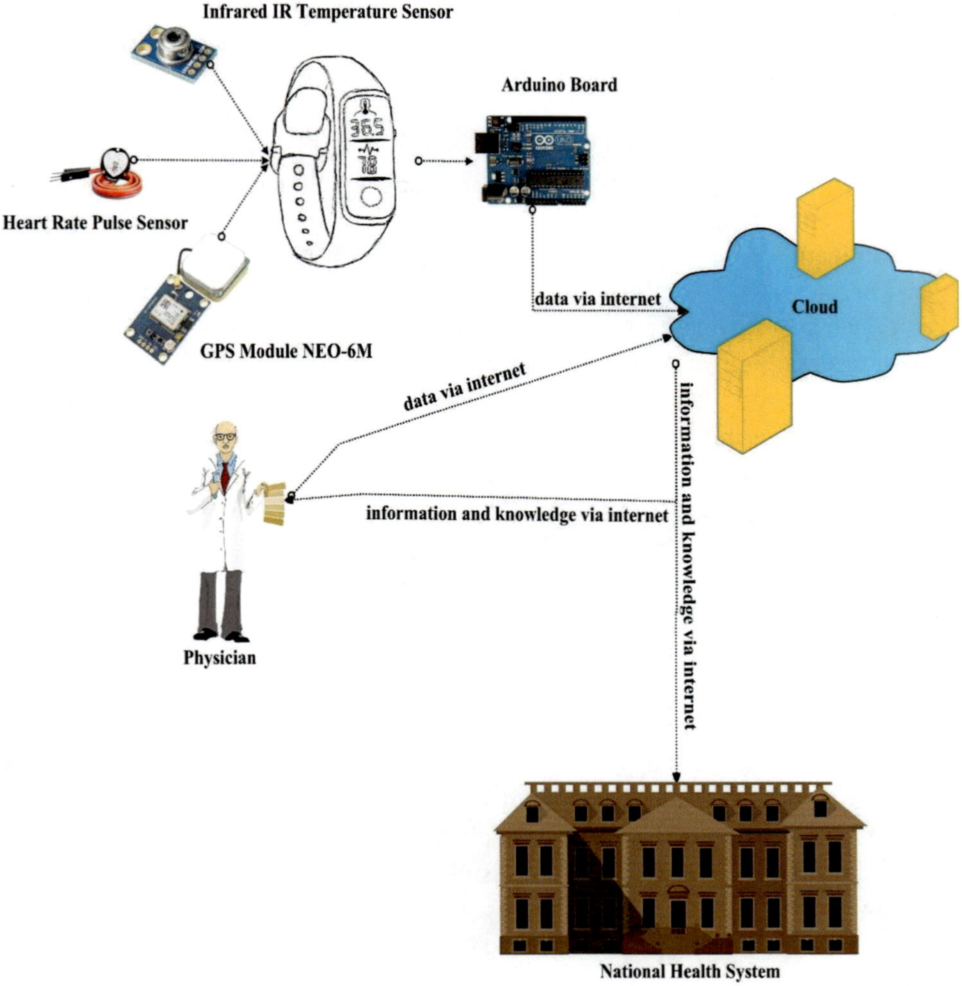

CONCLUSION

It is concluded that the IoT-Q-Band, with the included mobile application and cloud-based monitoring system, provides a scalable, low-cost solution to detect and track absconding COVID-19 quarantine subjects in real-time. The components of the wearable band, their mode of operation, and the battery are selected in such a way that they will remain operational throughout the quarantine time, which is also confirmed by the current consumption study. The reuse of IoT-Q-Band may be avoided due to the risk of contamination; hence, the cost of this prototype is maintained low by reusing various smartphone characteristics,

Integrating the benefits of tele retailing into an IoT system, such as the ability to access retail records through software and support for electronic communication channels between retailers and consumers, will upgrade our system towards a system that is not only suitable for the current crisis but also for long-term -useful in retail management systems.

The IoT-Q-Band could serve low-income areas of the world as a cost-effective option for keeping track of quarantine subjects. It's a new playbook for retailers, one that encourages them to move away from retail automation and toward retail customization.

This idea has potential to be intriguing. With the advent of AI marketing, traditional automated marketing approaches have been postponed to personalization, voice and image recognition, chat bots, churn forecasts, dynamic pricing and more consumer analytics entered the picture. Retailers must comprehend and support this item or concept to determine whether it is best for their business objectives and revenue generation, even when it takes a small investment.

Future Work

To gain a deeper knowledge of the influence of AI and IoT technology on business in retail supermarkets, this research must be completed with testimonials from business management to provide a more definitive image of AI's impact. Remote collaborations were used to conceptualise and construct the prototype while keeping a lockdown situation in mind. On the 24th of March 2020, India fell under complete lockdown, which was extended until the 14th of April 2020 (and was subsequently extended until the 3rd of May 2020). This severely hampered the supply of components and movement around the country. As a result, the prototype's current status throws up a slew of new possibilities for researchers.

Using data from biosensors connected to IoT-Q-Band and machine learning to estimate the likelihood of a person breaking out of quarantine would be the correct direction. It's also a good idea to look into device power optimization and proper battery research. Finally, we used electronic watch as a possible skeleton for the device, make the wearable comfortable enough to be worn across arms, on the other hand, by giving this devise to window shoppers who are visiting to retail supermarket we observe how this band will work it was successful experiment shoppers were constantly present, as proven throughout this paper, and understanding the influence on their lives is critical in future work.

ACKNOWLEDGMENT

The authors would like to thank the tech creators and technical staff for enabling remote collaboration of CMR – Institute of Technology, Bangalore department of ECS for their important contribution to this research. The authors are staunch believers in the use of wearable technologies, but only for humanitarian reasons. Any invasion of an individual's privacy through the use of a mobile device is unethical and strongly condemned.

REFERENCES

Aghenta, L. O., & Iqbal, M. T. (2019) Low-Cost, Open Source IoT-Based SCADA System Design Using Thinger. *IO and ESP32 Thing. Electronics, 8*(8), 1-24.

Boillat, T., Rivas, H., & Wac, K. (2018). "Healthcare on a Wrist": Increasing Compliance Through Checklists on Wearables in Obesity (Self-) Management Programs. Digital Health. Health Informatics, 65-81.

Brannon, E., Cushing, C., Crick, C., & Mitchell, T. (2016) the promise of wearable sensors and ecological momentary assessment measures for dynamical systems modeling in adolescents: a feasibility and acceptability study. *Translational Behavioral Medicine, 6*(4), 558–565.

Breakfast, S. (2020). *KwaZulu-Natal COVID-19 patient charged after absconding quarantine*. News, The South African.

Caruso, G. D. (2016) Free will skepticism and criminal behavior: A public health-quarantine model. *Southwest Philosophy Review, 32*(1), 25-48.

Deekshith, M. (2020). Covidiots everywhere: Cases of foreign returnees flouting home quarantine in rise. *Nation, Current Affairs, Deccan Chronicle*.

DiGiovanni, C., Conley, J., Chiu, D., & Zaborski, J. (2004). Factors influencing compliance with quarantine in Toronto during the 2003 SARS outbreak. *Biosecurity and bioterrorism: Biodefense strategy, practice, and science, 2*(4), 265-272.

Eden, A., Steinhart, E., Pearce, D., & Moor, J. (2012). *Singularity Hypotheses: An Overview*. Springer., doi:10.1007/978-3-642-32560-1

Espressif Systems. (2020). *ESP32 Series Datasheet*. Datasheet. Author.

Fitzsimmons, C. (2020). They haven't listened: Medical professionals skipped quarantine and flew interstate. *News, The Sydney Morning Herald*.

Indiatimes. (2020). Coronavirus suspects under home quarantine to have their left hand stamped in Maharashtra. *News, The Economic Times*.

Ivanov, D. (2020). Predicting the impacts of epidemic outbreaks on global supply chains: A simulation-based analysis on the coronavirus outbreak (COVID-19/SARSCoV-2) case. Transportation Research Part E: Logistics and Transportation Review, 136, 1-14.

Kietzmann, J., Paschen, J., & Treen, E. (2018). Artificial intelligence in advertising: How marketers can leverage artificial intelligence along the consumer journey. *Journal of Advertising Research, 58*(3), 263–267. doi:10.2501/JAR-2018-035

Liu, T. (2020) *Transmission dynamics of 2019 novel coronavirus (2019-nCoV)*. DOI: doi:10.1101/2020.01.25.919787

Loos, J. R., & Davidson, E. J. (2016). Wearable health monitors and physician-patient communication: the physician's perspective. *Proceedings of 2016 49th Hawaii International Conference on System Sciences (HICSS)*, 3389-3399. 10.1109/HICSS.2016.422

Mahale, A. (2020). Coronavirus | Western Railway deboards 17 passengers bearing home quarantine stamp. *News, The Hindu*.

Maier, A., Sharp, A., & Vagapov, Y. (2017). Comparative analysis and practical implementation of the ESP32 microcontroller module for the internet of things. In *Proceedings of 2017 Internet Technologies and Applications (ITA)* (pp. 143–148). IEEE. doi:10.1109/ITECHA.2017.8101926

MajumderM.MandlK. (2020). *Early Transmissibility Assessment of a Novel Coronavirus in Wuhan, China*. doi:10.2139/ssrn.3524675

Makridakis, S. (2017). The forthcoming Artificial Intelligence (AI) revolution: Its impact on society and firms. *Futures, 90*, 46–60. doi:10.1016/j.futures.2017.03.006

Mohammed, A., Abdul Kareem, K. H., Al-Waisy, A. S., Mostafa, S. A., Al-Fahdawi, S., Dinar, A. M., Alhakami, W., Baz, A., Al-Mhiqani, M. N., Alhakami, H., Arbaiy, N., Maashi, M. S., Mutlag, A. A., Garcia-Zapirain, B., & De La Torre Diez, I. (2020). Benchmarking methodology for selection of optimal COVID-19 diagnostic model based on entropy and TOPSIS methods. *IEEE Access: Practical Innovations, Open Solutions*, *8*, 99115–99131. doi:10.1109/ACCESS.2020.2995597

Mu-chun, S., & Kao, E. (2020). *6 suspected Vietnamese stowaways escape from quarantine*. Society, Focus Taiwan.

Pandey, A. (2020). *Coronavirus in India: Man stamped for quarantine in Mumbai caught at Secundarabad railway station*. News, India Today.

PRNewswire. (2018). *Despite the Buzz, Consumers Lack Awareness of the Broad Capabilities of AI*. https://www.prnewswire.com/news-releases/despite-the-buzz-consumers-lackaware ness-of-the-broad-capabilities-of-ai-300458237.html

Russell, S.J., & Norvig, P. (2016). *Artificial Intelligence: A Modern Approach*. Pearson Education Limited. doi:10.1016/j.artint.2011.01.005

Sarjerao, B. S., & Prakasarao, A. (2018). A Low Cost Smart Pollution Measurement System Using REST API and ESP32. *Proceedings of 2018 3rd International Conference for Convergence in Technology (I2CT)*, 1-5. 10.1109/I2CT.2018.8529500

Sethi & Sarangi. (2017). Internet of Things: Architectures, protocols, and applications (2017). *Journal of Electrical and Computer Engineering*, *2017*(1), 1–25.

Siau, K. L., & Yang, Y. (2017). Impact of artificial intelligence, robotics, and machine learning on sales and marketing. *Twelve Annual Midwest Association for Information Systems Conference*, 18–19.

Singh, V.K., Chandna, H., & Upadhyay, N. (2019). SmartPPM: An Internet of Things Based Smart Helmet,Design for Potholes and Air Pollution Monitoring. *EAI Endorsed Transactions on Internet of Things*, *5*(18), 1-9.

Sohrabia, C., Alsafib, Z., O'Neilla, N., Khanb, M., & Kerwanc, A. (2020). World health organization declares global emergency: A review of the 2019 novel coronavirus (COVID-19). *International Journal of Surgery*, *76*(4), 71–76. doi:10.1016/j.ijsu.2020.02.034 PMID:32112977

Sung, M., Marci, C., & Pentland, A. (2005). Wearable feedback systems for rehabilitation. Journal of NeuroEngineering and Rehabilitation, 2(17). doi:10.1186/1743-0003-2-17

Wilder-Smith, A., & Freedman, D.O. (2020). Isolation, quarantine, social distancing and community containment: pivotal role for old-style public health measures in the novel coronavirus (2019-nCoV) outbreak. *Journal of Travel Medicine, 27*(2), 1–4.

Ye, Z., Zhang, Y., Wang, Y., Huang, Z., & Song, B. (2020). Chest CT manifestations of new coronavirus disease 2019 (COVID-19): A pictorial review. *European Radiology, 30*(8), 4381–4389. doi:10.100700330-020-06801-0 PMID:32193638

Zhao, S. (2020) Preliminary estimation of the basic reproduction number of novel coronavirus (2019-nCoV) in China, from 2019 to 2020: A data-driven analysis in the early phase of the outbreak. International Journal of Infectious Diseases, 92, 214-217.

Zhong, R. Y., Xua, X., Klotz, E., & Newmanc, S. T. (2017). Intelligent manufacturing in the context of industry 4.0: A review. *Engineering, 3*(5), 616–630. doi:10.1016/J.ENG.2017.05.015

Chapter 12
Data Modeling in Finance Challenges

Prasanth Kumar Ra
https://orcid.org/0000-0001-5299-7701
University of Hyderabad, India

Santosh Kumar
PNC Financial Services, USA

Vikas Singh
Ministry of Consumer Affairs, Government of India, India

ABSTRACT

This chapter aims to draw readers' attention on the challenges of modeling in finance. The new quantitative methods offer extraordinary capabilities with the latest algorithms using AI, ML, etc., aided by high technological computational power. However, the adoption of the latest tools and techniques comes with many challenges that are limited by human resources and nuances of financial industries. Unlike the recommendation-based models in the technology industry, real money is at stake in the financial industry. Hence, it is not very prudent to accept the result of quantitative methods without understanding the inherited risks. Despite the hype created by data scientists, the financial industry cautiously adopted the highly complicated learning tools after due diligence because investor and shareholder money is at stake and experts want to strategize financial decisions based on the data model outputs. Further, the chapter brings the key highlights of financial models.

DOI: 10.4018/978-1-6684-4483-2.ch012

Copyright © 2023, IGI Global. Copying or distributing in print or electronic forms without written permission of IGI Global is prohibited.

INTRODUCTION

Quantitative methods have been applied in financial decisions quite for a long time. However, the application of quantitative methods has accelerated rapidly with the advancement of mathematical research and computational abilities. Modeling in finance using quantitative methods has provided a multitude of opportunities to enhance financial institutions' efficiency and risk management capabilities. However, it has its challenges while developing and deploying the financial models in the finance domain.

This chapter discusses the various challenges encountered in building models for financial institutions. It is important to note that financial modeling has been rapidly evolving recently, and the challenges are not limited to the issues listed in this chapter. Every new method and tuning the model using a new algorithm has its unique challenges. This chapter describes the most commonly encountered problems during the modeling process.

DATA CHALLENGES

The first step in the modeling process is to collect data from available sources. There are multiple considerations involved while building a suitable dataset for training a model.

Quantity of Data

Financial institutions have been collecting their customers' data for a very long time. However, the data was mainly in the paper format until the advancement of computer technology. Only the last few decades of data are available in a machine-readable format for modeling purposes. Further, the various financial institution adoption of data processing evolved over a while. Nevertheless, all financial institutions have not followed the same data process. Also, it is essential to note that the evolution of financial products has also changed over the period. Hence, some products do not have sufficient data history to perform modeling. Small banks and even large banks with specialized portfolios, like the utility industry in wholesale banking, always lack sufficient default data to perform modeling (Kiefer, N. M, 2009).

Quality of Data

The quality of data is key to building a robust financial model. Due to multiple reasons, the quality of historical data has to be compromised and unsuitable for

Data Modeling in Finance Challenges

modeling—some of the common issues in historical data caused by technological glitches in the past. The second issue could be an improper control process while collecting the data. The input data might be fed incorrectly without applied checks before saving it. Another critical issue could be that the data definition may have changed over time due to business reasons, and hence the data appropriateness can be questionable. The data quality could be compromised, and adopt alternative modeling processes to overcome the challenges (Bansal, A., Kauffman, R. J., & Weitz, R. R., 1993).

Availability of Data

Financial institutions often have no relevant data for modeling a specific scenario. As the banks and financial institutions launch new financial products, finding pertinent data modeling to match the requirement is problematic. It becomes necessary to look for data from external sources to perform such an exercise in such a situation. Another issue could be that banks could be collecting limited data from the existing product history, and now the banks were to add build-in financial models with more attributes. Financial modeling may require a combination of internal and external data to perform the analysis. It is challenging to build a model for the extreme economic situation, either great recession or great moderation (Keen, S., 2013).

Data Exclusions

In the modeling process, one may desire to use all the historical data collected to develop a model. However, under most circumstances, some data needs to be excluded before starting the model development. The exclusion could be that data was erroneously collected, or the portfolio mix may have changed over the period. Some components no longer reflect the current or expected future portfolio. Another vital issue could be missing multiple key attributes for some populations, and hence the exclusion may be warranted.

Economic Cycle

Ideally, the modeling data should contain sufficient variation so that the parameter estimates can capture the underlying behavior of crucial factors. To ensure that the financial data have sufficient variation, it must contain complete economic cycles with multiple recession periods. As the economic recession is few, maximum of one to two recessions in each decade, it is challenging to have multiple recessionary periods in the data. If the modeling does not contain any data from the recession

Data Modeling in Finance Challenges

period, the usability of the model dramatically reduces during adverse economic situations (Panoš, J., & Polák, P., 2019).

MODEL DEVELOPMENT CHALLENGES

Outliers Analysis

Data analysis is an essential step before training the model. The analysis begins with data distribution that has some outliers. The outliers in the data can result in model misspecification (Ané, T., Ureche-Rangau, L., Gambet, J. B., & Bouverot, J., 2008) and need to be capped and floored within the range bound to the real values. The bottom and top percentiles clipped during the process to make it more reasonable.

Missing Data Processing

Another step in data processing is to evaluate the missing data. Options include deleting observations with missing information or imputing ad hoc values that can potentially fail to deliver efficient and unbiased parameter estimates (Kofman, P., & Sharpe, I. G., 2003). The missing data can be assigned zero values or some other justifiable values derived from the proximate data point of the same borrower, as the borrower profile does not expect to change drastically within a short run. The model should ensure that the trend and relationship of the independent variable remain intact, which produces unbiased results due to the missing imputation process.

Data Trend Analysis

The independent variables are analyzed separately before building the model. The plotted variable distribution and trends enable us to inspect them visually and perform multiple tests for assessing the suitability of the variable. One such test is to find the stationarity of the variable. If the independent variable is not stationary, some transformation may be applied to achieve stationarity.

Variable Transformations

Independent variables in the raw forms are easier to interpret. However, it is beneficial to perform some data transformations on the input variables to get the most valuable output from the model development. As the transformation includes lead, lag, moving average, square, cubical, and logarithmic, the data size increases dramatically, creating more challenges in the model selection process. The lead-lag relationship

186

Data Modeling in Finance Challenges

in economic data is essential for many economic agents such as policymakers, traders in financial markets, and other market participants (Funashima, Y., 2017).

Relationship With Target Variable

The independent variables are tested against the target variable to understand their relationship. The relationship trend should show an intuitive pattern that can be justifiable by the business logic and experience in the past. Furthermore, the relationship should fulfill the requirement of the mathematical algorithm proposed in the model; for example, linear regression should use variables with factors having a linear relationship with the target variable. If the independent variable does not meet the requirement of the algorithm, then the variable needs to be transformed using suitable methods.

Segmentation and Clustering

The modeling population can mix multiple subsegments, each having some unique features; for example, a Middle market business portfolio could mix multiple industries. The clustering analysis helps better understand the data trends, and it varies across subpopulations upon the unique feature of each segment. Research shows that the Time series of financial asset returns often exhibit the volatility clustering property, which means significant changes in prices tend to cluster together (Cont, R., 2007). Such behavioral data analysis can help solve the problem and arrive at a more optimal solution.

Algorithm Selection

Mathematical methods have been improving systemically, and with the increased availability of computational technologies, most methods could be tested depending on the data size. It is important to note that some algorithms have high computational requirements, while others have more data requirements to avoid overfitting. However, some algorithms can provide better results than others, depending on the dataset. Furthermore, not all algorithms are equally transparent and explainable to interpret the results. Two primary model training methods used in financial risk analysis are supervised and unsupervised learning algorithms. It has demonstrated that supervised learning can achieve high accuracy, but it may not be helpful when the data have no predefined class labels. The other technique, i.e., Unsupervised learning methods, can find underlying structures in unlabeled data (Kou, G., Peng, Y., & Wang, G., 2014).

Final Model Selection

The selection of the final model is a very challenging task as it needs consideration of multiple dimensions, which will be explained more in detail in testing sections. Pretesting is essential before accepting a model. Performance metric, which could be multiple dimensions based on the mathematical functions, is just one challenge. Another aspect of the challenge is the choice of input factors. Are those the most critical factors, and do they have sufficient contributions? Another important consideration is the stability of the factors. Are the factors performing stable across periods in stressful situations?

Researchers have shown that the constrained Bayesian model averaging(BMA) approach potentially address several difficulties while conducting a stress-testing exercise: (a) Testing severe yet plausible forecasted scenario, (b) reasoning for any additional ex-post expert-based adjustments, and (c) the model specification adjustments with every new data point (Panoš, J., & Polák, P., 2019).

PERFORMANCE METRIC CHALLENGES

Subsegment Performance

The model should perform reasonably well across subsegments of the population.

a.   Performance across Industry segments

For example, the model built for the middle market should reasonably predict that all the industries contributing to the middle market portfolio are challenging, as some populations could be too small to perform the test.

b.   Out-of-sample and Out-of-Time population -

The model should have a good performance on population out of modeling population. The model estimates are based on the sample population to perform reasonably well. However, the model is extensively tested on Out-of-Sample and Out-of-Time datasets for validation purposes before deploying in the production environment (Aggarwal, V., & Rej, S. 2015).

Data Modeling in Finance Challenges

c.   Performance across different economic periods -

The models should perform reasonably well during the pre-recession, recession, and post-recession periods. As the modeling data consists of different stages of the economic cycle, the model should perform reasonably across all subsegments of the population based on the stages of the economic cycle.

Time Series Performance

The model should perform well in the time series dataset. The most straightforward visual analysis shows that the model performs reasonably well on the average population across the periods in the historical dataset. As the economic cycle changes over the period, it becomes difficult for the model to match the peak and trough of the observed characteristics. Besides, some models desired to be more stable instead of capturing the volatility of the economic cycle. It has been an accepted fact that financial time series forecasting is one of the most challenging and vital issues facing numerous financial analysts and decision makers (Khashei, M., & Hajirahimi, Z., 2017).

Goodness-of-Fit Test

Hosmer-Lemeshow's (HL) chi-squared goodness-of-fit test estimates the grouping values of estimated probabilities. It divides the ranked predicted probabilities into k groups (based on deciles) to compute the Pearson chi-squared statistic to compare the predicted and observed frequencies of the defaults (Gurny, M. 2015).

ROC Test

The model should assign a higher risk score to high-risk borrowers in the financial models. Such models need to be tested to meet the requirement. ROC (receiver operating characteristic) curves are one of the most powerful tools used to quantify the predictive power of models for the evaluation of credit defaults. A ROC curve plots the Type II error against one minus the Type I error (Gurny, M., 2015).

Factor Stability Test

The model factors should remain stable across periods and out-of-time samples to be usable under good and bad market conditions. Traditional statistical techniques designed to prevent overfitting tend to be unreliable and inaccurate, such as using hold-out. Newer methods like using k-fold cross-validation techniques test the robustness of models (Bailey, D. H., Borwein, J., Lopez de Prado, M., & Zhu, Q. J., 2016).

Factor Sensitivity Test

The model output should be sensitive to input factor changes and the output should change adequately with a reasonable amount of input factor changes. Banks are often required to estimate their losses under various macroeconomic scenarios. Quantitative models used for loss estimates are tested against macroeconomic sensitivity to assess a bank's vulnerability under difficult macroeconomic situations (Camara, B., Pessarossi, P., & Philippon, T., 2016).

Model Stress Test

The model should perform well in stress market conditions when multiple factors deteriorate simultaneously and evaluate the impact on output. The stress tests calibrate conservatively to overestimate the risks so that sufficient buffers are in place when adverse shocks materialize (Gersl, A., & Seidler, J., 2012).

Model Output Stability Test

The built models estimate the possible output in the foreseeable future. However, the future could be 1 quarter, 1 year, 5 years, or longer. Based on the business requirement, the model output needs testing if the model output remains stable to meet the forecast period.

Factor Contribution

The model output should have an adequate contribution from different key input factors. Also, the distribution of contributions should align with the business expectation. The challenges lie in measuring the contribution due to multiple methods, and also, business expectations are judgmental.

Table 1. Key highlights of the Data Modeling

Themes of Finance	Artificial Intelligence							
	Machine Learning Techniques							
	Supervised				Unsupervised			
	Purpose				Purpose			
	Pattern Recognition	Classification	Prediction	Optimization	Pattern Recognition	Classification	Prediction	Optimization
Algorithmic Trading	Hidden Markov Mode[i]	Markov decision process (MDP), linear inverse reinforcement learning (LIRL) and Gaussian Process IRL (GPIRL), hierarchical clustering[ii]	Reinforcement learning, K-NN, Random Forest, Support Vector Machine, Gaussian Naive Bayes, Logistic Regression, Generative Adversarial Networks	Robbins–monro algorithm[iii]		NLP (semantic analysis algorithm		
Arbitrage Trading Trading Strategy		Support Vector Regressors (SVR), Light Gradient Boosting (LGB)[iv]	Holt–Winters smoothing and ensemble learning[v], long short-term memory (LSTM) [vi]					Density-Based Spatial Clustering of Applications with Noise (DBSCAN), t-Distributed Stochastic Neighbor Embedding (t-SNE)[vii]
Asset Pricing			Recurrent Neural Network, LSTM			Autoencoder neural networks[viii]		
Asset Return								
Bankruptcy								

continues on following page

Table 1. Continued

Themes of Finance	Artificial Intelligence							
	Machine Learning Techniques							
	Supervised				Unsupervised			
	Purpose				Purpose			
	Pattern Recognition	*Classification*	*Prediction*	*Optimization*	*Pattern Recognition*	*Classification*	*Prediction*	*Optimization*
Credit Rating Credit Score Credit Risk Default Prediction Loan/Credit		N aive bayes classifier, Multi-Layer Perceptron Neural Networks, Extreme learning machine, Support Vector Machine[ix], decision tree, (Spiking Extreme Learning Machine (SELM), Q-generalized extreme learning machine, Radial basis neural network[x]), One-class Classification Driven Dynamical Ensemble Learning[xi]	Quadratic Unconstrained Binary Optimization (QUBO), Recurrent Neural Network, (Decsion Tree, gradient boosting[xii]), (Logistics Regression and Neural Network[xiii]), (random forests and artificial neural networks[xiv]			K-nearest neighbor, k-means[ix], fuzzy c-means (fcm)[xv]	NLP	
Derivative pricing Hedging								
Feature Selection	PCA		Quadratic Unconstrained Binary Optimization (QUBO)			NLP		
Financial crisis Financial distress								

continues on following page

Data Modeling in Finance Challenges

Table 1. Continued

Themes of Finance	Artificial Intelligence							
	Machine Learning Techniques							
	Supervised				Unsupervised			
	Purpose				Purpose			
	Pattern Recognition	Classification	Prediction	Optimization	Pattern Recognition	Classification	Prediction	Optimization
Financial Inclusion Financialization		Graph theory[xvi]	Logistic regression and support vector machine (SVM) [xvii], Graph Neural Networks(Graph Convolutional Neural Networks, GraphSage, Graph Attention Network, Topology Adaptive Graph Convolutional Networks)[xviii]					
Forex			ANN					
Fraud Detection		Boltzmann Machine					NLP	
Implied Volatility			Deep Quantum Neural Network					
Option Pricing Option Trading			quantum Generative Adversarial Network,					
Portfolio Management Portfolio Optimization Investment evaluation			Lasso regression					

continues on following page

Table 1. Continued

Themes of Finance	Artificial Intelligence							
	Machine Learning Techniques							
	Supervised				Unsupervised			
	Purpose				Purpose			
	Pattern Recognition	*Classification*	*Prediction*	*Optimization*	*Pattern Recognition*	*Classification*	*Prediction*	*Optimization*
Predictive Analysis			Ridge Logistic Regression, Lasso Logistics Regression, Decision Tree, Naive Bayes, Support Vector Machine					
Risk Management	Boruta algorithm[xix]		K Nearest Neighbors (KNN), Support Vector Machine (SVM), Regression Tree, Linear Regression, Stochastic Gradient Boosting. The random forest (RF)[xx], Deep neural netrwork[xxi]				support vector data description (SVDD) [xxii]	

[i] (Wu & Siwasarit, 2020); [ii] (Yang et al., 2015); [iii] (Cont & Kukanov, 2017); [iv] (Carta et al., 2021); [v] (Park et al., 2019); [vi] (Chang et al., 2021); [vii] (Tronvoll & Andersen, 2018); [viii] (Gu et al., 2021); [ix] (Pandey et al., 2018); [x] (Kuppili et al., 2020); [xi] (Li et al., 2021); [xii][xii] (Kokate & Chetty, 2021); [xiii] (Ashofteh & Bravo, 2021); [xiv] (Óskarsdóttir et al., 2018); [xv] (Pang et al., 2021); [xvi] (Roa et al., 2022); [xvii] (Akinnuwesi et al., 2020); [xviii] (Roa et al., 2022); [xix] (Shakhovska et al., 2022); [xx] (Shakhovska et al., 2022); [xxi] (Rönnqvist & Sarlin, 2017); [xxii] (Dionne, 2018).

Business Judgment Based on Additional Information

As the quantitative model relies on the input factors, it captures only limited information. The model outputs do not generate daily due to delayed information availability. The portfolio assessment takes place when the firm releases quarterly financial statements. Some information like macroeconomic data is available after quarter-end, while an event like Covid and bankruptcies can occur anytime during mid-quarter. Under these circumstances, the portfolio manager is provided with the flexibility to downgrade an obligor based on additional information not provided within the input factors based on standardized rules.

The key highlights of the data modeling in finance are exhibited in table 1.

CONCLUSION

Quantitative modeling provides enormous opportunities in the field of finance. Latest analytics algorithms and technologies are especially relevant in finance as numbers and data processes have always driven the financial industry. Financial institutions can leverage their data to enhance operational efficiency and mitigate risks. Financial institutions are also leveraging analytics tools to expand their business and create new opportunities. However, the quantitative methods and technologies involved are very sophisticated, requiring specialized and trained professionals. The modeling process is not about fitting the curve but involves a complete life cycle of development. The development process includes data preparation, variable analysis, algorithm selection, model selection, testing of the final selected model on multiple samples, and at the end, deployment and monitoring of the model. Understanding these aspects and overcoming those challenges can help create valuable and robust models. The appropriate financial models will allow institutions to gain an advantage over their peer institutions and compete in the crowded global financial industry.

REFERENCES

Aggarwal, V., & Rej, S. (2015). *Retail Credit Risk Model Validation: Performance and Stability Aspects*. Academic Press.

Akinnuwesi, B. A., Fashoto, S. G., Metfula, A. S., & Akinnuwesi, A. N. (2020). Experimental Application of Machine Learning on Financial Inclusion Data for Governance in Eswatini. In Lecture Notes in Computer Science (including subseries Lecture Notes in Artificial Intelligence and Lecture Notes in Bioinformatics): Vol. 12067 LNCS. Springer International Publishing. doi:10.1007/978-3-030-45002-1_36

Ané, T., Ureche-Rangau, L., Gambet, J. B., & Bouverot, J. (2008). Robust outlier detection for Asia–Pacific stock index returns. *Journal of International Financial Markets, Institutions and Money*, *18*(4), 326–343. doi:10.1016/j.intfin.2007.03.001

Ashofteh, A., & Bravo, J. M. (2021). A conservative approach for online credit scoring. *Expert Systems with Applications*, *176*(March), 114835. doi:10.1016/j.eswa.2021.114835

Bailey, D. H., Borwein, J., Lopez de Prado, M., & Zhu, Q. J. (2016). The probability of backtest overfitting. *Journal of Computational Finance*. Advance online publication. doi:10.21314/JCF.2016.322

Bansal, A., Kauffman, R. J., & Weitz, R. R. (1993). Comparing the modeling performance of regression and neural networks as data quality varies: A business value approach. *Journal of Management Information Systems*, *10*(1), 11–32. doi:10.1080/07421222.1993.11517988

Camara, B., Pessarossi, P., & Philippon, T. (2016). *Back-testing bank stress tests*. Stern School of Business, New York University.

Carta, S. M., Consoli, S., Podda, A. S., Recupero, D. R., & Stanciu, M. M. (2021). Ensembling and Dynamic Asset Selection for Risk-Controlled Statistical Arbitrage. *IEEE Access: Practical Innovations, Open Solutions*, *9*(i), 29942–29959. doi:10.1109/ACCESS.2021.3059187

Chang, V., Man, X., Xu, Q., & Hsu, C. H. (2021). Pairs trading on different portfolios based on machine learning. *Expert Systems: International Journal of Knowledge Engineering and Neural Networks*, *38*(3), 1–25. doi:10.1111/exsy.12649

Cont, R. (2007). Volatility clustering in financial markets: empirical facts and agent-based models. In *Long memory in economics* (pp. 289–309). Springer. doi:10.1007/978-3-540-34625-8_10

Cont, R., & Kukanov, A. (2017). Optimal order placement in limit order markets. *Quantitative Finance*, *17*(1), 21–39. doi:10.1080/14697688.2016.1190030

Dionne, G. (2018). *Machine Learning and Risk Management: SVDD Meets RQE*. Academic Press.

Funashima, Y. (2017). Time-varying leads and lags across frequencies using a continuous wavelet transform approach. *Economic Modelling*, *60*, 24–28. doi:10.1016/j.econmod.2016.08.024

Gersl, A., & Seidler, J. (2012). How to improve the quality of stress tests through backtesting. *Finance a Uver*, *62*(4), 325.

Gu, S., Kelly, B., & Xiu, D. (2021). Autoencoder asset pricing models. *Journal of Econometrics*, *222*(1), 429–450. doi:10.1016/j.jeconom.2020.07.009

Gurny, M. (2015). *Default probabilities in credit risk management: estimation, model calibration, and backtesting* [Doctoral dissertation]. Faculty of Business and Economics, Macquarie University.

Keen, S. (2013). A monetary Minsky model of the Great Moderation and the Great Recession. *Journal of Economic Behavior & Organization*, *86*, 221–235. doi:10.1016/j.jebo.2011.01.010

Khashei, M., & Hajirahimi, Z. (2017). Performance evaluation of series and parallel strategies for financial time series forecasting. *Financial Innovation*, *3*(1), 1–24. doi:10.118640854-017-0074-9

Kiefer, N. M. (2009). Default estimation for low-default portfolios. *Journal of Empirical Finance*, *16*(1), 164–173. doi:10.1016/j.jempfin.2008.03.004

Kofman, P., & Sharpe, I. G. (2003). Using multiple imputation in the analysis of incomplete observations in finance. *Journal of Financial Econometrics*, *1*(2), 216–249. doi:10.1093/jjfinec/nbg013

Kokate, S., & Chetty, M. S. R. (2021). Credit risk assessment of loan defaulters in commercial banks using voting classifier ensemble learner machine learning model. *International Journal of Safety and Security Engineering*, *11*(5), 565–572. doi:10.18280/ijsse.110508

Kou, G., Peng, Y., & Wang, G. (2014). Evaluation of clustering algorithms for financial risk analysis using MCDM methods. *Information Sciences*, *275*, 1–12. doi:10.1016/j.ins.2014.02.137

Kuppili, V., Tripathi, D., & Reddy Edla, D. (2020). Credit score classification using spiking extreme learning machine. *Computational Intelligence*, *36*(2), 402–426. doi:10.1111/coin.12242

Li, H., Qiu, H., Sun, S., Chang, J., & Tu, W. (2021). Credit scoring by one-class classification driven dynamical ensemble learning. *The Journal of the Operational Research Society*, *0*(0), 1–10. doi:10.1080/01605682.2021.1944824

Óskarsdóttir, M., Sarraute, C., Bravo, C., Baesens, B., & Vanthienen, J. (2018). Credit scoring for good: Enhancing financial inclusion with smartphone-based micro lending. *International Conference on Information Systems 2018, ICIS 2018*, 1–14.

Pandey, T. N., Jagadev, A. K., Mohapatra, S. K., & Dehuri, S. (2018). Credit risk analysis using machine learning classifiers. *2017 International Conference on Energy, Communication, Data Analytics and Soft Computing, ICECDS 2017*, 1850–1854. 10.1109/ICECDS.2017.8389769

Pang, P. S., Hou, X., & Xia, L. (2021). Borrowers' credit quality scoring model and applications, with default discriminant analysis based on the extreme learning machine. *Technological Forecasting and Social Change, 165*(November). doi:10.1016/j.techfore.2020.120462

Panoš, J., & Polák, P. (2019). *How to Improve the Model Selection Procedure in a Stress-testing Framework*. Czech National Bank, Economic Research Department.

Park, M., Kim, J., Won, D., & Kim, J. (2019). Development of a two-stage ESS-scheduling model for cost minimization using machine learning-based load prediction techniques. *Processes (Basel, Switzerland), 7*(6), 370. Advance online publication. doi:10.3390/pr7060370

Roa, L., Rodríguez-Rey, A., Correa-Bahnsen, A., & Arboleda, C. V. (2022). Supporting Financial Inclusion with Graph Machine Learning and Super-App Alternative Data. *Lecture Notes in Networks and Systems, 295*, 216–230. doi:10.1007/978-3-030-82196-8_16

Rönnqvist, S., & Sarlin, P. (2017). Bank distress in the news: Describing events through deep learning. *Neurocomputing, 264*, 57–70. doi:10.1016/j.neucom.2016.12.110

Shakhovska, N., Melnykova, N., Chopiyak, V., & Gregus Ml, M. (2022). An ensemble methods for medical insurance costs prediction task. *Computers. Materials and Continua, 70*(2), 3969–3984. doi:10.32604/cmc.2022.019882

Tronvoll, H., & Andersen, H. (2018). *Statistical Arbitrage Trading with Implementation of Machine Learning*. Academic Press.

Wu, P., & Siwasarit, W. (2020). Capturing the Order Imbalance with Hidden Markov Model: A Case of SET50 and KOSPI50. *Asia-Pacific Financial Markets, 27*(1), 115–144. doi:10.100710690-019-09285-1

Yang, S. Y., Qiao, Q., Beling, P. A., Scherer, W. T., & Kirilenko, A. A. (2015). Gaussian process-based algorithmic trading strategy identification. *Quantitative Finance, 15*(10), 1683–1703. doi:10.1080/14697688.2015.1011684

Chapter 13
Review of Machine Learning Techniques in the Supply Chain Management of Indian Industry:
A Future Research Agenda

Rashmi Ranjan Panigrahi
Siksha 'O'Anusandhan, India

Meenakshee Dash
Rajdhani College of Engineering and Management, India

Zakir Hossen Shaikh
https://orcid.org/0000-0003-4733-4166
Bahrain Training Institute, Bahrain

Mohammad Irfan
CMR Institute of Technology, India

ABSTRACT

The technologies have increased the role of IT in evolving the path for the future. A sense of belonging and significance to the market is felt by current industries. Procurement, assembly, and supply were affected by the digital revolt that has swept the world. Now machine learning is a hot area among scholars and industry professionals. Two decades ago, there were few publications of machine learning and supply chain management. SCM-related ML application research hasn't been thoroughly examined in the literature till date with respect to the Indian steel

DOI: 10.4018/978-1-6684-4483-2.ch013

Copyright © 2023, IGI Global. Copying or distributing in print or electronic forms without written permission of IGI Global is prohibited.

industry. As a result, this study examined articles from Jan. 2010 to Dec. 2020 in five major databases to present the latest research trends. A quantitative analysis of 112 shortlisted articles revealed that there were not enough publications to form a strong group force in this field. This study's comprehensive look at ML techniques used in SCM will help future research. A true reflection of today's industries, the chapter accurately reflects prospects to express feelings, thoughts, and contribute to future industries.

INTRODUCTION

The success of an industry is heavily dependent on the Supply Chain. It's a complicated integration of many different business units, each with their own unique set of technologies and resources. Despite the fact that the efficiency of a supply chain is reliant on a variety of factors, it appears to be difficult to design/develop a common platform that allows industry to respond quickly to market needs. In recent years, the world has entered a new era known as the "fourth industrial revolution," which is characterised by the "development of digitization", "information", "robotics", "communication technology", and "Artificial Intelligence (AI)" (Baryannis et al., 2019). In this day and age, robots are becoming intelligent enough to make judgments in place of people. These techniques are referred to as machine learning (ML), and This group is focused on automated systems that are capable of "learning" through their past usage (Pournader et al., 2021). Due to machines' rising ability to deal with large amounts of data over the last two decades, and some computers' even capability of finding hidden pathways and complicated relationships to make appropriate and reliable decisions on issues where humans were incapable or unwilling, machine learning (ML) was born (Toorajipour et al., 2021). According to research, robots are capable of providing more accurate outcomes than humans in a wide range of decision-making contexts (Hartley & Sawaya, 2019; Pournader et al., 2021).

The use of machine learning and its fundamental components can improve the prediction of SCM Performance Learning algorithm, deep learning, and optimization algorithms all contribute to machine learning's ability to continually seek for the SC performance-enhancing factors. For the fourth time, using visual machine learning over a SC network, ML may examine a broad spectrum of applications in physical asset management and physical inspection. Despite the fact that the applications of machine learning have numerous advantages and despite the fact that certain research have shown that ML has made its way into Supply Chain Management (SCM), including warehouse management (Makkar et al., 2020; Ni et al., 2020), Neural Networks (Golmohammadi et al., 2009; Ni et al., 2020), Support Vector Machine

(Ni et al., 2020; Prahathish et al., 2020), Logistic regression (H. Ma et al., 2018; Ni et al., 2020), Decision Tree (Estelles-Lopez et al., 2017) and Extreme Learning Machine(Martínez et al., 2020; Ni et al., 2020), One research found that just 15% of businesses had implemented ML including one or even more SC functions. The insufficient usage of machine learning in SC may be due to a lack of awareness of how ML may be implemented, a low level of acceptability in the business culture, and an inability to get appropriate data(Ni et al., 2020). An urgent systematic study is required to quantitatively examine the most recent research trends, to investigate the machine learning algorithms that are often employed in supply chain management, and to identify the SCM tasks that are most suited for ML(Sharma et al., 2021). As a result of noticing a lack of studies on the use of decision support systems for conducting supply chain management (SCM) investigations with regards to MI, we chose this study. The majority of studies have used fuzzy set theory, experience and understanding systems, multi-criteria methods, and/or minimization algorithms and situational optimization as primary methods, which we believe is insufficient. However, despite the fact that increasingly sophisticated artificial intelligence technologies such as "machine learning", "deep learning", and "image/text processing" are essential components of today's supply chains, the literature is still lagging behind the industry when it comes to studying their applications in manufacturing. At same time, our research showed important fragmentation in artificial intelligence (AI) research, stressing the necessity of a classification system that can guide operations and supply chain researchers in broadening their knowledge of supply chain management (SCM) AI research in the past, present, and future.

In practise, there has been an implied division of labour between people and machines. As automation enters the picture, this clear separation of tasks is becoming more ambiguous (Patel et al., 2017). When it comes to automation in manufacturing, for the past 100 years, the focus has been on automating activities, but now Machine Learning (ML) is entering in a new age in which decision-making (thought) is being automated. Machine learning and other machine learning are transforming manufacturing in a way that is unprecedented in human history. Knowledge base must be organised in a new way, gaps in understanding must be identified, and new information must be synthesised in order to fully realise a new paradigm's implications. Machine learning as well as other intelligent machines are transforming manufacturing in a fundamental way. It is usual for a new paradigm to be necessary to fully comprehend, organise, discover gaps in knowledge, guide future research and practise, and synthesise new information within a paradigm shift (Sharma et al., 2021). This is a major shift in thinking that prompts the issue of how ML will impact manufacturing Industry in India. India Steel Industry hasn't had a lot of attention paid to ML application research in the literature so far. The results of the study were based on a review of articles published between January 2010 and December

2020 in five major databases. This in turn leads to questions: RQ 1: Is it possible to manufacture products using machine learning? RQ 2: What are the research gaps concerning the machine learning in manufacturing? RQ 3: What are the research problem directions in machine learning applications in supply chain management?

In summary, academic research on machine learning in manufacturing is confronted with a double challenge: the unavailability of a thorough and detailed literature evaluation; and the inadequacy of a linked framework for directing both research and practise in the field. Using a two-stage blended literature review approach, this research discusses both of these challenges by incorporating a conceptual integration step. The descriptive literature review approach is employed during first step. (Sharma et al., 2021) is utilized in the performance of a systematic evaluation of the literature in order to identify interesting research themes.

REVIEW OF RECENT LITERATURE

A broad range of research fields benefit from systematic literature reviews (SLRs) (Arksey & O'Malley, 2005; Ni et al., 2020). SLRs were originally developed in the medical industry. Later, (Tranfield et al., 2003) customized SLRs to meet the specific objectives and features of management research (Durach et al., 2017). and to those of SCM research(Sawyerr & Harrison, 2020). These modifications are required due to the fact that each study field has its own set of criteria and features (Durach et al., 2017). However, there was no thorough review of the research development in the discipline of machine learning application, particularly in SCM in Indian manufacturing Industry.

Shopping in the present day is more disruptive and discontinuous than ever before due to digitalization of customers' purchases and purchasing behaviors. In order for businesses to remain competitive, they need to keep up with these developments in order to minimize unpredictability in demand and financial risk(Ni et al., 2020). In today's dynamic business environment, an organization's ability to acquire, convert, and deliver SC is vital(He et al., 2020). Many cutting-edge enterprises may exchange data with their SC partners (e.g. inventory, sales data) to improve visibility along the SC. Recognizing the growing relevance of data in SC, SCM academics and practitioners have tried everything to enhance data management along the SC(Wu et al., 2019). It is one of these instruments that has been used for some time but has not yet reached its full potential in supply chain management (SCM).According to one of the Forbes (Makkar et al., 2020) reports, adopting machine learning has shown to be the most critical choice for 61 percent of the firms tested. The following are a few critical aspects of supply chain management, as well as the applications where Machine Learning techniques are now in use.

- Predictive ML demand and sales (Feizabadi, 2020).
- Product suggestions that are customized to each other(Xiao & Benbasat, 2018).
- Pricing and marketing techniques to maximize revenues(Campbell et al., 2020).
- Inventory optimization with correct stock levels(Caggiano et al., 2009; Duan & Liao, 2013)
- The warehouse throughput optimization system(Makkar et al., 2020; Silva et al., 2017)
- Steel supply chain sustainability(Goyal & Routroy, 2021).
- Attaining improved environmental sustainability(Goyal & Routroy, 2021; R. Kumar et al., 2021).
- Cognitive services may help us gain vital customer insights. (such as sentiment analysis, preferences, and social listening).
- Shopfloor yield optimization Optimum stock levels are used to optimize inventory(Caggiano et al., 2009; Ni et al., 2020).
- In manufacturing, preventative equipment maintenance is used(Carvalho et al., 2019; Kaparthi & Bumblauskas, 2020).
- Predictive lead scoring can help in qualification, prioritization, and acquisition(L. Ma & Sun, 2020).
- Help with smart work area design(Kaparthi & Bumblauskas, 2020).

Problems With Existing Supply Chains

Traditional supply chain management has a negative influence on the efficiency of a firm. A lack of responsibility and visibility make traditional supply chain management a high-risk practice. The price range of each step in the supply chain may grow as a result of changes in market trends. In a typical supply chain management system, logistical estimate is less effective, which results in a high cost of management. A complicated supply chain structure may be created by a supply chain that includes many routes(A. Kumar et al., 2020). Managing both the ecommerce supply chain and the offline supply chain requires the adaptation of numerous supply chain techniques in recent times(Bressanelli et al., 2019). As a result, appropriate management of various channels and underlying channels is required to maintain accuracy in inventory control. The quality of customer service may be negatively impacted by poor inventory management. High-risk scenarios can arise as a result of fluctuating demand and supply in a market. In high-demand markets, supply chain management must be swift(Bressanelli et al., 2019; Burga & Rezania, 2017; Wisetsri et al., 2021). The quality of services and goods might be impacted if supply is managed in response to excessive demand. As a result, traditional supply chain management procedures may have problems maintaining both speed and quality while also being unable to accurately anticipate and govern the supply chain(Tirkolaee et al., 2021). Supply chain management in Indian steel manufacturing companies is concentrating on identifying possible supply chain bottlenecks. Each of these stumbling blocks is critical to the retailing industry and the country's overall economy(R. Kumar et al., 2021). Steel supply chain environmental sustainability needs to be a focus for ML in Indian industry specifically(Goyal & Routroy, 2021). Studies need to examined SCM strategy for small and medium-sized enterprises (SMEs). With the goal of enhancing industrial companies' responsiveness and flexibility, SCM has been widely accepted as a successful method. It appears that supply chain concerns are extensively studied in the context of major Indian corporations, but that SMEs receive less attention. Companies have a supply chain management (SCM) emphasis and describe the most essential AI based supply chain concerns in Indian manufacturing SMEs(Thakkar et al., 2012).

RESEARCH METHODOLOGY

Choosing the Best Approach for Doing a LR

An effective literature review is guided by the specific objectives of the study, that might vary from delivering a summary of the current status of the literature to contributing ideas for further investigation (Makkar et al., 2020; Sandelowski et al., 2007),the process of developing a narratives to justify a view(Kumaraguru et al., 2014), the process of developing a narrative to promote a position, a quantitative summary of the relevant literature(Kusiak, 2020), To discover and synthesize diverse streams of research, theme analysis must be used(Ni et al., 2020), putting up a foundation for discussion (Sharma et al., 2021).

Our literature study has two objectives: doing a literature review and then developing a methodical framework for choosing articles on the use of learning algorithms in Indian manufacturing industry. Due to the fact that these objectives necessitate various methodologies, a hybrid strategy was used for the literature evaluation. The descriptive literature review approach was used to review and report the current state of knowledge in this study. Researchers use this strategy to obtain and study relevant publications in order to summarize results, which is frequently driven by an overall framework. This strategy was chosen because it was necessary to conduct a thorough study and analysis of publications in order to gain a more nuanced grasp of the subject matter(Sharma et al., 2021).

The framework synthetic approach was employed in order to synthesize and expand the present state of knowledge. An a priori conceptual model is identified and then utilized to identify and organize the relevant literature(Sharma et al., 2021). Modifications to the conceptual model are made as a result of the literature study and are based on the results of the coding process. "an updated model that may incorporate both changed elements and additional factors not expected in the initial model" is the consequence of this approach(Dixon-Woods, 2011)

To summaries, we used a fusion literature review strategy focuses on descriptive literature review. Figure 1 depicts diagram of DLR and its phases.

Descriptive Literature Review (DLR)

Identifying patterns in the available literature is among the primary objectives of a DLR. Finding patterns in the available literature is one of the main objectives for conducting a Descriptive Literature Review (DLR). (Guzzo, R. A., Jette, R. D., & Katzell, 1985). Publications in a certain field of research are tagged in order to discover common themes. This can serve as a starting point for the construction of a system of classification in the future. The DLR method involves retrieval of documents, document inclusion/exclusion, classification/analysis, and the synthesis of results as part of the process.

Retrieval of Research Papers and Working Papers

The databases ScienceDirect, Emerald, WOS, Wiley, and Scopus were utilized to conduct the literature search. The terms used in the search were chosen to illustrate the wide range of possibilities in the manufacturing industry. As a result, in addition to manufacturing, terms such as maintenance, quality control, machining, and additive manufacturing were also included in the list of search results. The selection of these keywords was based on a preliminary assessment of the literature as well as our own observations and conclusions. Because of the broad span of the manufacturing area, the search was limited to publications published between January 2010 and December 2020.

Furthermore, the search was limited to solely review articles. These limitations were imposed in order to keep the quantity of results under control. A descriptive literature review approach, in particular, takes a great amount of time and effort in thoroughly reading and interpreting each publication.

If we consider the maintenance domain, our search word combination includes the terms "Review", "Manufacturing", "Maintenance", "Quality control", "Machining", "Supply Chain management", Similar search phrase combinations were utilized in other industrial domains to find similar results. Table 1 shows the number of first results for each search word combination, as well as the total number of results.

Table 1. Number of searches resulted from multiple Database in January 2010 and December 2020

Data Base	Searching Items	Result Count (in thousands)
ScienceDirect	Review + Manufacturing+ Maintenance + Supply Chain management	1,19,500
Emerald	Review + Quality control+ Machining,	1,42,500
WOS	Review + Additive manufacturing + Quality control	52,500
Wiley	Review + Supply Chain management Manufacturing+ Maintenance	18,500
Scopus	Review + Manufacturing+ Maintenance+ Quality control+ Machining+ Supply Chain management	9,500

Inclusive and Exclusive Criteria for Research Papers and Working Papers

In keeping with DLR's emphasis on article relevancy, the top 100 most relevant results from each domain were picked. The top 25 most referenced papers in each topic were chosen from among these 165 review articles. This resulted in a total of 165 review papers being found throughout the ML manufacturing domains that were examined. Each of these 112 review papers was then thoroughly examined, and a backward citation search was carried out in order to uncover other publications that were relevant to our study. A few articles Additionally, if they were judged to be pertinent to the scope of this review, they were included manual process. This resulted in the production of 500 articles in total. (Figure 2).

Final Evaluation of Research Papers and Working Papers

Our final result set included 112 papers that were each thoroughly analyzed and coded on a variety of variables such as "manufacturing function, manufacturing techniques, type of data, scanning technologies type, algorithm type, and data preparation technique". An in-depth investigation of how machine learning may be used in the manufacturing industries was conducted once this development activity was completed, after that, we'll go through the important findings of our research (Figure 2).

Figure 1. Methodology of DLR

Figure 2. Methodology in selection of research and working papers

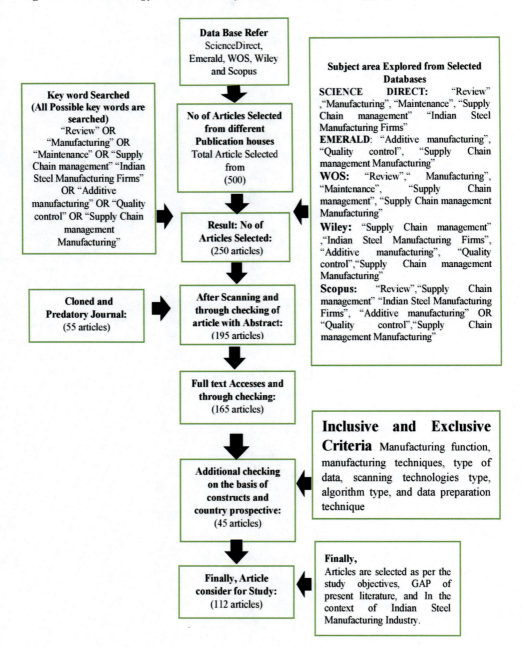

FINDINGS OF THE STUDY

Important Findings From the DLR

The existing literature on machine learning in manufacturing has taken one of three main perspectives: The following lenses are available: (a) a task-centric lens, (b) a digital lens, or (c) a manufacturing lens The first lens, referred to as 'work,' has varying degrees of coverage(Sharma et al., 2021). These levels are "Task Oriented", "Process Wise", "Functional Wise", and "Industry Wise", and they are listed in the following (table 2) in descending order of increasing scope. Studying individual tasks at the task-level is important allowing research to concentrate objectives, such as forecast of machined surface in extruded(W. Zhang, 2021) instead of using monitored ML to find production inefficiencies (Alexopoulos et al., 2020). Machine learning (ML) may be used to improve manufacturing structure such as machining, according to process-level studies(Kim et al., 2018), additive manufacturing(Kim et al., 2018). Some of the process level studies try to cover a broader range of topics than just specific manufacturing processes (Razvi et al., 2019). (Weichert et al., 2019) examine the application of machine learning in the optimization of manufacturing processes in general. Quality control (Escobar & Morales-Menendez, 2018) and predictive maintenance in "sustainable supply chain management" (Köksal et al., 2018) ML may be used to improve the performance of specific industrial operations in two instances of research at the function level. In addition, research conducted at the industry level look on the use of machine learning in specific areas, such as the process industry (Sharma et al., 2021; X.-D. Zhang, 2020).

ML Applicability in SCM in Indian Steel Industry

Industrial Engineering for Bringing Competitiveness for Iron and Steel

Integrated steelmaking processes, which include everything from ironmaking to the final steel classifications and shapes, are a complex industrial system in and of itself. Furthermore, decision-makers must have a thorough understanding of many areas of operations management, process execution, risk concerns and material handling considerations among other things in order to make informed decisions. It is necessary for the solution strategy to take into account trade-offs and uncertainties as well as several phases, multiple objectives, numerous decision factors, and limitations. Several Industrial Engineering approaches, such as multi-objective optimization, heuristics, evolutionary algorithms, simulations, lean six-sigma, and others, have been presented in the literature to address the iron and steel industry's complex problems, such as integrated production planning, in the iron and steel industry.

Table 2. Important Findings of Review with respect to Machine Learning in Manufacturing Supply Chain

Intensity of Study.	LR's Functions	Relevant Research Articles
(a) A Task-Centric Lens		
Industry Wise	Examining machine learning in industrial areas such as the process industry and the automobile industry	In the process industry, machine learning is utilised(Chen et al., 2018; Sharma et al., 2021).
Functional Wise	Examination of machine learning in manufacturing operations such as quality control, maintenance, and production planning	ML with the purpose of enhancing quality(Wisetsri et al., 2021)
Process Wise	An examination of machine learning in manufacturing processes such as casting, forming, machining, and additive manufacturing	ML in the machining industry (Kim et al., 2018)
Task Oriented	Review of machine learning techniques in particular applications such as defect identification, Supply Chain Complexity, surface roughness prediction	Predicting extrusion surface roughness (W. Zhang, 2021)
(b) Digital Lens		
Particularly technological component	Examining machine learning in the context of particular component technologies	Analysing ML in machine monitoring (Bramley & Ouzman, 2019; Tirkolaee et al., 2021)
Innovation in technology	Review of a single technology's applicability in a specialized domain	Improving machining performance with soft computing(Kim et al., 2018)
ML in Advanced SCM	Review of Advanced Supply Chain Management	SCM in conjunction with IT-enabled systems(Feizabadi, 2020; Huo et al., 2014; Tirkolaee et al., 2021)
(c) A Manufacturing Lens		
Transition in the industry	Examining the major transformations that have occurred in the manufacturing industry	Supply chain network disciplines using machine learning contextual intelligence (Jose & Shanmugam, 2019; Pahwa, 2020)
Manufacturing Industry Technologies	Review of manufacturing technologies	Industry 4.0 and associated technologies review(Buer et al., 2021; Valente & Neto, 2017)

An AHP and Fuzzy AHP Approach for Barrier Prioritization in the Indian Steel Industry

Identifying threats to the Indian steel industry supply chain and prioritizing them. The study analyzed 11 possible significant impediments. The Indian steel sector may face further hurdles. This study uses both AHP and FAHP to rate identified barriers.

SCP is Enhanced by the use Of Machine Learning in Production Planning and Control

Improving PPC operations can have a ripple effect throughout the company's production processes because of its cross-functional nature. ML techniques have become an enticing answer to industrial difficulties with the introduction of Industry 4.0's abundant data, high computational power, and big storage capacity.

Digitalization of the Capital Investment Cycle

Steel plants need engineering knowledge, flexibility, and productivity to alter their EBITDA trajectories. The capital investment cycle in steel factories is complex, both in terms of design and implementation. These risks increase the project financing risk premium and lower life cycle cash flows. This boosts capital costs, lowers sustainable EBITDA margins, and lowers return on capital utilized. Consideration of plant flexibility in the face of market and raw material uncertainty may result in plants that may change product mix, substitute raw materials and balance scope and scale economies in iron, steel, and downstream units. Real options models combined with market uncertainty modelling may produce realistic scenarios with better anticipated value and fewer risks.

Blockchain Enables a Robust Steel Supply Chain With COVID-19

COVID-19 triggered a supply chain breakdown affecting practically all manufacturers, retailers, and distributors, affecting various production processes. Steel, an energy-intensive sector, is advised to utilize digitalization technologies to optimize and sustain production. To deal with such a situation, industries have the chance to develop the supply chain towards sustainability.

SCM Distribution of ML Algorithms

By analyzing the development patterns of ML applications in SCM, as well as the most often used ML methods in SCM, it appears that ML's potential for solving complicated issues and retrieving data has not been completely explored.

When it comes to sales, demand, and the amount of inventory necessary, machine learning algorithms are capable of improving the accuracy of prediction and forecasting. The fact that ML algorithms are not as reliant on the accuracy of historical data as other traditional methods such as "moving average, exponential smoothing, time-series methods" and "Box-Jenkins methods" has led to their promotion as alternatives for demand and planning in supply chain management (SCM).

Customer satisfaction with low-cost, high-quality items delivered quickly is the cornerstone to every firm's purchasing and supply management success. Supplier evaluation and selection are the primary functions performed by machine learning applications in supply chain management. ML methods such as Support Vector Machines are frequently used to help in the decision-making process in the following scenarios because of the dynamism and complexity of the scenarios.

SC inventory management (SCIM) and storage are both extremely expensive efforts. The important objectives of SCIM are to expand product diversity, improve customer service, and reduce expenses, among other things. Traditional decision rules, on the other hand, find it difficult to properly estimate, anticipate, and gather the information necessary to achieve all of these objectives since it is mostly relied on the sound judgement and expertise of inventory managers themselves. Consequently, warehouses are regularly faced with dubious inventory input, necessitating the creation of a system that would aid people in overcoming this unpredictability. ML algorithms are capable of looking for input patterns that are similar to those found in warehouse data sets, which makes them ideal for data mining.

LIMITATIONS OF THE STUDY

In spite of the rigorous and well-established research methodologies used in our hybrid literature review, this publication still has significant limitations in terms of methodology. It was necessary to use inclusion and exclusion criteria to limit the amount of material studied because manufacturing is such a large area of study. Some papers may have been left out because of this, which is a common occurrence in literature reviews. Nevertheless, we believe that our manual inclusion and backward search for further relevant papers have minimized the likelihood that important work has been ignored. As a second point, despite the fact that our study has taken a methodical and thorough approach to identifying the relevant literature, the chance that our final list of articles reflects certain hidden biases cannot be disregarded. As a result, the final articles were thoroughly evaluated by each of the authors to ensure that they were relevant.

SCOPE FOR FUTURE RESEARCH

Our concentration was on manufacturing, supply chain management issues, and machine learning algorithms. These models may be used in future supply chain management studies. The present study focused on developing a conceptual framework for academic research on the function of ML in supply chains in Indian industry. It tried to answer the question, i.e. How important are different ML applications for supporting supply chain management as well operational flexibility in Indian context.

CONCLUSION OF THE STUDY

Today, companies must improve their supply chains for a variety of reasons, including gaining market share, attracting new customers, building a brand, and so on. The information in this paper shows how industries may make the most of their capabilities. When it comes to this, machine learning is one of the finest solutions because it may have both real and intangible benefits for businesses. The article presents different ML Algorithms and its Applicability in SCM in Indian Steel Industry and it depicts importance of ML in Manufacturing Industry. Machine learning allows all stakeholders to work toward a common objective while also taking their individual strengths and weaknesses into consideration. It has also aided in the development of risk management, supply and demand estimates, effective networking across several supply channels, and a stable supply chain. In essence, using sophisticated technology has increased profit margins and competitive advantage. Overall, the digital revolution and machine learning have proven tremendously favourable.

REFERENCES

Alexopoulos, K., Nikolakis, N., & Chryssolouris, G. (2020). Digital twin-driven supervised machine learning for the development of artificial intelligence applications in manufacturing. *International Journal of Computer Integrated Manufacturing*, *33*(5), 429–439. doi:10.1080/0951192X.2020.1747642

Arksey, H., & O'Malley, L. (2005). Scoping studies: Towards a methodological framework. *International Journal of Social Research Methodology*, *8*(1), 19–32. doi:10.1080/1364557032000119616

Baryannis, G., Validi, S., Dani, S., & Antoniou, G. (2019). Supply chain risk management and artificial intelligence: State of the art and future research directions. *International Journal of Production Research*, *57*(7), 2179–2202. doi:10.1080/00 207543.2018.1530476

Bramley, R. G. V., & Ouzman, J. (2019). Farmer attitudes to the use of sensors and automation in fertilizer decision-making: Nitrogen fertilization in the Australian grains sector. *Precision Agriculture*, *20*(1), 157–175. doi:10.100711119-018-9589-y

Bressanelli, G., Perona, M., & Saccani, N. (2019). Challenges in supply chain redesign for the Circular Economy: A literature review and a multiple case study. *International Journal of Production Research*, *57*(23), 7395–7422. doi:10.1080/0 0207543.2018.1542176

Buer, S. V., Semini, M., Strandhagen, J. O., & Sgarbossa, F. (2021). The complementary effect of lean manufacturing and digitalisation on operational performance. *International Journal of Production Research*, *59*(7), 1976–1992. do i:10.1080/00207543.2020.1790684

Burga, R., & Rezania, D. (2017). Project accountability: An exploratory case study using actor–network theory. *International Journal of Project Management*, *35*(6), 1024–1036. doi:10.1016/j.ijproman.2017.05.001

Caggiano, K. E., Jackson, P. L., Muckstadt, J. A., & Rappold, J. A. (2009). Efficient computation of time-based customer service levels in a multi-item, multi-echelon supply chain: A practical approach for inventory optimization. *European Journal of Operational Research*, *199*(3), 744–749. doi:10.1016/j.ejor.2008.08.002

Campbell, C., Sands, S., Ferraro, C., Tsao, H.-Y., & Mavrommatis, A. (2020). From data to action: How marketers can leverage AI. *Business Horizons*, *63*(2), 227–243. doi:10.1016/j.bushor.2019.12.002

Carvalho, T. P., Soares, F. A. A. M. N., Vita, R., Francisco, R. da P., Basto, J. P., & Alcalá, S. G. S. (2019). A systematic literature review of machine learning methods applied to predictive maintenance. *Computers & Industrial Engineering*, *137*, 106024. doi:10.1016/j.cie.2019.106024

Chen, N. C., Drouhard, M., Kocielnik, R., Suh, J., & Aragon, C. R. (2018). Using machine learning to support qualitative coding in social science: Shifting the focus to ambiguity. *ACM Transactions on Interactive Intelligent Systems*, *8*(2), 1–20. Advance online publication. doi:10.1145/3185515

Dixon-Woods, M. (2011). Using framework-based synthesis for conducting reviews of qualitative studies. *BMC Medicine*, *9*(1), 39. doi:10.1186/1741-7015-9-39 PMID:21492447

Duan, Q., & Liao, T. W. (2013). A new age-based replenishment policy for supply chain inventory optimization of highly perishable products. *International Journal of Production Economics*, *145*(2), 658–671. doi:10.1016/j.ijpe.2013.05.020

Durach, C. F., Kembro, J., & Wieland, A. (2017). A New Paradigm for Systematic Literature Reviews in Supply Chain Management. *The Journal of Supply Chain Management*, *53*(4), 67–85. doi:10.1111/jscm.12145

Escobar, C. A., & Morales-Menendez, R. (2018). Machine learning techniques for quality control in high conformance manufacturing environment. *Advances in Mechanical Engineering*, *10*(2), 168781401875551. doi:10.1177/1687814018755519

Estelles-Lopez, L., Ropodi, A., Pavlidis, D., Fotopoulou, J., Gkousari, C., Peyrodie, A., Panagou, E., Nychas, G.-J., & Mohareb, F. (2017). An automated ranking platform for machine learning regression models for meat spoilage prediction using multi-spectral imaging and metabolic profiling. *Food Research International*, *99*, 206–215. doi:10.1016/j.foodres.2017.05.013 PMID:28784477

Feizabadi, J. (2020). Machine learning demand forecasting and supply chain performance. *International Journal of Logistics Research and Applications*, 1–24. doi:10.1080/13675567.2020.1803246

Golmohammadi, D., Creese, R. C., Valian, H., & Kolassa, J. (2009). Supplier Selection Based on a Neural Network Model Using Genetic Algorithm. *IEEE Transactions on Neural Networks*, *20*(9), 1504–1519. doi:10.1109/TNN.2009.2027321 PMID:19695996

Goyal, S., & Routroy, S. (2021). Analyzing environmental sustainability enablers for an Indian steel manufacturing supply chain. *Journal of Engineering, Design and Technology, ahead-of-p*(ahead-of-print). doi:10.1108/JEDT-03-2021-0118

Guzzo, R. A., Jette, R. D., & Katzell, R. A. (1985). The effects of psychologically based intervention programs on worker productivity: A meta-analysis. *Personnel Psychology*, *38*(2), 275–291. doi:10.1111/j.1744-6570.1985.tb00547.x

Hartley, J. L., & Sawaya, W. J. (2019). Tortoise, not the hare: Digital transformation of supply chain business processes. *Business Horizons*, *62*(6), 707–715. doi:10.1016/j.bushor.2019.07.006

He, P., He, Y., & Xu, H. (2020). Buy-online-and-deliver-from-store strategy for a dual-channel supply chain considering retailer's location advantage. *Transportation Research Part E, Logistics and Transportation Review*, *144*, 102127. doi:10.1016/j.tre.2020.102127

Huo, B., Qi, Y., Wang, Z., & Zhao, X. (2014). The impact of supply chain integration on firm performance: The moderating role of competitive strategy. *Supply Chain Management*, *19*(4), 369–384. doi:10.1108/SCM-03-2013-0096

Jose, A., & Shanmugam, P. V. (2019). Supply chain issues in SME food sector: a systematic review. In Journal of Advances in Management Research (Vol. 17, Issue 1, pp. 19–65). doi:10.1108/JAMR-02-2019-0010

Kaparthi, S., & Bumblauskas, D. (2020). Designing predictive maintenance systems using decision tree-based machine learning techniques. *International Journal of Quality & Reliability Management*, *37*(4), 659–686. doi:10.1108/IJQRM-04-2019-0131

Kim, D.-H., Kim, T. J. Y., Wang, X., Kim, M., Quan, Y.-J., Oh, J. W., Min, S.-H., Kim, H., Bhandari, B., Yang, I., & Ahn, S.-H. (2018). Smart Machining Process Using Machine Learning: A Review and Perspective on Machining Industry. *International Journal of Precision Engineering and Manufacturing-Green Technology*, *5*(4), 555–568. doi:10.100740684-018-0057-y

Köksal, D., Strähle, J., & Müller, M. (2018). Social Sustainability in Apparel Supply Chains—The Role of the Sourcing Intermediary in a Developing Country. *Sustainability*, *10*(4), 1039. doi:10.3390u10041039

Kumar, A., Liu, R., & Shan, Z. (2020). Is Blockchain a Silver Bullet for Supply Chain Management? Technical Challenges and Research Opportunities. *Decision Sciences*, *51*(1), 8–37. doi:10.1111/deci.12396

Kumar, R., Tiwari, S., & Kansara, S. (2021). Barriers Prioritization of the Indian Steel Industry Supply Chain: Applying AHP and Fuzzy AHP Method. *Vision: The Journal of Business Perspective*. Advance online publication. doi:10.1177/09722629211065687

Kumaraguru, S., Kulvatunyou, B., & Morris, K. C. (2014). *Integrating Real-Time Analytics and Continuous Performance Management in Smart Manufacturing Systems*. doi:10.1007/978-3-662-44733-8_22

Kusiak, A. (2020). Convolutional and generative adversarial neural networks in manufacturing. *International Journal of Production Research*, *58*(5), 1594–1604. doi:10.1080/00207543.2019.1662133

Ma, H., Wang, Y., & Wang, K. (2018). Automatic detection of false positive RFID readings using machine learning algorithms. *Expert Systems with Applications*, *91*, 442–451. doi:10.1016/j.eswa.2017.09.021

Ma, L., & Sun, B. (2020). Machine learning and AI in marketing – Connecting computing power to human insights. *International Journal of Research in Marketing*, *37*(3), 481–504. doi:10.1016/j.ijresmar.2020.04.005

Makkar, S., Devi, G. N. R., & Solanki, V. K. (2020). Applications of Machine Learning Techniques in Supply Chain Optimization. In ICICCT 2019 – System Reliability, Quality Control, Safety, Maintenance and Management (pp. 861–869). Springer Singapore. doi:10.1007/978-981-13-8461-5_98

Martínez, A., Schmuck, C., Pereverzyev, S. Jr, Pirker, C., & Haltmeier, M. (2020). A machine learning framework for customer purchase prediction in the non-contractual setting. *European Journal of Operational Research*, *281*(3), 588–596. doi:10.1016/j.ejor.2018.04.034

Ni, D., Xiao, Z., & Lim, M. K. (2020). A systematic review of the research trends of machine learning in supply chain management. *International Journal of Machine Learning and Cybernetics*, *11*(7), 1463–1482. doi:10.100713042-019-01050-0

Pahwa, A. (2020). Agritech-towards transforming Indian agricutlure. *Ernst & Young LLP EY*, *8*, 1–53.

Patel, B. S., Samuel, C., & Sharma, S. K. (2017). Evaluation of agility in supply chains: A case study of an Indian manufacturing organization. *Journal of Manufacturing Technology Management*, *28*(2), 212–231. doi:10.1108/JMTM-09-2016-0125

Pournader, M., Ghaderi, H., Hassanzadegan, A., & Fahimnia, B. (2021). Artificial intelligence applications in supply chain management. *International Journal of Production Economics*, *241*, 108250. doi:10.1016/j.ijpe.2021.108250

Prahathish, K., Naren, J., Vithya, G., Akhil, S., Dinesh Kumar, K., & Sai Krishna Mohan Gupta, S. (2020). *A Systematic Frame Work Using Machine Learning Approaches in Supply Chain Forecasting*. doi:10.1007/978-3-030-39033-4_15

Razvi, S. S., Feng, S., Narayanan, A., Lee, Y.-T. T., & Witherell, P. (2019, August 18). A Review of Machine Learning Applications in Additive Manufacturing. *39th Computers and Information in Engineering Conference*. 10.1115/DETC2019-98415

Sandelowski, M., Voils, C. I., & Barroso, J. (2007). Comparability work and the management of difference in research synthesis studies. *Social Science & Medicine*, *64*(1), 236–247. doi:10.1016/j.socscimed.2006.08.041 PMID:17029691

Sawyerr, E., & Harrison, C. (2020). Developing resilient supply chains: lessons from high-reliability organisations. In Supply Chain Management (Vol. 25, Issue 1, pp. 77–100). Emerald Group Publishing Ltd. doi:10.1108/SCM-09-2018-0329

Sharma, A., Zhang, Z., & Rai, R. (2021). The interpretive model of manufacturing: A theoretical framework and research agenda for machine learning in manufacturing. *International Journal of Production Research*, *59*(16), 4960–4994. doi:10.1080/0 0207543.2021.1930234

Silva, J. C. F., Carvalho, T. F. M., Basso, M. F., Deguchi, M., Pereira, W. A., Sobrinho, R. R., Vidigal, P. M. P., Brustolini, O. J. B., Silva, F. F., Dal-Bianco, M., Fontes, R. L. F., Santos, A. A., Zerbini, F. M., Cerqueira, F. R., & Fontes, E. P. B. (2017). Geminivirus data warehouse: A database enriched with machine learning approaches. *BMC Bioinformatics*, *18*(1), 240. doi:10.118612859-017-1646-4 PMID:28476106

Thakkar, J., Kanda, A., & Deshmukh, S. G. (2012). Supply chain issues in Indian manufacturing SMEs: Insights from six case studies. *Journal of Manufacturing Technology Management*, *23*(5), 634–664. doi:10.1108/17410381211234444

Tirkolaee, E. B., Sadeghi, S., Mooseloo, F. M., Vandchali, H. R., & Aeini, S. (2021). Application of Machine Learning in Supply Chain Management: A Comprehensive Overview of the Main Areas. *Mathematical Problems in Engineering*, *2021*, 1–14. doi:10.1155/2021/1476043

Toorajipour, R., Sohrabpour, V., Nazarpour, A., Oghazi, P., & Fischl, M. (2021). Artificial intelligence in supply chain management: A systematic literature review. *Journal of Business Research*, *122*, 502–517. doi:10.1016/j.jbusres.2020.09.009

Tranfield, D., Denyer, D., & Smart, P. (2003). Towards a Methodology for Developing Evidence-Informed Management Knowledge by Means of Systematic Review. *British Journal of Management*, *14*(3), 207–222. doi:10.1111/1467-8551.00375

Valente, F. J., & Neto, A. C. (2017). Intelligent steel inventory tracking with IoT / RFID. *2017 IEEE International Conference on RFID Technology and Application, RFID-TA 2017*, 158–163. 10.1109/RFID-TA.2017.8098639

Weichert, D., Link, P., Stoll, A., Rüping, S., Ihlenfeldt, S., & Wrobel, S. (2019). A review of machine learning for the optimization of production processes. *International Journal of Advanced Manufacturing Technology*, *104*(5–8), 1889–1902. doi:10.100700170-019-03988-5

Wisetsri, W., Donthu, S., Mehbodniya, A., Vyas, S., Quiñonez-Choquecota, J., & Neware, R. (2021). An Investigation on the Impact of Digital Revolution and Machine Learning in Supply Chain Management. *Materials Today: Proceedings.* Advance online publication. doi:10.1016/j.matpr.2021.09.367

Wu, H., Cao, J., Yang, Y., Tung, C. L., Jiang, S., Tang, B., Liu, Y., Wang, X., & Deng, Y. (2019). Data Management in Supply Chain Using Blockchain: Challenges and a Case Study. *2019 28th International Conference on Computer Communication and Networks (ICCCN)*, 1–8. 10.1109/ICCCN.2019.8846964

Xiao, B., & Benbasat, I. (2018). An empirical examination of the influence of biased personalized product recommendations on consumers' decision making outcomes. *Decision Support Systems*, *110*, 46–57. doi:10.1016/j.dss.2018.03.005

Zhang, W. (2021). Surface Roughness Prediction with Machine Learning. *Journal of Physics: Conference Series*, *1856*(1), 012040. doi:10.1088/1742-6596/1856/1/012040

Zhang, X.-D. (2020). Machine Learning. In *A Matrix Algebra Approach to Artificial Intelligence* (pp. 223–440). Springer Singapore. doi:10.1007/978-981-15-2770-8_6

Chapter 14
The Effect of Good Corporate Governance on Financial Distress in Companies Listed in Sharia Stock Index Indonesia:
Machine Learning Approach

Sylva Alif Rusmita
Airlangga University, Indonesia

Moh.Saifin Ami An-Nafis
Airlangga University, Indonesia

Indria Ramadhani
Airlangga University, Indonesia

Mohammad Irfan
CMR Institute of Technology, India

ABSTRACT

This study aims to examine the effect of good corporate governance (GCG) on financial distress in companies listed on the Indonesian Sharia Stock Index. The purposive sampling method was used, obtaining 23 samples that met the criteria. Panel regression and machine learning were used to test the hypothesis. Based on the results, the variables of GCG, which consist of institutional ownership (IO), managerial ownership (MO), board of commissioners size (BoC), and proportion

DOI: 10.4018/978-1-6684-4483-2.ch014

Copyright © 2023, IGI Global. Copying or distributing in print or electronic forms without written permission of IGI Global is prohibited.

of independent commissioners (PI), affect financial distress simultaneously, whereas BoC and PI are partially the most significant variables. The machine learning method shows that extra trees is the best model to analyze financial distress. The model indicates the most significant variable is IO, followed by BoC and PI. From the result, Islamic issuers should manage their GCG by reducing the number of BoC, IO, and adding a proportion of PI to minimize the case of financial distress.

INTRODUCTION

The term Good Corporate Governance is commonly referred to as the governance of a company. Good Corporate Governance is regulation for companies helpful in carrying out control to add value-added to the company and its stakeholders. This can happen with Good Corporate Governance, which can form a pattern of management performance that makes management clean, transparent, and professional (Effendi, 2009).

Based on the data from Asian Development bank in 2013, Indonesia is ranked 5th at (54.55), far above the first ranked country, namely Thailand (75.39), Malaysia ranked second (71.69), Singapore ranked third (71.68). Furthermore, the Philippines ranked fourth at (57.99), while Vietnam ranked sixth at (33.87) (Asia Dev:elompent Bank, 2014). Good Corporate Governance is considered increasingly crucial with macro-scale financial problems. Further the data from the Ministry of Finance, state owned enterprises were threatened with financial distress, such as PT. Dirgantara Indonesia (-0.84), PT. Pindad (1.02), PT Indosutri Kereta Api (0.92), PT. Barata Indonesia (0.83), PT. Krakatau Steel (0.47), PT. Doc and Kodja Bahari (-1.72), PT. Dock and Shipping Surabaya (-1.23), PT Industri Kapal Indonesia (0.89), PT PAL Indonesia (-0.1) (Santoso & Kurniawan, 2019). The emergence of various kinds of problems that occur further strengthens the importance of applying good corporate governance.

The concept of corporate governance is promoted to realize corporate governance that is more open to users of financial statements. So, in the long term, the implementation of good corporate governance can affect the company's results, where the company's results will be linked to financial performance. If there is a problem with financial performance, it can damage the company's stability, and in the long run, it can lead to bankruptcy conditions (Ananto et al., 2017).

Symptoms of bankruptcy can be identified by conducting a bankruptcy analysis. Management will be better at minimizing bankruptcy if these symptoms are detected early. One of the symptoms of bankruptcy can be seen from financial distress.

Financial distress is a fundamental problem for a company to be aware of. According to Platt & Platt (2002), financial distress is a critical stage in financial decline and can signify more serious financial problems, including bankruptcy.

In this study examine the effect of GCG to financial distress from a group of companies listed on Indonesian Sharia Stock Index (ISSI). Researchers are interested in taking samples from ISSI because the considerations have more complex criteria. The Islamic capital market has its own charm for Muslim investors who avoid shares of companies that operate not according to sharia. This object is attractive because of the very fast development of investors. The shares listed on ISSI so far have more than 350 issuers joining ISSI, so it is interesting for the authors to conduct this research. In addition, ISSI constituents are selected (screening) 2 times a year, ISSI constituents are also determined by Indonesia financial Authority (OJK) that they do not have a non-halal portfolio, not only that, the issuer's financial ratio is a comparison ratio with a total legacy of less than 45% and the ratio of interest income / non-halal is limited to an optimal 10% of the total income and other income. With these criteria, listed companies must implement good corporate governance. This analyze the last 9 years period from 2011-2019. This research was also conducted to ensure the correctness of the inconsistent results between the influences of independent variables on the possibility of financial distress. The writing stage of this research begins with the introduction. The second is research background to describe the related theories. Next is the problem statement of research, which are includes the previous study, issues, problem statement, and the development of hypotheses. In the fourth part is the solutions and recommendations. Then, followed by future research directions. Finally, there is a conclusion.

BACKGROUND

Agency Theory

The agency deals with issues that arise when people intend to divide their authority to provide services for them, which is a kind of contract between management and shareholders (Jensen & Meckling, 1976). Agency theory suggests corporate governance could reduce agency conflicts which ultimately leads to improved corporate performance. The problem that occurs is known as a problem between two parties, namely shareholders and managers. The separation of control and ownership in a company's financial system led to agency problems and a number of corporate governance mechanisms were introduced to mitigate it.

The onset of profit management can be explained by the agency's theory. As an agent, managers are morally responsible for optimizing the profits of the owners and in return will be compensated in accordance with the contract. Thus there are two different interests within the company where each party strives to achieve or maintain the desired level of prosperity. Jensen & Meckling (1976) state that agency theory uses three assumptions of human nature, namely: (1) humans are generally self-interested, (2) humans have limited thinking about future perceptions (bounded rationality), and (3) humans always avoid risk (risk averse).

According to Jensen & Meckling (1976), companies whose ownership and managerial control are high then the cost of the agency is low. This is because between shareholders and managers there is the same goal. Agency problems arise due to the presence of: (1) information asymmetry, (2) potential welfare transfers made by managers from bondholders to shareholders through the acceptance of high-risk projects that generate high returns, (3) the error of accepting projects that provide positive net present value and consumption of remaining profits.

Financial Distress

Financial distress is the stage of a deterioration in the state of finance that occurs as a sign of bankruptcy or liquidation (Platt & Platt, 2002). Financial distress is reflected in the inability of the company or the unavailability of a fund to pay obligations that have matured. The procedure that can be used in recognizing how the financial state of an industry can use a mathematical model of prediction of financial difficulties (Altman, 1968).

Altman classifies financial distress into four parts:

1.   Economic Failure: A state where a company's income cannot cover its total costs, including its cost of capital. The sustainability of the company depends on the willingness of creditors to provide capital and the owner of the company is willing to accept the rate of return (rate of return) below the market.
2.   Business Failure: Occurs due to inability to generate profits. In other words, the business will fail if it does not provide cash flow for expenses.
3.   Technical Insolvency: Bankruptcy can occur if a company does not meet its obligations, even though the value of its assets exceeds the amount of its debt (temporary). And bankruptcy can occur when the value of the debt exceeds the market value of the asset and makes it possible to stop the business.
4.   Legal Bankruptcy: In this case it is more formal, or the company can be declared legally bankrupt if a formal lawsuit is filed under the law.

Financial distress can arise due to factors from within the company itself (internal) or from outside the company (external). Effendi (2009) states that the factors that cause financial distress from within the company are more micro, these factors include cash difficulties, the amount of debt, and losses in the company's operational activities.

If the company can overcome or cover the three things above, there is no guarantee that the company can avoid financial distress. Because there are still external factors of the company that cause financial distress. According to Effendi (2009) the company's external factors are more macro and the scope is wider. One of these external factors can be government policies that can add to the business burden borne by the company. In addition, there is also an increased loan interest rate policy that causes the interest expense borne by the company to increase.

Good Corporate Governance (GCG)

GCG is the principle that underlies the processes and mechanisms of corporate governance based on the provisions of laws and regulations and business ethics. The Organization for Economic Cooperation and Development (OECD) shares the basic principles of good corporate management consisting of 4 aspects, namely fairness, transparency, accountability, and responsibility. Indonesian companies monitor the implementation of good corporate governance supervised by the National Committee on Governance Policy (KNKG). KNKG issued the General Guidelines for Good Corporate Governance Indonesia to be used by companies as a reference in good company management, which is further known as GCG guidelines.

According to Agrawal and Knober (1996) in (Al-Najjar, 2010), the good corporate mechanism is divided into internal and external mechanisms, such as institutional ownership or the proportion of company shares owned by institutions or business entities or organizations, managerial ownership is the ownership of company shares owned by the company's own managers, the size of the board of commissioners as an organ of the company is collectively responsible for supervising and providing advice to the board of directors and ensure that the company implements GCG, and the proportions of independent commissioners determined by the general meeting of shareholders decisions by affiliated parties.

Panel Regression

Regression analysis of panel data in this study was used to see the same time period in several study samples using Eviews 9 software. The use of this model will result in different interceptions and slope coefficients in each company and each time period, so that there will be the following possibilities (Gujarati & Porter, 2009):

1. It is assumed that the interception and slope are fixed over time and the individual (company) and the difference in interception and slope is explained by the variable of the disorder
2. Assumed the slope is fixed but the interception is different between individuals Assumed the slope is fixed but the interception is different both between time and between individuals
3. It is assumed that the interception and the slope are different between individuals
4. It is assumed that the interception and the slope are different between times and between individuals.

In estimating the panel data regression model according to Gujarati & Porter (2009) there are several techniques including:

1. OLS (Ordinary Least Square)

The OLS regression model or known as the comman effect estimation method is calculated by combining data in time series and cross sections without paying attention to the difference between time and individuals or in other words, the assumption of company behavior is the same in various periods of time. The equation of the OLS model can be written as follows:

$$lny_{it} = \beta_0 + \beta_1 lnX_{1it} + \beta_2 \beta X_{2it} + e_{it}$$

2. Fixed effect

The fixed effect model refutes the assumption that interceptions and slopes are the same at any time between companies where in practice it will be very far from what happens in the field. The presence of variables that are not included in the model allows non-constant interceptions or changes to occur for each company and time. To overcome the intercept change, this model uses the dummy variable technique in trapping the differences in interceptions between companies. Here are the similarities of the fixed effect model:

$$lny_{it} = \beta_0 + \beta_1 lnX_{1it} + \beta_2 \beta X_{2it} + \beta_3 \beta X_{3it} + \beta_4 \beta X_{4it} + \beta_5 \beta X_{5it} + e_{it}$$

3. Random effect

The random effect model looks at the differences between companies and time through their error values. This method takes into account errors that may be correlated throughout the time series and cross sections, mathematically the equation can be formulated as follows:

$$y_{it} = \alpha + \alpha_i + \beta X_{it} + \varepsilon_{it} + u_{it}$$

To find out the panel data regression model that will be used, a test method is needed which is divided into three (Gujarati & Porter, 2009).

1. Chow test

To see the panel data regression technique with fixed effect is better than fixed effect models without dummy variables or OLS models, the Chow test can be used. The hypothesis of the Chow test is:

H0 = if alpha > 0.05 then using the Comman effect model
H1= if alpha < 0.05 then using the Fixed effect model

2. Hausman test

This test was carried out to compare the fixed effect model with the random effect. If on the chow test the results show that H1 is accepted, you must do the hausman test. The hypothesis formed in the Hausman test is:

H0 = if alpha > 0.05 then using the Random effect model
H1= if alpha < 0.05 then using the Fixed effect modelUji Lagrange Multiplier

3. Lagrange Multiplier test (LM)

This test aims to find out the exact model used between the OLS or Random effect, the LM test looks at the value of the chi-squares distribution with a degree of freedom of the number of independent variables. The hypothesis of the LM test is:

H0 = if alpha > 0.05 then using the Comman effect model
H1 = if alpha < 0.05 then using the Random effect model

Machine Learning

Machine learning method consists of several stages, namely:

1.   Dendrological Methods:

Decision Trees and Forest classification and regression tree (CART) is a model used to see how strongly the influence of each independent variable on its dependent variables by dividing data according to values for each independent variable used so that a decision will be obtained useful as a predictive value. (Athey & Imbens, 2019; Chen, 2021; Putra, 2019; Zurada et al., 2011)

2.   Bias Variance Tradeoff

To be able to improve accuracy on cart models, it is necessary to pay attention to the comparison between bias and variance. The presence of high bias values can have an impact on the lower the value of the sample loyal variance. There is no need for a tradeoff between bias and variance, as it is not possible together to achieve the lowest possible bias and variance values. The tradeoff solution offered is to look for models with low bias and low variance, so that there is an ideal balance between underfitting data (lowest variance) and overfitting (highest variance). (Athey & Imbens, 2019; Chen, 2021; Putra, 2019; Zurada et al., 2011). To reduce the bias, there are several steps that should be followed:

- Hyperparameter tuning

Looking for a good balance between bias values and variance can be done with hyperparameters tests that can be adjusted for value. How to customize the hyperparameter through grid search and random search. (Athey & Imbens, 2019; Chen, 2021; Putra, 2019; Zurada et al., 2011).

- Training, validation, and test data

When making adjustments the hyperparameter can consume all available data. The existence of large amounts of data is needed because it is useful to separate data into training data, validity, and testing subtests that can later be useful to find the optimal balance between bias and variance. (Athey & Imbens, 2019; Chen, 2021; Putra, 2019; Zurada et al., 2011).

3.   Ensemble and boosting methods

At this stage will be tested models both using training data that is the shaper of the model and the test data used to test the model. In machine learning there are several models that can be used, namely:

- Bagging and pasting

Determining the most appropriate CART value can be done by diversifying between training data and test data. Later training data can be replaced or not. Training data that is not replaced may be used as an additional validation of cart value determination for previously unobserved data. As for training data conducted replacement / bagging can improve training data and CART performance. (Chen, 2021)

- Random forest and extra trees

In this model is done inputting a large number of decisions using a variety of models (Extra trees, AdaBoost, XGBoost). The extra trees model is the simplest model in its use, which is done by tuning two hyperparameters which then randomizes each data included in the threshold. (Chen, 2021)

- Adaptive and gradient boosting

AdaBoost is a model that relies on a single decision, so the AdaBoost Model is done to update weights for each independent variable, this is what is difficult for AdaBoost to do because there needs to be learning from independent variables continuously. XGBoost or gradient boosting is more suitable for use because it can make decisions by offering many variant options. (Chen, 2021)

- Support vector machines and neural networks

Support vesctor machines and neural networks are two very different approaches to machine learning. Where for small to medium sized data sets are more suitable using the support model vesctor machines because it is flexible enough to handle tasks such as classification, error detection and fraud. (Ben-Hur et al. 2001). Neural networks can be used in the field of body language processing and robotics. (Chen, 2021)

4. Model selection

After selecting diverse models, data processing can be done to find out the comparison between training values and test scores in each model. The model with the best accuracy can be seen through the highest $R2$ value and the lowest RMSE value. A high $R2$ indicates the most powerful or accurate model with little data bias.

While the RMSE value indicates the error rate, the lower the value, the less errors that occur in the model. (Chen, 2021)

MAIN FOCUS OF THE CHAPTER

Issues, Controversies, Problems

There are several previous studies discussing the implementation of GCG on financial distress. Findings in Helena & Saifi (2018); Hussein & Al-Tamimi (2012); Li et al. (2008); Pramudena (2017); and Wardhani (2006) stated that there are several components of GCG that have an impact on financial distress. However, in the research of Widhiastuti et al. (2019) says that GCG has no direct or indirect influence on financial distress. Helena & Saifi (2018); and Pramudena (2017) state that institutional ownership also has an impact on financial distress. Meanwhile, in the research analysis of Widhiastuti et al. (2019) and (Yudha & Fuad, 2014). Institutional ownership as a GCG variable does not have an impact on financial failure. The managerial ownership variable has an effect on the probability of financial difficulties (Fathoni & Haryetti, Wijaya, 2014; Pramudena, 2017). On the other hand, Wardhani (2006) research says that there is a negative impact of managerial ownership on financial failure. Managerial ownership has no effect on financial failure (Widhiastuti et al., 2019). Ownership concentration was also found to be negative with the probability of financial distress/financial difficulty (Li et al., 2008).

The size of the board of commissioners affects the probability of bankruptcy (Helena & Saifi, 2018; Wardhani, 2006). Meanwhile, according to Mafiroh & Triyono (2016) and Yudha & Fuad (2014) that the board of commissioners has no influence on the collapse of bankruptcy. According to Helena & Saifi (2018); Pramudena (2017); Yudha & Fuad (2014) the portion of the Independent Commissioner has an influence on financial failure. Meanwhile, in the research of Fathoni et al. (2014) that the proportion of independent commissioners has a significant effect on the occurrence of financial difficulties.

In the study, Murhadi et al. (2018) argue that the size variable affects financial difficulties. However, a study by Santoso et al. (2018) stated that size does not affect forecasts of financial failure. Leverage affects the potential for financial difficulties, as shown by the studies of Mafiroh & Triyono (2016); Shahwan (2015). Mafiroh & Triyono (2016) stated that the leverage ratio has a significant positive effect on the possibility of a financial crisis.

The variety results describe the inconsistent results of these variables on financial distress analysis, so this encourages researchers to re-examine how the influence of GCG on the six indicators of institutional ownership, managerial ownership, board of commissioners' size, independent board of commissioners, size, and leverage. The reason the researcher chooses this variable is because according to several theories in previous research, it is illustrated that there are variables that cause financial difficulties.

In this study examine the effect of GCG to financial distress from a group of companies listed on Indonesian Sharia Stock Index (ISSI). Researchers are interested in taking samples from ISSI because the considerations have more complex criteria. The Islamic capital market has its own charm for Muslim investors who avoid shares of companies that operate not according to sharia. This object is attractive because of the very fast development of investors

Hypothesis One: The effect of institutional ownership on financial distress

Institutional ownership has a positive influence on financial distress (Fathonah, 2016). If you want to increase the value of the company, institutional owners are encouraged to make loans to management, this is intended to continue to improve their performance (Sujoko, 2007). According to Classens et al. (1999) in the research of Wardhani (2006) stated that the existence of company ownership can reduce the level of corporate bankruptcy. However, when the property is owned centrally, in other words, by a majority shareholder, the board is more likely to undertake research activities that can bring personal gain. In this case, the formulation of the hypothesis is as follows:

H0: institutional ownership has no effect on financial distress.
H1: institutional ownership has a significant effect on financial distress.
Hypothesis Two: The effect of managerial ownership on financial distress

Companies in which there is good managerial ownership can increase the value of the company because large management ownership can monitor company activities effectively (Jensen & Meckling, 1976). Michelberger (2016) also produces the same thing that the importance of ownership structure in the company. One solution to overcome agency costs is to increase managerial ownership, because when managerial ownership increases it can synchronize the interests of managers with the interests of shareholders (Jensen & Meckling, 1976).

H0: Managerial ownership has no effect on financial distress.
H2: Managerial ownership has a significant effect on financial distress.
Hypothesis Three: The effect of the size of the board of commissioners on financial distress

The higher the need for optimal external relations, the higher the need for governance (Wardhani, 2006). Meanwhile, increasing the number of administrators can also increase coordination and communication problems, which is followed by a decrease in the ability of administrators to exercise control over management, and can cause problems for agencies (Jensen, 1993). Then the hypothesis is:

H0: The size of the board of commissioners has no effect on financial distress.

H3: The size of the board of commissioners has a significant effect on financial distress.

Hypothesis Four: The effect of the proportion of the board of commissioners on financial distress

The higher the proportion of independent commissioners can improve monitoring and control on the performance of a company, this can be beneficial for reducing the potential for financial distress for the company (Salancik & Pfeffer, 1978). The formulation of the hypothesis is:

H0: The proportion of independent commissioners has no effect on financial distress.

H4: The proportion of independent commissioners has a significant effect on financial distress.

SOLUTIONS AND RECOMMENDATIONS

The method used in this study is a quantitative approach, a combination of economic analysis and experimental statistics, which are classified into specific categories to facilitate analysis. The assistance of computer statistics applications is used in the statistical calculation process of Eviews 9 for running panel data regression and R for machine learning method. The data used in this study are quantitative data taken from the Indonesia Stock Exchange (IDX) website www.idx.co.id, Indonesia financial service authority (OJK), and annual reports from various companies that are in line with this research, as well as sources of information relevant. The population of this study consisted of all companies listed on the Indonesian Sharia Stock Index (ISSI) for the period 2011 to 2019.

The sampling in this study used a purposive sampling method. The purposive sampling method is a sampling technique that fits certain criteria that the researcher wants to study (Etikan et al., 2016).

The criteria sample are:

1. Consist listed in ISSI form 2011-2029

1. The companies which generated profit (not negative profit)
2. Consist presenting data used in research

This study conducted data twice using different methods. The first method is regression of panel data to identify the effect of independent variables on dependent variables either simultaneously or partially. Another method used is machine learning, the selection of this method because it can identify several models, both traditional statistics and by using machine learning models (Chen, 2021). Later it can be seen the difference between the two research methods in looking at the most influential dependent variables.

Panel Regression Result and Discussion

This test aims to determine the effect of the independent variable on the dependent variable. The panel regression test used Fixed Effect Model (FEM):

Table 1. Panel Regression (FEM) Result

Variable	Coefficient	Std. Error	t-Statistic	Prob.
C	41.41879	14.34638	2.88706	0.00437
X1_IO	-1.842122	1.19926	-1.53604	0.12630
X2_MO	-2.29740	1.77309	-1.29570	0.19676
X3_BoC	-0.37836	0.16074	-2.353843	0.01967*
X4_IC	4.03510	1.79112	2.25284	0.02549*
X5_SIZE	-1.06526	0.47842	-2.22662	0.02723
X6_LEV	-0.79351	1.48953	-0.53272	0.59489

Source: Data Processed, 2022

The form of the multiple linear regression model equation can be rewritten as follows:

Financial Distress $= 41.41879 - 1.842122\,IO - 2.29740MO - 0.37836BoC + 4.03510IC - 1.06526SIZE - 0.79351LEV + e$

According to the theory Altman z score, a high Z-Score value indicates the smaller the possibility of financial distress. Based on the result above, the Institutional Ownership (X1_IO) with coefficient -1.84 and a probability level 0,12 describe a

Effect of Good Corporate Governance on Financial Distress in Companies Listed in Stock Index

negative relationship between institutional ownership and Z score. Each additional 1 unit in institutional ownership will reduce the Z-Score value by -1.84, meaning that the financial distress will increase. So, the increasing of Institutional ownership will deliver company into financial distress. The result is in line with Adityaputra (2017) who argues that institutional ownership is a temporary owner who focuses more on short-term profits; If this profit is considered less profitable, investors from other companies will liquidate a very large number of shares. Such actions can affect the value of shares, which will cause financial difficulties for the company in the future. The Indonesian Corporate Governance Forum (FCGI) states that companies with concentrated ownership structures, such as institutional ownership with large shares, can be a reflection of institutional strength. This condition allows institutions to intervene in the company's operations, to intervene with the aim of committing fraud/deviance which can result in a decrease in company efficiency which will result in financial difficulties.

Second, variable, Managerial Ownership (X2_MO) with a coefficient of -2.297 with a probability level (significance) of 0.19 which indicate no significant at 5% level. The managerial ownership is negatively on the Z.Score. Each additional 1 unit in managerial ownership will decrease the Z-Score value by -2.297 units. A high Z-Score value indicates the smaller the possibility of financial distress. So, it can be concluded that management ownership could add financial difficulties. This study is consistent with Fathoni et al. (2014); Pramudena (2017); and Yudha & Fuad (2014) which state that managerial ownership probability hold up of financial distress.

The Board of the Commissioner (X3_BoC) with a coefficient of -0.378 with a probability level (significance) of 0.019 or less than 5% (0.05), so statistically the independent board of commissioners has a negative relationship and a significant effect below 5% on the Z-Score. Each additional 1 unit on the independent board of commissioners will increase the Z-Score value by -0.378 units. A high Z-Score indicates a lower probability of financial distress, so it can be concluded that the size of the board of commissioners has a significantly add possibility negative effect on financial distress. The board of directors has full authority to direct the company's operational activities, and members of the board of directors can carry out their duties and responsibilities in accordance with the assigned division of duties and authorities. The ability of the board of directors affects the quality of decision making, which indirectly affects the size of the company's income. The higher the income received, the less likely it is to have financial difficulties (Radifan & Yuyetta, 2015). Unfortunately, the results show the size of the board director can result in the risk of bankruptcy, this explains that the company's internal parties sometimes make non-neutral decisions and the encouragement of corporate politics is in line with the agency's theory.

Next variable is the proportion of Independent Commissioners (X4_IC) shows a coefficient of 4.035 with a probability level (significance) of 0.025 or less than 5%, so statistically the proportion of independent commissioners has effect on the Z-Score. This means that the proportion of independent commissioners have a significant positive influence on financial problems. This shows that the number of independent commissioners in the company, the probability of financial difficulties can reduce financial distress. These results are in agreement with Helena & Saifi (2018) and Wardhani (2006). According to Helena & Saifi (2018), the significant relationship between the proportion of independent commissioners and financial distress conditions in the company shows that the existence of independent commissioners is still able to carry out effective supervision to prevent companies from financial distress,

The other controlling variable, Company Size (X6_SIZE) with a coefficient of -1.065 with a probability level (significance) of 0.027. Statistically the ownership of independent commissioners has a negative relationship and has a significant effect below 5% on Z-Score. Each additional 1 unit on the independent board of commissioners will reduce the Z-Score value by -1.065 units. A low Z-Score value indicates a higher probability of financial distress. It can be concluded that size has a significant positive effect on financial distress. This can happen because the bigger the company, the higher the cash flow and the bigger the company which will also cause agency problems, agency problems that can occur are free cash flow.

Leverage (X7_LEV), as a variable of control showed a coefficient of -0,79 with a probability level (significance) of 0.59 which indicate this variable is not significant. Each additional 1 unit on leverage will reduce the Z Score or in other words will increase financial distress. Thus, it can be concluded that leverage will inflict financial problems. This study is consistent with Miglani (2014) and Murhadi et al. (2018) that shows the greater the level of leverage in a company, the greater the probability of default occurring and can increase the possibility of financial distress.

Machine Learning Result and Discussion

The results of machine learning in this study used 8 models, including also comparing with traditional statistical models and 7 machine learning models as shown in the following table:

The results showed that the linearity model that describes classical statistics is not a suitable model. To determine the best model it is necessary to look at the test results with the highest R2 value and the lowest RMSE. R2 explains how accurate a model is to the research data, so to know the better model should selected the highest number of R square. While RMSE indicates an error that occurs in the model and selected that has the smallest value. Based on the table above, the Extra Tree model is the best model that can be used in this study. The extra trees model can indicate the most significant variables by using the mean decrease gini (Chen, 2021). Here are the results of the analysis per variable of the study:

Table 2. Machine Learning Result

Model	Training		Test	
	R^2	RMSE	R^2	RMSE
Linear	0.14383	0.93657	0.23020	0.83510
Decission Tree	0.43205	0.76280	0.20220	0.90148
Random Forest	0.85895	0.44773	0.56062	0.63334
Extra Tree	0.80876	0.50021	0.74441	0.50485
Bagging	0.91048	0.37034	0.57632	0.62252
XGBoost	0.86169	0.48790	0.70340	0.58420
Support Vector Machine	0.26146	0.90294	0.35608	0.78512
Neural Network	0.57363	0.66093	0.45814	0.78225

Based on the graph can be seen institutional ownership (X1) variables are the GCG variables that most affect financial distress, followed by variables Board of Commissioner size (X3) and Proportion of independent commissioners (X4). Although, managerial ownership (X2) variables have the weakest influence when compared to 3 other GCG variables. This indicates it is important for Islamic companies to pay attention to the proportion of these four variables, especially regarding institutional ownership that has the greatest influence. This means that the greater the proportion of institutional ownership of an Islamic company, can have an impact on fluctuations in bankruptcy risk, so it is important for Islamic companies to control.

FUTURE RESEARCH DIRECTIONS

Future research can used different independent variables as proxies of GCG, due to this paper just used 4 independent variables which represent 43%, which means there are 57% factors which did not include in this paper and had effect toward GCG. Afterwards, next research can focus in specific firm sectors or other counter. In the field of machine learning, this method such as extra trees is suitable to be implemented in economics and finance research and still rarely to be discussed.

Figure 1. Extra Trees Model.
Source: Data Processed, 2022

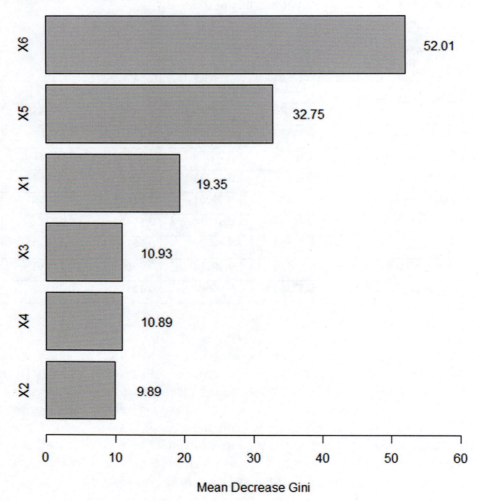

CONCLUSION

There are different results between panel data regression methods and machine learning using the extra trees model. On regression data panel found BoC variables have a significant negative effect and IC has a significant positive effect. Panel data results indicate to minimize the risk of bankruptcy, sharia companies can organize the proportion of GCG by reducing the number of boards of commissioners and increasing the proportion of independent commissioners. This result indicates that the function of an independent commissioner has a good effect on the sustainability of the company because it can provide neutral advice for the sustainability of the company, this is different from the duties of the board of commissioners that usually come from the company internally. The negative impact of the BoC indicates that more and more proportions of the BoC can actually lead to the risk of bankruptcy. This can indicate the existence of internal political interests of the company.

Other results found in the extra trees method indicate institutional ownership variables greatly affect the risk of corporate bankruptcy, which is then stacked with BoC and IC variables. Machine learning models cannot indicate the direction of significance, so there needs to be collaboration with panel data regression methods to see the negative or positive impact of a variable. Both models suggest io has a negative direction, meaning higher institutional ownership can result in a decreased risk of bankruptcy. The results of this study showed that the GCG variables consisting of IO, BoC, and IC were the most partially influential on the financial distress of Islamic companies.

REFERENCES

Adityaputra, S. A. (2017). The Effect of Corporate Governance Implementation on Financial Difficulties (Empirical Study on Manufacturing Companies Listed on the Indonesia Stock Exchange). *Jurnal ULTIMA Accounting*, *9*(2), 50–64. doi:10.31937/akuntansi.v9i2.729

Al-Najjar, B. (2010). Corporate Governance and Institutional Ownership: Evidence from Jordan. *Corporate Governance*, *10*(2), 176–190. doi:10.1108/14720701011035693

Altman, E. I. (1968). Financial Ratios, Discriminant Analysis, and the Prediction of Corporate Bankruptcy. *The Journal of Finance*, *23*(4), 589–609. doi:10.1111/j.1540-6261.1968.tb00843.x

Ananto, R. P., Mustika, R., & Handayani, D. (2017). The Effect of GCG, Leverage, Profitability and UP on FD on Consumer Goods Companies Listed on the Indonesia Stock Exchange. *Jurnal Ekonomi Dan Bisnis Dharma Andalas*, *19*(1), 92–105.

Athey, S., & Imbens, G. W. (2019). Machine Learning Methods That Economists Should Know about. *Annual Review of Economics*, *11*(1), 685–725. doi:10.1146/annurev-economics-080217-053433

Chen, J. M. (2021). An Introduction to Machine Learning for Panel Data. *International Advances in Economic Research*, *27*(1), 1–16. Advance online publication. doi:10.100711294-021-09815-6

Effendi, M. A. (2009). *The Power of Good Corporate Governance: Theory dan Implementations*. Salemba Empat.

Etikan, I., Musa, S. A., & Alkassim, R. S. (2016). Comparison of Convenience Sampling and Purposive Sampling. *American Journal of Theoretical and Applied Statistics*, *5*(1), 1–5. doi:10.11648/j.ajtas.20160501.11

Fathonah, A. N. (2016). The Effect of Good Corporate Governance Implementation on Financial Distress. *Jurnal Ilmiah Akuntansi, 1*(2), 133–150.

Fathoni, A. F., & Haryetti, W. E. Y. M. (2014). The Effect of Good Corporate Governance Mechanism, Financial Distress on Earning Management Behavior: Empirical Study in Property and Infrastructure Industry in Indonesian Stock Exchanges. *Jurnal Ekonomi*, *22*(1), 1–16.

Gujarati, D. N., & Porter, D. C. (2009). Basic Econometrics (5th ed.). McGraw-Hill.

Helena, S., & Saifi, M. (2018). The Impact of Corporate Governance Toward Financial Distress (Case Study: Transportation Companies Registered at Indonesia Stock Exchange 2013-2016). *Jurnal Administrasi Bisnis, 60*(2), 143–152. administrasibisnis. studentjournal.ub.ac.id%0A143

Hussein, A., & Al-Tamimi, H. (2012). The Effects of Corporate Governance on Performance and Financial Distress: The Experience of UAE National Banks. *Journal of Financial Regulation and Compliance*, *20*(2), 169–181. doi:10.1108/13581981211218315

Improving Lives Throughout Asia and The Pacific. (2014). https://www.adb.org/sites/default/files/institutional-document/158032/adb-annual-report-2014.pdf

Jensen, M. C. (1993). The Modern Industrial Revolution, Exit, and the Failure of Internal Control Systems. *The Journal of Finance*, *48*(3), 831–880. doi:10.1111/j.1540-6261.1993.tb04022.x

Jensen, M. C., & Meckling, W. H. (1976). Theory of The Firm: Managerial Behavior, Agency Costs, and Ownership Structure. *Journal of Financial Economics*, *3*(4), 305–360. doi:10.1016/0304-405X(76)90026-X

Li, H.-X., Wang, Z.-J., & Deng, X.-L. (2008). Ownership, Independent Directors, Agency Costs and Financial Distress: Evidence from Chinese Listed Companies. *Corporate Governance*, *8*(5), 622–636. doi:10.1108/14720700810913287

Mafiroh, A., & Triyono. (2016). The Effect of Financial Performance and Corporate Governance Mechanisms on Financial Distress (Empirical Study on Manufacturing Companies Listed on the Indonesia Stock Exchange 2011-2014 Period). *Riset Akuntansi Dan Keuangan Indonesia, 1*(1), 46–53.

Michelberger, K. (2016). Corporate Governance Effects on Firm Performance: A Literature Review. *Regional Formation and Development Studies, 20*(3), 84–95.

Miglani, S. (2014). Voluntary Audit Committee Characteristics in Financially Distressed and Healthy Firms: A Study of The Efficacy of The ASX Corporate Governance Council Recommendations. *Corporate Ownership & Control, 12*(1).

Murhadi, W. R., Tanugara, F., & Sutejo, B. S. (2018). The Influence of Good Corporate Governance on Financial Distress. *Advances in Social Science, Education and Humanities Research, 186*. doi:10.2991/insyma-18.2018.19

Platt, H. D., & Platt, M. B. (2002). Predicting Corporate Financial Distress: Reflections on Choice-Based Sample Bias. *Journal of Economics and Finance, 26*(2), 184–199. doi:10.1007/BF02755985

Pramudena, S. M. (2017). The Impact of Good Corporate Governance on Financial Distress in the Consumer Good Sector. *Journal of Finance and Banking Review, 10*(1), 46–55. http://journal.perbanas.id/index.php/jkp/article/view/192. doi:10.35609/jfbr.2017.2.4(6)

Putra, J. W. G. (2019). *The Introduction of Machine Learning and Deep Learning Consepts*. Computational Linguistics and Natural Language Processing Laboratory. https://www.researchgate.net/publication/323700644

Radifan, R., & Yuyetta, E. N. A. (2015). Good Corporate Governance Terhadap Kemungkinan Financial Distress. *Diponegoro Journal of Accounting, 4*(3), 1–11.

Salancik, G. R., & Pfeffer, J. (1978). A Social Information Processing Approach to Job Attitudes and Task Design. *Administrative Science Quarterly, 23*(2), 224–253. doi:10.2307/2392563 PMID:10307892

Santoso, G. A. P., Yulianeu, & Fathoni, A. (2018). Analysis of Effect of Good Corporate Governance, Financial Performance, and Firm Size on Financial Distress in Property and Real Estate Company Listed BEI 2012-2016. *Journal of Management, 4*(4).

Santoso & Kurniawan. (2019). List of State-Owned Enterprises Vulnerable to Bankruptcy. *Kontan*. https://nasional.kontan.co.id/news/ini-dia-daftar-bumn-yang-rentan-bangkrut

Shahwan, T. M. (2015). The Effects of Corporate Governance on Financial Performance and Financial Distress: Evidence from Egypt. *Corporate Governance, 15*(5), 641–662. doi:10.1108/CG-11-2014-0140

Sujoko. (2007). The Influence of Ownership Structure, Diversification Strategy, Leverage, Internal Factors, and External Factors on Firm Value (Empirical Study on Manufacturing and Non-Manufacturing Companies on the Jakarta Stock Exchange). *Ekuitas, 11*(2), 236–254.

Wardhani, R. (2006). Corporate Governance Mechanism in Financially Distressed Firms. *Simposium Nasional Akuntansi 9 Padang*, 23–26.

Widhiastuti, R., Nurkhin, A., & Susilowati, N. (2019). The Role of Financial Performance in Mediating The Effect of Good Corporate Governance on Financial Distress. *Journal of Economics, 15*(1), 34–47.

Yudha, A., & Fuad. (2014). Analysis of the Influence of the Implementation of Corporate Governance Mechanisms on the Possibility of Companies Experiencing Financial Distress Conditions (Empirical Study of Manufacturing Companies Listed on the Indonesia Stock Exchange 2010-2012). *Diponegoro Journal of Accounting, 3*(4), 1–12.

Zurada, J., Levitan, A. S., & Guan, J. (2011). A comparison of regression and artificial intelligence methods in a mass appraisal context. *Journal of Real Estate Research, 33*(3), 349–387. doi:10.1080/10835547.2011.12091311

KEY TERMS AND DEFINITIONS

Board of Commissioners Size: The company's parts are collectively responsible for supervising and advising the board of directors and ensuring that the company implements good corporate governance.

Extra Trees: One of the machine learning models, which classifies a type of ensemble learning technique that combines the results of several uncorrelated decision trees collected in the "forest" to produce the results of its classification.

Institutional Ownership: The proportion of company shares owned by institutions or business entities or organizations.

Islamic Issuers: Companies that are listed on the stock exchange and comply with sharia principles (financial statements and their business types).

Managerial Ownership: Ownership of company shares owned by the company's own managers.

Panel Regression: Quantitative research method that combines time series and cross sections which is useful for knowing the relationship between variables both simultaneously and partially.

Proportion of Independent Commissioners: Members of the commissioners are determined based on the decision of the GMS (General Meeting of Shareholders) by parties affiliated with the president director, board members, or other members of the commission.

Risk of Bankruptcy: The risk of failure for the company in carrying out its operations, can be caused by internal and external factors of the company.

Effect of Good Corporate Governance on Financial Distress in Companies Listed in Stock Index

APPENDIX 1

The result of panel regression model

Table 3. Chow Test

Effects Test	Statistic	d.f.	Prob.
Cross-section F	5.727878	(22,178)	0.0000
Cross-section Chi-square	110.804608	22	0.0000

Data Sources: Data Processed

Table 4. Hausman Test

Test Summary	Chi-Sq. Statistic	Chi-Sq. d.f.	Prob.
Cross-section random	18.180449	6	0.0058

Data Sources: Data Processed

Table 5. Fixed Effect Model

Dependent Variable: Y
Method: Panel Least Squares
Date: 03/07/22 Time: 13:02
Sample: 2011 2019
Periods included: 9
Cross-sections included: 23
Total panel (balanced) observations: 207

Variable	Coefficient	Std. Error	t-Statistic	Prob.
C	41.41879	14.34638	2.887056	0.0044
X1	-1.842122	1.199263	-1.536045	0.1263
X2	-2.297394	1.773089	-1.295702	0.1968
X3	-0.378360	0.160742	-2.353838	0.0197
X4	4.035091	1.791116	2.252836	0.0255
X5	-1.065265	0.478423	-2.226616	0.0272
X6	-0.793505	1.489530	-0.532722	0.5949

continues on following page

Effect of Good Corporate Governance on Financial Distress in Companies Listed in Stock Index

Table 5. Continued

Effects Specification			
Cross-section fixed (dummy variables)			
R-squared	0.509787	Mean dependent var	3.116935
Adjusted R-squared	0.432675	S.D. dependent var	2.425207
S.E. of regression	1.826690	Akaike info criterion	4.172146
Sum squared resid	593.9495	Schwarz criterion	4.639049
Log likelihood	-402.8171	Hannan-Quinn criter.	4.360957
F-statistic	6.610987	Durbin-Watson stat	1.055236
Prob(F-statistic)	0.000000		

Data Sources: Data Processed

APPENDIX 2

The result of machine learning model

Result 1 Linear Model

```
# Metode Linear
reg11=lm(Y~X1+X2+X3+X4+X5+X6,data=training1)
yhat=predict(reg11,newdata=test1)
### Nilai R^2 training
rsq(training1[,1],fitted(reg11))
### Nilai RMSE training
rmse(training1[,1],fitted(reg11))
### Nilai R^2 test
rsq(test1[,1],yhat)
### Nilai RMSE test
rmse(test1[,1],yhat)
df1=data.frame(o=c(training1[,1],test1[,1]),e=c(fitted(reg11),
yhat),group=c(rep("train",nrow(training1)),rep("test",nrow(te
st1))))

### Scatter plot
par(mar=c(5,4,4,8))
colors <- c("#66BD63", # Orange
            "Blue")
```

243

Effect of Good Corporate Governance on Financial Distress in Companies Listed in Stock Index

```
plot(df1$o, df1$e,xlab="Observed Value",ylab="Expected Value",
     pch = 19,
     col = colors[factor(df1$group)],main="Linear Regression")
lines(c(-1,max(training1[,1])-1),c(-1,max(yhat)+0.1),type="l",
lty=2)
legend("topleft",
       legend = levels(factor(df1$group)),
       pch = 19,
       col = colors)
legend("topleft",legend=c("Train:",expression(paste(r^2,"=
0.14383"))),"RMSE=0.93657","",
                        "Test:",expression(paste(r^2,"=
0.23020"))),"RMSE=0.83510"),
       inset=c(1,0), xpd=TRUE, bty="n")
```

Result 2 Decission Tree Model

```
## Decission Tree
tree1 = rpart(Y~.,
             data = training,
             method = "anova")
yhat.tr=predict(tree1,newdata=training)
yhat=predict(tree1,newdata=test)
### Nilai R^2 training
rsq(training[,1],yhat.tr)
### Nilai RMSE training
rmse(training[,1],yhat.tr)
### Nilai R^2 test
rsq(test[,1],yhat)
### Nilai RMSE test
rmse(test[,1],yhat)
df1=data.frame(o=c(training[,1],test[,1]),e=c(yhat.tr,yhat),gro
up=c(rep("train",nrow(training)),rep("test",nrow(test))))

### Scatter plot
par(mar=c(5,4,4,8))
colors <- c("#66BD63", # Orange
           "Blue")
plot(df1$o, df1$e,xlab="Observed Value",ylab="Expected Value",
     pch = 19,
```

244

```
        col = colors[factor(df1$group)],main="Decission Tree")
lines(c(-1.4,max(training1[,1])+1),c(-
0.7,1.9801),type="l",lty=2)
legend("topleft",
        legend = levels(factor(df1$group)),
        pch = 19,
        col = colors)
legend("topleft",legend=c("Train:",expression(paste(r^2,"=
0.43205")),"RMSE=0.76280","",
                            "Test:",expression(paste(r^2,"=
0.20220")),"RMSE=0.90148"),
        inset=c(1,0), xpd=TRUE, bty="n")
```

Result 3 Random Forest Model

```
## Random Forest
rf1= randomForest(Y~.,data = training,
                  mtry=5,importance =TRUE)
yhat1.tr=predict(rf1,newdata=training)
yhat1=predict(rf1,newdata=test)
### Nilai R^2 training
rsq(training[,1],yhat1.tr)
### Nilai RMSE training
rmse(training[,1],yhat1.tr)
### Nilai R^2
rsq(test[,1],yhat1)
### Nilai RMSE
rmse(test[,1],yhat1)
df1=data.frame(o=c(training[,1],test[,1]),e=c(yhat1.tr,yhat1),g
roup=c(rep("train",nrow(training)),rep("test",nrow(test))))

### Scatter plot
par(mar=c(5,4,4,8))
colors <- c("#66BD63", # Orange
            "Blue")
plot(df1$o, df1$e,xlab="Observed Value",ylab="Expected Value",
    pch = 19,
    col = colors[factor(df1$group)],main="Random Forest")
lines(c(-1.1,max(training1[,1])+1),c(-1,max(yhat1.
tr)+0.6),type="l",lty=2)
```

```
legend("topleft",
        legend = levels(factor(df1$group)),
        pch = 19,
        col = colors)
legend("topleft",legend=c("Train:",expression(paste(r^2,"=
0.85895"))),"RMSE=0.44773","",
                              "Test:",expression(paste(r^2,"=
0.56062"))),"RMSE=0.63334"),
        inset=c(1,0), xpd=TRUE, bty="n")
```

Result 4 Extra Trees Model

```
## Extra Tree
et <- ranger(Y~.,data = training,mtry=5,importance =
"impurity",
              splitrule="extratrees",num.random.splits=5)
yhat1.tr=predict(et,training)
yhat1=predict(et,test)
### Nilai R^2 training
rsq(training[,1],yhat1.tr$predictions)
### Nilai RMSE training
rmse(training[,1],yhat1.tr$predictions)
### Nilai R^2
rsq(test[,1],yhat1$predictions)
### Nilai RMSE
rmse(test[,1],yhat1$predictions)
df1=data.frame(o=c(training[,1],test[,1]),e=c(yhat1.tr$predicti
ons,yhat1$predictions),group=c(rep("train",nrow(training)),rep(
"test",nrow(test))))

### Scatter plot
par(mar=c(5,4,4,8))
colors <- c("#66BD63", # Orange
            "Blue")
plot(df1$o, df1$e,xlab="Observed Value",ylab="Expected Value",
     pch = 19,
     col = colors[factor(df1$group)],main="Extra Tree")
lines(c(-1.4,max(training1[,1])+1),c(-1.2,max(yhat1.tr$predicti
ons)+0.6),type="l",lty=2)
legend("topleft",
```

Effect of Good Corporate Governance on Financial Distress in Companies Listed in Stock Index

```
        legend = levels(factor(df1$group)),
        pch = 19,
        col = colors)
legend("topleft",legend=c("Train:",expression(paste(r^2,"=
0.80876")),"RMSE=0.50021","",
                          "Test:",expression(paste(r^2,"=
0.74441")),"RMSE=0.50485"),
        inset=c(1,0), xpd=TRUE, bty="n")
```

Resul 5 Bagging

```
## Bagging
bag = bagging(
  Y~.,data = training,
  nbagg = 100,
  coob = TRUE,
  control = rpart.control(minsplit = 2, cp = 0)
)
yhat3.tr=predict(bag,newdata=training)
yhat3=predict(bag,newdata=test)
### Nilai R^2 training
rsq(training[,1],yhat3.tr)
### Nilai RMSE training
rmse(training[,1],yhat3.tr)
### Nilai R^2
rsq(test[,1],yhat3)
### Nilai RMSE
rmse(test[,1],yhat3)
df1=data.frame(o=c(training[,1],test[,1]),e=c(yhat3.tr,yhat3),g
roup=c(rep("train",nrow(training)),rep("test",nrow(test))))

### Scatter plot
par(mar=c(5,4,4,8))
colors <- c("#66BD63", # Orange
            "Blue")
plot(df1$o, df1$e,xlab="Observed Value",ylab="Expected Value",
     pch = 19,
     col = colors[factor(df1$group)],main="Bagging")
lines(c(-1.4,max(training1[,1])+1),c(-1.2,max(yhat3.
tr)+0.6),type="l",lty=2)
```

```
legend("topleft",
       legend = levels(factor(df1$group)),
       pch = 19,
       col = colors)
legend("topleft",legend=c("Train:",expression(paste(r^2,"=
0.91048"))),"RMSE=0.37034","",
                          "Test:",expression(paste(r^2,"=
0.57632"))),"RMSE=0.62252"),
       inset=c(1,0), xpd=TRUE, bty="n")
```

Result 6 XGBoost

```
## XGBoost
xgb <- xgboost(data = data.matrix(training[,-1]),
               label = training[,1],
               eta = 0.1,
               max_depth = 15,
               nround=25,
               subsample = 0.5,
               colsample_bytree = 0.5,
               seed = 123,
)
yhat4.tr=predict(xgb,newdata=data.matrix(training[,-1]))
yhat4=predict(xgb,newdata=data.matrix(test[,-1]))
### Nilai R^2 training
rsq(training[,1],yhat4.tr)
### Nilai RMSE training
rmse(training[,1],yhat4.tr)
### Nilai R^2
rsq(test[,1],yhat4)
### Nilai RMSE
rmse(test[,1],yhat4)
df1=data.frame(o=c(training[,1],test[,1]),e=c(yhat4.tr,yhat4),g
roup=c(rep("train",nrow(training)),rep("test",nrow(test))))

### Scatter plot
par(mar=c(5,4,4,8))
colors <- c("#66BD63", # Orange
            "Blue")
plot(df1$o, df1$e,xlab="Observed Value",ylab="Expected Value",
```

```
    pch = 19,
    col = colors[factor(df1$group)],main="XGBoost")
lines(c(-1.3,max(training1[,1])+0.2),c(-0.9,max(yhat4.
tr)+0.2),type="l",lty=2)
legend("topleft",
       legend = levels(factor(df1$group)),
       pch = 19,
       col = colors)
legend("topleft",legend=c("Train:",expression(paste(r^2,"=
0.86169"))),"RMSE=0.48790","",
                        "Test:",expression(paste(r^2,"=
0.70340"))),"RMSE=0.58420"),
       inset=c(1,0), xpd=TRUE, bty="n")
```

Result 7 Support Vector Machine

```
## SVM (SUpport Vector Machine)
svm1 = svm(Y~.,data = training)
yhat5.tr=predict(svm1,newdata=training)
yhat5=predict(svm1,newdata=test)
### Nilai R^2 training
rsq(training[,1],yhat5.tr)
### Nilai RMSE training
rmse(training[,1],yhat5.tr)
### Nilai R^2
rsq(test[,1],yhat5)
### Nilai RMSE
rmse(test[,1],yhat5)
df1=data.frame(o=c(training[,1],test[,1]),e=c(yhat5.tr,yhat5),g
roup=c(rep("train",nrow(training)),rep("test",nrow(test))))

### Scatter plot
par(mar=c(5,4,4,8))
colors <- c("#66BD63", # Orange
            "Blue")
plot(df1$o, df1$e,xlab="Observed Value",ylab="Expected Value",
     pch = 19,
     col = colors[factor(df1$group)],main="Support Vector
Machine")
lines(c(-1.2,max(training1[,1])-1),c(-1.2,1),type="l",lty=2)
```

```
legend("topleft",
       legend = levels(factor(df1$group)),
       pch = 19,
       col = colors)
legend("topleft",legend=c("Train:",expression(paste(r^2,"=
0.26146"))),"RMSE=0.90294","",
                              "Test:",expression(paste(r^2,"=
0.35608"))),"RMSE=0.78512"),
       inset=c(1,0), xpd=TRUE, bty="n")
```

Result 8 Neural Network

```
## Neural Network
nn <- neuralnet(Y~.,data = training,hidden = 5,linear.output =
TRUE)
yhat6.tr = compute(nn, training[,2:7])
yhat6 = compute(nn, test[,2:7])
### Nilai R^2 training
rsq(training[,1],yhat6.tr$net.result)
### Nilai RMSE training
rmse(training[,1],yhat6.tr$net.result)
### Nilai R^2
rsq(test[,1],yhat6$net.result)
### Nilai RMSE
rmse(test[,1],yhat6$net.result)
df1=data.frame(o=c(training[,1],test[,1]),e=c(yhat6.tr$net.
result,yhat6$net.result),
                 group=c(rep("train",nrow(training)),rep("test",n
row(test))))

### Scatter plot
par(mar=c(5,4,4,8))
colors <- c("#66BD63", # Orange
            "Blue")
plot(df1$o, df1$e,xlab="Observed Value",ylab="Expected Value",
     pch = 19,
     col = colors[factor(df1$group)],main="Neural Network")
lines(c(-1.3,max(training1[,1])-1),c(-2.3,2.3),type="l",lty=2)
legend("topleft",
       legend = levels(factor(df1$group)),
```

```
        pch = 19,
        col = colors)
legend("topleft",legend=c("Train:",expression(paste(r^2,"=
0.57363")),"RMSE=0.66093","",
                          "Test:",expression(paste(r^2,"=
0.45814")),"RMSE=0.78225"),
        inset=c(1,0), xpd=TRUE, bty="n")
```

Compilation of References

A peer-to-peer electronic cash system. (n.d.). Retrieved December 13, 2022, from https://bitcoin.org/en/bitcoin-paper

Abad-Segura, E., González-Zamar, M.-D., Meneses, E., & Vázquez-Cano, E. (2020). Financial Technology: Review of Trends, Approaches and Management. *Mathematics.*, 8, 951. doi:10.3390/math8060951

Abideen, S. (2017). Blockchain E-Book. Cybrosys Technology.

Acharya, S., & Joshi, S. (2020). Impact of Cyber-Attacks on Banking Institutions in India: A Study of Safety Mechanisms and Preventive Measures. *Palarch's Journal of Archaeology of Egypt/Egyptology, 17*(6), 4656-4670.

Adityaputra, S. A. (2017). The Effect of Corporate Governance Implementation on Financial Difficulties (Empirical Study on Manufacturing Companies Listed on the Indonesia Stock Exchange). *Jurnal ULTIMA Accounting, 9*(2), 50–64. doi:10.31937/akuntansi.v9i2.729

Afolabi, O. J., & Onifade, M. K., & F, O. O. (2017). *Evaluation of the Role of Inventory Management in Logistics Chain of an Organisation* . doi:10.1515/logi-2017-0011

Agarrwal, K. (2021, May 22). AI, machine learning help investors gain 'edge' while investing. *Money Control.* https://www.moneycontrol.com/news/business/markets/ai-machine-learning-help-investors-gain-edge-while-investing-6922331.html

Agarwal, S., Amromin, G., Ben-David, I., Chomsisengphet, S., & Evanoff, D. (2010). Financial Literacy and Financial Planning: Evidence from India. *Journal of Housing Economics, 27.* doi:10.2139srn.1728831

Agbo, C. C., Mahmoud, Q. H., & Eklund, J. M. (2019). Blockchain technology in healthcare: a systematic review. In Healthcare, 7(2), p. 56.

Aggarwal, V., & Rej, S. (2015). *Retail Credit Risk Model Validation: Performance and Stability Aspects.* Academic Press.

Aghenta, L. O., & Iqbal, M. T. (2019) Low-Cost, Open Source IoT-Based SCADA System Design Using Thinger. *IO and ESP32 Thing. Electronics, 8*(8), 1-24.

Compilation of References

Akinnuwesi, B. A., Fashoto, S. G., Metfula, A. S., & Akinnuwesi, A. N. (2020). Experimental Application of Machine Learning on Financial Inclusion Data for Governance in Eswatini. In Lecture Notes in Computer Science (including subseries Lecture Notes in Artificial Intelligence and Lecture Notes in Bioinformatics): Vol. 12067 LNCS. Springer International Publishing. doi:10.1007/978-3-030-45002-1_36

Alahmari, S. A. (2020). Predicting the price of cryptocurrency using support vector regression methods. *Journal of Mechanics of Continua and Mathematical Sciences*, *15*(4), 313–322. doi:10.26782/jmcms.2020.04.00023

Alexandre, M., Silva, T. C., Connaughton, C., & Rodrigues, F. A. (2021). The drivers of systemic risk in financial networks: A data-driven machine learning analysis. *Chaos, Solitons, and Fractals*, *153*, 111588.

Alexopoulos, K., Nikolakis, N., & Chryssolouris, G. (2020). Digital twin-driven supervised machine learning for the development of artificial intelligence applications in manufacturing. *International Journal of Computer Integrated Manufacturing*, *33*(5), 429–439. doi:10.1080/09 51192X.2020.1747642

Al-Najjar, B. (2010). Corporate Governance and Institutional Ownership: Evidence from Jordan. *Corporate Governance*, *10*(2), 176–190. doi:10.1108/14720701011035693

Alqaryouti, O., Siyam, N., Alkashri, Z., & Shaalan, K. (2020a). Cryptocurrency Usage Impact on Perceived Benefits and Users' Behaviour. In M. Themistocleous & M. Papadaki (Eds.), *Information Systems. EMCIS 2019. Lecture Notes in Business Information Processing* (Vol. 381). Springer. doi:10.1007/978-3-030-44322-1_10

Alqaryouti, O., Siyam, N., Alkashri, Z., & Shaalan, K. (2020b). Users' knowledge and motivation on using cryptocurrency. *Information Systems Lecture Notes in Business Information Processing*, *381*, 113–122. doi:10.1007/978-3-030-44322-1_9

Altman, E. I. (1968). Financial Ratios, Discriminant Analysis, and the Prediction of Corporate Bankruptcy. *The Journal of Finance*, *23*(4), 589–609. doi:10.1111/j.1540-6261.1968.tb00843.x

Alt, R., Beck, R., & Smits, M. T. (2018). FinTech and the transformation of the financial industry. *Electronic Markets*, *28*, 235–243. https://doi.org/10.1007/s12525-018-0310-9

AmetranoF. M. (2016). Hayek money: The cryptocurrency price stability solution. *Social Science Research Network*.

Anantharaman, A. (2019). How artificial intelligence is enabling financial inclusion in India. *YourStory*. https://yourstory.com/2019/05/artificial-intelligence-enabling-financial-inclusion

Ananto, R. P., Mustika, R., & Handayani, D. (2017). The Effect of GCG, Leverage, Profitability and UP on FD on Consumer Goods Companies Listed on the Indonesia Stock Exchange. *Jurnal Ekonomi Dan Bisnis Dharma Andalas*, *19*(1), 92–105.

Anbalagan, G. (2015). New Technological Changes in Indian Banking Sector. *International Journal of Scientific Research and Management*, *5*(9), 7016–7021.

Ané, T., Ureche-Rangau, L., Gambet, J. B., & Bouverot, J. (2008). Robust outlier detection for Asia–Pacific stock index returns. *Journal of International Financial Markets, Institutions and Money*, *18*(4), 326–343. doi:10.1016/j.intfin.2007.03.001

Angraal, S., Krumholz, H. M., & Schulz, W. L. (2017). Blockchain technology: Applications in health care. *Circulation: Cardiovascular Quality and Outcomes*, *10*(9), e003800. doi:10.1161/CIRCOUTCOMES.117.003800 PMID:28912202

Archuleta, K. L., Britt, S. L., & Klontz, B. T. (2016). Financial therapy. In *Handbook of consumer finance research* (pp. 73–82). Springer. https://link.springer.com/chapter/10.1007/978-3-319-28887-1_6

Archuleta, K. L., & Grable, J. E. (2011). The future of financial planning and counselling: An introduction to financial therapy. In *Financial planning and counselling scales* (pp. 33–59). Springer. https://link.springer.com/chapter/10.1007/978-1-4419-6908-8_3

Arivazhagan, R., Geetha, P., Parthasarathy, R., Weatherspoon, D. D., & Oehmke, J. F. (2012). Analysis of Sources of Fruit Wastages in Retail outlets in Chennai, Tamilnadu, India. Academic Press.

Ariwala, P. (2019). 5 Ways ai is transforming the finance industry. *Maruti Techlabs*. https://marutitech.com/ways-ai-transforming-finance/

Arksey, H., & O'Malley, L. (2005). Scoping studies: Towards a methodological framework. *International Journal of Social Research Methodology*, *8*(1), 19–32. doi:10.1080/1364557032000119616

Arora, S., & Nabi, T. (2022). Blockchain Adoption in Banking Systems: A Boon or Bane? In Applications, Challenges, and Opportunities of Blockchain Technology in Banking and Insurance (pp. 19-42). IGI Global. doi:10.4018/978-1-6684-4133-6.ch002

Asebedo, S. D. (2019). Psychosocial Attributes and Financial Self-Efficacy Among Older Adults. *Journal of Financial Therapy*, *10*(1), 2. doi:10.4148/1944-9771.1196

Ashofteh, A., & Bravo, J. M. (2021). A conservative approach for online credit scoring. *Expert Systems with Applications*, *176*(March), 114835. doi:10.1016/j.eswa.2021.114835

Athey, S., & Imbens, G. W. (2019). Machine Learning Methods That Economists Should Know about. *Annual Review of Economics*, *11*(1), 685–725. doi:10.1146/annurev-economics-080217-053433

Atzori, M. (2015). *Blockchain technology and decentralized governance: Is the state still necessary?* Working Paper. Available at: http://nzz-filesprod.s3-website-eu-west1.amazonaws.com/files/9/3/1/blockchain+Is+the+State+Still+Necessary_1.18 689931.pdf

Ayn, D. J. (2019). Robo-advisors and Artificial Intelligence – Comparing 5 Current Apps. *Emerj*. https://emerj.com/ai-applicationcomparisons/robo-advisors-artificial- intelligencecomparing-5-current-apps/

Ayn, D. J. (2019). Robo-advisors and Artificial Intelligence –Comparing 5 Current Apps. *Emerj*.

254

Compilation of References

Bailey, D. H., Borwein, J., Lopez de Prado, M., & Zhu, Q. J. (2016). The probability of backtest overfitting. *Journal of Computational Finance*. Advance online publication. doi:10.21314/JCF.2016.322

Balraj, N. (2016). Issues and Challenges in the Supply Chain of Fruits & Vegetables Sector in India: A Review. *Splint International Journal of Professionals*, *3*(8), 113–118. doi:10.5121/ijmvsc.2015.6205

Bamrara, A., Bhatt, M., & Singh, G. (2013). Cyber Attacks and Defense Strategies in India: An Empirical Assessment of Banking Sector. *International Journal of Cyber Criminology*, *7*(1), 49–61. doi:10.2139srn.2488413

Bansal, A., Kauffman, R. J., & Weitz, R. R. (1993). Comparing the modeling performance of regression and neural networks as data quality varies: A business value approach. *Journal of Management Information Systems*, *10*(1), 11–32. doi:10.1080/07421222.1993.11517988

Barik, R., & Sharma, P. (2019). Analysing the progress and prospects of financial inclusion in India. *Journal of Public Affairs*, *19*(4), e1948. https://onlinelibrary.wiley.com/doi/abs/10.1002/pa.1948

Baron, O., Berman, O., & Perry, D. (2010). Continuous review inventory models for perishable items ordered in batches. *Mathematical Methods of Operations Research*, *72*(2), 217–247. doi:10.100700186-010-0318-1

Baryannis, G., Validi, S., Dani, S., & Antoniou, G. (2019). Supply chain risk management and artificial intelligence: State of the art and future research directions. *International Journal of Production Research*, *57*(7), 2179–2202. doi:10.1080/00207543.2018.1530476

Bashir, I., & Qureshi, I. H. (2022). *A Systematic Literature Review on Personal Financial Well-Being: The Link to Key Sustainable Development Goals 2030*. FIIB Business Review. doi:10.1177/23197145221106862

Baur, A. W., Bühler, J., Bick, M., & Bonorden, C. S. (2015). Cryptocurrencies as a Disruption? Empirical Findings on User Adoption and Future Potential of Bitcoin and Co. In Lecture Notes in Computer Science: Vol. 9373. *Open and Big Data Management and Innovation. I3E 2015*. Springer. doi:10.1007/978-3-319-25013-7_6

Begina, & M. A, ., Hickingbottom, J., Luttrull, E. G., McCoy, M., & Klontz, B. (2018). Identify and Understand Clients' Money Scripts: A Framework for Using the KMSI-R. *Journal of Financial Planning*, *31*(3), 46–55.

Benigno, P. (2019). *Monetary policy in a world of cryptocurrencies*. Voxeu.org. https://voxeu.org/article/monetary-policy-world-cryptocurrencies

Best, R. (2022, December 13). *Bitcoin price history Apr 2013 - Dec 12, 2022*. Retrieved December 13, 2022, from https://www.statista.com/statistics/326707/bitcoin-price-index/

Bharadwaj, K. V. (2015, january 27). Retrieved from The Hindu: https://www.thehindu.com/news/cities/bangalore/the-rise-and-fall-of-hopcoms/article6826063.ece

Bharadwaj, R. (2019). AI in the Indian financial sector – current traction, opportunities and challenges. Retrieved from: https://emerj.com/ai-sector-overviews/ai-in-the-indian-financial-sectorcurrent-traction-opportunities-and-challenges/ on 28.12.2019

Bharadwaj, S., & Deka, S. (2021, December). Behavioural intention towards investment in cryptocurrency: an integration of Rogers' diffusion of innovation theory and the technology acceptance model. In Forum Scientiae Oeconomia, 9(4), 137-159.

Bharucha, J. P. (2019). Determinants of financial literacy among Indian youth. In *Dynamic Perspectives on Globalization and Sustainable Business in Asia* (pp. 154–167). IGI Global. https://www.igi-global.com/chapter/determinants-of-financial-literacy-among-indian-youth/215111

Bharucha, J. P. (2019). Determinants of Financial Literacy Among Indian Youth. In P. Ordoñez de Pablos (Ed.), *Dynamic Perspectives on Globalization and Sustainable Business in Asia* (pp. 154–167). IGI Global. doi:10.4018/978-1-5225-7095-0.ch010

Bhat, S. A., Khan, F. A., & Narayan, S. (2017). *Storage Methods for Fruits and Vegetables.* Retrieved from https://www.researchgate.net/publication/317014767_Storage_Methods_for_Fruits_and_Vegetables

Bhatia, A., Chandani, A., & Chhateja, J. (2020). Robo advisory and its potential in addressing the behavioral biases of investors — A qualitative study in Indian context. *Journal of Behavioral and Experimental Finance, 25,* 100281, ISSN 2214-6350, doi:10.1016/j.jbef.2020.100281

Bhatia, A., Chandani, A., Atiq, R., Mehta, M., & Divekar, R. (2021). Artificial intelligence in financial services: a qualitative research to discover robo-advisory services. *Qualitative Research in Financial Markets, 13*(5), 632-654. doi:10.1108/QRFM-10-2020-0199

BI India Bureau. (2021, July 28). Equalisation levy on crypto exchanges in India will not apply to investors, according to the Finance Minister. *Business Insider India.* https://www.businessinsider.in/cryptocurrency/news/the-indian-government-has-no-data-on-how-many-crypto-exchanges-and-investors-working-on-cryptocurrency/articleshow/84821709.cms#:~:text=In%20addition%20to%20exchanges%2C%20India,owned%20by%20crypto%20giant%20Binance

Boillat, T., Rivas, H., & Wac, K. (2018). "Healthcare on a Wrist": Increasing Compliance Through Checklists on Wearables in Obesity (Self-) Management Programs. Digital Health. Health Informatics, 65-81.

Borate, N. (2021). India has just around 2,000 certified financial planners: Rajesh Krishnamoorthy. *Mint.* https://www.livemint.com/money/personal-finance/india-has-just-around-2-000-certified-financial-planners-rajesh-krishnamoorthy-11616600959703.html

Bordo, M., & Levin, A. (2017). *Central Bank Digital Currency and the Future of Monetary Policy.* Hoover. https://www.hoover.org/sites/default/files/bordo-levin_bullets_for_hoover_may2017.pdf

Bouri, E., Gupta, R., Tiwari, A. K., & Roubaud, D. (2017). *Does Bitcoin hedge global uncertainty? Evidence from wavelet-based quantile-in-quantile regressions.* Finance. doi:10.1016/j.frl.2017.02.009

Compilation of References

Bouri, E., Shahzad, S. J. H., & Roubaud, D. (2020). Cryptocurrencies as hedges and safe-havens for US equity sectors. *The Quarterly Review of Economics and Finance*, *75*, 294–307. doi:10.1016/j.qref.2019.05.001

Bramley, R. G. V., & Ouzman, J. (2019). Farmer attitudes to the use of sensors and automation in fertilizer decision-making: Nitrogen fertilization in the Australian grains sector. *Precision Agriculture*, *20*(1), 157–175. doi:10.100711119-018-9589-y

Brannon, E., Cushing, C., Crick, C., & Mitchell, T. (2016) the promise of wearable sensors and ecological momentary assessment measures for dynamical systems modeling in adolescents: a feasibility and acceptability study. *Translational Behavioral Medicine, 6*(4), 558–565.

Breakfast, S. (2020). *KwaZulu-Natal COVID-19 patient charged after absconding quarantine.* News, The South African.

Bressanelli, G., Perona, M., & Saccani, N. (2019). Challenges in supply chain redesign for the Circular Economy: A literature review and a multiple case study. *International Journal of Production Research*, *57*(23), 7395–7422. doi:10.1080/00207543.2018.1542176

Brown. (2015). Validation of the Intermountain patient perception of quality (PPQ) survey among survivors of an intensive care unit admission: A retrospective validation study Quality, performance, safety and outcomes. *BMC Health Services Research*, *15*(1), 155.

Buer, S. V., Semini, M., Strandhagen, J. O., & Sgarbossa, F. (2021). The complementary effect of lean manufacturing and digitalisation on operational performance. *International Journal of Production Research*, *59*(7), 1976–1992. doi:10.1080/00207543.2020.1790684

Burga, R., & Rezania, D. (2017). Project accountability: An exploratory case study using actor–network theory. *International Journal of Project Management*, *35*(6), 1024–1036. doi:10.1016/j.ijproman.2017.05.001

ButerinV. (2014). A next-generation smart contract and decentralized application platform. Available at: https://www.intgovforum.org/cms/wks2015/uploads/proposal_background_pa per/SSRN-id2580664.pdf\

Caggiano, K. E., Jackson, P. L., Muckstadt, J. A., & Rappold, J. A. (2009). Efficient computation of time-based customer service levels in a multi-item, multi-echelon supply chain: A practical approach for inventory optimization. *European Journal of Operational Research*, *199*(3), 744–749. doi:10.1016/j.ejor.2008.08.002

Camara, B., Pessarossi, P., & Philippon, T. (2016). *Back-testing bank stress tests*. Stern School of Business, New York University.

Campbell, C., Sands, S., Ferraro, C., Tsao, H.-Y., & Mavrommatis, A. (2020). From data to action: How marketers can leverage AI. *Business Horizons*, *63*(2), 227–243. doi:10.1016/j.bushor.2019.12.002

Çapar, H. (2021). Using cryptocurrencies and transactions in medical tourism. *Journal of Economic and Administrative Sciences*, *37*(4), 677–693. doi:10.1108/JEAS-07-2019-0080

Carstens, A. (2021). *Digital currencies and the future of the monetary system: Remarks by Agustín Carstens.* Bank for International Settlements. https://www.bis.org/speeches/sp210127.pdf

Carta, S. M., Consoli, S., Podda, A. S., Recupero, D. R., & Stanciu, M. M. (2021). Ensembling and Dynamic Asset Selection for Risk-Controlled Statistical Arbitrage. *IEEE Access: Practical Innovations, Open Solutions, 9*(i), 29942–29959. doi:10.1109/ACCESS.2021.3059187

Caruso, G. D. (2016) Free will skepticism and criminal behavior: A public health-quarantine model. *Southwest Philosophy Review, 32*(1), 25-48.

Carvalho, T. P., Soares, F. A. A. M. N., Vita, R., Francisco, R. da P., Basto, J. P., & Alcalá, S. G. S. (2019). A systematic literature review of machine learning methods applied to predictive maintenance. *Computers & Industrial Engineering, 137,* 106024. doi:10.1016/j.cie.2019.106024

ChainAnlysis Team. (2021). *The 2021 Global Crypto Adoption Index.* Chainalysis.com. https://blog.chainalysis.com/reports/2021-global-crypto-adoption-index

Chandorkar, A., & Misra, K. (2019). How financial services industry in India is set for ai makeover. Retrieved from: https://www.financialexpress.com/industry/how-financial-services-industryin-india-is-set-for-ai-makeover/1723836/ on 26.12.2019.

Chandrashekar, H. M. (2018). *Farmers Participatory Approach towards Role of the HOPCOMS Development of Agribusiness Management in Karnataka.* Academic Press.

Chang, M. C., & Park, D. (2020). How can blockchain help people in the event of pandemics such as the COVID-19? *Journal of Medical Systems, 44*(5), 1–2. doi:10.100710916-020-01577-8 PMID:32300906

Chang, V., Man, X., Xu, Q., & Hsu, C. H. (2021). Pairs trading on different portfolios based on machine learning. *Expert Systems: International Journal of Knowledge Engineering and Neural Networks, 38*(3), 1–25. doi:10.1111/exsy.12649

Chatterjee, S., & Fan, L. (2021). Older Adults' Life Satisfaction: The Roles of Seeking Financial Advice and Personality Traits. *Journal of Financial Therapy, 12*(1), 4. https://doi.org/10.4148/1944-9771.1253

Chemkha, R., BenSaïda, A., Ghorbel, A., & Tayachi, T. (2021). Hedge and safe haven properties during COVID-19: Evidence from Bitcoin and gold. *The Quarterly Review of Economics and Finance.*

Chen, H. S., Jarrell, J. T., Carpenter, K. A., Cohen, D. S., & Huang, X. (2019). Blockchain in healthcare: A patient-centered model. *Biomedical Journal of Scientific & Technical Research, 20*(3), 15017. PMID:31565696

Chen, H.-K., Hsueh, C.-F., & Chang, M.-S. (2009). Production scheduling and vehicle routing with time windows for perishable food products. *Computers & Operations Research, 36*(7), 2311–2319. doi:10.1016/j.cor.2008.09.010

Compilation of References

Chen, J. M. (2021). An Introduction to Machine Learning for Panel Data. *International Advances in Economic Research*, *27*(1), 1–16. Advance online publication. doi:10.100711294-021-09815-6

Chen, N. C., Drouhard, M., Kocielnik, R., Suh, J., & Aragon, C. R. (2018). Using machine learning to support qualitative coding in social science: Shifting the focus to ambiguity. *ACM Transactions on Interactive Intelligent Systems*, *8*(2), 1–20. Advance online publication. doi:10.1145/3185515

Chiu, J., & Koeppl, T. V. (2017). The Economics of Cryptocurrencies Bitcoin and Beyond. *Electronic Journal*. doi:10.2139/ssrn.3048124

Christopher, M. (2000). The Agile Supply Chain. *Industrial Marketing Management*, *29*(1), 37–44. doi:10.1016/S0019-8501(99)00110-8

Cichosz, S. L., Stausholm, M. N., Kronborg, T., Vestergaard, P., & Hejlesen, O. (2019). How to use blockchain for diabetes health care data and access management: An operational concept. *Journal of Diabetes Science and Technology*, *13*(2), 248–253. doi:10.1177/1932296818790281 PMID:30047789

Claeys, A., Demertzis, M., & Efstathiou, K. (2018). *Cryptocurrencies and monetary policy.* ECON Committee. https://www.europarl.europa.eu/cmsdata/150000/BRUEGEL_FINAL%20 publication.pdf

Clauson, K. A., Breeden, E. A., Davidson, C., & Mackey, T. K. (2018). Leveraging Blockchain Technology to Enhance Supply Chain Management in Healthcare: An exploration of challenges and opportunities in the health supply chain. *Blockchain in healthcare today*.

Cocco, L., Marchesi, M., & Pinna, A. (2017). Banking on Blockchain: Costs Savings Thanks to the Blockchain Technology. *Future Internet*, *9*(25), 1–20. doi:10.3390/fi9030025

Coin Ranking. (2018). *WazirX Exchange.* Coinranking. https://coinranking.com/exchange/ W9qIIHDJ_+wazirx

Congressional Research Service. (2018). Cryptocurrency: The Economics of Money and Selected Policy Issues. *CRS Report*. https://fas.org/sgp/crs/misc/R45427.pdf

Conlon, T., Corbet, S., & McGee, R. J. (2020). Are cryptocurrencies a safe haven for equity markets? An international perspective from the COVID-19 pandemic. *Research in International Business and Finance*, *54*, 101248. doi:10.1016/j.ribaf.2020.101248 PMID:34170988

Cont, R. (2007). Volatility clustering in financial markets: empirical facts and agent-based models. In *Long memory in economics* (pp. 289–309). Springer. doi:10.1007/978-3-540-34625-8_10

Cont, R., & Kukanov, A. (2017). Optimal order placement in limit order markets. *Quantitative Finance*, *17*(1), 21–39. doi:10.1080/14697688.2016.1190030

Crosby, M., Pattanayak, P., Verma, S., & Kalyanaraman, V. (2016). *Blockchain technology: Beyond Bitcoin*. Applied Innovation Review. Available at https://j2-capital.com/wp-content/ uploads/2017/11/AIR2016-Blockchain.pdf

Culinda. (2022). Medical Device Tracking on Blockchain. *Culinda*. https://www.culinda.io/wp-content/uploads/2020/10/Medical-devices-Blockchain.pdf

Das, S. C. (2016). Financial literacy among Indian millennial generation and their reflections on financial behaviour and attitude: An explanatory research. *The Indian Journal of Commerce*, *69*(4). https://www.researchgate.net/publication/320009228_Financial_Literacy_among_Indian_Millennial_Generation_and_their_Reflections_on_Financial_Behaviour_and_Attitude_An_Explanatory_Research_By

Deekshith, M. (2020). Covidiots everywhere: Cases of foreign returnees flouting home quarantine in rise. *Nation, Current Affairs, Deccan Chronicle*.

Delgadillo, L. M. (2016). Financial Counseling and Financial Health. In J. Xiao (Ed.), *Handbook of Consumer Finance Research*. Springer. doi:10.1007/978-3-319-28887-1_7

Digalaki, E. (2019). The impact of artificial intelligence in the banking sector & how AI is being used in 2020. *Business Insider*. https://www.businessinsider.in/finance/news/the-impact-of-artificial-intelligence-in-the-banking-sector-how-ai-is-being-used 2020/articleshow/72860899.cms

DiGiovanni, C., Conley, J., Chiu, D., & Zaborski, J. (2004). Factors influencing compliance with quarantine in Toronto during the 2003 SARS outbreak. *Biosecurity and bioterrorism: Biodefense strategy, practice, and science, 2*(4), 265-272.

Dionne, G. (2018). *Machine Learning and Risk Management: SVDD Meets RQE*. Academic Press.

Disli, M., Nagayev, R., Salim, K., Rizkiah, S. K., & Aysan, A. F. (2021). In search of safe haven assets during COVID-19 pandemic: An empirical analysis of different investor types. *Research in International Business and Finance*, *58*, 101461. doi:10.1016/j.ribaf.2021.101461

Dixon-Woods, M. (2011). Using framework-based synthesis for conducting reviews of qualitative studies. *BMC Medicine*, *9*(1), 39. doi:10.1186/1741-7015-9-39 PMID:21492447

Dolgorukov, D. (2021). How AI and ML Will Be Transforming Banking and Finance. *Finextra*. https://www.finextra.com/blogposting/19774/how-ai-and-ml-will-be-transforming-banking-and-finance

Donepudi, P. K. (2017). Machine learning and artificial intelligence in banking. *Engineering International*, *5*(2), 83–86. doi:10.18034/ei.v5i2.490

DqIndia. (2021). Overcoming the challenges in AI deployment for financial sector. *DqIndia*. https://www.dqindia.com/overcoming-challenges-ai-deployment-financial-sector/

Duan, Q., & Liao, T. W. (2013). A new age-based replenishment policy for supply chain inventory optimization of highly perishable products. *International Journal of Production Economics*, *145*(2), 658–671. doi:10.1016/j.ijpe.2013.05.020

Durach, C. F., Kembro, J., & Wieland, A. (2017). A New Paradigm for Systematic Literature Reviews in Supply Chain Management. *The Journal of Supply Chain Management*, *53*(4), 67–85. doi:10.1111/jscm.12145

Compilation of References

Dyhrberg, A. H. (2016). Bitcoin, gold and the dollar – A GARCH Volatility Analysis. *Finance Research Letters*, *16*, 85–92. doi:10.1016/j.frl.2015.10.008

Economic Times. (2021, May 20). *Cryptocurrency has risen despite the pandemic & is expected to continue*. The Economic Times. https://economictimes.indiatimes.com/markets/cryptocurrency/cryptocurrency-has-risen-despite-the-pandemic-is-expected-to-continue/articleshow/82800680.cms?from=mdr

Eden, A., Steinhart, E., Pearce, D., & Moor, J. (2012). *Singularity Hypotheses: An Overview*. Springer., doi:10.1007/978-3-642-32560-1

Effendi, M. A. (2009). *The Power of Good Corporate Governance: Theory dan Implementations*. Salemba Empat.

Ehrenstein, V., Kharrazi, H., & Lehmann, H. (2019). Obtaining Data From Electronic Health Records. In: Gliklich RE, Leavy MB, Dreyer NA, (eds.) *Tools and Technologies for Registry Interoperability, Registries for Evaluating Patient Outcomes: A User's Guide*, (3rd ed). Agency for Healthcare Research and Quality.https://www.ncbi.nlm.nih.gov/books/NBK551878/

El-Gazzar, R., & Stendal, K. (2020). Blockchain in health care: Hope or hype? *Journal of Medical Internet Research*, *22*(7), e17199. doi:10.2196/17199 PMID:32673219

Engelhardt, M. A. (2017). Hitching healthcare to the chain: An introduction to blockchain technology in the healthcare sector. *Technology Innovation Management Review*, *7*(10), 22–34. doi:10.22215/timreview/1111

Escobar, C. A., & Morales-Menendez, R. (2018). Machine learning techniques for quality control in high conformance manufacturing environment. *Advances in Mechanical Engineering*, *10*(2), 168781401875551. doi:10.1177/1687814018755519

Espressif Systems. (2020). *ESP32 Series Datasheet*. Datasheet. Author.

Estelles-Lopez, L., Ropodi, A., Pavlidis, D., Fotopoulou, J., Gkousari, C., Peyrodie, A., Panagou, E., Nychas, G.-J., & Mohareb, F. (2017). An automated ranking platform for machine learning regression models for meat spoilage prediction using multi-spectral imaging and metabolic profiling. *Food Research International*, *99*, 206–215. doi:10.1016/j.foodres.2017.05.013 PMID:28784477

Etikan, I., Musa, S. A., & Alkassim, R. S. (2016). Comparison of Convenience Sampling and Purposive Sampling. *American Journal of Theoretical and Applied Statistics*, *5*(1), 1–5. doi:10.11648/j.ajtas.20160501.11

Eyal, I., & Sirer, E. G. (2014). Majority is not enough: Bitcoin mining is vulnerable. In *Proceedings of International Conference on Financial Cryptography and Data Security*, (pp. 436–454). IEEE.

Fairfield, J. (2014). *Smart contracts, Bitcoin bots, and consumer protection*. https://scholarlycommons.law.wlu.edu/cgi/viewcontent.cgi?article=1003&context=wlulr-online

261

Fan, K., Wang, S., Ren, Y., Li, H., & Yang, Y. (2018). Medblock: Efficient and secure medical data sharing via blockchain. *Journal of Medical Systems*, *42*(8), 1–11. doi:10.100710916-018-0993-7 PMID:29931655

Fanning, K., & Centers, D. (2016). Blockchain and its coming impact on Financial Services. *Journal of Corporate Accounting & Finance*, *27*(August), 53–57. Advance online publication. doi:10.1002/jcaf.22179

Fathonah, A. N. (2016). The Effect of Good Corporate Governance Implementation on Financial Distress. *Jurnal Ilmiah Akuntansi, 1*(2), 133–150.

Fathoni, A. F., & Haryetti, W. E. Y. M. (2014). The Effect of Good Corporate Governance Mechanism, Financial Distress on Earning Management Behavior: Empirical Study in Property and Infrastructure Industry in Indonesian Stock Exchanges. *Jurnal Ekonomi, 22*(1), 1–16.

Feizabadi, J. (2020). Machine learning demand forecasting and supply chain performance. *International Journal of Logistics Research and Applications*, 1–24. doi:10.1080/13675567.2020.1803246

Ferreira, P., Kristoufek, L., & Pereira, J.D.A.E. (2020). ADCCAand DMCA Correlations of Cryptocurrency Markets. *Physica A, 545*(C). . doi:10.1016/j.physa.2019.123803

FICCI. (2020). *Revamping India's health insurance sector with blockchain and smart contracts*. PwC. https://www.pwc.in/assets/pdfs/healthcare/revamping-indias-health-insurance-sector-with-blockchain-and-smart-contracts.pdf

Finanse. (2018). *Portal Podatkowy*. Available at: https://www.finanse.mf.gov.pl/c/document_library/get_file?uuid=589b1960-46fd-41f2-bf17-4adf96ae2e13&groupId=764034

Finder. (n.d.). Cryptocurrency adoption rates. *Finder Crypto Report*. https://dvh1deh6tagwk.cloudfront.net/finder-us/wp-uploads/sites/5/2021/06/Crypto_Adoption_final-compressed-1.pdf

Fitzsimmons, C. (2020). They haven't listened: Medical professionals skipped quarantine and flew interstate. *News, The Sydney Morning Herald*.

Flore, M. (2018). *How Blockchain-Based Technology Is Disrupting Migrants' Remittances: A Preliminary Assessment*. https://core.ac.uk/download/pdf/186490943.pdf

Funashima, Y. (2017). Time-varying leads and lags across frequencies using a continuous wavelet transform approach. *Economic Modelling*, *60*, 24–28. doi:10.1016/j.econmod.2016.08.024

Gallo, A. (2021, May 25). *Central Bank Digital Currencies Will Fix Bad Policy*. Bloomberg. https://www.bloomberg.com/opinion/articles/2021-05-25/central-bank-digital-currencies-will-fix-bad-monetary-policy

Garrett, P., & Seidman, J. (2011) EMR vs EHR – What is the Difference? *Health IT*. https://www.healthit.gov/buzz-blog/electronic-health-and-medical-records/emr-vs-ehr-difference

Compilation of References

Gersl, A., & Seidler, J. (2012). How to improve the quality of stress tests through backtesting. *Finance a Uver*, *62*(4), 325.

Gkillas, K., & Katsiampa, P. (2018). An Application of Extreme Value Theory to Cryptocurrencies. *Economics Letters*, *164*, 109–111. doi:10.1016/j.econlet.2018.01.020

Glaser, F. (2017). Pervasive decentralisation of digital infrastructures: a framework for blockchain enabled system and use case analysis. In *50th Hawaii International Conference on System Sciences*. HICSS. Available at: https://pdfs.semanticscholar.org/859d/0535e16095f274df4d69df54954b2 1258a13.pdf

Global Data Healthcare. (2021). *Blockchain's potential in the medical device and healthcare industries.* Medical device Network https://www.medicaldevice-network.com/comment/blockchain-medical-device-healthcare-industries/

Goel, I., & Khanna, S. R. (2014). Financial education as tool to achieve financial literacy. *ZENITH International Journal of Multidisciplinary Research*, *4*(12), 73–81.

Golmohammadi, D., Creese, R. C., Valian, H., & Kolassa, J. (2009). Supplier Selection Based on a Neural Network Model Using Genetic Algorithm. *IEEE Transactions on Neural Networks*, *20*(9), 1504–1519. doi:10.1109/TNN.2009.2027321 PMID:19695996

Goodell, J. W., & Goutte, S. (2021). Diversifying equity with cryptocurrencies during COVID-19. *International Review of Financial Analysis*, *76*, 101781. doi:10.1016/j.irfa.2021.101781

Goyal, S., & Routroy, S. (2021). Analyzing environmental sustainability enablers for an Indian steel manufacturing supply chain. *Journal of Engineering, Design and Technology, ahead-of-p*(ahead-of-print). doi:10.1108/JEDT-03-2021-0118

Griggs, K. N., Ossipova, O., Kohlios, C. P., Baccarini, A. N., Howson, E. A., & Hayajneh, T. (2018). Healthcare blockchain system using smart contracts for secure automated remote patient monitoring. *Journal of Medical Systems*, *42*(7), 1–7. doi:10.100710916-018-0982-x PMID:29876661

Gu, S. (2013). *Research and Analysis on Issued Inventory Valuation Methods of Enterprises.* Academic Press.

Guiso, L., Jappelli, T., Padula, M., & Pagano, M. (2004). Financial market Integration and Economic Growth in the EU. *Economic Policy*, *19*(40), 524–577. doi:10.1111/j.1468-0327.2004.00131.x

Gujarati, D. N., & Porter, D. C. (2009). Basic Econometrics (5th ed.). McGraw-Hill.

Gundewadi, B. B., Storage, K. C., Campus, R., Shivajinagar, N., Maharashtra, S., & West, S. (2013). *Role and Performance of Cold Storages in Indian Agriculture.* Academic Press.

Gunjan, V. K., Kumar, A., & Avdhanam, S. (2013, September 21-22). *A survey of cyber crime in India.* [Paper presentation]. 15th International Conference on Advanced Computing Technologies (ICACT), Rajampet, India. 10.1109/ICACT.2013.6710503

Guo, R., Shi, H., Zhao, Q., & Zheng, D. (2018). Secure attribute-based signature scheme with multiple authorities for blockchain in electronic health records systems. *IEEE Access: Practical Innovations, Open Solutions*, 6, 11676–11686. doi:10.1109/ACCESS.2018.2801266

Guo, X., Lu, F., & Wei, Y. (2021). Capture the contagion network of bitcoin–Evidence from pre and mid-COVID-19. *Research in International Business and Finance*, 58, 101484. doi:10.1016/j.ribaf.2021.101484 PMID:34518717

Gurny, M. (2015). *Default probabilities in credit risk management: estimation, model calibration, and backtesting* [Doctoral dissertation]. Faculty of Business and Economics, Macquarie University.

Gu, S., Kelly, B., & Xiu, D. (2021). Autoencoder asset pricing models. *Journal of Econometrics*, 222(1), 429–450. doi:10.1016/j.jeconom.2020.07.009

Guzzo, R. A., Jette, R. D., & Katzell, R. A. (1985). The effects of psychologically based intervention programs on worker productivity: A meta-analysis. *Personnel Psychology*, 38(2), 275–291. doi:10.1111/j.1744-6570.1985.tb00547.x

Habiba, U. E., Peilong, S., Zhang, W., & Hamid, K. (2020). International Stock Markets Integration and Dynamics of Volatility Spillover between the USA and South Asian Markets: Evidence from Global Financial Crisis. *Journal of Asia Business Studies*, 14(5), 779–794. doi:10.1108/JABS-03-2019-0071

Halder, P., & Pati, S. (2011). A need for paradigm shift to improve supply chain management of fruits & Vegetables in India. *Asian Journal of Agriculture and Rural Development*, 1(1), 1–21. http://search.proquest.com/docview/1416221058?accountid=13771

Hartley, J. L., & Sawaya, W. J. (2019). Tortoise, not the hare: Digital transformation of supply chain business processes. *Business Horizons*, 62(6), 707–715. doi:10.1016/j.bushor.2019.07.006

Hashemi Joo, M., Nishikawa, Y., & Dandapani, K. (2020). Cryptocurrency, a successful application of blockchain technology. *Managerial Finance*, 46(6), 715–733. doi:10.1108/MF-09-2018-0451

Helena, S., & Saifi, M. (2018). The Impact of Corporate Governance Toward Financial Distress (Case Study: Transportation Companies Registered at Indonesia Stock Exchange 2013-2016). *Jurnal Administrasi Bisnis*, 60(2), 143–152. administrasibisnis.studentjournal.ub.ac.id%0A143

He, P., He, Y., & Xu, H. (2020). Buy-online-and-deliver-from-store strategy for a dual-channel supply chain considering retailer's location advantage. *Transportation Research Part E, Logistics and Transportation Review*, 144, 102127. doi:10.1016/j.tre.2020.102127

Hölbl, M., Kompara, M., Kamišalić, A., & Nemec Zlatolas, L. (2018). A systematic review of the use of blockchain in healthcare. *Symmetry*, 10(10), 470. doi:10.3390ym10100470

Holtmeier, M., & Sandner, P. (2019). *The impact of crypto currencies on developing countries*. Frankfurt School Blockchain Center. http://explore-ip.com/2019_The-Impact-of-Crypto-Currencies-on-Developing-Countries.pdf

HOPCOMS. (2018). *HOPCOMS Report*. HOPCOMS.

Compilation of References

Huo, B., Qi, Y., Wang, Z., & Zhao, X. (2014). The impact of supply chain integration on firm performance: The moderating role of competitive strategy. *Supply Chain Management*, *19*(4), 369–384. doi:10.1108/SCM-03-2013-0096

Hussein, A. F., ArunKumar, N., Ramirez-Gonzalez, G., Abdulhay, E., Tavares, J. M. R. S., & de Albuquerque, V. H. C. (2018). A medical records managing and securing blockchain based system supported by a genetic algorithm and discrete wavelet transform. *Cognitive Systems Research*, *52*, 1–11. doi:10.1016/j.cogsys.2018.05.004

Hussein, A., & Al-Tamimi, H. (2012). The Effects of Corporate Governance on Performance and Financial Distress: The Experience of UAE National Banks. *Journal of Financial Regulation and Compliance*, *20*(2), 169–181. doi:10.1108/13581981211218315

Hussien, H. M., Yasin, S. M., Udzir, N. I., Ninggal, M. I. H., & Salman, S. (2021). Blockchain technology in the healthcare industry: Trends and opportunities. *Journal of Industrial Information Integration*, *22*, 100217. doi:10.1016/j.jii.2021.100217

Hypersonix. (2021). *AI in Inventory Management: Putting AI to work to optimize inventory.* https://hypersonix.ai/resources/blog/ai-in-inventory-management/

IBM. (2021). Artificial Intelligence in Finance: Opportunities and Challenges *IBM*. https://community.ibm.com/community/user/datascience/blogs/stephen-crenshaw/2021/11/14/artificial-intelligence-in-finance-opportunities-a

icommunity. (2022). Blockchain technology for the prevention of pandemics such as the corona virus. *iCommunity.* https://icommunity.io/en/blockchain-technology-for-the-prevention-of-pandemics-such-as-the-coronavirus/

Iman, N. (2020) The rise and rise of financial technology: The good, the bad, and the verdict. *Cogent Business & Management, 7*(1). doi:10.1080/23311975.2020.1725309

Iman, N. (2020). The rise and rise of financial technology: The good, the bad, and the verdict. *Cogent Business & Management, 7*(1), 1725309.

Improving Lives Throughout Asia and The Pacific. (2014). https://www.adb.org/sites/default/files/institutional-document/158032/adb-annual-report-2014.pdf

Indiatimes. (2020). Coronavirus suspects under home quarantine to have their left hand stamped in Maharashtra. *News, The Economic Times.*

Institute of Medicine (US) Committee on Health Research and the Privacy of Health Information. (2009). The HIPAA Privacy Rule; Nass SJ, Levit LA, Gostin LO, (eds.), *Beyond the HIPAA Privacy Rule: Enhancing Privacy, Improving Health Through Research.* National Academies Press (US); https://www.ncbi.nlm.nih.gov/books/NBK9579/

International Money Fund. (2018). *Central Bank Monetary Policy in the Age of Cryptocurrencies - IMF F&D Magazine, 55*(2). Imf.org. https://www.imf.org/external/pubs/ft/fandd/2018/06/central-bank-monetary-policy-and-cryptocurrencies/he.htm

Introduction to the FinTech Ecosystem Technology & Law 69 Department of Justice Journal of Federal Law and Practice 2021. (2021, March 8). HeinOnline; heinonline.org. https://heinonline.org/HOL/LandingPage?handle=hein.journals/usab69&div=36&id=&page=

Investing. (2021). *Bitcoin Historical Data.* Investing.com. https://www.investing.com/crypto/bitcoin/historical-data

Investopedia. (n.d.). https://www.investopedia.com/tech/most-important-cryptocurrencies-other-than-bitcoin/#:text=One%20reason%20for%20this%20is,communities%20of%20backers%20and%20investors

Ionescu, L., & Berger, G. (2018). Applied Analysis of the Impact of Inventory Valuation Methods on the Financial Situation and Financial Performance. *Applied Analysis of the Impact of Inventory Valuation Methods on the Financial Situation and Financial Performance.*, *9*(1), 67–76. doi:10.2478/vjes-2018-0007

Ivanov, D. (2020). Predicting the impacts of epidemic outbreaks on global supply chains: A simulation-based analysis on the coronavirus outbreak (COVID-19/SARSCoV-2) case. Transportation Research Part E: Logistics and Transportation Review, 136, 1-14.

Jaccard, J. J., & Nepal, S. (2014). A survey of emerging threats in cybersecurity. *Journal of Computer and System Sciences*, *80*(5), 973–993. doi:10.1016/j.jcss.2014.02.005

Jayawardhana, A., & Colombage, S. (2020). Does Blockchain Technology Drive Sustainability? An Exploratory Review. In Governance and Sustainability. Emerald Publishing Limited. doi:10.1108/S2043-052320200000015002

Jensen, M. C. (1993). The Modern Industrial Revolution, Exit, and the Failure of Internal Control Systems. *The Journal of Finance*, *48*(3), 831–880. doi:10.1111/j.1540-6261.1993.tb04022.x

Jensen, M. C., & Meckling, W. H. (1976). Theory of The Firm: Managerial Behavior, Agency Costs, and Ownership Structure. *Journal of Financial Economics*, *3*(4), 305–360. doi:10.1016/0304-405X(76)90026-X

Jiang, Y., Lie, J., Wang, J., & Mu, J. (2021). Revisiting the roles of cryptocurrencies in stock markets: A quantile coherency perspective. *Economic Modelling*, *95*, 21–34. doi:10.1016/j.econmod.2020.12.002

Jose, A., & Shanmugam, P. V. (2019). Supply chain issues in SME food sector: a systematic review. In Journal of Advances in Management Research (Vol. 17, Issue 1, pp. 19–65). doi:10.1108/JAMR-02-2019-0010

Kaparthi, S., & Bumblauskas, D. (2020). Designing predictive maintenance systems using decision tree-based machine learning techniques. *International Journal of Quality & Reliability Management*, *37*(4), 659–686. doi:10.1108/IJQRM-04-2019-0131

Kassem, H. S., Alotaibi, B. A., Ghoneim, Y. A., & Diab, A. M. (2021). Mobile-based advisory services for sustainable agriculture: Assessing farmers' information behavior. *Information Development*, *37*(3), 483–495. https://doi.org/10.1177/0266666920967979

266

Compilation of References

Kaur, H., Alam, M. A., Jameel, R., Mourya, A. K., & Chang, V. (2018). A proposed solution and future direction for blockchain-based heterogeneous medicare data in cloud environment. *Journal of Medical Systems*, *42*(8), 1–11. doi:10.100710916-018-1007-5 PMID:29987560

Kaya, O., & Schildbach, J. AG, D. B., & Schneider, S. (2019). Artificial intelligence in banking: A lever for profitability with limited implementation to date. *EU Monitors Global financial markets.https://*www.dbresearch.com/PROD/RPS_ENPROD/PROD0000000000495172/Artificial_intelligence_in_banking%3A_A_lever_for_pr.pdf?undefined&realload=VhsiDhBWr~jzgZ~OD9X1XXylwp5O2UH6Q/fscdzc1KSVG4FsZDR0MPXIR1rxXSk2

Kee, D. M. H., Syazwan, M. A., Rusydi, M. D., Anwar, M. A., Islah, M. H., Khan, Y. F., & Ganatra, V. (2021). Trust, Perceived Support and Organizational Citizenship Behavior Among Undergraduate Students in Universiti Sains Malaysia. [APJME]. *Asia Pacific Journal of Management and Education*, *4*(3), 49–60.

Keen, S. (2013). A monetary Minsky model of the Great Moderation and the Great Recession. *Journal of Economic Behavior & Organization*, *86*, 221–235. doi:10.1016/j.jebo.2011.01.010

Khan, K. A., Akhtar, M. A., Dey, S. K., & Ibrahim, R. (2020). Financial Anxiety, Financial advice, and E-payment use: Relationship and perceived differences between males & females of Generation Z. *Journal of Critical Reviews,*. *7*(18). https://www.jcreview.com/index.php?mno=96289

Khan, N. A., Brohi, S. N., & Zaman, N. (2020). Ten Deadly Cyber Security Threats Amid COVID-19 Pandemic. TechRxiv *Powered by IEEE. file:///C:/Users/DELL/Downloads/Ten%20Deadly%20Cyber%20Security%20Threats%20Amid%20COVID-19%20Pandemic.pdf*

Khasanah, U., & Irawati, Z. (2022, June 13). The Effect of Financial Literacy, Financial Attitude, and the Use of Financial Technology on the Financial Management of SMEs. *Atlantis Press*. https://www.atlantis-press.com/proceedings/icoebs-22/125975151

Khashei, M., & Hajirahimi, Z. (2017). Performance evaluation of series and parallel strategies for financial time series forecasting. *Financial Innovation*, *3*(1), 1–24. doi:10.118640854-017-0074-9

Khezr, S., Moniruzzaman, M., Yassine, A., & Benlamri, R. (2019). Blockchain technology in healthcare: A comprehensive review and directions for future research. *Applied Sciences (Basel, Switzerland)*, *9*(9), 1736. doi:10.3390/app9091736

Khurshid, A. (2020). Why Banks need artificial intelligence? *Wipro.* https://www.wipro.com/business-process/why-banks-need-artificial-intelligence/

Kiefer, N. M. (2009). Default estimation for low-default portfolios. *Journal of Empirical Finance*, *16*(1), 164–173. doi:10.1016/j.jempfin.2008.03.004

Kietzmann, J., Paschen, J., & Treen, E. (2018). Artificial intelligence in advertising: How marketers can leverage artificial intelligence along the consumer journey. *Journal of Advertising Research*, *58*(3), 263–267. doi:10.2501/JAR-2018-035

Kim, D.-H., Kim, T. J. Y., Wang, X., Kim, M., Quan, Y.-J., Oh, J. W., Min, S.-H., Kim, H., Bhandari, B., Yang, I., & Ahn, S.-H. (2018). Smart Machining Process Using Machine Learning: A Review and Perspective on Machining Industry. *International Journal of Precision Engineering and Manufacturing-Green Technology*, *5*(4), 555–568. doi:10.100740684-018-0057-y

Kim, S.-J. (2005). Information Leadership in the Advanced Asia–Pacific Stock Markets: Return, Volatility and Volume Information Spillovers from the US and Japan. *Journal of the Japanese and International Economies*, *19*(3), 338–365. doi:10.1016/j.jjie.2004.03.002

Klein, T., Thu, H. P., & Walther, T. (2018). Bitcoin is not the New Gold–A comparison of volatility, correlation, and portfolio performance. *International Review of Financial Analysis*, *59*, 105–116. doi:10.1016/j.irfa.2018.07.010

Kliber, A., Marszałek, P., Musiałkowska, I., & Świerczyńska, K. (2019). Bitcoin: Safe haven, hedge or diversifier? Perception of bitcoin in the context of a country's economic situation—A stochastic volatility approach. *Physica A*, *524*, 246–257. doi:10.1016/j.physa.2019.04.145

Klontz, B., Zutphen, N., & Fries, K. (2016). Financial Planner as Healer: Maximizing the Role of Financial Health Physician. *Journal of Financial Planning*, *29*, 52–59.

Kofman, P., & Sharpe, I. G. (2003). Using multiple imputation in the analysis of incomplete observations in finance. *Journal of Financial Econometrics*, *1*(2), 216–249. doi:10.1093/jjfinec/nbg013

Kokate, S., & Chetty, M. S. R. (2021). Credit risk assessment of loan defaulters in commercial banks using voting classifier ensemble learner machine learning model. *International Journal of Safety and Security Engineering*, *11*(5), 565–572. doi:10.18280/ijsse.110508

Köksal, D., Strähle, J., & Müller, M. (2018). Social Sustainability in Apparel Supply Chains—The Role of the Sourcing Intermediary in a Developing Country. *Sustainability*, *10*(4), 1039. doi:10.3390u10041039

Kolady, D., Krishnamoorthy, S., & Narayanan, S. (2008). *Small-scale producers in modern agrifood markets Marketing cooperatives in a new retail context : A case study of HOPCOMS*. Academic Press.

Kosba, A., Miller, A., Shi, E., Wén, Z., & Papamanthou, C. (2016). Hawk: The blockchain model of cryptography and privacy-preserving smart contracts. in *Proceedings of IEE Symposium on Security and Privacy (SP)*, (pp. 839–858). IEEE.

Kou, G., Chao, X., Peng, Y., Alsaadi, F. E., & Herrera-Viedma, E. (2019). Machine learning methods for systemic risk analysis in financial sectors. *Technological and Economic Development of Economy*, *25*(5), 716–742. doi:10.3846/tede.2019.8740

Kou, G., Peng, Y., & Wang, G. (2014). Evaluation of clustering algorithms for financial risk analysis using MCDM methods. *Information Sciences*, *275*, 1–12. doi:10.1016/j.ins.2014.02.137

Compilation of References

Krause, S. K., Natarajan, H., & Gradstein, H. L. (2017). Distributed Ledger Technology (DLT) and Blockchain. In *The World Bank*. The World Bank., https://documents1.worldbank.org/curated/en/177911513714062215/pdf/122140-WP-PUBLIC-Distributed-Ledger-Technology-and-Blockchain-Fintech-Notes.pdf

Krejcie, R. V., & Morgan, D. W. (1970). Determining sample size for research activities. *Educational and Psychological Measurement, 30*(3), 607–610.

Krishna, K. M., & Mokshapathy, S. (2013). Performance and Prospects of HOPCOMS in Karnataka—A Direct Link between Farmers and Consumers. *International Journal of Research in Commerce, Economics and Management, 3*(2), 114–117. http://search.proquest.com/docvie w/1373419092?accountid=13042%5Cnhttp://oxfordsfx.hosted.exlibrisgroup.com/oxford?url_ ver=Z39.88-2004&rft_val_fmt=info:ofi/fmt:kev:mtx:journal&genre=article&sid=ProQ:ProQ :econlitshell&atitle=Performance+and+Prospects+of+HOP

Kuckreja, J., Nigde, P., & Patil, P. (2021). Health Insurance Claim Using Blockchain. *International Research Journal of Engineering and Technology, 8*(5), 2406–2409.

Kumar, A., Liu, R., & Shan, Z. (2020). Is Blockchain a Silver Bullet for Supply Chain Management? Technical Challenges and Research Opportunities. *Decision Sciences, 51*(1), 8–37. doi:10.1111/deci.12396

Kumaraguru, S., Kulvatunyou, B., & Morris, K. C. (2014). *Integrating Real-Time Analytics and Continuous Performance Management in Smart Manufacturing Systems.* doi:10.1007/978-3-662-44733-8_22

Kumar, R., Tiwari, S., & Kansara, S. (2021). Barriers Prioritization of the Indian Steel Industry Supply Chain: Applying AHP and Fuzzy AHP Method. *Vision: The Journal of Business Perspective.* Advance online publication. doi:10.1177/09722629211065687

Kunt, A.D., Klapper, L., Singer, D., Ansar, S., & Hess, J. (2017). *The Global Findex Database: Measuring Financial Inclusion and the Fintech Revolution.* World Bank Group. file:///C:/Users/DELL/Downloads/9781464812590.pdf

Kuppili, V., Tripathi, D., & Reddy Edla, D. (2020). Credit score classification using spiking extreme learning machine. *Computational Intelligence, 36*(2), 402–426. doi:10.1111/coin.12242

Kusiak, A. (2020). Convolutional and generative adversarial neural networks in manufacturing. *International Journal of Production Research, 58*(5), 1594–1604. doi:10.1080/00207543.201 9.1662133

Kutub, T., Meikang, Q., Gai, K., & Ali, M. L. (2015, November, 3-5). *An Investigation on Cyber Security Threats and Security Model.* [Paper presentation]. IEEE 2nd International Conference on Cyber Security and Cloud Computing, New York, NY, USA. 10.1109/CSCloud.2015.71

Kwela, H. A. (2015). *The effectiveness of the Personal Financial Management Programme on the well-being of employees in the Department of Rural Development and Land Reform in the Pietermaritzburg region* [Doctoral dissertation, University of Pretoria, South Africa].

Lappetito, C. (2021). AI And ML Can Transform Financial Services, But Industry Must Solve Data Problem First. *Forbes*. https://www.forbes.com/sites/forbesfinancecouncil/2021/10/13/ai-and-ml-can-transform-financial-services-but-industry-must-solve-data-problem-first/?sh=1eb612a96ea3

Latha, L. (2017). Inventory valuation methods in Indian manufacturing sector SMES - an empirical study. *Abhinav National Monthly Refereed Journal of Research, 6*(12).

Law, K. & Zuo, L. (2022, June 1). How Does the Economy Shape the Financial Advisory Profession? *Management Science*. doi:10.1287/mnsc.2020.3655

Law, K. K., & Zuo, L. (2022). Public concern about immigration and customer complaints against minority financial advisors. *Management Science, 68*(11), 8464–8482. doi:10.1287/mnsc.2021.4283

Lee Kuo Chuen, D. (2015). *Handbook of Digital Currency*, (1st ed). Elsevier. http://EconPapers.repec.org/RePEceee:monogr:9780128021170

Le, L.-T., Yarovaya, L., & Nasir, M. A. (2021). Did COVID-19 change spillover patterns between Fintech and other asset classes? *Research in International Business and Finance, 58*, 101441. doi:10.1016/j.ribaf.2021.101441 PMID:34518714

Li, H., Qiu, H., Sun, S., Chang, J., & Tu, W. (2021). Credit scoring by one-class classification driven dynamical ensemble learning. *The Journal of the Operational Research Society, 0*(0), 1–10. doi:10.1080/01605682.2021.1944824

Li, H.-X., Wang, Z.-J., & Deng, X.-L. (2008). Ownership, Independent Directors, Agency Costs and Financial Distress: Evidence from Chinese Listed Companies. *Corporate Governance, 8*(5), 622–636. doi:10.1108/14720700810913287

Li, H., Zhu, L., Shen, M., Gao, F., Tao, X., & Liu, S. (2018). Blockchain-based data preservation system for medical data. *Journal of Medical Systems, 42*(8), 1–13. doi:10.100710916-018-0997-3 PMID:29956058

Lipton, A., Hardjono, T., & Pentland, A. (2018). Digital Trade Coin: Towards more stable digital currency. *Royal Society Open Science, 5*(7), 180155. doi:10.1098/rsos.180155 PMID:30109071

Liu, T. (2020) *Transmission dynamics of 2019 novel coronavirus (2019-nCoV)*. Doi:10.1101/2020.01.25.919787

Loos, J. R., & Davidson, E. J. (2016). Wearable health monitors and physician-patient communication: the physician's perspective. *Proceedings of 2016 49th Hawaii International Conference on System Sciences (HICSS)*, 3389-3399. 10.1109/HICSS.2016.422

Lounds, M. (2020). Blockchain and its Implications for the Insurance Industry. *Munich Re*. https://www.munichre.com/us-life/en/perspectives/underwriting/blockchain-implications-insurance-industry.html

Lowery, C. (2020). What is digital health and what do I need to know about it? *Obstetrics and Gynecology Clinics, 47*(2), 215–225. doi:10.1016/j.ogc.2020.02.011 PMID:32451013

Compilation of References

Luther, W., & White, L. (2014). *Can Bitcoin become a major currency?* Working Paper. Available at: http://bahler.co/wpcontent/uploads/2016/11/Can-Bitcoin-Become-a-Major-Currency.pdf

Mafiroh, A., & Triyono. (2016). The Effect of Financial Performance and Corporate Governance Mechanisms on Financial Distress (Empirical Study on Manufacturing Companies Listed on the Indonesia Stock Exchange 2011-2014 Period). *Riset Akuntansi Dan Keuangan Indonesia, 1*(1), 46–53.

Ma, H., Wang, Y., & Wang, K. (2018). Automatic detection of false positive RFID readings using machine learning algorithms. *Expert Systems with Applications, 91*, 442–451. doi:10.1016/j.eswa.2017.09.021

Mahale, A. (2020). Coronavirus | Western Railway deboards 17 passengers bearing home quarantine stamp. *News, The Hindu.*

Mahapatra, M., & De, A. (2017). A Study on Influence of Financial Cognition on Personal Financial Planning of Indian Households. *Academic Research Colloquium for Financial Planning and Related Disciplines.* https://ssrn.com/abstract=3040807 or doi:10.2139/ssrn.3040807

Maier, A., Sharp, A., & Vagapov, Y. (2017). Comparative analysis and practical implementation of the ESP32 microcontroller module for the internet of things. In *Proceedings of 2017 Internet Technologies and Applications (ITA)* (pp. 143–148). IEEE. doi:10.1109/ITECHA.2017.8101926

Majumder, A., Routh, M., & Singha, D. (2019). A Conceptual Study on the Emergence of Cryptocurrency Economy and Its Nexus with Terrorism Financing. In The Impact of Global Terrorism on Economic and Political Development. Emerald Publishing Limited. doi:10.1108/978-1-78769-919-920191012

MajumderM.MandlK. (2020). *Early Transmissibility Assessment of a Novel Coronavirus in Wuhan, China.* doi:10.2139/ssrn.3524675

Majuri, Y. (2019). Overcoming economic stagnation in low-income communities with programmable money. *The Journal of Risk Finance, 20*(5), 594–610. doi:10.1108/JRF-08-2019-0145

Makkar, S., Devi, G. N. R., & Solanki, V. K. (2020). Applications of Machine Learning Techniques in Supply Chain Optimization. In ICICCT 2019 – System Reliability, Quality Control, Safety, Maintenance and Management (pp. 861–869). Springer Singapore. doi:10.1007/978-981-13-8461-5_98

Makridakis, S. (2017). The forthcoming Artificial Intelligence (AI) revolution: Its impact on society and firms. *Futures, 90*, 46–60. doi:10.1016/j.futures.2017.03.006

Ma, L., & Sun, B. (2020). Machine learning and AI in marketing – Connecting computing power to human insights. *International Journal of Research in Marketing, 37*(3), 481–504. doi:10.1016/j.ijresmar.2020.04.005

Malali, A., & Gopalakrishnan, S. (2020). Application of Artificial Intelligence and Its Powered Technologies in the Indian Banking and Financial Industry: An Overview. *Journal of the Humanities and Social Sciences, 25*(4), 55–60.

271

Marbouh, D., Abbasi, T., Maasmi, F., Omar, I. A., Debe, M. S., Salah, K., Jayaraman, R., & Ellahham, S. (2020). Blockchain for COVID-19: Review, opportunities, and a trusted tracking system. *Arabian Journal for Science and Engineering*, *45*(12), 1–17. doi:10.100713369-020-04950-4 PMID:33072472

Martínez, A., Schmuck, C., Pereverzyev, S. Jr, Pirker, C., & Haltmeier, M. (2020). A machine learning framework for customer purchase prediction in the non-contractual setting. *European Journal of Operational Research*, *281*(3), 588–596. doi:10.1016/j.ejor.2018.04.034

McNew, S. (2020). How Blockchain Can Solve Today's Medical Supply Chain Flaws And Improve Responses For Future Crises. *Forbes*. https://www.forbes.com/sites/forbesbusinessdevelopmentcouncil/2020/04/29/how-blockchain-can-solve-todays-medical-supply-chain-flaws-and-improve-responses-for-future-crises/?sh=1f475ee9750a

Meghani, K. (2020). Use of Artificial Intelligence and Blockchain in Banking Sector: A Study of Scheduled Commercial Banks in India. *Indian Journal of Applied Research*, *10*(8), 1–4.

Menold, N., & Bogner, K. (2016). *Design of Rating Scales in Questionnaires (Version 2.0)*. doi:10.15465/gesis-sg_en_015

Michelberger, K. (2016). Corporate Governance Effects on Firm Performance: A Literature Review. *Regional Formation and Development Studies, 20*(3), 84–95.

Miglani, S. (2014). Voluntary Audit Committee Characteristics in Financially Distressed and Healthy Firms: A Study of The Efficacy of The ASX Corporate Governance Council Recommendations. *Corporate Ownership & Control, 12*(1).

Mills, D., Wang, K., Malone, B., Ravi, A., Marquardt, J., Chen, C., Badev, A., Brezinski, T., Fahy, L., Liao, K., Kargenian, V., Ellithorpe, M., Ng, W., & Baird, M. (2016). Distributed Ledger Technology in Payments, Clearing, and Settlement. *Finance and Economics Discussion Series, 2016*(095). doi:10.17016/FEDS.2016.095

Milojević, N., & Redzepagic, S. (2021). Prospects of artificial intelligence and machine learning application in banking risk management. *Journal of Central Banking Theory and Practice*, *10*(3), 41–57. doi:10.2478/jcbtp-2021-0023

Ministry of Health & Family. (2016). Standards for India. *MOHFW*. https://main.mohfw.gov.in/sites/default/files/EMR-EHR_Standards_for_India_as_notified_by_MOHFW_2016_0.pdf

Mishra, A. S. S. (2021) Study on Blockchain-Based Healthcare Insurance Claim System. *Asian Conference on Innovation in Technology (ASIANCON)*, 1-4. IEEE. 10.1109/ASIANCON51346.2021.9544892

Mizerka, J., Stróżyńska-Szajek, A., & Mizerka, P. (2020). The role of Bitcoin on developed and emerging markets–on the basis of a Bitcoin users graph analysis. *Finance Research Letters*, *35*, 101489. doi:10.1016/j.frl.2020.101489

Compilation of References

Mohammed, A., Abdul Kareem, K. H., Al-Waisy, A. S., Mostafa, S. A., Al-Fahdawi, S., Dinar, A. M., Alhakami, W., Baz, A., Al-Mhiqani, M. N., Alhakami, H., Arbaiy, N., Maashi, M. S., Mutlag, A. A., Garcia-Zapirain, B., & De La Torre Diez, I. (2020). Benchmarking methodology for selection of optimal COVID-19 diagnostic model based on entropy and TOPSIS methods. *IEEE Access: Practical Innovations, Open Solutions*, 8, 99115–99131. doi:10.1109/ACCESS.2020.2995597

Mohanta, G., & Dash, A. (2022). Do financial consultants exert a moderating effect on savings behavior? A study on the Indian rural population. *Cogent Economics & Finance*, 10(1), 2131230.

Mosteanu, N. R. (2020). Artificial Intelligence and Cyber Security–A Shield against Cyberattack as a Risk Business Management Tool–Case of European Countries. *Quality-Access to Success*, 21(175).

Mu-chun, S., & Kao, E. (2020). *6 suspected Vietnamese stowaways escape from quarantine*. Society, Focus Taiwan.

Munohsamy, T. (2015). Personal. *Financial Management*.

Murhadi, W. R., Tanugara, F., & Sutejo, B. S. (2018). The Influence of Good Corporate Governance on Financial Distress. *Advances in Social Science, Education and Humanities Research*, 186. doi:10.2991/insyma-18.2018.19

Murphy, D., & Yetmar, S. (2010). Personal financial planning attitudes: A preliminary study of graduate students. *Management Research Review*, 33, 811–817. doi:10.1108/01409171011065617

Murthy, D. S., Gajanana, T. M., Sudha, M., & Dakshinamoorthy, V. (2009). *Marketing and Post-Harvest Losses in Fruits : Its Implications on Availability and Economy*. Academic Press.

Murugesan, R., & Manohar, V. (2019). AI in Financial Sector–A Driver to Financial Literacy. *Shanlax International Jou*, 66-70.

Musthafa, M. (2021). Cyber Threats To The Banking Sector To Watch Out For. *Claysys*. https://www.claysys.com/blog/cyber-threats-to-the-banking-sector/

Naeem, M. A., Hasan, M., Arif, M., & Shahzad, S. J. H. (2020). Can bitcoin glitter more than gold for investment styles? *SAGE Open*, 10(2). doi:10.1177/2158244020926508

Naik, D. S. (n.d.). Survey of Hopcoms Employees In Karnataka. *Introduction. Research Methodology*, 2(12), 249–257.

Nakamoto, S. (2008). Bitcoin: A peer-to-peer electronic cash system. *Bitcoin*.

Nakamoto, S. (2008). Bitcoin: a Peer-to-Peer Electronic Cash System. *Bitcoin.org*. https://bitcoin.org/bitcoin.pdf

NDTV Gadgets 360. (2021). *Cryptocurrency Prices in India Today (24th August 2021)*. NDTV Gadgets 360. https://gadgets.ndtv.com/finance/crypto-currency-price-in-india-inr-compare-bitcoin-ether-dogecoin-ripple-litecoin

Negi, S. (2014). Supply Chain Efficiency: An Insight from Fruits and Vegetables Sector in India. *Journal of Operations and Supply Chain Management*, 7(2), 154. doi:10.12660/joscmv7n2p154-167

Nethravathi, K. G. A. T. O. (2014). *Analysis of consumer's preferences in purchasing fruits and vegetables across selected marketing organizations in Bangalore rural and urban districts.* Academic Press.

Nguyen, Q. K. (2016). Blockchain - A Financial Technology for Future Sustainable Development. *3rd International Conference on Green Technology and Sustainable Development (GTSD),* (pp. 51-54). IEEE. 10.1109/GTSD.2016.22

Ni, D., Xiao, Z., & Lim, M. K. (2020). A systematic review of the research trends of machine learning in supply chain management. *International Journal of Machine Learning and Cybernetics*, 11(7), 1463–1482. doi:10.100713042-019-01050-0

Nugent, T., Upton, D., & Cimpoesu, M. (2016). Improving data transparency in clinical trials using blockchain smart contracts. *F1000 Research*, 5, 5. doi:10.12688/f1000research.9756.1 PMID:28357041

Oberoi, S., & Kansra, P. (2022). Blockchain Technology in the Insurance Industry. In Applications, Challenges, and Opportunities of Blockchain Technology in Banking and Insurance (pp. 160-172). IGI Global. doi:10.4018/978-1-6684-4133-6.ch009

Oberoi, S., & Kansra, P. (2021). Motivating Antecedents and Consequences of Blockchain Technology in the Insurance Industry. In *Blockchain Technology and Applications for Digital Marketing* (pp. 276–285). IGI Global. doi:10.4018/978-1-7998-8081-3.ch017

Ødegård, A. T., & Volden, T. M. (2020). *Cryptocurrency entering uncharted territory: a combined deductive and inductive study into the mechanisms of institutional demand for cryptocurrencies and an examination of Bitcoin's safe haven capabilities* (Master's thesis).

Óskarsdóttir, M., Sarraute, C., Bravo, C., Baesens, B., & Vanthienen, J. (2018). Credit scoring for good: Enhancing financial inclusion with smartphone-based micro lending. *International Conference on Information Systems 2018, ICIS 2018*, 1–14.

Othman, A. H. A., Alhabshi, S. M., & Haron, R. (2019). The effect of symmetric and asymmetric information on volatility structure of crypto-currency markets: A case study of bitcoin currency. *Journal of Financial Economic Policy*, 11(3), 432–450. doi:10.1108/JFEP-10-2018-0147

Ozturan, M., Atasu, I., & Soydan, H. (2019). Assessment of blockchain technology readiness level of banking industry: Case of Turkey. *International Journal of Business Marketing and Management (IJBMM), 4*(12), 01-13.

Pahwa, A. (2020). Agritech-towards transforming Indian agricutlure. *Ernst & Young LLP EY*, 8, 1–53.

Compilation of References

Pal, A., Sharma, S. S., & Gupta, K. P. (2021). The Role of Analytics and Robo-Advisory in Investors' Financial Decisions and Risk Management: Review of Literature Post-Global Financial Crisis. [IJBAN]. *International Journal of Business Analytics, 8*(2), 46–62. https://doi.org/10.4018/IJBAN.2021040104

Palmie, M., Wincent, J., Parida, V., & Caglar, U. (2020). The evolution of the financial technology ecosystem: An introduction and agenda for future research on disruptive innovations in ecosystems. *Technological Forecasting and Social Change, 151*, 119779. doi:10.1016/j.techfore.2019.119779

Pandey, A. (2020). *Coronavirus in India: Man stamped for quarantine in Mumbai caught at Secundarabad railway station.* News, India Today.

Pandey, M., Agarwal, R., Shukla, S. K., & Verma, N. K. (2021). Security of Healthcare Data Using Blockchains. *Survey (London, England)*, 1–40.

Pandey, T. N., Jagadev, A. K., Mohapatra, S. K., & Dehuri, S. (2018). Credit risk analysis using machine learning classifiers. *2017 International Conference on Energy, Communication, Data Analytics and Soft Computing, ICECDS 2017*, 1850–1854. 10.1109/ICECDS.2017.8389769

Pang, P. S., Hou, X., & Xia, L. (2021). Borrowers' credit quality scoring model and applications, with default discriminant analysis based on the extreme learning machine. *Technological Forecasting and Social Change, 165*(November). doi:10.1016/j.techfore.2020.120462

Panoš, J., & Polák, P. (2019). *How to Improve the Model Selection Procedure in a Stress-testing Framework.* Czech National Bank, Economic Research Department.

Park, M., Kim, J., Won, D., & Kim, J. (2019). Development of a two-stage ESS-scheduling model for cost minimization using machine learning-based load prediction techniques. *Processes (Basel, Switzerland), 7*(6), 370. Advance online publication. doi:10.3390/pr7060370

Patel, A. & Kumar, S. (2016). Awareness & Attitude Of Investors Regarding Personal Financial Planning. *Paripex-Indian Journal of Research, 5*(11).

Patel, B. S., Samuel, C., & Sharma, S. K. (2017). Evaluation of agility in supply chains: A case study of an Indian manufacturing organization. *Journal of Manufacturing Technology Management, 28*(2), 212–231. doi:10.1108/JMTM-09-2016-0125

Patel, V. (2019). A framework for secure and decentralized sharing of medical imaging data via blockchain consensus. *Health Informatics Journal, 25*(4), 1398–1411. doi:10.1177/1460458218769699 PMID:29692204

Phimolsathien, T. (2021). Determinants of the use of financial technology (Fintech). In *Generation Y Utopía y Praxis Latinoamericana, 26*(2), Universidad del Zulia, Venezuela. https://www.redalyc.org/articulo.oa?id=27966514003

Platt, H. D., & Platt, M. B. (2002). Predicting Corporate Financial Distress: Reflections on Choice-Based Sample Bias. *Journal of Economics and Finance, 26*(2), 184–199. doi:10.1007/BF02755985

Pournader, M., Ghaderi, H., Hassanzadegan, A., & Fahimnia, B. (2021). Artificial intelligence applications in supply chain management. *International Journal of Production Economics*, *241*, 108250. doi:10.1016/j.ijpe.2021.108250

Prahathish, K., Naren, J., Vithya, G., Akhil, S., Dinesh Kumar, K., & Sai Krishna Mohan Gupta, S. (2020). *A Systematic Frame Work Using Machine Learning Approaches in Supply Chain Forecasting*. doi:10.1007/978-3-030-39033-4_15

Pramudena, S. M. (2017). The Impact of Good Corporate Governance on Financial Distress in the Consumer Good Sector. *Journal of Finance and Banking Review*, *10*(1), 46–55. http://journal.perbanas.id/index.php/jkp/article/view/192. doi:10.35609/jfbr.2017.2.4(6)

PricewaterhouseCoopers. (2015). *Understanding the evolving cryptocurrency market: PwC*. PwC. https://www.pwc.com/us/en/industries/financial-services/library/cryptocurrency-evolution.html

PRNewswire. (2018). *Despite the Buzz, Consumers Lack Awareness of the Broad Capabilities of AI*. https://www.prnewswire.com/news-releases/despite-the-buzz-consumers-lackaware ness-of-the-broad-capabilities-of-ai-300458237.html

Putra, J. W. G. (2019). *The Introduction of Machine Learning and Deep Learning Consepts*. Computational Linguistics and Natural Language Processing Laboratory. https://www.researchgate.net/publication/323700644

PwC. (2020). Financial services technology 2020 and beyond: embracing disruption. *PwC*. https://www. PwC. Com/gx/en/financial-services/assets/pdf/technology2020-and-beyond.Pdf.

Qin, M., Su, C. W., & Tao, R. (2021). BitCoin: A new basket for eggs? *Economic Modelling*, *94*, 896–907. doi:10.1016/j.econmod.2020.02.031

Radifan, R., & Yuyetta, E. N. A. (2015). Good Corporate Governance Terhadap Kemungkinan Financial Distress. *Diponegoro Journal of Accounting*, *4*(3), 1–11.

Raghvan, A. R., & Partibhan, L. (2014). The effect of cybercrime on a Bank's finances. *International Journal of Current Research and Academic Review*, *2*(2), 173–178.

RahaR. (2018, September 4). https://thesoftcopy.in/2018/09/04/lack-of-cold-storage-facility-hinders-hopcoms-profit/

Ram, A. J. (2019). Bitcoin as a new asset class. *Meditari Accountancy Research*, *27*(1), 147–168. doi:10.1108/MEDAR-11-2017-0241

Rao, N. H. (2018). *A framework for implementing information and communication technologies in agricultural development in India*. doi:10.1016/j.techfore.2006.02.002

Ratta, P., Kaur, A., Sharma, S., Shabaz, M., & Dhiman, G. (2021). Application of blockchain and internet of things in healthcare and medical sector: Applications, challenges, and future perspectives. *Journal of Food Quality*, *2021*(1), 1–20. doi:10.1155/2021/7608296

Compilation of References

Raymaekers, W. (2015, March 1). Cryptocurrency Bitcoin: Disruption, challenges and opportunities. *Journal of Payments Strategy & Systems, 9*(1).

Razvi, S. S., Feng, S., Narayanan, A., Lee, Y.-T. T., & Witherell, P. (2019, August 18). A Review of Machine Learning Applications in Additive Manufacturing. *39th Computers and Information in Engineering Conference.* 10.1115/DETC2019-98415

Research and Markets. (2018, June 18). Global Algorithmic Trading Market 2018-2022 with Citadel, Optiver, Tower Research Capital, Two Sigma Investments & Virtu Financial Dominating. *GlobeNewswire.* https://www.globenewswire.com/news-release/2018/06/18/1525672/0/en/Global-Algorithmic-Trading-Market-2018-2022-with-Citadel-Optiver-Tower-Research-Capital-Two-Sigma-Investments-Virtu-Financial-Dominating.html

Reserve Bank of India. (2013). *Press Releases.* Rbi.org.in. https://www.rbi.org.in/Scripts/BS_PressReleaseDisplay.aspx?prid=30247

Reserve Bank of India. (2016). *Function Wise Monetary.* Rbi.org.in. https://m.rbi.org.in/scripts/FS_Overview.aspx?fn=2752

Reserve Bank of India. (2017). *FAQs.* Rbi.org.in. https://m.rbi.org.in/scripts/FS_FAQs.aspx?Id=112&fn=5

Reserve Bank of India. (2018). *Notifications.* Rbi.org.in. https://www.rbi.org.in/scripts/FS_Notification.aspx?Id=11243&fn=2&Mode=0

Revanna, N. (2020). Blockchain in Healthcare. *International Research Journal of Engineering and Technology., 7*(4), 3218–3224.

Reza, T. (2018). A Study on Digital Currency: The Safety of Future Money. *JurnalTransparansi, 1*(1), 134–139. doi:10.31334/trans.v1i1.145

Roa, L., Rodríguez-Rey, A., Correa-Bahnsen, A., & Arboleda, C. V. (2022). Supporting Financial Inclusion with Graph Machine Learning and Super-App Alternative Data. *Lecture Notes in Networks and Systems, 295*, 216–230. doi:10.1007/978-3-030-82196-8_16

Roehrs, A., Da Costa, C. A., & da Rosa Righi, R. (2017). OmniPHR: A distributed architecture model to integrate personal health records. *Journal of Biomedical Informatics, 71*, 70–81. doi:10.1016/j.jbi.2017.05.012 PMID:28545835

Rönnqvist, S., & Sarlin, P. (2017). Bank distress in the news: Describing events through deep learning. *Neurocomputing, 264*, 57–70. doi:10.1016/j.neucom.2016.12.110

Rose, J. W., Andrews, K., & Kenny, K. (2021). Introduction to the FinTech Ecosystem. *Dep't of Just. J. Fed. L. & Prac., 69*, 23.

Rout, D. (2021). *CEO Insights.* .CEO Insights. https://www.ceoinsightsindia.com

Rudd, B. N., & Beidas, R. S. (2020). Digital mental health: The answer to the global mental health crisis? *JMIR Mental Health, 7*(6), e18472. doi:10.2196/18472 PMID:32484445

277

Russell, S.J., & Norvig, P. (2016). *Artificial Intelligence: A Modern Approach*. Pearson Education Limited. doi:10.1016/j.artint.2011.01.005

S, F., & M, R. (2021). Performance of Machine Learning Techniques in the Prevention of Financial Frauds. *International Journal of Computer Sciences and Engineering*, 27-29.

Sabharwal, M. (2014). The use of Artificial Intelligence (AI) based technological applications by Indian Banks. *International Journal of Artificial Intelligence and Agent Technology*, 2, 1–5.

Sabir, L. B. (2016). Managing Fruits And Vegetables Inventory : A Study Of Retail. *SAJMMR*.

Sabir, L., & Farooquie, J. A. (2017). Effect of Different Dimensions of Inventory Management of Fruits and Vegetables on Profitability of Retail Stores : An Empirical Study. *Sage (Atlanta, Ga.)*, *19*(1), 99–110. doi:10.1177/0972150917713278

Sadgali, I., Sael, N., & Benabbou, F. (2019). Performance of machine learning techniques in the detection of financial frauds. *Procedia Computer Science*, *148*, 45–54. doi:10.1016/j.procs.2019.01.007

Salancik, G. R., & Pfeffer, J. (1978). A Social Information Processing Approach to Job Attitudes and Task Design. *Administrative Science Quarterly*, *23*(2), 224–253. doi:10.2307/2392563 PMID:10307892

Sandeep Sachdeva, T. R. (2013). Increasing Fruit and Vegetable Consumption: Challenges and Opportunities. *Indian Journal of Community Medicine*, *38*(4), 192–197. doi:10.4103/0970-0218.120146 PMID:24302818

Sandelowski, M., Voils, C. I., & Barroso, J. (2007). Comparability work and the management of difference in research synthesis studies. *Social Science & Medicine*, *64*(1), 236–247. doi:10.1016/j.socscimed.2006.08.041 PMID:17029691

Santoso & Kurniawan. (2019). List of State-Owned Enterprises Vulnerable to Bankruptcy. *Kontan*. https://nasional.kontan.co.id/news/ini-dia-daftar-bumn-yang-rentan-bangkrut

Santoso, G. A. P., Yulianeu, & Fathoni, A. (2018). Analysis of Effect of Good Corporate Governance, Financial Performance, and Firm Size on Financial Distress in Property and Real Estate Company Listed BEI 2012-2016. *Journal of Management*, *4*(4).

Saranya, R., & Murugan, A. (2021). A systematic review of enabling blockchain in healthcare system: Analysis, current status, challenges and future direction. *Materials Today: Proceedings*. doi:10.1016/j.matpr.2021.07.105

Sarjerao, B. S., & Prakasarao, A. (2018). A Low Cost Smart Pollution Measurement System Using REST API and ESP32. *Proceedings of 2018 3rd International Conference for Convergence in Technology (I2CT)*, 1-5. 10.1109/I2CT.2018.8529500

Compilation of References

Saurabh, K., & Nandan, T. (2019). Role of financial knowledge, financial socialisation and financial risk attitude in financial satisfaction of Indian individuals. *International Journal of Indian Culture and Business Management, Inderscience Enterprises Ltd, 18*(1), 104–122. doi:10.1504/IJICBM.2019.096925

Sawyerr, E., & Harrison, C. (2020). Developing resilient supply chains: lessons from high-reliability organisations. In Supply Chain Management (Vol. 25, Issue 1, pp. 77–100). Emerald Group Publishing Ltd. doi:10.1108/SCM-09-2018-0329

Schmelzer, R., & Tucci, L. (June, 2021). The top 5 benefits of AI in banking and finance. *TechTarget.* https://searchenterpriseai.techtarget.com/feature/AI-in-banking-industry-brings-operational-improvements

Schwabe, G., & Matter, P. (2009). Why information technology is not being used for financial advisory. *17th European Conference on Information Systems,* 1524-1535. ECIS.

Senbekov, M., Saliev, T., Bukeyeva, Z., Almabayeva, A., Zhanaliyeva, M., Aitenova, N., Toishibekov, Y., & Fakhradiyev, I. (2020). The recent progress and applications of digital technologies in healthcare: A review. *International Journal of Telemedicine and Applications, 2020,* 2020. doi:10.1155/2020/8830200 PMID:33343657

Sethi & Sarangi. (2017). Internet of Things: Architectures, protocols, and applications (2017). *Journal of Electrical and Computer Engineering, 2017*(1), 1–25.

Shah, N. H. (2014). *Ordering Policy For Inventory Management When Demand Is Stock-Dependent And A Temporary Price Discount.* Academic Press.

Shahwan, T. M. (2015). The Effects of Corporate Governance on Financial Performance and Financial Distress: Evidence from Egypt. *Corporate Governance, 15*(5), 641–662. doi:10.1108/CG-11-2014-0140

Shahzad, S. J. H., Bouri, E., Roubaud, D., Kristoufek, L., & Lucey, B. (2019). Is Bitcoin a better safe-haven investment than gold and commodities? *International Review of Financial Analysis, 63,* 322–330. doi:10.1016/j.irfa.2019.01.002

Shakhovska, N., Melnykova, N., Chopiyak, V., & Gregus Ml, M. (2022). An ensemble methods for medical insurance costs prediction task. *Computers. Materials and Continua, 70*(2), 3969–3984. doi:10.32604/cmc.2022.019882

Sharma, U. (2017). *Blockchain in Healthcare Patient Benefits and more.* IBM. https://www.ibm.com/blogs/blockchain/2017/10/blockchain-in-healthcare-patient-benefits-and-more/

Sharma, A., Zhang, Z., & Rai, R. (2021). The interpretive model of manufacturing: A theoretical framework and research agenda for machine learning in manufacturing. *International Journal of Production Research, 59*(16), 4960–4994. doi:10.1080/00207543.2021.1930234

Sharma, P. K. (2016). Perishable inventory systems: A literature review since 2006. *International Journal of Applied Research, 2*(9), 150–155.

Shi, S., He, D., Li, L., Kumar, N., Khan, M. K., & Choo, K. K. R. (2020). Applications of blockchain in ensuring the security and privacy of electronic health record systems: A survey. *Computers & Security, 97*, 101966. doi:10.1016/j.cose.2020.101966 PMID:32834254

Siau, K. L., & Yang, Y. (2017). Impact of artificial intelligence, robotics, and machine learning on sales and marketing. *Twelve Annual Midwest Association for Information Systems Conference*, 18–19.

Sillaber, C., & Waltl, B. (2017). Life Cycle of Smart Contracts in Blockchain Ecosystems. *Datenschutz Datensich, 41*, 497–500. doi:10.1007/s11623-017-0819-7

Silva, J. C. F., Carvalho, T. F. M., Basso, M. F., Deguchi, M., Pereira, W. A., Sobrinho, R. R., Vidigal, P. M. P., Brustolini, O. J. B., Silva, F. F., Dal-Bianco, M., Fontes, R. L. F., Santos, A. A., Zerbini, F. M., Cerqueira, F. R., & Fontes, E. P. B. (2017). Geminivirus data warehouse: A database enriched with machine learning approaches. *BMC Bioinformatics, 18*(1), 240. doi:10.118612859-017-1646-4 PMID:28476106

Simeon, E. D., & John, O. (2018). Implication of Choice of Inventory Valuation Methods on Profit. *Tax and Closing Inventory., 3*(07), 1639–1645. doi:10.31142/afmj/v3i7.05

Simom, J. (2016). The End of Big Banks. *Project sandicate.*

Singh, S. S. (2018). How blockchain will change the way you trade in stock markets. *Economic Times.* https://economictimes.indiatimes.com/markets/stocks/news/how-blockchain-will-change-the-way-you-trade-in-stock-markets/articleshow/62161610.cms?from=mdr, 2018

Singh, S., & Aggarwal, L. (2019). *Pros and Cons of Artificial Intelligence in Banking Sector of India.* [Paper presentation]. 14th India-Japan International Conference on Economic and Industrial Growth through Recent Innovations and Advancement, Jaipur, India. https://link.springer.com/book/10.1007/978-981-16-6332-1?noAccess=true

Singh, V.K., Chandna, H., & Upadhyay, N. (2019). SmartPPM: An Internet of Things Based Smart Helmet,Design for Potholes and Air Pollution Monitoring. *EAI Endorsed Transactions on Internet of Things, 5*(18), 1-9.

Singh, M. H. (2020). A Study of Block Chain-Based Electronic HealthCare Record System. *International Journal of Advanced Research in Science & Technology, 5*(5), 75–81.

Singh, V., Md, H., Zaman, P., & Meher, J. (2014). Postharvest Technology of Fruits and Vegetables. *An Overview., 02*(02), 124–135.

Singhvi, S. (2021). Understanding the Emerging Role and Importance of Robo-advisory: A Case Study Approach. In: Al Mawali N.R., Al Lawati A.M., S A. (eds) *Fourth Industrial Revolution and Business Dynamics.* Palgrave Macmillan. doi:10.1007/978-981-16-3250-1_3

Słapczyński, T. (2019). Blockchain Technology and Cryptocurrencies – legal and tax aspects. *ASEJ - Scientific Journal of Bielsko-Biala School of Finance and Law, 23*(1). doi:10.5604/01.3001.0013.2653

Compilation of References

Sohail, N., & Sheikkh, T. H. (2018). *A Study of Inventory Management System Case Study*. Academic Press.

Sohrabia, C., Alsafib, Z., O'Neilla, N., Khanb, M., & Kerwanc, A. (2020). World health organization declares global emergency: A review of the 2019 novel coronavirus (COVID-19). *International Journal of Surgery, 76*(4), 71–76. doi:10.1016/j.ijsu.2020.02.034 PMID:32112977

Song, X. H., Hu, Z.-H., Du, J.-G., & Sheng, Z.-H. (2014). Application of Machine Learning Methods to Risk Assessment of Financial Statement Fraud. *Journal of Forecasting, 33*(8), 611–626. doi:10.1002/for.2294

Spenkelink, H. (2014). *The adoption process of cryptocurrencies. Identifying factors that influence the adoption of cryptocurrencies from a multiple stakeholder perspective*. Google Scholar.

Srivastav, S. (2021, June 29). *History of the cryptocurrency market in India*. CNBCTV18. https://www.cnbctv18.com/photos/cryptocurrency/history-of-the-cryptocurrency-market-in-india-9816081-5.htm

Stars, D. (2019). 6 examples of ai in financial services. *DJangostars*. https://djangostars.com/blog/6-examples-ai-financial-services/

Statista. (2021). (2021). Most popular cryptocurrency apps India 2021. *Statista*. . https://www.statista.com/statistics/1209741/most-popular-cryptocurrency-wallets-india/

Statista. (n.d.). Retrieved from https://www.statista.com/statistics/326707/bitcoin-price-index/

Stensas, A., Nygaard, M. F., Kyaw, K., & Treepongkaruna, S. (2019). Can Bitcoin be a diversifier, hedge or safe haven tool? *Cogent Economics and Finance, 7*(1), 1593072. doi:10.1080/23322 039.2019.1593072

Sujoko. (2007). The Influence of Ownership Structure, Diversification Strategy, Leverage, Internal Factors, and External Factors on Firm Value (Empirical Study on Manufacturing and Non-Manufacturing Companies on the Jakarta Stock Exchange). *Ekuitas, 11*(2), 236–254.

Sung, M., Marci, C., & Pentland, A. (2005). Wearable feedback systems for rehabilitation. Journal of NeuroEngineering and Rehabilitation, 2(17). doi:10.1186/1743-0003-2-17

Sun, J., Ren, L., Wang, S., & Yao, X. (2020). A blockchain-based framework for electronic medical records sharing with fine-grained access control. *PLoS One, 15*(10), e0239946. doi:10.1371/journal.pone.0239946 PMID:33022027

Susan, A. (2016). 5 ways digital currencies will change the world. *World Economic Forum, Khoa Tran Trans*. Bitcoin Vietnam.

Susilo, D., Wahyudi, S., Pangestuti, I. R. D., Nugroho, B. A., & Robiyanto, R. (2020). Cryptocurrencies: Hedging opportunities from domestic perspectives in Southeast Asia emerging markets. *SAGE Open, 10*(4), 2158244020971609. doi:10.1177/2158244020971609

Szabo, N. (1997). *Smart contracts: Formalizing and securing relationships on public networks.* Available at: https://firstmonday.org/article/view/548

Tang, Y., Xiong, J., Becerril-Arreola, R., & Iyer, L. (2020). Ethics of blockchain: A framework of technology, applications, impacts, and research directions. *Information Technology & People, 33*(2), 602–632. doi:10.1108/ITP-10-2018-0491

Thakkar, J., Kanda, A., & Deshmukh, S. G. (2012). Supply chain issues in Indian manufacturing SMEs: Insights from six case studies. *Journal of Manufacturing Technology Management, 23*(5), 634–664. doi:10.1108/17410381211234444

The World Bank. (2021). *Personal remittances received (current US$) - India* [Data set]. Worldbank. org. https://data.worldbank.org/indicator/BX.TRF.PWKR.CD.DT?locations=IN

Thenmozhi, M., Dhanalakshmi, R., Geetha, S., & Valli, R. (2021). Implementing blockchain technologies for health insurance claim processing in hospitals. *Materials Today: Proceedings.* doi:10.1016/j.matpr.2021.02.776

Thomas, D. L. (2021). Blockchain Applications in Healthcare. *News Medical Life Sciences* https://www.news-medical.net/health/Blockchain-Applications-in-Healthcare.aspx

Thornton, G. (2020). Financial inclusion in rural India. *Grant Thornton.* https://www.vakrangee.in/pdf/reports_hub/financial-inclusion-in-rural-india-28-jan.pdf

Tirkolaee, E. B., Sadeghi, S., Mooseloo, F. M., Vandchali, H. R., & Aeini, S. (2021). Application of Machine Learning in Supply Chain Management: A Comprehensive Overview of the Main Areas. *Mathematical Problems in Engineering, 2021*, 1–14. doi:10.1155/2021/1476043

Toorajipour, R., Sohrabpour, V., Nazarpour, A., Oghazi, P., & Fischl, M. (2021). Artificial intelligence in supply chain management: A systematic literature review. *Journal of Business Research, 122*, 502–517. doi:10.1016/j.jbusres.2020.09.009

Trabelsi, N. (2018). Are there any volatility spill-over effects among cryptocurrencies and widely traded asset classes? *Journal of Risk and Financial Management, 11*(4), 66. doi:10.3390/jrfm11040066

Tranfield, D., Denyer, D., & Smart, P. (2003). Towards a Methodology for Developing Evidence-Informed Management Knowledge by Means of Systematic Review. *British Journal of Management, 14*(3), 207–222. doi:10.1111/1467-8551.00375

Tronvoll, H., & Andersen, H. (2018). *Statistical Arbitrage Trading with Implementation of Machine Learning.* Academic Press.

Tyagi, S. E. B. I. (2020, Jan 23). 7 Benefits of AI/ML in the Financial Services Industry.. *The Hindu Business Line.* https://www.thehindubusinessline.com/markets/social-media-key-tool-for-market-manipulation-ajay-tyagi/article30633275.ece

Compilation of References

Valente, F. J., & Neto, A. C. (2017). Intelligent steel inventory tracking with IoT / RFID. *2017 IEEE International Conference on RFID Technology and Application, RFID-TA 2017*, 158–163. 10.1109/RFID-TA.2017.8098639

Vargas, R. (2021). 7 Benefits of AI/ML in the Financial Services Industry. *Encora*. https://www.encora.com/insights/7-benefits-of-ai/ml-in-the-financial-services-industry

Vazirani, A. A., O'Donoghue, O., Brindley, D., & Meinert, E. (2020). Blockchain vehicles for efficient medical record management. *NPJ Digital Medicine, 3*(1), 1–5. doi:10.103841746-019-0211-0 PMID:31934645

Veiga, R. T., Avelar, C., Moura, L.C., & Higuchi, A. K. (2019). Validation of Scales to Research the Personal Financial Management. *Revista Brasileira de Gestão de Negócios, 21*(2), 332-348. doi:10.7819/rbgn.v21i2.3976

Venkatesh, V. (2000). Determinants of Perceived Ease of Use: Integrating Control, Intrinsic Motivation, and Emotion into the Technology Acceptance Model. *Information Systems Research, 11*(4), 342–365. doi:10.1287/isre.11.4.342.11872

Wang, H., & Song, Y. (2018). Secure cloud-based EHR system using attribute-based cryptosystem and blockchain. *Journal of Medical Systems, 42*(8), 1–9. doi:10.100710916-018-0994-6 PMID:29974270

Wang, P., Zhang, W., Li, X., & Shen, D. (2019). Is cryptocurrency a hedge or a safe haven for international indices? A comprehensive and dynamic perspective. *Finance Research Letters, 31*, 1–18. doi:10.1016/j.frl.2019.04.031

Wardhani, R. (2006). Corporate Governance Mechanism in Financially Distressed Firms. *Simposium Nasional Akuntansi 9 Padang*, 23–26.

Weichert, D., Link, P., Stoll, A., Rüping, S., Ihlenfeldt, S., & Wrobel, S. (2019). A review of machine learning for the optimization of production processes. *International Journal of Advanced Manufacturing Technology, 104*(5–8), 1889–1902. doi:10.100700170-019-03988-5

Wiatr, M. (2014). *Bitcoin as a Modern Financial Instrument*. https://rep.polessu.by/bitstream/123456789/5570/1/30.pdf

Widhiastuti, R., Nurkhin, A., & Susilowati, N. (2019). The Role of Financial Performance in Mediating The Effect of Good Corporate Governance on Financial Distress. *Journal of Economics, 15*(1), 34–47.

Wilder-Smith, A., & Freedman, D.O. (2020). Isolation, quarantine, social distancing and community containment: pivotal role for old-style public health measures in the novel coronavirus (2019-nCoV) outbreak. *Journal of Travel Medicine, 27*(2), 1–4.

Wisetsri, W., Donthu, S., Mehbodniya, A., Vyas, S., Quiñonez-Choquecota, J., & Neware, R. (2021). An Investigation on the Impact of Digital Revolution and Machine Learning in Supply Chain Management. *Materials Today: Proceedings*. Advance online publication. doi:10.1016/j.matpr.2021.09.367

Wong, M. C., Yee, K. C., & Nøhr, C. (2018). Socio-technical considerations for the use of blockchain technology in healthcare. In *Building Continents of Knowledge in Oceans of Data: The Future of Co-Created eHealth* (pp. 636–640). IOS Press.

Worldbank. (2011). *Average transaction cost of sending remittances to a specific country (%) - India* [Data set]. Worldbank.org. https://data.worldbank.org/indicator/SI.RMT.COST. IB.ZS?locations=IN

Writ Petition (Civil) No.528 of 2018 INTERNET AND MOBILE ASSOCIATION OF INDIA Petitioner Versus RESERVE BANK OF INDIA Respondent WITH Writ Petition (Civil) No.373 of 2018. https://main.sci.gov.in/supremecourt/2018/19230/19230_2018_4_1501_21151_Judgement_04-Mar-2020.pdf

Wu, H., Cao, J., Yang, Y., Tung, C. L., Jiang, S., Tang, B., Liu, Y., Wang, X., & Deng, Y. (2019). Data Management in Supply Chain Using Blockchain: Challenges and a Case Study. *2019 28th International Conference on Computer Communication and Networks (ICCCN)*, 1–8. 10.1109/ICCCN.2019.8846964

Wu, P., & Siwasarit, W. (2020). Capturing the Order Imbalance with Hidden Markov Model: A Case of SET50 and KOSPI50. *Asia-Pacific Financial Markets*, *27*(1), 115–144. doi:10.100710690-019-09285-1

Wu, W., Tiwari, A. K., Gozgor, G., & Leping, H. (2021). Does Economic Policy Uncertainty Affect Cryptocurrency Markets? Evidence from Twitter-Based Uncertainty Measures. *Research in International Business and Finance*, *58*, 101478. doi:10.1016/j.ribaf.2021.101478

Xiao, B., & Benbasat, I. (2018). An empirical examination of the influence of biased personalized product recommendations on consumers' decision making outcomes. *Decision Support Systems*, *110*, 46–57. doi:10.1016/j.dss.2018.03.005

Xunfa, L. U., Liu, S. K., San Liang, X., Zhang, Z., & Hairong, C. U. I. (2020). The break point-dependent causality between the cryptocurrency and emerging stock markets. *Economic Computation and Economic Cybernetics Studies and Research*, *54*(4), 203–216. doi:10.24818/18423264/54.4.20.13

Y, S. (2021). Machine Learning Applied in the Financial Industry. *Financial Forum*, 239.

Yang, S. Y., Qiao, Q., Beling, P. A., Scherer, W. T., & Kirilenko, A. A. (2015). Gaussian process-based algorithmic trading strategy identification. *Quantitative Finance*, *15*(10), 1683–1703. doi:10.1080/14697688.2015.1011684

Ye, Z., Zhang, Y., Wang, Y., Huang, Z., & Song, B. (2020). Chest CT manifestations of new coronavirus disease 2019 (COVID-19): A pictorial review. *European Radiology*, *30*(8), 4381–4389. doi:10.100700330-020-06801-0 PMID:32193638

Yu, S., Lv, K., Shao, Z., Guo, Y., Zou, J., & Zhang, B. (2018). A High Performance Blockchain Platform for Intelligent Devices. *1st International Conference on Hot Information-Centric Networking (HotICN)*, (pp.260-261). IEEE.. 10.1109/HOTICN.2018.8606017

Compilation of References

Yudha, A., & Fuad. (2014). Analysis of the Influence of the Implementation of Corporate Governance Mechanisms on the Possibility of Companies Experiencing Financial Distress Conditions (Empirical Study of Manufacturing Companies Listed on the Indonesia Stock Exchange 2010-2012). *Diponegoro Journal of Accounting, 3*(4), 1–12.

Yuneline, M. H. (2019). Analysis of cryptocurrency's characteristics in four perspectives. *Journal of Asian Business and Economic Studies, 26*(2), 206–219. doi:10.1108/JABES-12-2018-0107

Zhang, P., White, J., Schmidt, D. C., Lenz, G., & Rosenbloom, S. T. (2018). FHIRChain: Applying blockchain to securely and scalably share clinical data. *Computational and Structural Biotechnology Journal, 16*, 267–278. doi:10.1016/j.csbj.2018.07.004 PMID:30108685

Zhang, W. (2021). Surface Roughness Prediction with Machine Learning. *Journal of Physics: Conference Series, 1856*(1), 012040. doi:10.1088/1742-6596/1856/1/012040

Zhang, X.-D. (2020). Machine Learning. In *A Matrix Algebra Approach to Artificial Intelligence* (pp. 223–440). Springer Singapore. doi:10.1007/978-981-15-2770-8_6

Zhao, S. (2020) Preliminary estimation of the basic reproduction number of novel coronavirus (2019-nCoV) in China, from 2019 to 2020: A data-driven analysis in the early phase of the outbreak. International Journal of Infectious Diseases, 92, 214-217.

Zheng, Z., Xie, S., Dai, H., Chen, X., & Wang, H. (2017). An Overview of Blockchain Technology: Architecture, Consensus, and Future Trends. *International Congress on Big Data (BigData Congress)*, (pp.557-564). IEEE. 10.1109/BigDataCongress.2017.85

Zhong, R. Y., Xua, X., Klotz, E., & Newmanc, S. T. (2017). Intelligent manufacturing in the context of industry 4.0: A review. *Engineering, 3*(5), 616–630. doi:10.1016/J.ENG.2017.05.015

Zurada, J., Levitan, A. S., & Guan, J. (2011). A comparison of regression and artificial intelligence methods in a mass appraisal context. *Journal of Real Estate Research, 33*(3), 349–387. doi:10.1080/10835547.2011.12091311

About the Contributors

Mohammad Irfan is presently working as an Associate Professor at CMR Institute of Technology, Bangalore. Prior joining to CMRIT, he was associated with the School of Business, AURO University, Surat, Gujarat for five years. He is MBA (Finance and Marketing) and M.Com (Account and Law). Dr. Irfan has done this Ph.D. from the Central University of Haryana. He has qualified UGC-SRF/NET in Management and UGC-NET in Commerce. Dr. Irfan has also qualified NSEs (NCFM) and BSEs Certification. He has experience of fifteen years in the area of Financial Management, Portfolio Management, Data Analysis for Business, Financial Engineering, Financial Analytics, Fintech, Financial modeling in Excel, Green Finance, and Alternative Finance. He has to his credit various research papers published in Scopus Indexed Journals. He is an editorial board member/reviewer in several national and international journals. Dr. Irfan presented papers in IIM-A, IIM-C, IIM-Indore, IIM-Shillong, IIT-Roorkee, Indonesia, Malaysia, Nigeria, Switzerland.

Salina Kassim has a great passion in writing scholarly articles in various areas of Islamic banking and finance. She has published extensively in academic journals with nearly 200 scholarly articles in the areas of her research interests. She has also published several books mainly in the areas of Islamic finance. In recognition to her dynamic role as a subject matter expert, she has been appointed as member of the editorial boards of several reputable international and local journals. At present, she is supervising (and has supervised) nearly 80 post-graduate candidates at the PhD and Masters levels. She has also served as internal and external examiners for Masters and PhD theses in several universities, apart from being appointed as Adjunct Professor, Visiting Research Fellow and trainer at several universities and institutes, locally and abroad.

* * *

About the Contributors

Raghavendra A. N. is presently working as Associate Professor in the School of Business and Management, CHRIST (Deemed to be University), Bangalore. He received his Master of Business Administration (MBA) degree in 1999 from Bangalore University with Human Resource Management Specialization. He qualified the eligibility test for lecturers (UGC-NET) in the year 2011. He has completed PhD from Visvesvaraya Technological University (VTU), Belgaum on the Topic "Reengineering Expatriate Deployment Model for efficient Supply Chain Practices in Indian IT Industry" in November 2017. He has authored more than 20 publications including research papers and articles in the national and international journals of repute along with e-journals. He has working knowledge of EXCEL, SPSS, SAS, AMOS, TABLEAU, PYTHON and R Softwares and has conducted many workshops/training programmes for MBA students and faculty members.

Meenakshee Dash (ORCID ID- 0000-0002-9665-1267) has four years of teaching experience to both UG and PG students as well as 2 years of corporate experiences. She has taught subjects called Financial Management, Financial Accounting, Business studies, management, etc. at Rajdhani College of Sc.Tech. &Management, Bhubaneswar, Odisha, India. She has published one paper (Book Chapters) in reputed publication houses of T&F. Her area of research is general management and supply chain management.

Omvir Gautam is working as an Assistant Professor in the Faculty of Commerce and Management, Vishwakarma University, Pune, Maharashtra, India. He has more than 13 years of experience in teaching, research, and administration. His area of interest in research includes digital marketing, consumer research, social media analytics, and entrepreneurship and business analytics. He is a passionate researcher and presented papers in various national and international conferences. He has fair number of good publications in Scopus and ABDC indexed journals to his credit.

Babita Jha is working as an Assistant professor in Christ University, Uttar Pradesh, India.

Pooja Kansra is Head of Department, Mittal School of Business, Lovely Professional University, Punjab, India.

Niranjan Kulkarni is working as an Assistant Professor in the Faculty of Commerce and Management, Vishwakarma University, Pune, Maharashtra, India. He has more than 12 years of experience of corporate and teaching. His area of interest in research includes Entrepreneurship and Financial management.

About the Contributors

Sunil Kumar is working as an Assistant Professor, School of IT, AURO University, Surat.

Mohan N. is presently working as an Associate Professor at CMR Institute of Technology, Bangalore. Prior joining to CMRIT, at Dr Kariappa School of Art & Design Management, Bengaluru, India. He has done his MBA at Sikkim Manipal University. He obtained his MPhil and PhD from Bharathiar University, Coimbatore. He has total 8 years as Academician 8 years in Retail, FMCG and Building Material industry Exposers. He has published various research papers published in UGC Indexed Journals including International of Business International Journal of Business Excellence, He is an editorial board member/reviewer in several national and international journals. Dr. Mohan.N presented papers in the National and International conferences organized by leading institutions like SDM-IIM,PESCE, and many more. He is specialized in Managerial Economics, Legal Subjects and Business Environment, Analytics and Marketing Management.

Rashmi Ranjan Panigrahi (Research Associate, FMS, IBCS, SOA-DU) (ORCID ID- 0000-0002-2199-293X) has 10-years of academic as well as administrative experience and 1-year of corporate experience. He teaches different finance and core papers of master's degree students such as financial management, statistics for managers, Research methodology, corporate restructuring, merchant banking & financial services, and inventory management. he had published around 10 research papers in Scopus and WOS index journal. and two papers also in ABDC/ABS Indexed Journal along with Two book publications also in his credit. he is also a reviewer of three Scopus Index Journal journals of Inderscience Publication House.

Indria Ramadhani has completed her bachelor's degree from Airlangga University, Indonesia. Majored in Islamic Economics with a minor subject in finance, her research interest included Islamic capital market, Islamic financial management, and halal industrial economy.

Sylva Alif Rusmita is an assistant professor at The Faculty of Economics and Business from Airlangga University, Indonesia. She holds a master's degree from INCEIF Malaysia and is currently pursuing her Ph.D. at Universiti of Malaya. Her research focuses on Islamic financial institutions and Islamic capital market. She also contributed to Jurnal Ekonomi dan Bisnis Islam (JEBIS) as an executive editor and lecturer in Sharia Economics Department.

About the Contributors

Swapnil Shah is director at FinoGlobin Financial Services Pvt. Ltd., Pune, Maharashtra, India. He has been in the financial services domain since 2006. Handled large corporates, families and high net worth individuals investments across the product spectrum.

Zakir Hossen Shaikh is a Faculty of Islamic Banking and Finance, Commercial Studies Division under Ministry of Education, Kingdom of Bahrain since 2015. Prior to this, he worked more than 15 years in commercial and academic industry. He has published numerous articles in referred journals and presented many papers in various conferences, both local and abroad exclusively in the different area of Accounting, management and Islamic Banking and Finance. He has also participated in a variety of seminars, forums, workshops and international conferences. He obtained his Ph.D. (Islamic Banking and Finance) from India in 2018. His doctoral thesis explored the entrepreneurial phenomenon from an Islamic perspective and argued for profit and loss sharing (PLS) contracts as viable alternatives to conventional interest-based financing instruments. He holds Master degree in Commerce, Business Administration & Finance and Control. He is a member of Chartered Institute of Islamic Finance Professionals (CIIF), Malaysia; Indian Accounting Association; Orissa Commerce Association, India and associated with Accounting & Auditing Organization for Islamic Financial Institution (AAOIFI), Bahrain.

Sudhi Sharma is serving as an assistant professor in FIIB Delhi.

Parag Shukla (M.Com, PGDMM, UGC-NET, and SET) is a PhD Scholar and working as an Assistant Professor in the Faculty of Commerce at the M.S. University of Baroda, Department of Commerce and Business Management, Gujarat, India. He received his Bachelors and Masters Degree with specialization in Marketing Management from the M.S. University of Baroda, India. His area of research is in the field of Retailing. His experience includes content analysis with the television and media research industry. He currently teaches courses of management in various under graduate and post graduate levels in the University. He has presented and published several research papers in different areas of Retailing and Marketing in various National and International refereed Journals and conference proceedings. He has also received other accolades in his research papers from various academia. Mr. Shukla is the recipient of the Best Business Academic of the Year Award (BBAY)where he won the Silver Medal for his research paper in 68th International All India Commerce Conference, which is widely recognized in Indian Education and Retail Industry.

About the Contributors

Madhvendra Pratap Singh works as an assistant professor at the KNIPSS Management Institute in Sultanpur (Uttar Pradesh), India. His research interests span a wide range of topics, including business research, service marketing, and consumer centred research. He has ten years of expertise in the fields of teaching and research. He has authored a number of research papers that have been published in prestigious peer-reviewed publications.

Rohit Singh is working as a Pro-Vice Chancellor in Royal Global University, Guwahati, Assam.

Sanjeev Thalari is a result oriented professional with 20+ years of rich experience that includes 17 years teaching UG and PG levels in the area of Business Management and Psychology and 3+ years in Industry. Working as Associate Professor in CMR Institute of Technology, Bangalore from Sept 27 to till now. PhD from SK University, 2021 titled "Human Capital Management Practices and their impact on Employee Performance in select Retail Outlets in select Cities". M.B.A (Marketing & systems) from S.K.University, 2005. M.Sc (Psychology) from S.V.University, 2009. UGC NET, 2019. APSET, 2012. PGDCA from CAT Information & Communication Pvt Ltd, Hyderabad. Certified Master Trainer, Bodhih Training Solutions Pvt Ltd, Bangalore. Certified e-Trainer, Scooppin Trainers Academy, Bangalore. Certified Soft skills trainer, Globerena Technologies Pvt, Ltd, Hyderabad. Participated in National and International level conferences and presented papers. Attended different FDP, SDP, and STTP programs sponsored by UGC and AICTE.

Miklesh Prasad Yadav is an Assistant Professor at Amity College of Commerce and Finance. He has work experience of 12 years and contributed acclaimed publications in ABDC-A, ABS3*, and Scopus indexed journal. He is also a guest editor of International Journal of Public Sector Performance Management (SCOPUS Indexed).

Index

A

AI-Powered Demand Forecasting 115
Algorithms 2, 6-8, 14, 33, 45-46, 48-49, 136, 157-164, 167, 183, 187, 195, 197, 200-201, 204, 209, 212-213, 217
Applications 1-5, 9-10, 13, 18, 21-22, 24-25, 27, 29, 32, 46-48, 53, 63-64, 81-83, 88-89, 92-93, 135, 137-138, 143-144, 155-158, 160, 167, 172, 174-176, 180-181, 196, 198, 200-202, 212-213, 215, 217, 231
Artificial Intelligence 1-9, 11-14, 16-17, 43-44, 46-49, 51-55, 57, 63, 73-76, 79, 115, 117, 121, 156, 163, 165-168, 170, 180-181, 195, 200-201, 213-214, 217-219, 240

B

Banking 1-3, 5, 8-9, 11, 13-17, 25, 33, 38, 43-54, 62-63, 74, 79, 89, 92, 134, 144, 146, 150-151, 157-158, 160-161, 165, 184, 239
BITW 94-96, 99-100, 103-110
Block Chain 43, 51, 146, 152
Blockchain Technology 19, 21, 25-26, 28-30, 33, 52, 79, 82, 84, 86-93, 136, 138, 142-146, 152-155
Board of Commissioners Size 220, 240

C

Corporate Finance 1
COVID-19 45, 53, 89, 91, 98, 111-112, 156, 166-167, 171-172, 178-182, 211
Cryptocurrency 18-19, 25, 31-35, 38-42, 76, 94-97, 111, 113-114, 134-140, 142, 144, 146-147, 149, 152-155
Cyber Threats 43-46, 53

D

Data Science 14, 159
Decentralised Finance 132
Decentralization 21, 28, 81-82, 84, 87-88
Decision Making 15, 156-157, 164, 219, 233
Digital Finance 132, 134, 140, 146
Digital Transformation 158, 216
Distributed Ledger 18, 21, 24, 26, 33, 41, 138, 142-143
Distributed Ledger Technology 24, 33, 41, 138, 143
Doctor-Patient 81, 86-88

E

Exchange 21, 31, 34-35, 39-40, 64, 133-136, 141, 143, 145, 149-150, 202, 231, 237-240
Extra Trees 220-221, 228, 234-237, 240, 246
Extra Trees Model 220, 228, 234, 236, 246

F

FIFO 118, 120, 127
Financial Advisory 55, 57, 59-62, 64, 68, 70-71, 73, 78, 80, 156-158

Index

Financial Freedom 55-56
Financial Inclusion 53, 55-58, 61, 73-76, 80, 149-151, 195, 197-198
Financial Modeling 183-185
Financial Planning 56-57, 59-63, 75-76, 78-79
Financial Sector 4, 17, 27, 47, 76, 132-133, 140, 143, 156, 158, 164-165
Fintech 53, 56-57, 63, 75, 78, 80, 98, 111-112, 142, 151
Future Research Trends 199

H

Health Insurance 81, 87-88, 90-91, 93
Healthcare 24-25, 28, 82-93, 140, 167, 172, 179

I

Indian Industry 199, 204, 213
Indian Monetary System 31
Industry 4.0 182, 211
Institutional Ownership 220, 224, 229-230, 232-233, 235, 237, 240
Insurance 16, 18, 24-25, 27, 57, 81-83, 87-93, 145, 198
Inventory Valuation Methods 115, 118, 124, 127-131
IoT 24, 166-170, 173-178, 218
Islamic Issuers 221, 240

L

LIFO 118, 120
Limitations 43, 49, 51, 136, 138, 205, 209, 212

M

Machine Learning 1-14, 16-17, 44, 48, 55, 73-74, 156-165, 178, 181, 195-202, 206, 209-221, 226-228, 231-232, 234-237, 239-240, 243
Managerial Ownership 220, 224, 229-230, 233, 235, 240
Medical Records 82-83, 86-87, 90, 93
Medical Supplies 81, 83, 87-88

MSCI Emerging Markets Index 94, 96, 99-100, 102-103, 105-110
MSCI World Index 94, 96, 99-100, 102-110

O

Optimal Order Policy 118-120, 124, 127
Order Fulfillment 115, 124, 128

P

Pandemic 35, 41, 53, 56-57, 59, 97-98, 111, 132-133, 156, 166-167, 171, 177
Panel Regression 220, 224, 232, 241-242
Panel Regression Model 220, 242
Perishable 115-118, 120-121, 127-129, 131, 215
Personal Financial Management 55-56, 59-61, 63-64, 71, 73-75, 78, 80
Proportion of Independent Commissioners 229, 231, 234-236, 241

Q

Qualitative Concept Research 166
Quantitative Methods 183-184, 195
Quarantines 166

R

Regulations 13-14, 32, 49, 135-136, 142, 146, 150, 152, 224
Retail Industry 166, 169
Retailers 115-120, 122-124, 127-128, 168-170, 178, 211
Risk Analytics 183
Risk of Bankruptcy 233, 236-237, 241

S

Smart Contract 18, 24-27, 153
Stock Markets 30, 97-99, 112, 114
Supply Chain 18, 27, 89, 91, 115-119, 127-130, 168-169, 199-205, 209-219

U

Utilization 43, 48, 61, 73

Recommended Reference Books

IGI Global's reference books can now be purchased from three unique pricing formats:
Print Only, E-Book Only, or Print + E-Book.
Shipping fees may apply.

www.igi-global.com

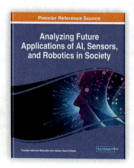

Analyzing Future Applications of AI, Sensors, and Robotics in Society

ISBN: 9781799834991
EISBN: 9781799835011
© 2021; 335 pp.
List Price: US$ 225

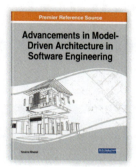

Advancements in Model-Driven Architecture in Software Engineering

ISBN: 9781799836612
EISBN: 9781799836636
© 2021; 287 pp.
List Price: US$ 215

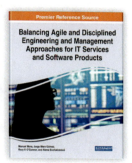

Balancing Agile and Disciplined Engineering and Management Approaches for IT Services and Software Products

ISBN: 9781799841654
EISBN: 9781799841661
© 2021; 354 pp.
List Price: US$ 225

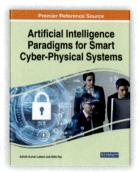

Artificial Intelligence Paradigms for Smart Cyber-Physical Systems

ISBN: 9781799851011
EISBN: 9781799851028
© 2021; 392 pp.
List Price: US$ 225

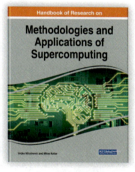

Methodologies and Applications of Supercomputing

ISBN: 9781799871569
EISBN: 9781799871583
© 2021; 393 pp.
List Price: US$ 345

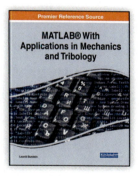

MATLAB® With Applications in Mechanics and Tribology

ISBN: 9781799870784
EISBN: 9781799870807
© 2021; 368 pp.
List Price: US$ 195

Do you want to stay current on the latest research trends, product announcements, news, and special offers?
Join IGI Global's mailing list to receive customized recommendations, exclusive discounts, and more.
Sign up at: **www.igi-global.com/newsletters.**

Publisher of Timely, Peer-Reviewed Inclusive Research Since 1988

IGI Global
PUBLISHER of TIMELY KNOWLEDGE

www.igi-global.com | Sign up at www.igi-global.com/newsletters | facebook.com/igiglobal | twitter.com/igiglobal

Ensure Quality Research is Introduced to the Academic Community

Become an Evaluator for IGI Global Authored Book Projects

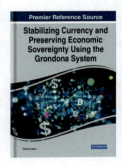 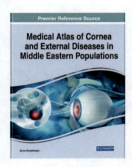  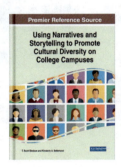

The overall success of an authored book project is dependent on quality and timely manuscript evaluations.

Applications and Inquiries may be sent to:
development@igi-global.com

Applicants must have a doctorate (or equivalent degree) as well as publishing, research, and reviewing experience. Authored Book Evaluators are appointed for one-year terms and are expected to complete at least three evaluations per term. Upon successful completion of this term, evaluators can be considered for an additional term.

If you have a colleague that may be interested in this opportunity, we encourage you to share this information with them.

Easily Identify, Acquire, and Utilize Published Peer-Reviewed Findings in Support of Your Current Research

IGI Global OnDemand

Purchase Individual IGI Global OnDemand Book Chapters and Journal Articles

For More Information:
www.igi-global.com/e-resources/ondemand/

Browse through 150,000+ Articles and Chapters!

Find specific research related to your current studies and projects that have been contributed by international researchers from prestigious institutions, including:

- Accurate and Advanced Search
- Affordably Acquire Research
- Instantly Access Your Content
- Benefit from the InfoSci Platform Features

"*It really provides* **an excellent entry into the research literature of the field**. *It presents a manageable number of* **highly relevant sources** *on topics of interest to a wide range of researchers. The sources are* **scholarly, but also accessible** *to 'practitioners'.*"

– Ms. Lisa Stimatz, MLS, University of North Carolina at Chapel Hill, USA

Interested in Additional Savings?

Subscribe to
IGI Global OnDemand *Plus*

Learn More

Acquire content from over 128,000+ research-focused book chapters and 33,000+ scholarly journal articles for as low as US$ 5 per article/chapter (original retail price for an article/chapter: US$ 37.50).

6,600+ E-BOOKS.
ADVANCED RESEARCH.
INCLUSIVE & ACCESSIBLE.

IGI Global e-Book Collection

- **Flexible Purchasing Options** (Perpetual, Subscription, EBA, etc.)
- Multi-Year Agreements with **No Price Increases** Guaranteed
- **No Additional Charge** for Multi-User Licensing
- No Maintenance, Hosting, or Archiving Fees
- Transformative **Open Access Options** Available

Request More Information, or Recommend the IGI Global e-Book Collection to Your Institution's Librarian

Among Titles Included in the IGI Global e-Book Collection

Research Anthology on Racial Equity, Identity, and Privilege (3 Vols.)
EISBN: 9781668445082
Price: US$ 895

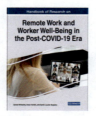

Handbook of Research on Remote Work and Worker Well-Being in the Post-COVID-19 Era
EISBN: 9781799867562
Price: US$ 265

Research Anthology on Big Data Analytics, Architectures, and Applications (4 Vols.)
EISBN: 9781668436639
Price: US$ 1,950

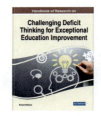

Handbook of Research on Challenging Deficit Thinking for Exceptional Education Improvement
EISBN: 9781799888628
Price: US$ 265

Acquire & Open

When your library acquires an IGI Global e-Book and/or e-Journal Collection, your faculty's published work will be considered for immediate conversion to Open Access *(CC BY License)*, at no additional cost to the library or its faculty *(cost only applies to the e-Collection content being acquired)*, through our popular **Transformative Open Access (Read & Publish) Initiative**.

For More Information or to Request a Free Trial, Contact IGI Global's e-Collections Team: eresources@igi-global.com | 1-866-342-6657 ext. 100 | 717-533-8845 ext. 100

Have Your Work Published and Freely Accessible
Open Access Publishing

With the industry shifting from the more traditional publication models to an open access (OA) publication model, publishers are finding that OA publishing has many benefits that are awarded to authors and editors of published work.

Freely Share Your Research

Higher Discoverability & Citation Impact

Rigorous & Expedited Publishing Process

Increased Advancement & Collaboration

Acquire & Open

When your library acquires an IGI Global e-Book and/or e-Journal Collection, your faculty's published work will be considered for immediate conversion to Open Access *(CC BY License)*, at no additional cost to the library or its faculty *(cost only applies to the e-Collection content being acquired)*, through our popular **Transformative Open Access (Read & Publish) Initiative**.

Provide Up To 100% OA APC or CPC Funding

Funding to Convert or Start a Journal to Platinum OA

Support for Funding an OA Reference Book

IGI Global publications are found in a number of prestigious indices, including Web of Science™, Scopus®, Compendex, and PsycINFO®. The selection criteria is very strict and to ensure that journals and books are accepted into the major indexes, IGI Global closely monitors publications against the criteria that the indexes provide to publishers.

WEB OF SCIENCE™  **Scopus®**

PsycINFO®

Learn More Here: For Questions, Contact IGI Global's Open Access Team at openaccessadmin@igi-global.com

www.igi-global.com

Are You Ready to Publish Your Research

IGI Global offers book authorship and editorship opportunities across 11 subject areas, including business, computer science, education, science and engineering, social sciences, and more!

Benefits of Publishing with IGI Global:

- Free one-on-one editorial and promotional support.
- Expedited publishing timelines that can take your book from start to finish in less than one (1) year.
- Choose from a variety of formats, including Edited and Authored References, Handbooks of Research, Encyclopedias, and Research Insights.
- Utilize IGI Global's eEditorial Discovery® submission system in support of conducting the submission and double-blind peer review process.
- IGI Global maintains a strict adherence to ethical practices due in part to our full membership with the Committee on Publication Ethics (COPE).
- Indexing potential in prestigious indices such as Scopus®, Web of Science™, PsycINFO®, and ERIC – Education Resources Information Center.
- Ability to connect your ORCID iD to your IGI Global publications.
- Earn honorariums and royalties on your full book publications as well as complimentary copies and exclusive discounts.

Join Your Colleagues from Prestigious Institutions, Including:

Learn More at: www.igi-global.com/publish
or by Contacting the Acquisitions Department at: acquisition@igi-global.com

Easily Identify, Acquire, and Utilize Published
Peer-Reviewed Findings in Support of Your Current Research

IGI Global OnDemand

Purchase Individual IGI Global OnDemand Book Chapters and Journal Articles

For More Information:
www.igi-global.com/e-resources/ondemand/

Browse through 150,000+ Articles and Chapters!

Find specific research related to your current studies and projects that have been contributed by international researchers from prestigious institutions, including:

- Accurate and Advanced Search
- Affordably Acquire Research
- Instantly Access Your Content
- Benefit from the InfoSci Platform Features

❝ It really provides **an excellent entry into the research literature of the field**. It presents a manageable number of **highly relevant sources** on topics of interest to a wide range of researchers. The sources are **scholarly, but also accessible** to 'practitioners'. ❞

- Ms. Lisa Stimatz, MLS, University of North Carolina at Chapel Hill, USA

Interested in Additional Savings?

Subscribe to
IGI Global OnDemand *Plus*

Learn More

Acquire content from over 128,000+ research-focused book chapters and 33,000+ scholarly journal articles for as low as US$ 5 per article/chapter (original retail price for an article/chapter: US$ 37.50).

Printed in the United States
by Baker & Taylor Publisher Services